SOMETHING BETTER

GOD'S

GRACIOUS

PROVISIONS

FOR OUR

DAILY

DECISIONS

Also by Calvin Rock:
Perspectives

To order, **call 1-800-765-6955**.
Visit us at **www.reviewandherald.com** for information
on other Review and Herald® products.

CALVIN B. ROCK

SOMETHING
BETTER

GOD'S

GRACIOUS

PROVISIONS

FOR OUR

DAILY

DECISIONS

REVIEW AND HERALD® PUBLISHING ASSOCIATION

Since 1861 | www.reviewandherald.com

Copyright © 2014 by Review and Herald® Publishing Association

Published by Review and Herald® Publishing Association, Hagerstown, MD 21741-1119

Review and Herald® titles may be purchased in bulk for educational, business, fund-raising, or sales promotional use. For information, e-mail SpecialMarkets@reviewandherald.com.

The Review and Herald® Publishing Association publishes biblically based materials for spiritual, physical, and mental growth and Christian discipleship.

Unless otherwise noted, Bible texts in this book are from the New King James Version. Copyright © 1979, 1980, 1982 by Thomas Nelson, Inc. Used by permission. All rights reserved.

Bible texts credited to Amplified are from *The Amplified Bible*, Old Testament copyright © 1965, 1987 by Zondervan Corporation. The *Amplified New Testament* copyright © 1958, 1987 by The Lockman Foundation. Used by permission.

Texts credited to ASV are from *The Holy Bible*, edited by the American Revision Committee, Standard Edition, Thomas Nelson & Sons, 1901.

Bible texts credited to Goodspeed are from Smith and Goodspeed, *The Complete Bible: An American Translation*. Copyright 1939 by the University of Chicago Press.

Bible texts credited to Moffatt are from: *The Bible: A New Translation*, by James Moffatt. Copyright by James Moffatt 1954. Used by permission of Harper & Row, Publishers, Incorporated.

Scripture quotations marked NASB are from the *New American Standard Bible*, copyright © 1960, 1962, 1963, 1968, 1971, 1972, 1973, 1975, 1977, 1995 by The Lockman Foundation. Used by permission.

Texts credited to NEB are from *The New English Bible*. © The Delegates of the Oxford University Press and the Syndics of the Cambridge University Press 1961, 1970. Reprinted by permission.

Scripture quotations credited to NIV are from the *Holy Bible, New International Version*. Copyright © 1973, 1978, 1984, 2011 by Biblica, Inc. Used by permission. All rights reserved worldwide.

Verses marked TLB are taken from *The Living Bible*, copyright © 1971 by Tyndale House Publishers, Wheaton, Ill. Used by permission.

Texts credited to Weymouth are from Richard Francis Weymouth, *The New Testament in Modern Speech* (London: James Clarke & Co., 1903).

This book was
Edited by Paula Webber
Copyedited by Jeremy J. Johnson and Ted Hessel
Designed by Daniel Anez / Review and Herald® Design Center
Cover art by Thinkstock.com
Typeset: Minion Pro 10.5/13.5

PRINTED IN U.S.A.

18 17 16 15 14   5 4 3 2 1

Library of Congress Cataloging-in-Publication Data
Rock, Calvin B.
Something better : God's gracious provisions for our daily decisions / Calvin Rock.
pages cm
ISBN 978-0-8280-2751-9
1. Bible—Meditations. 2. Devotional calendars. I. Title.
        BS491.5.R63 2014
        242'.2—dc23
                              2014009305

ISBN 978-0-8280-2751-9

DEDICATION

In memory of my mother,
a woman of exceptional talents,
kindness, and courage
whom I hope to see
in that Better Day. Thank you.

CONTENTS

JANUARY
A Better Passover

FEBRUARY
A Better Covenant

MARCH
A Better Sanctuary

APRIL
A Better High Priest

MAY
A Better Temple

JUNE
A Better Moses

JULY
A Better Adam

AUGUST
A Better Witness

SEPTEMBER
A Better Priority

OCTOBER
A Better Righteousness

NOVEMBER
A Better Resurrection

DECEMBER
A Better Reward

JANUARY

A Better Passover

A Nation Is Born

Now the Lord spoke to Moses and Aaron in the land of Egypt,
saying, "This month shall be your beginning of months;
it shall be the first month of the year to you." Ex. 12:1, 2.

In terms of drama, emotion, and historical significance there has never been anything quite like it! Finally, after more than four centuries of bondage they were free. The journey from promise to peoplehood had devastated their morale as well as their reputation and culture. Seventeen generations lived and died without the fulfillment of God's pledge to Abraham, but now at last—at long last—"it came to pass"!

God's Word always "comes to pass." There are times His blessings are delayed (as with Israel's 40-year trek through the wilderness) in order that the recipients of His mercy might be conditioned to receive His goodness. But, always unfailingly, His Word comes to pass.

It is not just the dependability of God's promises that our text reinforces—it is the strength and wisdom of His directives. Moses and Aaron could not mistake their instructions; they were to regard the month in which their slavery ended as the beginning of their statehood. God's Word gave the alert to "start counting now."

What better counsel for us on this, the first day of the new year, to start counting now. Last year's successes and failures have been graded. This year is a brand-new unit of reckoning. While the next 12 months will undoubtedly be influenced by past experiences, this year will be a chapter of its own—a different engagement, a fresh opportunity, a time to correct and improve, the chance to start again. It is our privilege and God's desire that we "start counting now."

What shall we count? Let's begin with each day's blessing. We shall not take for granted God's mercies. We shall pray for His protection, His guidance, and His forgiveness. As He answers our petitions, we shall chronicle them in our logbook of gratitude. Beginning today, we shall not, like the nine lepers in the Scripture, receive healing and forget to give thanks. Most of all, we shall count our personal growth: our growth in knowledge, in patience, in self-control, in faith, and in all the other fruits of the Spirit that involve our most important activity of the year—our development in the likeness of Christ.

From Now On

And Moses said to the people: "Remember this day in which
you went out of Egypt, out of the house of bondage; for by strength
of hand the Lord brought you out of this place. . . . On this day
you are going out, in the month of Abib." Ex. 13:3, 4.

Four times in this passage Moses tried to prepare the children of Israel for complete separation from Egypt. He emphasized repeatedly going "out," or leaving behind the conditions that had suppressed and depressed them for so long. That day, the tenth day of the month of Abib, was to celebrate the day of their transition from the indignities of the past to a glorious future. So complete would be their separation from the evils of Egypt that their 400 years of bondage was not to be counted as part of their formal chronology.

The need to cut ties with the past and bravely step into the future is vital to the success of our churches and our families, and to us as individuals. One's willingness to turn the page on yesterday's woes and do their best from now on is the key to complete separation from the past.

We all need new beginnings—a time for fresh starts; times that we abandon life's accumulated baggage, psychological and otherwise, and optimistically and enthusiastically engage the future. It is time for us to move on not only from past failures, but also past triumphs that may lessen our present zeal and motivation.

At the beginning of each new year our heavenly Father provides us the ideal time for restatement of our goals and renewal of our zeal. Of course, we do not have to wait for the new year to begin this process; we can mark any life event as a time for refocused determination. For example, Enoch refocused when his son was born, Jacob's mind-set shifted after a dream, Elijah also refocused after an epiphany in a cave, so did Isaiah after King Uzziah's death, David experienced this following Nathan's rebuke, and Peter certainly did upon the realization of his denial.

Ellen G. White says of the apostle Paul: "If ever his ardor in the path of duty flagged for a moment, one glance at the cross caused him to gird up the loins of his mind and press forward in the way of self-denial" (*The Ministry of Healing*, p. 500).

By his example we are reminded that the cross of Christ is not only our most potent source of inspiration, but also our most available.

Be Ready

And thus you shall eat it: with a belt on your waist,
your sandals on your feet, and your staff in your hand.
So you shall eat it in haste. It is the Lord's Passover. Ex. 12:11.

"Eat in haste"? Not a prescription for good digestion, is it? No parent or physician would recommend such a dining posture. And yet the Israelites were instructed by God to eat the Passover meal in a hurry—in traveling shoes, fully dressed, with staff in hand. This is not a formula for healthy dining, but a wonderful lesson regarding everyday readiness for the return of our Lord.

The moment had arrived—after 400 years of slavery and all the drama of the plagues, deliverance was imminent; God had not forgotten them! Their prayers and dreams were coming true, and the heart of every anxious Hebrew throbbed with happy anticipation. Actually, under these conditions we could understand if they had no appetite at all.

God's people, in this time of earth's history, are similarly positioned. We too look back upon many generations of believers for whom the promise was not made a reality—"They without us were not made perfect" (see Heb. 11:40) or recipients of final victory. However, can we say we are more hopeful today than generations past? We must stay ready—poised for deliverance—always looking up, for our redemption draweth nigh!

Do we know precisely when He will appear? No. Do we know for a fact that He will return in this generation or even in our lifetime? No. What we do know is that the circumstances are right and that His promises are sure; that He will someday "cut short" His work in righteousness. In the meantime we must faithfully endure the tension between promise and fulfillment, the ready and the not ready.

Meanwhile, the hope of imminent deliverance from this sin-cursed world is a strong motivation for the daily contemplation of His Word that produces holy living and holy boldness in sharing His grace with others.

The Firstborn Slain

And it came to pass at midnight that the Lord struck
all the firstborn in the land of Egypt, from the firstborn of Pharaoh
who sat on his throne to the firstborn of the captive who was
in the dungeon, and all the firstborn of livestock. Ex. 12:29.

Recompense postponed is not recompense removed! Centuries of cruelty toward other nations, especially the Israelites, and weeks of hard-hearted resistance to warnings that God's cup of wrath was now overflowing finally culminated in the worst of plagues—the chilling death of the firstborn in every Egyptian household.

Sin has its consequences. Not only in the naturally debilitating effects it produces in human relationships, but also in death—the legal punishment that God issues as a consequence of disobedience.

God hates sin! Why? Sin is arrogance; it is rebellion, disloyalty, and irreverence, and it is extremely contagious. Because sin is contrary to righteousness and cannot exist eternally amid God's perfect handiwork, He cannot—will not—allow this repulsive, life-sapping perversity to disfigure His harmonious creation forever.

The refusals of the Egyptians to heed God's warnings remind us that "because the sentence against an evil work is not executed speedily, therefore the heart of the sons of men is fully set in them to do evil" (Eccl. 8:11); that there will always be "payday—someday"; that God does have punishment reserved for those who persistently ignore His invitations of grace.

The good news is that Christ's death has spared us the fate of eternal doomed. He has paid the penalty for our sins. He has died the second death. By this unfathomably unselfish act, He delivered us from its necessity. Hellfire is prepared not for humans, but for the devil and his angels, who will then be burned up "root" and "branch" (Mal. 4:1).

Our most precious thought today and every day should be that Christ, the firstborn of heaven, has rescued us from the pit of destruction; and by the gift of His humiliation, we are "passed over" into honor and glory.

Are All the Children In?

Now the blood shall be a sign for you on the houses where you are.
And when I see the blood, I will pass over you; and the plague shall
not be on you to destroy you when I strike the land of Egypt. Ex. 12:13.

The individual households of the children of Israel were specific units of focus during the Passover event. Moses was told that the angel of death would inspect each residence with solemn scrutiny. Each house must have the Lamb's blood sprinkled upon the doorpost, and each family was to gather in prayerful anticipation of the promised judgment.

This should be the case with all families that anticipate Christ's second coming and the exodus of God's people into heavenly Canaan. We are often tempted to hold the church and the school responsible for the dreadful conditions of society and the continued delay of His return. But revival, reformation, and our eventual rescue from sin's domain are linked to the quality of spirituality in our homes more than to the influence of any other institution.

This reality demands that this year, this month, this day, the call to solemn assembly should be heard in each home. As the Israelites, in preparation for their deliverance, gathered their children from the streets and fields of Egypt and led their households in earnest supplication, we must do the same.

So what is the condition of your home? Are all the children in? Are they gathering daily in family devotion? Are they sheltered under the superior banner of Christian education? What about our single-parent and single-person households? Is the Lamb's blood marking these dwellings as well? Are we, as a Christian body, living united in prayerful anticipation of Christ's return?

The day of His appearing will bring swift and terrible judgment upon sin and sinners. Jesus Himself said that when His angels come to reap the harvest of earth, the nations will mourn, and that there will be "weeping and gnashing of teeth" (Matt. 8:12). The prophet John was even more graphic. His description was that the sky will recede like a "scroll rolling up," that "every mountain and island shall be moved from its place" and that those not rightfully prepared for His coming will unsuccessfully flee the wrath of the avenging God (see Rev. 6:14-16). Whether or not we live to see Christ come in royal splendor or shall rise from our rest to greet Him is a reality that we cannot control. What we can control and what we must effect daily is the consecration of our households and ourselves to prepare us for either outcome.

January 6

Why a Lamb?

Speak to all the congregation of Israel, saying: "On the tenth
of this month every man shall take for himself a lamb, according
to the house of his father, a lamb for a household." Ex. 12:3.

Lambs were not Israel's only choice of sacrifice. A wide variety of creatures, including oxen, goats, and doves, was utilized in sacrificial offerings—each representing important aspects of Christ's service on our behalf. The dove symbolized His gentleness; the ox His strength and dependability; and the goat was His sin-bearing substitution. But no other creature captured the essence of His life like the lamb. In the docile, obedient lamb is seen the gentleness, the willingness, the sincerity of our Lord. Sheep are meek and submissive; they have a nonthreatening, defenseless presence; they are proverbial for innocence and acceptance of mistreatment. Even death at the hands of humans is suffered without anger or attempts at retaliation. One is hard pressed to imagine a more loving and trusting animal.

This is why the lamb, more than any other creature or object, best represents Jesus. He is our Savior, meek and mild. In the words of the prophet Isaiah: "He was led as a lamb to the slaughter, and as a sheep before her shearers is dumb, so he openeth not his mouth" (Isa. 53:7).

The Negro spiritual says it well:
"O, they crucified my Lord and
  He never said a mumbling word.
  Not a word, not a word, not a word.
  O, they nailed Him to the tree, and
  He never said a mumbling word.
  Not a word, not a word, not a word."

In addition to the portrayal of Christ's meekness, the lamb typified a number of other very important and practical aspects of His ministry. In some cultures sheep are utilized for food (1 Sam. 25:18), for milk (1 Cor. 9:7), for clothing (Prov. 31:13), as well as for gifts (2 Sam. 17:27-29). These examples remind us of Christ: He is our daily sustainer, the source of our constant well-being, our covering of righteousness, the gift of the Father who through the Son gives us strength for today and hope for every tomorrow.

A Young Lamb

Now this is what you shall offer on the altar: two lambs
of the first year, day by day continually. Ex. 29:38.

Israel's sacrificial system called for youthful victims. The people were commanded
to slay young lambs, young bullocks (Lev. 4:3), young calves (Lev. 9:2), and young
kids (verse 3), and, if they were too poor, they used an animal of their choice—for
example, young pigeons (Lev. 14:30).

Jesus' death at age 33 was not unusual for the era in which He lived. The 4,000
years of sin that transpired between Eden and Bethlehem had depreciated human
vitality, and during Christ's generation few people survived beyond their 30s.

However, humanity did not lose its vitality all at once. When we look back
over the first 1,500 years of time, Adam lived to be 930 years; Noah, whose life span
bridged the Flood, lived to be 950. So longevity was maintained close to 1,000 years.

But after the Flood, escalating iniquity contributed to declining longevity.
Abraham, whose birth occurred about the time of Noah's death, lived 175 years.
David, who ministered six centuries before Christ, reckoned 70 to be a ripe old age
and 80 a possible but painful extension. By the time we get to the Bethlehem era,
sin's ravage had brought life expectancy to the lowest point in human history—a
scant 22 years.

No, the age on Jesus' death certificate is not unique for His day. It is, however,
unique to human history in general. He was a young sacrifice. Young, because at
the time of His crucifixion His capacity for doing good was at its peak; young, because His health was perfect and His will undimmed; young, because in the light of
God's original plans for the human race, He barely existed.

He could have delayed His death far beyond its occurrence or escaped its ter-
rors altogether. The fact that He did not is a daily reminder of His incomparable
sacrifice on our behalf and the ultimate inspiration of our devotion.

A Male Lamb

Your lamb shall be without blemish, a male of the first year.
You may take it from the sheep or from the goats. Ex. 12:5.

In biblical days the choice of a male lamb as a sacrifice foreshadowed a number of critical aspects of the ministry of Jesus.

From the beginning the male was assigned the role of priest, provider, and protector of the family. Jesus is all that for the needy human race. As our priest He functions daily in the courts above; He is our "go-between," our worthy, trusted arbitrator before the Father. As our provider, He grants our daily sustenance by the guidance of Scripture, and gives gifts of seed time and harvest so the righteous are never seen forsaken or their seed "begging bread" (Ps. 37:25). As our protector He guides us by His angels through and around the physical dangers by which Satan could destroy our churches, our children, and our lives.

He protects us spiritually as well. That is what David had in mind when he wrote: "Your word I have hidden in my heart, that I might not sin against You" (Ps. 119:11).

The male, created first in Eden, was tasked to care for his wife and children. His superior height and physical prowess were to be utilized in guaranteeing their comfort and happiness. In this sense, Eve's status was not simply compatible with his, but actually more privileged in that her welfare was to be guaranteed by his servanthood.

Jesus, Son of God and Son of man, is guarantor for the whole human race. He was born of the flesh (Rom. 8:3) in a process that Ellen White describes as "mysterious" and "painful" (*The Upward Look,* p. 90). He was born to serve. His commission was one of self-abnegation, self-denial, and selfless sacrifice. The gender of Jesus promotes, not a state of superiority, but an assignment of service. In God's scheme of things, males are called to perform acts of care that are required to insure the safety of family and society. The term husband or "house-band," itself, is a connotation of service and sacrifice, which was expected of Adam and all his gender likeness.

This is a view quite different from the mind-set that drives many males to function in their relationship to the opposite gender and each other. But this is the mind-set and the example of Jesus, our sacrificial Lamb and loving Lord.

A Perfect Lamb

If his offering as a sacrifice of a peace offering to the Lord is of the flock, whether male or female, he shall offer it without blemish. Lev. 3:6.

The Paschal lamb, or the Passover lamb, as with all of the ritual sacrifices, could have no deformities, no diseases, no discoloration or imperfections. By its purity is represented in the sinless Christ—our righteous sacrifice.

He was absolutely holy in the eternity of His existence before Bethlehem. He has, since His ascension to the Father's right hand, remained the fountainhead of all universal purity. But it was His experience in His earthly life that is symbolized by the spotless lamb. His victory over sin was complete. He was, in the words of Scripture, "holy, harmless, undefiled" (Heb. 7:26). A lesser sacrifice would not have been sufficient. Satan's claim, that the law could not be kept, needed to be disproved. Only after Christ proved that God's law is reasonable and reliable could He die for those who were, by their breach of the law, locked under its condemnation.

His obedience here on earth and His obedience in the courts above were not relatively perfect, they were absolutely, infinitely, completely perfect; perfect without asterisk or possibility of higher gradation. They were not comparatively perfect; they were imminently, totally, and enduringly so.

There are, in religious circles today, a number of theories concerning Christian perfection. Some say it means maturity in action; others describe it as relative obedience; and living without mistake or misjudgment.

How does Christ's life compare with such guidelines? Contrasted with any and all of these, His life on earth was "more than wonderful!" His obedience proved mature without regression, relevant without omission, and absolutely faultless. By all measures His performance in thought, word, and deed exceeds all of our most stringent definitions of purity and perfection.

It is this victory that He shares with us in the form of His righteous blood that cancels our sins and His righteous robe that covers our unholy flesh. By these priceless gifts He is accepted by His Father as our perfect, priceless, Paschal lamb of deliverance.

A Proven Lamb

Now Josiah kept a Passover to the Lord in Jerusalem, and they slaughtered the Passover lambs on the fourteenth day of the first month. 2 Chron. 35:1.

The four days allotted the Hebrew family, between the selection of the Paschal lamb and the slaying, was a period of intense examination of the animal's physical condition. This was ample time to reveal any illness that may have incubated in the animal's flesh or any sickness or deformity that might not have been visible at the moment of initial inspection.

The period of detailed scrutiny of the typical lamb is suggestive of the intense scrutiny that our Lord, the antitypical sacrifice, endured during His earthly ministry. Satan understood the consequences of Christ living a sinless existence and dying a perfect sacrifice, so he utilized all his arsenal of evil to cause Jesus to transgress. Satan sent peers to tease Him, lawyers to trap Him, women to tempt Him, the Sanhedrin to test Him, lawyers to try Him, rulers to threaten Him, the mob to taunt Him, soldiers to terrorize Him, and demons to tear His flesh. Before they violently thrust the cross into the stony ground, they grossly maligned His character and greatly misrepresented His mission.

But "when He was reviled," He "did not revile in return" (1 Peter 2:23). He "was in all points tempted as we are, yet without sin" (Heb. 4:15). "He had done no violence, nor was any deceit in His mouth" (Isa. 53:9). Peter's conclusive testimony was: He "committed no sin" (1 Peter 2:22); He was our spotless sacrifice.

And the Father "shall see the labor of His soul, and be satisfied" (Isa. 53:11). By His triumph over evil, He spoiled the tempter's scheme. He dispelled the tempter's lie and provided for us the example and goal of our daily living. The consequence: by His blood He forgives our sins and makes His perfect obedience the covering gift of our salvation.

We will never prove ourselves worthy. Our natures are too vile, our spiritual constitutions too frail. However, we must try—violently, wholeheartedly—to do so, knowing that our salvation is attained, not by reaching a goal, but by being recipients of the gift of His perfect obedience.

An Innocent Lamb

And you shall offer on that day, when you wave the sheaf, a male lamb of the first year, without blemish, as a burnt offering to the Lord. Lev. 23:12.

The Passover has remained a perpetual reminder to Hebrew descendants of their escape from Egypt. Even today, Orthodox Jewry celebrates these beginnings and relives the miraculous way in which God engineered His people's deliverance. For these modern-day children of Abraham, expectations of final freedom are still rooted in their understandings of the ancient sacrificial rituals.

The lambs, of course, had done nothing worthy of death. They were innocent. Christ, however, was not just innocent in the sense of having done nothing worthy of death; He was innocent in the sense that He had spent His entire life doing nothing but good. And if ever a human deserved to live, it was He.

Pilate pronounced Him guiltless no less than three times during His trials. First, at daybreak on Friday morning when the Sanhedrin took their case to him; second, when Jesus was returned to Pilate following His examination by Herod; and third, as he yielded to the cries of the bloodthirsty mob, asking in fear, "Why, what hath He done? I find no fault in Him at all" (see Luke 23:22). And yet they killed Him. What a miscarriage of justice! What a failure of fairness! What a reversal of right! What a travesty of truth! In essence, Pilate said, "I declare Him innocent . . . crucify Him!"

"Were you there when they crucified my Lord?" the song asks. Yes, we were there. For his death was not simply something done for us; it was an act committed by us. "But he was pierced for our transgressions, he was crushed for our iniquities; the punishment that brought us peace was on him, and by his wounds we are healed" (Isa. 53:5, NIV).

He paid a debt He did not owe because we owed a debt we could not pay. And because of this, He is our blessed Passover worthy of our daily gratitude and surrender.

A Substitute Lamb

Then Moses called for all the elders of Israel and said to them,
"Pick out and take lambs for yourselves according to your families,
and kill the Passover lamb." Ex. 12:21.

Imagine the pain to parents and children caused by the slaying of the lamb. Often the creature sacrificed was not simply one of the flock, but a lamb that had been observed and nurtured for weeks and months; a lamb known for its physical characteristics and personality traits; a lamb that had been named, petted, and teased and had learned to follow the family at work and play.

Now the unsuspecting creature is cradled in the father's arms. His head is pulled back and the furry neck exposed for the strike. His trusting eyes lock onto those of his lifelong benefactor who clinches his teeth and plunges the jagged blade through the thick fur and flesh of the lamb; and swiftly, deftly draws the knife across its jugular vein, instantly producing a pulsating stream of rich, warm blood. As the animal's eyes close in death, its system convulses in grotesque contortions while the tearful executioner bows his head in hopeless sorrow.

It was thus at Calvary where our sacrifice died. Throughout His life here on earth He and the Father had been one. They had worked together and functioned in tandem as partners in the great plan of salvation. But there in the Garden of Gethsemane He took our sins upon Himself, and the God who has promised to punish sin wherever He finds it regarded Him as the enemy. By pulling our sins and transgressions over His perfect being, He became the object of the Father's wrath. The Father, who hates sin and is dedicated to its eradication from His otherwise-pure universe, punished Him as sin—Jesus, "who knew no sin to be sin for us" (2 Cor. 5:21).

The Father could not save Him and us, so He punished us through Him and endured the pain of ordering and witnessing His Son's shameful death. There is no greater love, no dearer sacrifice, and no higher stimulus for our daily consecration.

What is our response to this sacrifice? It should be a life that reveals to others both His grace to forgive and His power to cleanse.

The All-conquering Lamb

Saying with a loud voice: "Worthy is the Lamb who was slain
to receive power and riches and wisdom, and strength
and honor and glory and blessing." Rev. 5:12.

In speaking of the cosmic, all-pervasive consequences of Jesus' victory on our behalf, John, the beloved disciple who gave us the picturesque revelations of the final book of the Bible, describes Jesus as our Lamb:

Who stands upon Mount Zion (see Rev. 5:6).

Whose death purchases our salvation (verse 9)

Before whom the elders bow (verse 12).

Who is worthy to be praised (verse 12).

To whom thanks is forever given (verse 13).

Who opens the seals (Rev. 6:1).

Who sits upon the throne (verse 16).

From whose wrath the wicked flee (verse 16).

Whose blood makes white the robes of the saved (Rev. 7:14).

By whose blood the saints overcome (Rev. 12:11).

Who was slain from the foundation of the world (Rev. 13:8).

Who the redeemed will follow (Rev. 14:4).

Before whom the saved will gather (see Rev. 17:9).

Who inhabits the temple above (Rev. 21:22).

Who opens the "Book of Life" (verse 27).

Whose presence cancels the need for sun or moon (verse 23).

Our text states that the redeemed, forever enamored with the benefits of salvation provided by the Lamb, will follow Him whithersoever He shall go. But in order for that to happen, we must love and obey Him now. We do this by accepting the gracious offer of His righteousness and by conforming to His will, i.e., by consciously applying His righteous principles to our daily decisions.

All of the triumphs and tributes above accent how our great God became our lowly servant and successfully rescued us from destruction. All praise be to the Lamb today, every day, and forever!

The Lamb Consumed

Then they shall eat the flesh on that night; roasted in fire, with unleavened bread and with bitter herbs they shall eat it. Ex. 12:8.

Every detail of the Passover experience had significant meaning for Israel's relationship to God. However, it was essential that the flesh must be eaten. Killing the lamb was not enough; roasting the lamb was not enough; the lamb must be consumed.

This act symbolized the need of each believer to ingest the Word of God. Purchasing beautiful Bibles is not enough; having various versions of the Word on the family bookshelf is not enough; going to church on Sabbath and listening to the Word taught by those who have studied Scripture more is not enough. We must individually, thoughtfully, prayerfully consume its contents.

The Word is the source of infinite power. The power that brought light from darkness and founded our world (Ps. 33:9) is now resident in the written Word that makes saints of sinners. The Word is not just a source of conversion; it is the only source of conversion. Without the life-giving power of the Word, no hard hearts can be broken, no stubborn wills brought to surrender, no filthy lives cleansed.

The power that creates also sustains. Our world was not brought into being and left to the vagaries of time and space. Planet Earth is upheld and controlled in its orbit by the superior will of its Creator, God. We are not re-created (redeemed) and left alone. Strength and wisdom for our daily journey are abundantly provided in His Word; we can receive it if we eat His flesh not in ritualistic compliance or marginally measured bites, but with the zeal of David, who said: "I will delight myself in Your statutes; I will not forget Your Word" (Ps. 119:16). And with Jeremiah, who happily observed: "Your words were found, and I ate them, and Your word was to me the joy and rejoicing of my heart" (Jer. 15:16).

I like the motto of the young evangelist I heard admonishing his recently baptized converts: "no Bible—no breakfast; no Bible—no bed." This simply stated principle is absolutely essential for converts old and new.

The Whole Lamb

You shall let none of it remain until morning, and what remains of it until morning you shall burn with fire. Ex. 12:10.

In most climates the onslaught of bodily decay takes place approximately 72 hours after breath leaves the body—a period twice as long as Jesus' sojourn in the tomb. Consequently, there was no spoiling of the Master's flesh. His spiritual nature was susceptible to sinning, and His physical flesh, without the nourishment of flowing blood and an active nervous system, was susceptible to souring, but that was not to be. Flesh that had not sinned would not sour.

Jesus rose according to His own prediction (John 2:19), frustrating Satan's attempts to reduce His body to nothingness. Even if His human body deteriorated, His divine being would still have survived into eternity. Since it was critical to His high priestly function on our behalf that His humanity be preserved, He suffered no bodily decay.

The preservation of Christ's body speaks grandly not only to His present ministry, but also to our reverence for His Word. No part of the Bible is to be thought of lightly or left to languish. "All Scripture is given by inspiration of God, and is profitable for doctrine, for reproof, for correction, for instruction in righteousness" (2 Tim. 3:16).

"The Old Testament is the New Testament concealed; the New Testament is the Old Testament revealed!" While changing times and cultures make some biblical laws and customs nonapplicable for our day, there is no part of Scripture that is not instructive for us today. Even Moses' laws and ceremonies, no longer binding, shed valuable light upon the character and will of God. None of His Word is to be discarded as irrelevant or unnecessary.

The Word is life: the revelation of the mind of God. It is the promise and pledge of salvation that not only exalts and glorifies the Lamb of God, but also provides us motivation and power to do His will. This is why David wrote of God's statutes: "More to be desired are they than gold. . . . Moreover by them Your servant is warned, and in keeping them there is great reward" (Ps. 19:10, 11).

Sharing the Lamb

And if the household is too small for the lamb, let him and his neighbor next to his house take it according to the number of the persons; according to each man's need you shall make your count for the lamb. Ex. 12:4.

Selfishness is the fundamental human fault. It is the wellspring of egotism, envy, hatred, materialism, pride, racism, tribalism, and all other ungodliness. Selflessness, on the other hand, is the most distinguishing characteristic of the mind of God. It was selfless love that caused the Father to share His Son, the Son to share His life, and the Holy Spirit to share His powers in guiding us to acknowledgment and obedience of truth.

Every aspect of the Passover experience accents this unselfish love that is so different from the greed that afflicts the human heart. However, no part of the ceremony speaks more poignantly of God's love than the command to share one's lamb with households too small or too poor to afford the sacrifice. After all, it is because we are incapable of satisfying the demands of justice and forgiveness that Jesus, our lamb, was sacrificed. The resources of humanity are far too meager to afford and far too polluted to deserve His mercies.

He has died for us, and we must share the Lamb! We err when we selfishly contain the good news of salvation. When we are truly redeemed, that is, truly impacted by the liberating news of Jesus love, we cannot and will not be silent. Hearts and homes in which Jesus dwells will share the Lamb. Christ's love cannot be hidden or hoarded by those whom He has touched. We need no plaques or certificates of performance to stimulate their witness. They are motivated by Christ's love; God's goodness always finds expression in the grateful heart.

We share the Lamb not as a means of salvation. Our sharing the Lamb is an irrepressible consequence of our rescue by His love. It is when that love is eclipsed by "the lusts of other things entering in" (Mark 4:19, KJV) that our zeal flags, our ardor is blunted, and our joy is lost. When, in our daily devotion, the truths of the slaughtered Lamb are renewed in our hearts, "the love of Christ compels us" (2 Cor. 5:14) to joyful, selfless sharing in word and deed.

The Bitter Herbs

Then they shall eat the flesh on that night; roasted in fire, with
unleavened bread and with bitter herbs they shall eat it. Ex. 12:8.

The bitter herbs spoke to the suffering of both the deliverer (the true Lamb of God) and the delivered (His people, Israel). They also remind us of the certainty of suffering in the life of each believer today. This suffering of the saints has many categories. One is the natural consequence of our human condition: the state of the physical debility produced by Adam's transgression and ours—the illnesses and deformities that are the consequences of the Fall.

Another is brought on by Satan as a means to frustrate God's people and His program. Satan's tactics are often more subtle than in prior centuries, but they are no less savage and certain. In fact, they are multiplied and intensified as he sees his end approaching (Rev. 12:12).

Another source of suffering is that of our own doings. Scripture's declaration "Blessed are those who are persecuted for righteousness' sake" (Matt. 5:10) reminds us that not all suffering is the result of unavoidable consequences of the Fall or imposed by specified attacks by Satan. Some suffering results from our own conscious misdeeds and is peculiarly damaging to our confidence.

There is yet another cause of suffering: the pain that God Himself inflicts—the fiery trials He ordains to burn away the dross from the raw diamonds (which symbolize His people) and thus prepare us for use in His service now and in the kingdom to come.

No matter what the source or category, Scripture reminds us that all our trials can be agents of spiritual growth. If we will bear trustingly our unavoidable pain and learn humbly from our avoidable errors, we will discover that "all things work together for good to those who love God" (Rom. 8:28). We will also be inspired to remember that there is a better day coming—a day of complete release from the bitter perplexities and pain of this life. A day of roses without thorns, life without death, and time without end; this joyous prospect makes today and every day a hopeful prelude to "something better."

The Unleavened Bread

For seven days no leaven shall be found in your houses,
since whoever eats what is leavened, that same person shall
be cut off from the congregation of Israel. Ex. 12:19.

Leaven is an additive: a substance included in the breadmaking process with the primary purpose of making it (the bread) attractive in size and shape. Leaven is not used for nutritional purpose; its real value is cosmetic, not substantive. Thus, the absence of leaven from the Passover bread left it much less attractive, but no less nutritional. From this fact we gain valuable spiritual lessons.

The first is that God sees the heart. Others may judge by appearance and outward show, but not God; He values our internal state of being. God is not oblivious to beauty; after all, He is the Creator of the incandescent hue of the rainbow that spans the sky above, the multicolored fish that inhabit the ocean below, and the attractive wings of an infinite variety of butterflies flying around. The lesson of the loaves reminds us that external appearance does not equate to internal goodness and that we are mistaken when we project form above substance.

The second lesson is that pride is the basic sin. It is the lifting up of the heart, the swelling of the ego that underlies all transgressions. Pride is the reason we refuse to submit to an exterior although superior being. Pride is the cause of us holding our own intelligence as sufficient for life's battles. Pride is the emotion that exalts our opinions, our looks, our possessions, even our desires, as better than those of others.

The third lesson of the leavened bread is that God delights to use the weak and ordinary. The Savior of the world had "no beauty that we should desire Him" (Isa. 53:2)—He came into the world without the appearance or the trappings of power that drew attention. He came in a servant's garb "as a root out of a dry ground" and lived a life of Spartan humility in order to know our condition at its lowest. He accepted the limitations of our denigration that we might one day be joined with Him in heavenly places. His sacrifice is not only a path we follow as Christians, but also a provision that makes our living worthwhile and joyous.

No Bones Broken

In one house it shall be eaten; you shall not carry any of the flesh outside the house, nor shall you break one of its bones. Ex. 12:46.

In reflecting upon the way in which Christ's death fulfilled this element of the Passover process, John wrote: "But when they came to Jesus and saw that He was already dead, they did not break His legs. . . . For these things were done that the Scripture should be fulfilled, 'Not one of His bones shall be broken'" (John 19:33-36).

Why were His legs not to be broken? Because had death been induced in that manner the process of His dying in our behalf would have been aborted—He was destined, by our sins, to die from a broken heart, not from broken bones. In addition, the body that He offered for our sins would not have been acceptable by the Father were it lame or limp or defective in any way. It was required that our Lord die physically as well as spiritually unimpaired.

True, the violence He suffered during His passion marred His physical exterior. But the crucified Christ had no structural deficiencies, except in the end His broken heart. The whip that gouged flesh from His back, the nails that forced blood from His veins, the crown that penetrated His noble brow, and the sword that pierced His tender side defaced a body that carried no disease or malfunctions. He died not only a willing but also a complete sacrifice.

Jesus was complete not only with respect to His individual person. He was complete with respect to His identity with needy humanity. Scripture is clear on this point: "But when the fullness of the time had come, God sent forth His Son, born of a woman, born under the law, to redeem those who were under the law, that we might receive the adoption as sons" (Gal. 4:4, 5). In other words, He was one of us; He was and is, in the truest sense, "bone of [our] bone and flesh of [our] flesh" (Gen. 2:23), subject as are we to temptation and death, but the sinless conqueror of both.

However, that which gives tactical completeness to His services on our behalf is none of the above. It is His present ministry as our advocate before the Father. The pleading of His cleansing blood and the offering of His righteous robe are the acts whereby He finalized (completes) our salvation and sustains our hopes in the fulfillment of His pledge to come again.

The Hyssop Also

And you shall take a bunch of hyssop, dip it in the blood that is in the basin, and strike the lintel and the two doorposts with the blood that is in the basin. And none of you shall go out of the door of his house until morning. Ex. 12:22.

Bible scholars and botanists express uncertainty as to what kind of hyssop was available to the Hebrews in the above reference. However, there is one common agreement: all hyssop by itself or in combination with other plants or trees (i.e., cedar wood) used in the purification rites of lepers (Lev. 14:3-6) was symbolic of healing. This is because hyssop in many of its varieties contains distinct purification (disinfectant properties).

It was this that David prayed: "Purge me with hyssop, and I shall be clean; wash me, and I shall be whiter than snow" (Ps. 51:7). This message is as pertinent today as it was to ancient Israel. Purity is still required of all who would effectively proclaim fellowship with Jesus. Isaiah said it clearly: "Be clean, you who bear the vessels of the Lord" (Isa. 52:11).

The broader lesson is that the blood itself cleanses. The righteous blood, shed on Calvary, is the legal tender that atones for our transgressions. The blood that Christ gave in response to Heaven's rule—"the wages of sin is death" (Rom. 6:23)— is what brings forgiveness and reconciliation and deliverance.

Those who handle the blood (who proclaim salvation to others) must be cleansed or wholly consecrated to God. In answer to the prophet's demanding challenge, "Who may ascend into the hill of the Lord? Or who may stand in His Holy place?" the clear clarion response rings: "He who has clean hands and a pure heart, who has not lifted up his soul to an idol, nor sworn deceitfully" (Ps 24:3, 4).

Today we have another opportunity to be effective witnesses for our Lord. We must do so by remembering that the quality of that witness is tied to the depth of our consecration and that one's consecration is very much dependent upon one's habits of prayerful devotion. Why not deepen the consecration and brighten our witness today by being more focused, more solemn, more dedicated to the attention of His Word?

The Prominence of the Blood

And they shall take some of the blood and put it on the two doorposts and on the lintel of the houses where they eat it. Ex. 12:7.

Actually, the avenging angel would have known who the obedient were no matter where the blood was positioned. But as a test of their trust in God's promises and their willingness to strictly comply with His directions, He ordained that the blood be placed on the posts and lintels that framed the entrance to each family residence.

The critical need to follow faithfully the instructions concerning the sprinkling of the blood reminds us that we were created with free wills—not as robots programmed to obey in routine, mechanical fashion. The Creator desires services of love and willing obedience. The tree of the knowledge of good and evil was the test for our first parents. The Sabbath and the tithing plan is a test for us today.

There was an even greater reason for the sprinkling of the blood in such obvious positions. By this visible display of the blood, the nation of Israel and its spiritual descendants were to be forever reminded of the centrality of Christ's sacrifice.

How vital is His blood for our salvation? It is totally responsible. As our physical organism is made alive and sustained by the life-bearing qualities distributed throughout our bodies in an intricate system of arteries and veins, so are we spiritually quickened and sustained by Jesus' blood. It is because life is in the blood that God decreed the shedding to symbolize Christ's sacrifice. He is our Pascal lamb, and our appreciation and dependence upon His blood must be abundantly evident. It should garland all our teachings, highlight all our testimonies, and resound in all our preaching. The dominant note of our witness, the dearest thought of our hearts, the daily joy of our lives should be the essence of the musical strain that declares:

"The blood that Jesus shed for me,
   way back on Calvary;
   the blood that gives me strength from day to day,
   it will never lose its power."

The Place of the Blood

Now the blood shall be a sign for you on the houses where you are. And when I see the blood, I will pass over you; and the plague shall not be on you to destroy you when I strike the land of Egypt. Ex. 12:13.

Notice, it was not on the church walls or the school doors that the blood was to be sprinkled, but on the portals of their homes. What a potent reminder of the vital role of family life to individual and corporate prosperity!

The importance of the home to social welfare is also embodied in the biblical mandate "Keep your heart with all diligence, for out of it spring the issues of life" (Prov. 4:23). The heart of the community and the nation is the home. It (the home) is the factory whose product (the individual citizen) builds our communities. When that factory is faulty in the processing, it issues products (children) that are disrespectful, dispirited, undisciplined, and ill-intentioned. The result is seen in the frightening chaos of our pleasure-mad, materialistic age.

The essential tie between family life and personal as well as societal well-being is noted by the fact that family focus is given in no less than six of the 10 tenants of the moral law. Home influences are involved in commandments 2, 4, 5, 6, 9, and 10. The home is also amplified in the imagery by which Scripture references the associations of church membership: God is our Father, Jesus His Son is our brother, the church itself is the family of God, we believers are brothers and sisters, and all of us are children in the household of faith."

Further establishing Scripture's family emphasis is the fact that the church is referred to as "a house of prayer for all nations" (Isa. 56:7). The saved are spoken of as "adopted through the blood of Christ" (see Eph. 1:5), our returning Lord is called the "coming groom," the pure church is His "waiting bride" and the Second Coming is "the marriage of the Lamb."

The success of our individual family units, the family groups that make up our congregations, and the church families that constitute the world body of believers depends directly on our daily application of His blood to all our endeavors.

The Power of the Blood

And it came to pass at midnight that the Lord struck all the
firstborn in the land of Egypt, from the firstborn of Pharaoh who
sat on his throne to the firstborn of the captive who was
in the dungeon, and all the firstborn of livestock. Ex. 12:29.

The prominence and place of the blood have their special meaning. But nothing about the Passover speaks more loudly to our salvation than the power of the blood.

How radically did the Passover blood rearrange the landscape of those it affected? To the Egyptians, its absence meant death, with utter chaos and sorrow. But for Israel and all those in Egypt who did believe and follow Jehovah's commands, it meant approval and rescue and the inexpressible joy of participating in the fulfillment of His special pledge to Abraham. The parallels for us are unmistakable. For all who accept Christ's blood and obey, there is life everlasting. For those who reject His sacrifice, there is awesome condemnation from which there is no appeal.

As with Pharaoh, rejection did not come summarily; it was only after his refusal to heed the warnings of the first nine plagues that ultimate judgment was executed upon the land of Egypt. The long-suffering Creator does not quickly abandon the sinner. He extends heaven's choicest offerings over lengthy periods seeking to win the hearts of those who do not know Him or who have met Him but still refuse to obey.

For the righteous, the blood is the source of a lengthy list of deliverances. It is by the blood that we have forgiveness (Eph. 1:7) and cleansing (1 John 1:7) and justification (Rom. 5:9) and sanctification (Heb. 13:12) and victory (Rev. 15:2) and communion (1 Cor. 10:16) and purchase (Acts 20:28) and redemption (Col. 1:14).

Only His blood is rich enough, rare enough, and righteous enough to buy back the lost dominion to satisfy the claims of justice and to still the swift sword of the avenger.

The hymnologist was inspired to ask, "Would you be free from the burden of sin?" And to respond: "There is pow'r, pow'r, wonder-working pow'r in the precious blood of the Lamb."

The End of the Beginning

Now you shall keep it until the fourteenth day of the same month. Then the whole assembly of the congregation of Israel shall kill it at twilight. Ex. 12:6.

Dawn begins the second half of God's most basic temporal gifts to the human race: the 24-hour cycle that we call day. In Creation week, what began as darkness issued into the light and beauty of a world made bright by the Creator's presence and power. However, in the Passover design, the lamb was slain at twilight or just as the lengthening shadows heralded the arrival of darkness. It was as the rotating earth began to obscure the shining sun that the lamb was slain. This act foreshadowed the deep depression and dark consternation experienced by Christ's followers in the wake of His crucifixion.

But this sadness and sorrow notwithstanding, Jesus' death was, in truth, the beginning of a better day. Jesus, our better Passover, died at the ninth hour or at 3:00 p.m. on Friday—the day of His crucifixion. In respect for the Sabbath, His friends asked for and received permission to take His body down from the cross, and they tenderly, tearfully laid Him in the grave. He was in Joseph's new tomb on a portion of Friday, He rested all day Saturday (the Sabbath), and He rose early in the morning of the first day (Sunday). He died just as light gave way to darkness—now He rose just as the darkness broke forth to light!

The depression that weighed upon His despairing disciples and the gloom that enveloped the angelic host (each of whom would have gladly died in His place) was not the beginning of the end; it was only the end of the beginning—He rose! In sparkling, blinding brightness, He rose!

His triumph reminds us that "weeping may endure for a night, but joy comes in the morning" (Ps. 30:5); that whatever our night of trial, "He restores [our souls]" (Ps. 23:3); that no matter how crushing the problem or disappointment, we have prospects of a better day in a better world. All this is made possible because our Passover lamb is risen, and reigns not only as monarch of the universe but also as Lord of our lives.

God's People Organized

So God led the people around by way of the wilderness
of the Red Sea. And the children of Israel went up in
orderly ranks out of the land of Egypt. Ex. 13:18.

Notice how the second sentence reads: "And the children of Israel went up in orderly ranks out of the land of Egypt." Unshackled but not unfocused, the Israelites, 600,000 men besides women and children, left the bitter circumstances of slavery and headed for their home in Canaan. They did not leave Egypt helter-skelter or in disarray; they went out in prescribed arrangements with clear instructions regarding rank and process. Their later encounters with the nations through whose territory they marched and whose armies they conquered was a testimony to their adherence to the strict requirements of marshaled marching. They were, Moses states, "harnessed" (KJV).

The orderly exodus of Israel has been a shining example for the people of God throughout history. Ours is a God of order. The universe, with its dependable laws, its predictable seasons, and its codifiable principles of operation, reminds us that "God is not the author of confusion" (1 Cor. 14:33) and that success in His cause, as in any other, is to a great extent in proportion to our attention to details and our submission to justifiable authority.

The modern push for radical individualism; the conversion of the legitimate good of freedom to legal forms of license in contemporary society—these have no place in the church of the living God. The task of gospel proclamation demands efforts of a people unified in doctrine, regulated in policy, and led by the Holy Spirit, who blesses unity and rejects disorder.

However, unity is not unison. They err, those who demand that believers march through this wilderness of waiting "lockstepped" or in mindless uncreative, unimaginative conformity of sameness. The God of order is also a God of diversity and freedom from the slavery of stifling sameness and tired tradition. God's people are to go forward harnessed in the sense of cooperation with wholesome rules and regulations, but never suppressed or stymied in terms of legitimate creativity.

Jewels in Egypt

And the Lord had given the people favor in the
sight of the Egyptians, so that they granted them what they
requested. Thus they plundered the Egyptians. Ex. 12:36.

The children of light and the lovers of darkness functioned by different rules. The devotees of Babylon and the disciples of Christ are led by contrasting principles. The family of God is not comfortable as hostages to the mores of Egypt and its deities; neither is heaven pleased. We cannot be surprised at scriptures that command, "Come out of her" and be separate (Rev. 18:4).

And yet, as Israel's exodus demonstrates, the command to leave Egypt is not a command to ignore its resources that will benefit the work of God. Egypt was no longer to be Israel's home, but many of its materials (see Ex. 12:35) became useful in their economic and social development.

Secular society today lives just as contrary to God's will as did Pharaoh and his people. Our age is rightly described as heathenistic, materialistic, and crassly irreverent. The biblical predictions of evil times apply to this generation as none other. Ours is the world that mirrors all too sadly the descriptions in Matthew 24:36-44, 2 Timothy 3:1-7, and other scriptures that mark this generation as ripe for harvesting by an avenging Lord.

There are jewels in Egypt! There are elements of knowledge to be gained in some of its universities. There are methods of administration to be modeled in its industrialized complexes. There is literature and art and music to be appreciated in its galleries. There is technology helpful to the spreading of the gospel, science that augments our care of the sick, and finance capable of benefiting the advance of God's kingdom.

All good comes from God, and there is some good in the kingdom of darkness that God is waiting to extricate and convert for His kingdom of light. But we must be discriminating. It is when we exalt the secular above the sacred, the finite above the infinite, and the temporary above the eternal that we lose focus and are victims of greed instead of rescuers of good. Riveting our eyes upon Jesus, our superior Passover, is an unfailing antidote to spiritual drift and the key to recognizing and properly utilizing the gems within the society about us.

A Day to Remember

And Moses took the bones of Joseph with him, for he had placed
the children of Israel under solemn oath, saying, "God will surely visit you,
and you shall carry up my bones from here with you." Ex. 13:19.

As the children of Israel left Egypt, they took with them the bones of Joseph—who had made this dying request hundreds of years before (Gen. 50:25). Amid all the signs and wonders that accompanied their departure, they remembered to honor this request of the ancient patriarch. What a wonderful demonstration of fidelity to their elders. Their preparation to move to a better circumstance did not negate their fidelity to their predecessors, nor should it for us.

As the twentieth century recedes in the rearview mirror of our daily experience and we move inexorably deeper into this first century of a new millennium, ever closer to the end of earth's history, we must not allow present wonders to obscure appreciation for the contributions of who made our current state possible.

We owe much to the pioneers who have gone before. The inspiration of past deeds wrought by the people of God is vital to the certainty and purpose of present laborers. As we remember the way God has led in the past, we are mindful of the prophet's words: "In reviewing our past history, having traveled over every step of advance to our present standing, I can say, Praise God! As I see what the Lord has wrought, I am filled with astonishment, and with confidence in Christ as leader. We have nothing to fear for the future, except as we shall forget the way the Lord has led us, and His teaching in our past history" (*Counsels for the Church*, p. 359).

There are some bridges that need to be burned; some yesterdays should be forgotten; some former events excised from our contemplation; some past that should be deleted from the screen of our memory, but never those personalities and victories that positively define our heritage. We stand upon the shoulders of spiritual giants whose contributions to our individual and corporate lives can and should serve as special inspiration as we go forward in faith confident that the future with Christ, our better Passover, is secure in His nail-pierced hands.

Partners in Salvation

Speak to all the congregation of Israel, saying: "On the tenth
of this month every man shall take for himself a lamb, according
to the house of his father, a lamb for a household." Ex. 12:3.

Because we are commanded to neither add nor subtract from the Word of God
(Rev. 22:18, 19), we must be careful not to read more symbolism into the use
of numbers than those scriptures intend. To insist dogmatically that any number
always represents a particular aspect of the divine scheme for humanity is to transgress in this regard. However, when in Scripture a number bears similar emphasis
in multiple instances, we are both justified and blessed by discerning similarities of
meaning.

The number 10 emphasized in our text today is one of several having high priority in the Bible. There were 10 days given to prove the superior fitness of Daniel
and his companions (Dan. 1:12-16); a 10-degree reversal of the sundial provided
Hezekiah as a sign of God's mercy (Isa. 38:8); 10 virgins are mentioned as anticipating the wedding event (Matt. 25:1-13); 10 coins are assiduously sought by the
determined householder (Luke 15:8); there were 10 lepers who begged the Master
for healing (Luke 17:12); 10 minas were issued to the servants by the householder
as a test of their fidelity (Luke 19:13); and, of course, the Ten Commandments were
given as guides for morality and standards of judgment (see James 2:10-12).

What meaning do we discern in this collection of incidents and circumstances
each structured with the use of the number 10? We learn: (a) that God is the great
giver of opportunity and talent; (b) that we are individually accountable to Him for
the development and deployment of His gifts; (c) that the rewards of faithfulness
are infinitely superior to the short-term benefits of capitulation to lesser impulses;
(d) that while all true blessings come from God, there is a direct correlation between effort and success; and (e) that God's plans for our accomplishments are
always higher than our limited designs. How fortunate we are to be reminded by
these means of heaven's offerings and our grateful response.

Assurances of Salvation

Remember the Sabbath day, to keep it holy. Six days you shall labor
and do all your work, but the seventh day is the Sabbath of the Lord
your God. In it you shall do no work: you, nor your son, nor your daughter,
nor your male servant, nor your female servant, nor your cattle, nor your
stranger who is within your gates. For in six days the Lord made the heavens
and the earth, the sea, and all that is in them, and rested the seventh day.
Therefore the Lord blessed the Sabbath day and hallowed it. Ex. 20:8-11.

Seven is another "high visibility" number in the Bible. Its most prominent use, of course, is attached to the Sabbath instituted by God in Eden as a memorial of Creation and reaffirmed by Jesus' rest in Joseph's new tomb.

Seven is also the number used to describe the years that Jacob pledged to work for Rachel (Gen. 29:20), Naaman's washing in the Jordan (2 Kings 5:10), the year of Israel's harvest cycle (Ex. 23:10, 11), the applying of blood upon the horns of the altar (Lev. 16:19), the calculation of Christ's instruction regarding forgiveness (Matt. 18:22), the churches addressed in Revelation (Rev. 1:11), the lampstands among which the Spirit moves (verse 13), and the stars held in God's right hand (verse 16).

In these usages and others it is possible to see: (a) the everlasting nature of God's merciful covenanting toward his creatures; (b) God's assurances of doing a complete or finished work of restoration for this world of sin; (c) the fact that God's mercy does not negate our requirement of obedience; and (d) the sacredness of divine commands.

But again, the most memorable use of the number 7 is its place in the weekly cycle, where it is literally the "sacred seventh" or the holy Sabbath day—the only day that God blessed, sanctified, and hallowed.

What makes the seventh day of worship all the more meaningful is our diligent stewardship on the six days of labor that precede it. The "sacred seventh" cannot be fully enjoyed unless one has faithfully cultivated the "secular six." By living God's way, that day like no other brings riches of rest and reward.

Symbols of Salvation

Hear, O Israel: The Lord our God, the Lord is one! Deut. 6:4.

The numbers 10 and 7 used in the Passover experience and elsewhere are not the only ones with visible symbolism in the Word of God. There is also the number one, which is stressed in God's wish for Adam and Eve's compatibility (Gen. 2:24), in His characterization of the togetherness of the Godhead (Deut. 6:4), and in Christ's wish for the unity of His disciples (John 17:21). These and other uses speak to the attention of Divinity to order and cooperation and unity.

Then there is the number 3, which is employed in the Trinity (1 John 5:7), in the three personages who appeared on the Mount of Transfiguration (Mark 9:5), and in the three crosses erected upon Calvary (Luke 23:32, 33). These uses speak eloquently to the balance of God's character and His redemptive gifts to humanity.

And there is the number 4, comprising the word YHWH, or Jehovah (Ps. 83:18); also seen in the number of rivers in Eden (Gen. 2:10); the total quarters of the earth (Rev. 7:1); the wheels of Ezekiel's vision of majesty (Eze. 10:9); the walls of the new Jerusalem (Rev. 21:16); the world kingdoms of history (Dan. 2); the days Lazarus laid in the grave prior to Christ's arrival (John 11:17); and the gospels of the New Testament—all of which speak to the power and majesty of God.

Then there is the number 12 utilized in Israel's tribal arrangements (Gen. 25:26), in the loaves placed by the priest upon the table of showbread (Lev. 24:5, 8), in the number of stones placed in the Jordan (Joshua 4:8), in the totality of disciples Jesus chose (Matt. 10:1), in the number of baskets that remained after the miracle of the feeding (Matt. 14:20), in the number of thrones upon which the righteous will sit (Matt 19:28), and in the fruit borne annually in the Holy City (Rev. 22:2). All are reminders of God's active compassion, his willingness and ability not only to adopt us into the family of the redeemed, but also to empower and finally to sustain and reward the faithful in both this world and the next.

Such study confirms that God's Word is a treasure trove of object lessons of salvation that, seen with the eye of faith, is a marvelous unveiling of the beauty and wisdom of its Author.

The New Passover

And He said, "Go into the city to a certain man, and say to him,
'The Teacher says, "My time is at hand; I will keep the Passover
at your house with My disciples."'" Matt. 26:18.

As the Passover service foreshadowed the sacrifice of our earthly Messiah, the Communion service that He instituted just before He died points to His glorious second coming. By partaking of the broken bread and unfermented wine, we join our Lord in the pledge that someday soon we will eat and drink with Him in fellowship above.

The ordinance of humility that precedes the eating and drinking is a time of confession and repentance—a time for spiritual confession and rededication. The lapping of the water on one's feet symbolizes cleansing from sin; it is a "mini baptism," a plea to God for the washing away of the dust of sins and shortcomings that may have accumulated upon our hearts since our last celebration of this rite.

But when we come to the table, we should come, not with sorrow or remorse, but with joyful anticipation. As we engage this part of the service, we are not to "lament [our] shortcomings" or dwell upon past failures. The foot-washing phase embraced all of that. During this phase of the ceremony, God's people "are not to stand in the shadow of the cross, but in its saving light. They are to open the soul to the bright beams of the Sun of Righteousness" (*The Desire of Ages,* p. 659).

The ancient Passover service with all its pageantry and drama has ended. The Communion sacrament that Christ has given in its place is much less dramatic, but it is just as meaningful and just as much a requirement for His followers. It is true that none should participate in this service unworthily (1 Cor. 11:27, 29), i.e., with sins not confessed or premeditated evil in one's heart.

Since the opportunity for refreshing precedes the moments of rejoicing, each one can freely participate in these services, and each can leave revived, restored, and rededicated to "daily partaking of the bread of life" and "receiving His Word and doing His will" (*The Seventh-day Adventist Bible Commentary,* Ellen G. White Comments, vol. 5, p. 1140).

FEBRUARY

A Better Covenant

Something New

To Jesus the Mediator of the new covenant, and to the blood
of sprinkling that speaks better things. Heb. 12:24.

Scripture contains many prospects of something new. God's Word provides us the promises of a new birth (John 3:3-5), becoming a new creation (2 Cor. 5:17), inheriting a new heaven (Rev. 21:1), occupying a new earth (2 Peter 3:13), acquiring a new name (Rev. 2:17), singing a new song (Rev. 5:9), and, as stated by Christ Himself, being partakers of the new covenant (Matt. 26:28).

Old is not always bad. Old friendships, old memories, old values, and sometimes even old books, old clothes, old cars, and other such objects delight our senses and enhance our comfort zone, bringing pleasurable feelings and memories.

But oldness is always tied to the steady, stealthy flow of time. It is a sure indicator of our temporariness: a sign of our perishability; the certain evidence of the mortal succession that binds the human race—the fact that "time and tide wait for no man."

Newness, on the other hand, speaks to beginning again: the hope of better relations, improved performance, enhanced joys—the prospects of satisfactions never experienced before. God's new covenant is the vehicle by which all such spiritual and physical good is fulfilled.

Not that the old covenant established at Sinai is without value for us today—its legal arrangements are no longer valid, but its spiritual lessons should never be lost. We learn from it that God is to be reverenced, respected, and revered; that God is a faithful provider for the needs of His people; that God is utterly dependable in fulfillment of His promises; and that true success demands on human response to divine initiatives.

We also learn that human vows and victories, no matter how grandiose, are not of themselves qualifiers for heaven's approval; that to "talk the talk" is not to "walk the walk," and that only by the illumination of the Divine Spirit is true obedience sustainable.

This is precisely what the covenant sealed at Calvary—the New Testament of His blood intends (Matt. 26:28). By this sacrifice, sanctification is the gift of Christ's righteousness; not the earnings of our efforts. Our most urgent priority is accepting this rich and ennobling gift.

February 2

The Covenanting God

This is the history of the heavens and the earth when they were created, in the day that the Lord God made the earth and the heavens. Gen. 2:4.

The character of the Creator who covenants with the human race is mirrored in the names by which He introduces Himself in the Genesis account. First, He is spoken of in Genesis 1:1 as God, the Hebrew word *"Elohim,"* suggesting a *Being* of long-suffering and tender regard toward His creatures—in other words, a God of mercy.

Second, He is presented in Genesis 2:4 as not simply God, but Lord God. Lord in the Hebrew is *"Yahew,"* the one who relates to His subjects with exactitude and accountability—in other words, a *Being* of justice.

Thus, in the combination of these terms, Yahew and Elohim, or Lord God, a name that appears 11 times in Genesis 2, we are presented the full scale of God's personality. Together, the words "Lord God" constitute the essence of His nature, the twin spheres of His character, and the dual principles of His covenanting relationship with humanity.

There are many other names used later in Scripture. Among them: *El Shaddai*, the provider of blessings to His people; *El Elyon*, the possessor of heaven and earth; *Adonai,* the Lord and master of all created beings, and *El Olam*, the God who works His will through eternity.

It is in this original designation, Lord God, or the Creator, who is both absolutely just and wholly merciful, that we see the all-encompassing totality of His being.

In numerous accounts of the Old Testament we are given memorable emphasis of God's impeccable justice. In the New Testament, however, we are impressed by God's mercy highlighted at Calvary. It should be noted that it was there on the cross that these opposite prerogatives were eternally reconciled; there, at the vortex of history, "mercy and truth have met together; righteousness and peace have kissed" (Ps. 85:10); there, in the form of the bleeding lamb, the universe beheld the perfect blend of justice (Jesus punished on behalf of sinners) and mercy (Jesus punished as a sinner Himself).

What should our response be? How about beginning with daily thanksgiving for His manifold goodness, and daily surrender to His manifest grace.

The Creation Covenant

And the Lord God commanded the man, saying,
"Of every tree of the garden you may freely eat;
but of the tree of the knowledge of good and evil you shall not eat,
for in the day that you eat of it you shall surely die." Gen. 2:16, 17.

God did not create sinners. He created beings in His own image who lost their status by disobedience. Neither did He create sickness or death or the pollution-riddled planet on which we now live. All that is the souring of the perfection He established in Eden; the consequences of the broken covenant of life—a souring that we do not truly understand, for to understand or logically explain it (sin) would be to excuse it.

The covenant arrangement was simple and straightforward. God would provide the perfection of Eden, our first parents would provide loving obedience, and, in that happy relationship, humanity would revel and heaven rejoice.

And it worked! We are not certain for how many days or weeks or years, but it was there until Eve naively wandered from Adam's side and Adam consciously yielded to temptation; the Eden covenant was in fruitful force.

While the Creation covenant aborted by sin is no longer binding, its principles still exist. God still delights in trusting relationships with His creatures and His creatures are still promised everlasting life when they are faithful to His will. Life in "Eden restored" will be no less grand and attractive than life in "Eden lost." As with our first parents, it is our exercise of the power of choice that determines our citizenship there; our choice constitutes the deciding vote. Immortality is still an option for the human race.

Though that immortality is preceded by the sleep of death, it is no less a reality. Jesus' death and resurrection is prototype and pledge for those who will awaken from the enduring darkness of the grave to the unending joys of eternity. His words "He who believes in Me, though he may die, he shall live" (John 11:25) are but the restatement of His original pledge to our species and the grand assurance that brings daily hope to our otherwise hopeless existence.

The Covenant of Life

Then the man said, "The woman whom You gave
to be with me, she gave me of the tree, and I ate." And the Lord God
said to the woman, "What is this you have done?" The woman said,
"The serpent deceived me, and I ate." Gen. 3:12, 13.

In structuring the terms of the original covenant with Adam and Eve, God did not desire to hide from them the history of evil. He intended that they learn of sin and its consequences, but not as participants or victims of the process. They were, over time, to be adequately introduced to the secrets of the tree. By yielding to Satan's wishes, they shortened the process; their eyes were opened, but their promises were broken, and the covenant of life was annulled.

Hosea describes our first parents' breach of contract succinctly: "But they like Adam have transgressed the covenant: there have they dealt treacherously against me" (Hosea 6:7, ASV).

What a bargain God had arranged—what a deal! For their trusting obedience, everlasting life in an atmosphere of absolute perfection! But they failed amid the beauty of paradise. And, as our prophet reminds us, when the first parents sinned, they were not even hungry (*Signs of the Times,* Apr. 4, 1900). The text revealed they made excuses, but actually there was no reasonable reason. There is never any reasonable excuse for sin. Sin is explainable only in terms of our idolatrous efforts at self-gratification rather than self-abnegation and trusting in God.

While the relationship that you and I have with God carries far less than the cosmic consequences that were involved in the case of Adam and Eve, it is no less important to Him and no less meaningful to our personal destiny. God will always keep His promises. This is the realization that caused Jeremiah to write: "It is of the Lord's mercies that we are not consumed, because his compassions fail not. They are new every morning: great is thy faithfulness. The Lord is my portion, saith my soul; therefore will I hope in him" (Lam. 3:22-24, KJV). And it is that thought that should and must inspire us this day to live in joyful obedience to His will.

The Covenant With Noah

Then God spoke to Noah and to his sons with him,
saying: . . . "Thus I establish My covenant with you:
Never again shall all flesh be cut off by the waters of the flood;
never again shall there be a flood to destroy the earth." Gen. 9:8-11.

An early demonstration of God's covenanting with humanity was His rainbow pledge to Noah. Just as God had given hope to Adam and Eve by accompanying their pronouncements of punishment with a promise of the Redeemer (Gen. 3:15), He gave assurances to Noah above the carnage of the floodwaters when He spanned the rainbow as a dramatic and delightful declaration of His love.

By the rainbow was seen God's mercy in sparing the righteous (Noah and his family), but in the destruction that it overarched we also see His fearsome justice. The rainbow's soft but stunning beauty is a reminder that the destruction of His creatures is God's "strange act" (Isa. 28:21, KJV), that death and dying are not His wish for the human race, that it is our sins that separate us from Him and necessitate His displeasure.

The rainbow is still with us. The primary message of its beauty is that trouble won't last always; that above the den of human confusion and misery there is a loving God waiting and ruling upon the circle of the universe. No matter how bad or how painful our lives, God sees, God knows, that His stern justice is balanced by His great mercy; and beyond the terror of this life there is a better day ahead.

The good doctor who, for 50 years, served selflessly in the little town labored from his office under a modest shingle that directed patients to his second-floor facilities. When he died, his family provided unique tribute to his memory by placing the words of that shingled sign upon the headstone to mark his grave. It read: "J. J. Murdock, Office Upstairs."

Jesus, our Redeemer, spent His life in selfless, sacrificial ministry for our doomed and dying world. He is no longer with us, but from His "office upstairs" He sees our sorrows, hears our prayers, and fulfills His promises to provide life and joy and peace to all who honor Him.

The Covenant With Abraham

"And I will make My covenant between Me and you,
and will multiply you exceedingly." . . . "As for Me, behold,
My covenant is with you, and you shall be a father of many nations.
No longer shall your name be called Abram, but your name shall be
Abraham; for I have made you a father of many nations." Gen. 17:2-5.

Genesis 17 is regarded as the covenant chapter. More than 10 times in this passage the word "covenant" is used by God to describe the unique pact that He established with Abraham.

It is actually five chapters prior in Genesis 12:1-3 that the agreement is sealed. And what was His servant's response to God's challenge? Verse 4 of chapter 12 reads: "So Abram departed as the Lord had spoken to him."

What a wonderful demonstration of friendship! God trusted Abram, and Abram trusted Him; he left the comforts of family and country and tribe in blind obedience to God's command. So trusting was his faith that it was "counted . . . to him for righteousness" (Gen. 15:6, KJV). But Abram's faith was not perfect. His faith, though mighty, was not invincible; it was seen in his disbelief of the promise of a son in his old age (Gen. 17:16, 17).

However, as he witnessed the miracle-working power of God in Isaac's birth, his faithful trust, already mighty, was perfected. Thus he was able to pass the supreme test: the willingness to sacrifice the child of promise (Gen. 22:1-16). How did God respond to Abram's demonstration of completed trust? The promise of the covenant was repeated, and his name was changed from Abram to Abraham.

God changed Abram's name to Abraham; Jacob's name to Israel; and Saul's name to Paul. However, this did not indicate their having reached a state of absolute or finished perfection. Both their faith and their character were amenable to growth. They were often thereafter tried, and, in some cases, they failed. But they persisted and were used by God as instruments of salvation.

Everyday providence brings us all into situations requiring trustful obedience. Though we, as they, sometimes falter, if we persist in daily devotion and obedience to His Word, we too will become and remain friends of God—heirs of the offerings of the covenant of life.

The Sign of Agreement

And God said to Abraham: "As for you, you shall keep My covenant,
you and your descendants after you throughout their generations.
This is My covenant which you shall keep, between Me and you and your
descendants after you: Every male child among you shall be circumcised;
and you shall be circumcised in the flesh of your foreskins, and it
shall be a sign of the covenant between Me and you." Gen. 17:9-11.

We are not surprised that God instituted a memorial or sign as a way of seal-ing the agreement between Himself and Abraham. Shortly before Abraham's birth God provided, in the wake of the Flood, the rainbow as a reminder, to the populace, of His covenanting presence. Later, in Israel's desert wanderings, He gave the pillar of cloud by day and the pillar of fire by night, as well as various blood sacrifices, as symbols of His covenant relationship with His people.

But why was circumcision a sign to to signify His covenant with Abraham? Because this painful ritual that was performed upon each male of Hebrew heritage and imposed upon each male adopted into their society was rife with spiritual les-sons. Among them: the casting aside of the flesh (Rom. 2:27, 28), the putting off of unnecessary habits and weights (Heb.12:1), the call to cleanliness of heart (Rom. 2:29), and, the most poignant of all, the pain and suffering of Jesus, who ratified His Father's "better covenant" by His submission to the painful horrors of Calvary.

One of the soldiers who beheld that act exclaimed: "Truly this Man was the Son of God" (Mark 15:39). When we who are circumcised of heart also cry out in sur-render to His gift of immeasurable love for us, this acknowledgment is recognized in heaven as the signature act that opens to us all the privileges and promises of contractual relationship with our God.

In what act of obvious obedience do we most clearly express our continuing covenant relationship with our Lord? By honoring His holy Sabbath day. This is the meaning of Ezekiel's words: "I am the Lord your God: Walk in My statutes, keep My judgments, and do them; hallow My Sabbaths, and they will be a sign between Me and you, that you may know that I am the Lord your God" (Eze. 20:19, 20).

The Rewards of Faith

As for Me, behold, My covenant is with you,
and you shall be a father of many nations. Gen. 17:4.

Abraham's willingness to slay Isaac, the child of promise, was the ultimate act of surrender. He believed that God would either bring him back to life or give to him and Sarah another son through whom the covenant promises would be fulfilled. His passing that test earned him the title "The Father of the Faithful" and qualified him for inclusion in Hebrew's gallery of Old Testament heroes and heroines (Heb. 11:8-12).

The act that Abraham was asked to perform is not a likely challenge for modern Christians. However, the quality of faith that he demonstrated is still required. Ours is not a faith-friendly era. Our age of scientism and technology exalts empirical evidence: hard data—readable, tangible, logical proof. This is not an age of trust. We believe what we can see and what has been proven in the test tubes of our laboratories; we don't believe what someone postulates, especially if that postulation demands deferred gratification—sacrifice of present joys for future rewards.

Jesus anticipated the lack of confidence in matters eternal that this generation would experience and asked: "When the Son of Man comes, will He really find faith on the earth?" (Luke 18:8).

The answer to that question is: "Yes, but not much!" As in the days of Noah, the days of the end will find few who are faith-filled. There will, however, be a remnant. John saw this and wrote: "Then I looked, and behold, a Lamb standing on Mount Zion, and with Him one hundred and forty-four thousand, having His Father's name written on their foreheads" (Rev. 14:1). Paul had this same faithful number in mind when he wrote: "Then we who are alive and remain shall be caught up together with them in the clouds to meet the Lord in the air" (1 Thess. 4:17).

You and I cannot prove that we will be alive to welcome our returning Lord, but we can and must be like Father Abraham and believe that He is the God of both the resurrection and translation promises and live out our days in surrendered covenant compliance.

The Covenant With Moses

Now therefore, if you will indeed obey My voice and
keep My covenant, then you shall be a special treasure to
Me above all people; for all the earth is Mine. Ex. 19:5.

God's covenant with Israel was affected under the most dramatic of circumstances. Imagine the scene: there at Sinai, just three months out of Egypt, the
pilgrim people gathered with apprehensive anticipation of God's directions for
their future. They had exited Egypt with high hopes of a quick trip to Canaan. But
now doubts began to rise—they saw ahead difficult terrain, hostile tribes and the
prospects of unfriendly elements of weather. They wanted and needed reassurance,
and this God gave. His words were: "You have seen what I did to the Egyptians,
and how I bore you on eagles' wings and brought you to Myself. Now therefore; if
you will indeed obey My voice and keep My covenant, then you shall be a special
treasure to Me above all people; for all the earth is Mine" (Ex. 19:4, 5).

How did the people respond? "Then all the people answered together and said,
'All that the Lord has spoken we will do.' So Moses brought back the words of the
people to the Lord" (verse 8).

They did not do what the Lord had said. They repeatedly failed. They expressed
their disloyalty toward God by faithless murmuring and complaining, by frequently
adopting the habits of the heathen about them and by often berating their leader.
Faithfulness would have brought them far better blessings than they could have
projected; faithlessness eventuated in far greater difficulty than they could have
imagined.

The same is true for us today—corporately and individually. Both the benefits
of fidelity and the bitterness of disobedience greatly exceed our knowing. We cannot measure either consequence. But we can, in trusting simplicity, accept God's
gracious terms of agreement and make each day an ever-ripening relationship with
Him. It is a simple but profoundly meaningful message that the song portrays:

"When we walk with the Lord in the light of His word,
What a glory He sheds on our way!
While we do His good will, He abides with us still,
And with all who will trust and obey.
Trust and obey, for there's no other way
To be happy in Jesus, but to trust and obey."

Moses the Intercessor

Now when the people saw that Moses delayed
coming down from the mountain, the people gathered together
to Aaron, and said to him, "Come, make us gods that shall go before us;
for as for this Moses, the man who brought us up out of the land of Egypt,
we do not know what has become of him." And Aaron said to them,
"Break off the golden earrings which are in the ears of your wives,
your sons, and your daughters, and bring them to me." Ex. 32:1, 2.

Six weeks after their promise to do "all that God said," the people ruptured the terms of their covenant agreement by faithlessly engaging in idolatrous worship.

When Moses returned from communion with God and saw the shameful scene, he threw down the tablets of stone upon which God had written the moral law, and commanded that the golden calf be ground to powder and that its ashes be mixed in the people's drinking water. After this he sternly rebuked them and called for rededication of their loyalties to the true God.

God's displeasure toward the disobedient tribes is reflected in His statement to Moses: "Your people whom you brought out of the land of Egypt" (Ex. 32:7). In other words, He completely disavowed them, attributing both their identity and deliverance to Moses and not Himself.

When Moses appealed to God in verse 13, pleading: "Remember Abraham, Isaac, and Israel, Your servants, to whom You swore by Your own self, and said to them, I will multiply your descendants as the stars of heaven; and all this land that I have spoken of I give to your descendants, and they shall inherit it forever." His intercession was effective. God accepted his petition; the people were spared, and the covenant continued.

As Israel's mediator, Moses represents Christ, the intercessor for us all. We have all "corrupted" ourselves (verse 7); "All have sinned and fall short" (Rom. 3:23). "As it is written: 'There is none righteous, no, not one'" (verse 10). We all need an intercessor. Jesus is our Moses—our lawgiver, our redeemer, our go-between.

Whatever pains and problems of yesterday, its miscues and mistakes, faults, foibles, and failures, we can today express anew our surrender to God knowing that He, because of Jesus, our mediator and friend, will hear our prayers, heal our pain, and honor our faith.

Rules for Living

So he was there with the Lord forty days and forty nights;
he neither ate bread nor drank water. And He wrote on the tablets
the words of the covenant, the Ten Commandments. Ex. 34:28.

What a great God we serve! Not only does He reach down to relate to us in our lost condition, but also He provides by His own hand the rules, if properly observed, that will give maximum health and happiness to those who obey. David was emphatic about that when he wrote: "The law of the Lord is perfect, converting the soul; the testimony of the Lord is sure, making wise the simple; the statutes of the Lord are right, rejoicing the heart; the commandment of the Lord is pure, enlightening the eyes; . . . the judgments of the Lord are true and righteous altogether. More to be desired are they than gold, yea, than much fine gold" (Ps. 19:7-10).

The Ten Commandments constitute the only part of the Bible written by God. The other parts of Scripture was written by humans as they were inspired by God—"Holy men of God spoke as they were moved by the Holy Spirit" (2 Peter 1:21). However, the Decalogue (the moral law) was not simply inspired or dictated or authorized by the Creator, it was written by Him and given to Moses to give to Israel and through Israel, His people, the entire human race.

Some accused Christ, by whose death the ceremonial laws of Moses were abolished, as also aborting the moral law or the Ten Commandments. But Scripture states otherwise. Jesus Himself said, "If you love Me, keep My commandments" (John 14:15); James warns that to break one of the commandments is to break them all (James 2:10); and through John the revelator, in the benedictory chapter of the Bible, we are told, "Blessed are those who do His commandments, that they may have a right to the tree of life" (Rev. 22:14).

Through the Ten Commandments (Ex. 20:3-17) God makes clear His will regarding our relationship to Him. The first four commandments (verses 3-11) detailed our vertical response to His reality; the last six commandments (verses 12-17) outline our horizontal duties to one another. In other words His commandments are clear, comprehensive, and wonderfully compelling for spiritual dedication and practical duty.

Why not make it a conscious guide for living this day and every day?

The Law of the Covenant

And the Lord spoke to you out of the midst of the fire.
You heard the sound of the words, but saw no form;
you only heard a voice. So He declared to you His covenant
which He commanded you to perform, the Ten Commandments;
and He wrote them on two tablets of stone. Deut. 4:12, 13.

Before Sinai, the terms of the covenant, which were to guide their relationship to their Creator and to each other, were spoken—handed down by word of mouth. At Sinai they were penned by God and presented to His people in written form. No longer satisfied to trust the memories of humans now diminished by 2,000 years of sin, God detailed His moral law on stone.

Adam and Eve understood their covenant responsibility of loving obedience to their Maker. Their abrogation of this privileged relationship is signaled in the question with which the Creator confronted them, "Have you eaten from the tree of which I commanded you that you should not eat?" (Gen. 3:11).

The history of their successive generations is no better. The record of God's people's covenanting between Eden and Sinai bears baleful evidence of the many ways in which the human signatories of those eras failed to live up to their contractual obligation. By having other gods before them, by Sabbathbreaking, murdering, stealing, etc., the patriarchs and their lineage were often found guilty of breaching their contract with God.

Had God's chosen people been faithful, they would not have suffered the dire calamities that dogged their existence—obedience would have minimized their sicknesses, modified their pain, maximized their longevity, and magnified their witness.

The terms of the moral law, reinforced in the words and life of Jesus Himself, still stand—"Obey and live!" Our modern society, stricken with false concepts of freedom and obsessed with desires for self-gratification, is not readily amendable to the laws spoken in Eden, written at Sinai, and modeled in the life of Christ. Just think, God has done all that and, in addition, suffered with His Son on Calvary in order that through His "better covenant" we are now forgiven, have a "better life" today, and have a "better tomorrow" in the world to come.

The Ark of the Covenant

Which had the golden censer and the ark of the covenant
overlaid on all sides with gold, in which were the golden pot that had manna,
Aaron's rod that budded, and the tablets of the covenant. Heb. 9:4.

The ark was distinguished for many reasons, one of which was the nature of its contents. It housed the golden pot, which preserved a sampling of the manna by which God fed His people for 40 years. It contained the rod by which God, through His servant Aaron, confounded Pharaoh and his magicians; and it held the tables on which were written the Ten Commandments penned by God Himself.

Each spoke eloquently to the people regarding God's covenant relationship with them. The manna was to remind them of God's power to supply their physical needs; the rod was His authority over all other gods as well as over all human authority; and the Ten Commandments were His care of their spiritual as well as their social welfare.

More specifically the ark represented the very throne of God and was the central object of the tabernacle. On its tabletop, beneath the golden wings of the hovering angels, was the Shekinah light of the presence of God. Once a year the high priest came to seek forgiveness and approval for the nation.

Because the ark spoke to the creatures' frailties as well as the Creator's power, it demonstrated, as no other sanctuary piece, the divine/human relationship and the covenant it represented. It illumined in sacred, solemn tones the people's dependence upon God's will, their means of forgiveness of sin, and, ultimately, for the perpetuation of life itself.

The earthly ark is no longer with us. However, the heavenly form, which is our model, is where we daily kneel seeking forgiveness and favor. Because Jesus our Savior is there and because judgment is given to Him (John 5:22), we may "come boldly to the throne" (Heb. 4:16) knowing that in His presence is "fullness of joy; at [His] right hand [is] pleasures forever more" (Ps. 16:11), that He who keeps Israel "shall never slumber nor sleep" (Ps. 121:4), and that "He always lives to make intercession for [us]" (Heb. 7:25).

The Blood of the Covenant

And Moses took the blood, sprinkled it on the people,
and said, "This is the blood of the covenant which the Lord
has made with you according to all these words." Ex. 24:8.

The essence of Moses' charge to the people as he sealed their solemn promise to fulfill their covenant obligations was "Behold the blood!" And that, in summary, has been the Father's primary charge to lost humanity since Eden's tragic fall.

"Behold the blood" continued as salvation's clarion call from the beginning of Eden's altars to the abolishing of physical sacrifices when the true Lamb shed His blood. As the oblivious priest raised his knife to slay yet another sacrifice and the Savior cried, "It is finished," the earth quaked and the substitute sacrifice escaped while the real sacrifice expired.

But while the meeting of "type with antitype" ended the old covenant and sealed the new, it did not lessen the role of the blood it highlighted. "For if the blood of bulls and goats . . . , sprinkling the unclean, sanctifies for the purifying of the flesh, how much more shall the blood of Christ?" (Heb. 9:13, 14).

But why blood? Because blood is the carrier of life; its flow through the system vitalizes and sustains consciousness and energy. Blood, properly constituted and well distributed, guards against decay and disease, guaranteeing human vitality. It is like no other substance or system; it speaks to the life-giving properties of Jesus' gift of His life. This is the reason that Cain's offering was not acceptable; vegetation cannot yield blood. It was the blood of Jesus that the sacrifices were to magnify; the blood was the fundamental focus of each element of the sacrificial system and the contract with God that it magnified.

We no longer build altars and slay animals to represent Christ's sacrifice of Himself. Still, our efforts in His behalf must be stamped: "Behold the blood!" This should be the theme of all our gospel endeavors, the dominant role of all our teaching, all our planning, and all our living. It will be accomplished not so much by what we say, but by the practical demonstration of the principles provided in the life and death of the Lamb of God.

The Faulty Response

Then he took the Book of the Covenant and read
in the hearing of the people. And they said, "All that the Lord
has said we will do, and be obedient." Ex. 24:7.

It was not that the children of Israel were insincere in their declaration of loyalty and obedience; they meant it when they declared their absolute fidelity; they really intended to do it.

However, their good intentions reveal a pattern of weakness and failure—from their well-documented rebellions through the centuries of their survival from the Passover exodus to the stoning of Stephen. They did not obey perfectly. Why? Because they trusted in their own powers of obedience; they depended upon their own strength of reserve and resolve; they relied upon their human prowess and failed to emphasize the role of the very Redeemer that their sacrificial system honored. The tragic result of their misplaced loyalties constitutes a major percentage of Old Testament history.

On the other hand, while proper obedience would have earned them all the earthly benefits of the covenants given to Abraham and Moses, it would not have given them the greatest prize of all—eternal life. That is because human obedience, at its best, while making heaven happy, does not make heaven happen! Only Christ's impeccable, holy obedience earned by His life of suffering can do that.

Our needs today are no less dire than those who earnestly covenanted at the base of Sinai. But our opportunities are greatly enhanced—that is because we have their unhappy example as well as the reassurances of Jesus' life not simply prophesied, but proven and available for our redemption.

What specifically does this example tell us? It tells us that our vows, be they ever so sincere, can be kept only as we remain anchored in firm relationship with God. It tells us that our best is not good enough—that the perfume of Christ's righteousness is needed to make our obedience acceptable. It tells us that God is longsuffering and merciful, "not willing that any should perish" (2 Peter 3:9), but that all should be saved. It tells us that we are participants of "something better"—the new and living covenant built upon better promises (Heb. 8:6) that the "fault" has been superseded (overcome) by the unspeakable generosity of the Son of God.

Mutual Fidelity

Faithful is He Who is calling you [to Himself]
and utterly trustworthy, and He will also do it [fulfill His call
by hallowing and keeping you]. 1 Thess. 5:24, Amplified.

The new agreement that Jesus built does not engage one particular race, as conduit of His will. He now covenants with humanity without regard to race or status or stature. The privileges once reserved for Abraham's seed are now showered upon any and all who believe.

What are the benefits His followers receive? He gives them sunshine and rain, seedtime and harvest, our daily bread and our daily breath. But doesn't He also provide these for those who do not know Him? Does not the rain also fall upon the just and unjust? Yes. But what they do not—cannot—know is peace in the storms of life, joy amid sorrow, assurance in pain, His hand to guide and comfort in "the valley of the shadow of death" (Ps. 23:4). All He requires of us in return is loving obedience.

How has it been for us thus far this year? Does the beginning of a new month in the new year reveal that we have been true to our part of the contract? If not, why not begin again today? God never tires of sincere repentance and new beginnings; He never fails to accept us whenever and wherever we seek Him. Whether our relationship to past agreements has been faithful or faithless, He is always willing and waiting to engage the honest in heart in covenant regard. It is only our lack of belief and trust that can deny or abort God's covenant blessings. Calvary proves that He is faithful. The question is: Are we?

One of history's most stunning examples of covenant fidelity is the case of Onoda, the Japanese soldier who was discovered on an obscure Pacific island in 1974 conducting guerrilla warfare for a cause he was not sure had ended. Haggard and hungry, he was not just surprised; he was angry and bitterly ashamed that his government had surrendered to the Allies, ending World War II 30 years earlier.

We are called to fight in the conflict of the ages: the battle between Christ and Satan. As loyal soldiers for the cause of truth it is our duty to make this day and every day another unit of victory in the cause of Christ, who has never lost a battle and whose original purposes for the human race will someday soon be reinstated.

Christian the Seed

Now to Abraham and his Seed were the promises made.
He does not say, "And to seeds," as of many, but as of one,
"And to your Seed," who is Christ. Gal. 3:16.

The promise to Abraham is fulfilled in two ways. The first is the blessing bestowed upon the many millions of his lineage—his physical descendants. The second is the individual personage of Jesus Himself. He is, as Paul indicates, the true seed—the real deal! As the Seed of Abraham and the "Seed of the woman," Jesus is the kernel or depository of eternal wisdom and power. The small bundle of life that came from Mary's womb was God wrapped up in the covering of humanity.

Jesus was the seed not only in His position as the promised one, the one historically anticipated, the one most highly sought, the one expected throughout time's long journey from Eden through Huron to Sinai and on to Bethlehem. He was and is also the seed because in Him was contained all the elements of perfect eternity that we lost in the garden—and more; in Him were the materials of unconditional permanence. Why? Because in Him was all the fullness of the Godhead bodily (Col. 2:9).

He was indeed the root of Jesse, the lily of the valley, the rose of Sharon— born of the tribe of David according to the flesh (Rom. 1:3). He, the "seed of the woman," is also the dynamo of all intelligence, the wellspring of all righteousness, the author of our faith, the genesis of all right desires, the source of all true love, the fountain of all truth, the generator of all our energies for right action, the sustainer of our faith, and the active high priest of our confession.

From His inauspicious beginning in Bethlehem, where, ignored by the populace, Jesus entered our sphere and began the earthly sojourn by which our dying humanity was revived to His glorious ascent from Mount Olivet, where, escorted by the angelic host, He returned triumphant to glory, He was our perfect provider.

As our living Lord, He is still our only true source of life and light and loving obedience. The poet was right:

"Christ is the righteous bread we need,
His is the righteous voice we heed.
Christ is the righteous truth indeed.
He is our righteous living Seed."

Signed, Sealed, and Delivered

And I will put enmity between you and the woman,
and between your seed and her Seed; He shall
bruise your head, and you shall bruise His heel. Gen. 3:15.

Paradoxically, the key scripture in Genesis, and perhaps in the entire Bible, is spoken not to humans but to Lucifer. While the fallen angel is the direct object of God's words, the fallen race is the happy recipient of their force.

It was right there on the scene of the crime as they cowered in numbed shock and guilt, our first parents were given the hope of a Redeemer, the promise of forgiveness and rescue from their unspeakably tragic circumstances.

The fulfillment of that promise did not take place for 4,000 years. "But in the fullness of time," when sin's consequences had depressed earth's populace to its lowest level, when humans, debased by millennia of sin, looked and acted more like the animals of the forest than the God in whose likeness they were made, a voice in heaven was heard, saying: "Sacrifice and offering You did not desire, but a body You have prepared for Me" (Heb. 10:5).

Christ's birth at Bethlehem began dramatic fulfillment of the promise made in Eden. It was not easy. His entry, to be credible, had to satisfy both the laws of nature and the demands of justice. The personage of the Being who would tabernacle with us must, while being equal with God, also exist on the level of humanity. Christ overcoming these physical and ethical logistics is the most tactically brilliant, strategically stunning accomplishment ever. His becoming the God-man is an act that bewilders the devil, amazes the angels, delights the Father, and is the joy and salvation of all those who sincerely accept and faithfully obey His Word.

Not only was His entry and later ministry fully accomplished, but also the promise of Satan's ire toward His mission. That hatred resulted in the sacrifice of His life on Calvary. There His heel was bruised, His blood was shed, and by that blood the better covenant was signed, sealed, and delivered.

The Meeting at Calvary

Surely His salvation is near to those who fear Him,
that glory may dwell in our land. Mercy and truth have met
together; righteousness and peace have kissed. Ps. 85:9, 10.

The salvation covenant made in heaven between God the Father and God the
Son before the creation of the world and revealed to our fallen parents in the
Garden of Eden is called the new covenant, as stated in the book of Hebrews. This
is because the covenant made with the nation of Israel at Sinai, while actually a later
agreement, ended before the one announced to Adam and Eve.

It was on the cross that the two covenants met. Here, they intersected as type
(the Sinai covenant) and antitype (the Eden covenant). The blood of Jesus, while
ratifying or sealing the original but new covenant, was foreshadowed by the blood
of animals that the faithful had offered for 4,000 years as they honored the old but
second covenant—the one provided to Israel. The cross is where the two covenants
converged, where promise met fulfillment and shadow met substance; hope met
reality, anticipation met actuality; time met eternity, and Satan, the archenemy of
Prince Emmanuel, met his doom.

Ellen White gives animation to this confluence of events by stating that at
Calvary, "justice moved from its exalted throne, and with all the armies of heaven
approached the cross. There it saw One equal with God bearing the penalty for all
injustice and sin. With perfect satisfaction Justice bowed in reverence at the cross,
saying, It is enough" (*The Seventh-day Adventist Bible Commentary*, Ellen G. White
Comments, vol. 7, p. 936).

Yes, it was enough! Enough suffering, enough bloodshed, enough pain, enough
sacrifice, enough loneliness, enough heartbreak and enough demonstration of
compassion of the Godhead for the human race. The Father saw "the travail of his
soul, and [was] satisfied"! (Isa. 53:11, KJV).

What is not, nor can ever be sufficient is our gratitude; we cannot thank Him
enough. A thousand lifetimes of obedient service could not repay His one lifetime
of sacrifice. Eternity itself will not be sufficient to comprehend fully the fullness of
His love or to express redemption's joys adequately.

A Better Confirmation

For he is not a Jew who is one outwardly,
nor is circumcision that which is outward in the flesh;
but he is a Jew who is one inwardly; and circumcision
is that of the heart, in the Spirit, not in the letter; whose praise
is not from men but from God. Rom. 2:28, 29.

God's choice for Israel's expression of agreement with the covenant's terms was circumcision—a bloody and (because of the lack of sterile instruments) very risky ritual.

A sharp stone was better than a dull one, but at its best, this ordinance was painful for the child and his parents. What was difficult for Israel's young boys was even more dreaded by those males who joined the nation as adolescents or adults.

The painful act by which the old covenant was sealed paled into insignificance in comparison to the pain and sacrifice by which the new covenant was ratified. Those were dull, blunt nails driven with heavy-headed hammers that tore through the hands and feet of Jesus. His flesh was lacerated for our sins. He bled profusely and died proactively for us. It was not pretty. The artists are kind but probably inaccurate to place a loincloth about the midsection of the dying Lord. Scholars almost universally agree that it did not happen that way. The crucified in Christ's day usually died stripped of all clothing, mocked by the people, tormented by the elements, and relentlessly assaulted by swarming insects and creeping vermin.

As the weight of their torso gradually sank upon their weakening abdomen, breathing became so difficult that even the strongest, within 72 hours, lost the will and ability to push upward on painful feet and gasp for breath. The crucified died in humiliating, inescapable, indescribable agony.

Of course, this prisoner could have escaped! He could have called 10,000 angels! He could have, with a word or look or thought, slain His enemies and delivered Himself from this gruesome fate. But He thought of us and of His promise to the Father and of the new and better covenant He had come to confirm. By His blood He sealed forever the deal of our lifetime and the pledge of eternity. Can we do less than love and serve such a God?

Baptism: A Better Sign

Therefore we were buried with Him through baptism into death,
that just as Christ was raised from the dead by the glory of the Father,
even so we also should walk in newness of life. Rom. 6:4.

By His death, burial, and resurrection Christ annulled the Mosaic laws with their many ordinances (Col. 2:12-15). But through the same act, He ratified His new way of relating to His followers; the sacrifice that doomed the old covenant now illumines the new. How do we communicate Calvary's events? By baptism! By submitting to the rite of baptism, we Christians declare our death to sin, our burial of past disobedience, and our resurrection to a new life directed and sustained by the Word of God. Baptism is a public statement of our renunciation of our former life of ungodly living and our determination to live henceforth, by His grace, in faithful conformity to Christ's will.

Baptism does not cleanse us. It does not give us new power. It produces neither justification nor sanctification. It is not itself a saving act, but rather a declaration of intent regarding our responses to Jesus' gracious offerings of everlasting life.

Is rebaptism sometimes appropriate? Yes. It is appropriate for those already baptized whose lifestyle has flagrantly transgressed God's law; it is appropriate for those whose need for rededication, although not suggesting flagrant violation of God's commandments, inspires to rededication stronger than that afforded by foot-washing ritual. And since Christ's commission to baptize was accompanied with the injunction to teach "all things," it is most appropriate for those Christians who were baptized before learning "all things" (all truths essential to salvation). These essentials include the characteristics of the Ten Commandments: the Sabbath, the state of the dead, and the second coming of Jesus.

Whether baptism is engaged the first time in response to hearing God's call, or another time upon learning the full gospel, or as reentry into church fellowship following apostasy, or simply as the surrender of a life in need of serious rededication, it is refreshing to the candidate, is reviving to the beholder, and brings rejoicing to the Trinity in whose name it is done.

Church Membership: A Covenant

Go therefore and make disciples of all the nations, baptizing them in the name of the Father and of the Son and of the Holy Spirit. Matt. 28:19.

Baptism is one's covenant pledge to God and in addition one's covenant commitment to His visible body on earth, the organized church.

As the gateway to church membership, it is one's statement of sincere intent to honor the church's laws and leaders, and to work faithfully for its success. Because of this, it binds the believers in solemn obligation to work together for the best interest of one another as well as the institutional good. Baptism is not only a firm renunciation of the kingdom of darkness, but also a proclamation of wholehearted support for the kingdom of light and its objectives.

The covenant commitment to the church includes, among other things, personal witness in our daily activities, organized soul-winning activities, the use of identified spiritual gifts in the work of the church, and the sharing of our material holdings (our finances) to support church programs. The membership covenant that we seal with baptism often calls for self-denial and sacrifice. We should, if the love of Christ burns brightly in our hearts, cheerfully regard the church, its facilities, its auxiliaries, and its outreach initiatives as our spiritual call to arms—our reasonable obligation in the contractual relationship we have made with Christ.

Our covenant with the church means that we will respect its rules, protect its name, support its mission, and represent its Lord with all our heart, mind, and soul. To be baptized without such determination is not to be buried and risen with Him. To be baptized with that understanding and desire is to rise from the water as enlightened, committed, effective soldiers of the cross, productive epistles of grace, vigorous conduits of His cause, and loyal soldiers in the army of truth.

The Heart: A Better Place

For this is the covenant that I will make with the house of Israel after those days, says the Lord: I will put My laws in their mind and write them on their hearts; and I will be their God, and they shall be My people. Heb. 8:10.

A major problem with the first covenantal arrangement is that the children of Israel never internalized the law written on stone. There were a few who grasped the spirit as well as the letter of the rules God had given. They had bias and another agenda: They wanted food and favor, privilege and power, status and security, but they valued the ways of the heathen who surrounded them above the will of the God who promised these.

Their disobedience resulted not only in military defeats and physical ills, but also in social decline, intellectual decay, and gross self-delusion. This lack of trust in God and disregard for His commandments always brings disaster.

The good news for us is that since "all these things happened to them as examples, and they were written for our admonition, upon whom the ends of the ages have come" (1 Cor. 10:11), we are privileged to benefit from their mistakes. We cannot expect all who claim the name of Jesus to walk as true disciples, but we can and must individually determine to never abandon the vows of our covenant with our God.

Some years ago a well-known businessman stood before the graduating class of Pine Forge Academy in eastern Pennsylvania and delivered the shortest but perhaps most profound commencement address ever given at this historic institution. His unforgettable two-minute speech consisted of the repetition of three words— "never give up." Only at the conclusion did he vary, saying, "never, never, give up!"

That undying determination must be the motto of every child of God. How does one, in spite of all the temptations, pause or stop or quit—never give up? By staying in constant contact with God's Word—the source of both our motivation and power to obey. Then, in spite of the pressures of the lesser, lower, and, in the final analysis, lethal standards of the society about us, we can and will succeed in faithful, honorable, ethical life-giving partnership with our Lord.

An Individual Matter

And the remnant who have escaped of the house of Judah
shall again take root downward, and bear fruit upward.
For out of Jerusalem shall go a remnant, and those who escape
from Mount Zion. The zeal of the Lord of hosts will do this. 2 Kings 19:30, 31.

Does the fact of Israel's rejection mean that the many millions who lived under the old covenant provisions will be lost? No. It does mean that they were rejected as a corporate vehicle for the continued display of God's purposes to the human race.

This is not strange. It is not the case at all that the majority of a nation or a people subscribe to obedience. The few in Noah's day who were saved are paralleled by the few in Sodom and Gomorrah, the few who appreciated Christ during His ministry, the few faithful of the wilderness church of the Dark Ages, and the few who will be saved when Christ returns (Luke 17:26-28).

What we learn from Israel's failure (and ours as well) is that salvation is an individual matter. Laws written in gospel books and on church walls, painted above the rostrums or baptistries for all to read, are well positioned and rightfully made prominent. But this is not redemptive; God's law must be inscribed upon our hearts. What exactly does this mean? It means that they must be in our memory, in our consciences—the framework and substance of the worldview that guides our every action.

The Ten Commandments are not a set of rules to be remembered simply during a Week of Prayer or a special day of worship, or boldly hung upon the pulpit as reminders of our duty. Nor are they a constitution or code to be referenced in an occasional study or debate. They must become our constant companion—the guide that informs all provinces of our living: the church, the home, the school, as well as in our recreation, our work, and even in our leisure.

God's remnants who escape the awful judgments of evil in time's last hour are not a physical race or denomination, but a spiritual aggregate—His invisible church of every race and denomination, upon whose hearts His law has been inscribed and His love enthroned.

Choosing to Be Faithful

And if it seems evil to you to serve the Lord, choose for yourselves this day whom you will serve, whether the gods which your fathers served that were on the other side of the River, or the gods of the Amorites, in whose land you dwell. But as for me and my house, we will serve the Lord. Joshua 24:15.

There are no neutral grounds or demilitarized zones—no islands of "in between" where one can retreat in isolation from the battles of good and evil. Life is a combat lived in covenant with God or with Satan. There is no middle ground. We are either children of God growing toward perfection and maturity (completeness) or we are devotees of evil. Jesus said to His disciples, "No one can serve two masters; for either he will hate the one and love the other, or else he will be loyal to the one and despise the other. You cannot serve God and mammon" (Matt. 6:24).

How is it that we as professed Christians serve mammon? We do so by "pitching our tents toward Sodom"; by claiming the name of Christ while walking the way of sin; by becoming so accustomed to society's ways that its sights and sounds no longer shock us; by lapsing from the fervency of first love to the lackadaisical performances of "business as usual."

It is not necessarily by demonstration or dramatic pronouncement that we choose to side with evil. Most often our covenanting with death is a slow descent from the exhilarating fellowship of our conversion experience into the pit of sin that is the holding place of disbelief.

Rarely do we leap into temptation and error. We do so in single acts of neglect that sap our energies and skew our allegiance. The lure of lesser priorities and poisonous undergrowth of secular values are the culprits that rob our spiritual vitality and turn us to wrong allegiances, false attractions, and covenants with death.

We cannot escape the sights and sounds, the temptations and allurements of society about us; we are citizens of this present world of darkness. But we can and must die daily to sin and, though we are occupants in this evil environment, keep our affections focused on things above.

The Better Covenant

But now He has obtained a more excellent ministry,
inasmuch as He is also Mediator of a better covenant,
which was established on better promises. Heb. 8:6.

Better covenant? Better promises? Yes, precisely! The covenant that Jesus made before our world's creation (that He articulated in the garden and ratified on Calvary) is infinitely better than the one expressed at Sinai or any other. This is because the human variable of this covenant equation is not the obedience of sinners, even though saved by grace, but that of Jesus, the God-man, who conquered sin perfectly in our behalf.

In all the other covenants the creature's response to the Creator's pledge, though well meaning, was of itself impossible. Because all human works are faulty, no human works can adequately fulfill the obedience requirements of the divine contract. The deficiency of unholy flesh guarantees the insufficiency of our posture with God. We simply cannot offer a product or performance valuable enough, clean enough, righteous enough, and pure enough that it qualifies as adequate response to the bargain elements that God provides.

We creatures cannot deliver a performance that fulfills the sober vows of our longing but limited hearts. How can we expect or how dare we project contributions to the covenant relationship judged as worthy? We cannot; we do not. But Jesus does in our behalf.

He alone lived the life on earth that is acceptable. He alone says to the Father, "All that Thou commanded—I did!" And it is that life that the Father accepts in our stead, and it is the better promise upon which is built the better covenant—the covenant of grace.

We sign notes and contracts: house notes, car notes, real estate contracts, and the like, and if we are wise, we are faithful to the obligation that these material promises assume. How more diligent and dedicated should we be in fulfilling our contract with Jesus? Since He has already met the terms for us, there is need to neither fear nor fail. This is because, when we are in Christ Jesus, He becomes "for us wisdom from God—and righteousness and sanctification and redemption" (1 Cor. 1:30). The promises are better, the terms are surer, and the rewards are secured by His gift of righteousness.

The Original Covenant Fulfilled

He indeed was foreordained before the foundation of the world,
but was manifest in these last times for you. 1 Peter 1:20.

The very first or original covenant, the "covenant of all covenants—the everlasting covenant," is not the one made to Adam and Eve, or to Abraham or to Moses or to any of the other patriarchs. It was made by the personages of the Trinity on our behalf before the world was created. Inspiration records: "Before the foundations of the earth were laid, the Father and the Son had united in a covenant to redeem man if he should be overcome by Satan. They had clasped their hands in a solemn pledge that Christ should become the surety for the human race" (*The Desire of Ages,* p. 834).

What was the essence of this agreement? It was formed that if humans should fail, He, Jesus, would condescend to be our Redeemer.

Evidences that Christ understood His sojourn on earth to fulfill this mission is seen in His many statements to His Father's will. His words are "The Father who sent Me" (John 12:49); "I always do those things that please Him" (John 8:29); "I must be about My Father's business" (Luke 2:49); "I must work the works of Him who sent Me" (John 9:4); and "I have not spoken on My own authority; but the Father who sent Me" (John 12:49). And when He had successfully accomplished His mission, He could say to the Father: "I desire that they also whom You gave Me be with Me where I am" (John 17:24). To us, "Let not your heart be troubled; you believe in God, believe also in Me. In My Father's house are many mansions; if it were not so, I would have told you. I go to prepare a place for you. And if I go and prepare a place for you, I will come again and receive you unto Myself; that where I am, there you may be also" (John 14:1-3).

Because He who has called us is faithful, we can today and every day, live in the bright light of joyful hope and expectation. By the successful completion of His pledge made in eternity past, we have promises of life together with Him in eternity future. By that love and grace we are stabilized, inspired, and sustained in the turbulence of our everyday living.

His Unchangeable Will

Brethren, I speak after the manner of men;
Though it be but a man's covenant, yet if it be confirmed,
no man disannulleth, or addeth thereto. Gal. 3:15, KJV.

As attested in our scripture, even those covenants (contracts or wills) confirmed by humans are to be strictly and honorably regarded. Hebrews 9:16, 17 states the case for the binding nature of covenant or testament agreement this way: "For where there is a testament, there must also of necessity be the death of the testator. For a testament is a force after men are dead, since it has no power at all while the testator lives."

The everlasting (original) covenant, in addition to being God's first promise of redemption, is also His final will for humanity. When He died upon Calvary, He sealed His covenant will. Had He not died, His will could not be available. Because He died, it is not subject to abrogation or amendment; it cannot be subtracted from or added to (nor should it be nor can or need it be). Everything our salvation requires—all the principles, promises, and procedures necessary for our present and eternal good are included.

There are some items, such as baptism, the Lord's Supper, the Ten Commandments (including the holy seventh-day Sabbath), with which various religionists disagree: sprinkling instead of immersion, eating and drinking the bread and wine but not washing feet, reducing the Ten Commandments to the idea of love without specific rules, and substituting the first day as the seventh day of worship. None of these substitutions and amendments are allowable; they are attempted on the wrong side of Calvary, and therefore not confirmed by the Testator whose word the covenant is and whose death the covenant seals.

What then is our proper relationship to Christ's will? It is absolute surrender, dying daily to self, and, while trusting and obeying, "walking by faith and not by sight" (see 2 Cor. 5:7).

Even then, with this everyday behavior, we do not qualify for heaven. This is because "nothing but the righteousness of Christ can entitle us to one of the blessings of the covenant of grace. . . . We must not think that our own merits will save us; Christ is our only hope of salvation" (*Patriarchs and Prophets*, p. 431). It is by this mercy alone that our covenant with Christ is not only acceptably signed, but also forever sealed and, at His coming, finally delivered.

MARCH

A Better Sanctuary

A Symbol Needed

And let them make Me a sanctuary, that I may dwell among them. Ex. 25:8.

By the manifestation of His glory at Sinai, God sought to impress upon His people the awesome grandeur of His being. They were to see Him as the God of justice and mercy by whose power they would be protected and by whose wisdom they would be nurtured to premiere status among the nations.

But they were slow to comprehend. "Accustomed as they had been in Egypt to material representations of the Deity, and these of the most degrading nature, it was difficult for them to conceive of the existence or the character of the Unseen One. In pity for their weakness, God gave them a symbol of His presence. 'Let them make Me a sanctuary,' He said" (*Education,* p. 35).

How about us today? Are we any better than they? Yes, better equipped—we have all the trappings of modernity to enhance our witness; and, yes, better informed—we have their example to warn us. However, could it be that the gods of materialism, pleasure, and pride that claim the allegiance of society about us have claimed our worship as well?

"Thou shalt have no other gods before me" (Ex. 20:3, KJV) is an injunction not only against worship of sculptured idols, or the mandate to give God first place in our lives, it is also the Creator's command that there be absolutely no "God sharing" in our hearts. He is not to be our highest God—but the only God; He would be Lord of all or not at all!

It is reported that Napoleon once ordered his celebrating soldiers to complete silence while he placed his ear to the ground and listened intently. After several minutes he arose and ordered his troops back to their defensive positions. Why? Because what the wily general heard in the distance warned of imminent danger. Although it was the piping of French music that had buoyed their spirits, it was the tread of English marching that shook the earth and signaled an ambush just ahead.

Israel's Canaan entrance was delayed largely because they sought to share God's space with other deities. Modern Israel is just as guilty and similarly deluded and delayed. Corporate redemption was not a reality then, nor is it now. He still dwells within the hearts of those who give Him exclusive devotion and who, by that commitment, match their marching with their music, their walk with their talk, and their performance with their profession.

Alone With God

*So Moses went into the midst of the cloud and went up into the mountain.
And Moses was on the mountain forty days and forty nights. Ex. 24:18.*

Commenting upon the place where Moses was shown the sanctuary pattern, Ellen White states: "It was in the mount with God that Moses beheld the pattern of that wonderful building which was to be the abiding place of His glory. It is in the mount with God—in the secret place of communion—that we are to contemplate His glorious ideal for humanity" (*Education,* p. 258).

But how and when and where are we able to do this? The vast majority of us do not live near mountains, and those of us who do are caught up in the dizzying draft of daily duty and have little time for mountain meditation. We have planes, trains, and buses to catch, traffic jams to negotiate, meetings to attend, children to pick up and deliver, meals to ready, the yard to clean, classwork to finish, and the need to return all those calls logged on our voice mail, our beepers, and our e-mail screens. Mountaintop communion with God is not easy to come by, and yet it is vital for spiritual strength and direction.

Of course, God can and does speak to us amid the daily din—while we are driving our cars, fixing our meals, etc. But of special importance are the quiet moments when we can close our eyes and commune with Him. We can ask ourselves, When does this happen? Is it during family devotion, in public worship, or in solitary (private) prayer and meditation? When are these experiences best enjoyed? Is it before our morning peace is disturbed by telephones ringing? before any family duties impinge? Or is it before any other activity engages our attention? Setting time apart for personal, private communion with God requires stern discipline—the kind that refuses to allow anyone or anything to rob us of those precious moments.

By stern discipline we can and must make that engagement our first and consistent priority. There is no circumstance for which prayer (most often the silent kind) is not in order. It is, however, the "mountaintop" experience of private devotion that presents Him clearly and in a way that we pilgrims most dearly need.

The Sanctuary Beautiful

According to all that I show you, that is, the pattern of the tabernacle and the pattern of all its furnishings, just so you shall make it. Ex. 25:9.

With its exterior walls covered with attractive animal skin and its interior walls of glistening gold, reflecting in rainbow hue upon the curtains inwrought with cherubims, the sanctuary offered a glistening testimony to the God it portrayed. "A structure of surpassing splendor, demanding for its construction the most costly material and the highest artistic skill, was to be erected in the wilderness, by a people just escaped from slavery" (*Education*, p. 36).

Our God is a God of beauty. He created a world that was lavished in dazzling color and perfect symmetry. Even now, after six millennia of sin's degradation, nature reveals His love for variety, color, proportionality, and attractiveness. We see it in the soft colors of flowers, in the striking markings of birds, in the neon glow of fish beneath the surface of ocean waters, and in the incandescent lights of the sky above.

How then should we worship God? "In the beauty of holiness" (Ps. 29:2). Our Creator understands those situations where political or economic conditions prevent congregations from erecting a building or upgrading its physical plant to truly reflect the beauty of His mind and character. He is deeply offended and misrepresented in instances in which members could do better but settle for second-class facilities for worship. This is especially so when their personal homes, clothing, etc., demonstrate that they have the capacity and not the concern to build the best for Him.

Congregations that have built or are building attractive houses of worship for Him are clearly instrumental by the quality of the tabernacle God ordered His people to erect. Building the sanctuary for His honor, even to death, was the quality of the tabernacle God ordered His people to erect. Building a sanctuary for Him means making whatever sacrifice necessary to insure that the place where we worship is not only functional, but also attractive. This includes providing Him not only an attractive church, but also an attractive church school, an attractive conference office, or an attractive campground. Not all congregations are able to build with costly design and materials. However, God is not honored unless these facilities bearing His name (no matter how humble) reflect His glory to the very highest of our ability.

Working Together

Then everyone came whose heart was stirred, and everyone whose spirit was willing, and they brought the Lord's offering for the work of the tabernacle of meeting, for all its service, and for the holy garments. Ex. 35:21.

One of the primary lessons God taught in the construction of the sanctuary was that of cooperation. "In the preparation of the sanctuary and in its furnishing, all the people were to cooperate. There was labor for brain and hand. A great variety of material was required, and all were invited to contribute as their own hearts prompted" (*Education,* p. 37).

God's work, and, more important, our soul salvation, demands a cooperative spirit. Cooperation is a lesson that begins at home. It must be taught to our children by diligent instruction and practiced by them from adult example. The lack of cooperation in our churches is assured by the lack of cooperation in our homes.

Selfishness is the culprit. Wanting to have it our way; wishing failure on others so that we might look good or important; hoping for a disaster on those endeavors that are not planned with our input or approval—this describes attitudes that are carried into church relationships from the family circle. It is impossible to sing, "What a fellowship, what a joy divine" on Sabbath morning and truly mean it when one has indulged such selfish attitudes during the week.

The role of all Israel in bringing gifts for the sanctuary construction and the appointment of artisans of various skills from differing tribes for its building reminds us that each one has a part to play in God's work. We all have a variety of gifts; these talents and ideas should complement (not nullify) one another, and it is important to regard one another's gifts and opinions as being as valuable as ours.

Paul does say, "Covet earnestly the best gifts" (1 Cor. 12:31, KJV). By doing this, he is urging the acquirement and development of spiritual prowess, not envy toward another's talents or the destructive competitiveness of individual pride.

Satan seeks to confuse our loyalties and skew a wholesome vision of reality and relationships. But collaboration of the Trinity, whose blessed three wrought our creation and brought us redemption, stands as both example and empowerment for our attitudes and actions.

Stirred to Serve

All the women who were gifted artisans spun yarn
with their hands and brought what they had spun, of blue,
purple, and scarlet, and fine linen. Ex. 35:25.

O f special note is the prominent participation of women in the sanctuary construction. Given the second-class status of females in ancient Jewish society,
their willing and productive participation in the construction of the sanctuary is
truly remarkable. Unfortunately the millennia that have transpired since those days
of gender disadvantage have not brought females equal status in either the church
or society in general. In most of the world's societies women still suffer from attitudes that deny them equal pay, equal status, equal opportunity—in short, equal
worth in the scale of human creation.

Demonstration of this bias is seen in the fact that in many countries female
babies are regularly abandoned and, in some cases, destroyed. Their rejection
is fueled by their lesser economic value or earning capacity compared to that of
males. Female sexual abuse is rampant in most cultures, as is abuse (physical and
psychological) of other kinds, including murder—most often at the hands of their
husbands or declared lovers. Sadly, the populace still functions with the belief that
God creates males to rule, and females, by definition, are inferior in brain as well
as strength.

In spite of such obvious disadvantage (often perpetuated in the name of God)
women through the centuries have played a dominant role in the work of the
church, and they still do. In fact, today they are, by the virtue of education and with
sheer courage and the love of God, equipped to not only "spin yarn" for curtain
decoration, but direct temple affairs as well.

As children of God we have a duty to war against laws, conditions, and systems
that rob us of the talents suppressed by gender discrimination. We are challenged
by Scripture, as stated in our text today, to act in practical ways to nurture and empower females in their quest of equality and full participation both in the church
and community about us.

Giving Freely

And they spoke to Moses, saying, "The people bring much more than enough for the service of the work which the Lord commanded us to do." Ex. 36:5.

What a wonderful state of affairs! The people responded so willingly that they had to be restrained in their giving. The sanctuary was finished "debt free." There were no heavy loans to pay, no long-term mortgages with mounting interest.

Incurring loans of reasonable amounts in the prosecution of God's work is not a sin. But how much better or easier could the journey be when, by personal and corporate sacrifice, His people are able to free themselves of debt altogether? Israel's sanctuary contribution reminds us that when God's people are truly motivated, the spirit of sacrifice will be much more evident among us. The list of evils that stymie the spirit of sacrifice includes attitudes of suspicion, the lack of faith, the grip of materialism, and a greater priority for the "pride blossoms" of individual achievement and possession.

The prophet Ellen White gives the following encouragements regarding building plans grounded in sacrifice and a determination to avoid lingering debt. Her warnings include: (a) "The building erected for the worship of God will not be left crippled with debt. It will appear almost like a denial of your faith to allow such a thing" (*Counsels on Stewardship*, p. 260); (b) "It is dishonoring to God for our churches to be burdened with debt. This state of things need not exist. It shows wrong management from beginning to end, and it is a dishonor to the God of heaven" (*ibid.*, p. 261); and (c) "In some cases a continual debt is upon the house of God, and continual interest to be paid. These things should not and need not be" (*ibid.*, p. 263).

Printing names in the bulletin, having banquets and dinners, and giving trophies and awards in recognition of sacrificial stewardship are all legitimate forms of recognition. But these are not the true motivation for faithful, sacrificial giving. Not the fear of hell, not the longing for the tree of life, not even readiness for the Second Coming should be our primary stimulus. Our highest motivation for giving to God's cause must ever be—"For God so loved the world that He gave His only begotten Son, that whoever believes in Him should not perish but have everlasting life" (John 3:16).

God in the Midst

And I will dwell among the children of Israel and will be their God. Ex. 29:45.

Ancient Israel's sanctuary service was conducted in two primary areas: the outer court (an area 75 feet wide and 150 feet long) and the enclosed tabernacle (15 feet wide and 45 feet long), which contained the holy and Most Holy Place. Originally the tent was portable—its parts being interconnected as to allow for easy dismantling and reassembling by the nomadic nation. Centuries later, in the time of Solomon, the portable sanctuary was replaced by the permanent Temple named after Solomon, its distinguished builder, and, when it needed repair, by Zerubbabel.

The sanctuary's location during the long years of Israel's itinerate sojourn was the center of her tribal arrangements. To the east were camped the tribes of Judah, Issachar, and Zebulun; to the west, the tribes of Ephraim, Manasseh, and Benjamin; to the south, the tribes of Reuben, Simeon, and Gad; and to the north, the tribes of Dan, Ashur, and Naphtali. God literally dwelt in the middle or their midst.

There is no longer need for a portable or permanent building where blood is offered and bearded priests talk to God on behalf of waiting congregants. Nevertheless, God still dwells in the midst of His people. Modern Israel is no less the object of His concern than were the ancient tribes. It is true with us as it was with them, that in spite of our shortcomings and failures, we are still the "only object upon earth upon which Christ bestows His supreme regard" (*Testimonies to Ministers*, p. 49).

How does He dwell among us? Through His Holy Spirit! None of the parts and particles that made the sanctuary such an impressive structure remains today. The God who spoke through those ceremonies now speaks through His Spirit— who, while evidenced before Calvary, has since assumed His special office as our counselor and guide. Our safety and success as individuals, as families, as churches, and as institutions are directly proportionate to our willingness to recognize and faithfully respond to His presence among us. It is "not by might nor by power, but by [His] Spirit" (Zech. 4:6) that our daily lives are made lastingly happy and productive.

The Outer Court

And he put the altar of burnt offering before the door of the tabernacle
of the tent of meeting, and offered upon it the burnt offering and
the grain offering, as the Lord had commanded Moses. Ex. 40:29.

The outer court was the killing zone of sanctuary operations. It was here that the sacrifices were slain and burned.

Our world constitutes the outer area or slaughter field of the universe. Since Cain (enraged by God's rejection of his improper sacrifice) slew his brother, Abel, this planet has been distinguished from all others by its rule of death.

We all die—and deservedly so. The wages of sin is death, and we have all sinned. Even those prisoners executed for crimes they did not commit deserved to die, because the wages of sin is death, and all have sinned (Rom. 6:23; Rom. 3:23).

No matter how death comes, whether by violent accident, crippling disease, or other incidence, it is the distinguishing element of our blood-soaked existence on this painful planet.

Jesus did not deserve to die. He was our innocent sacrifice. He died in the outer court of this world far from the holy places of His eternal dwelling—the righteous dying for the unrighteous. It captivates our hearts when we remember that while scarcely would one die for a good person, He died for us while we were yet sinners, hostile to His love and grace.

Unlike the bleeding lambs, He died knowingly. The unsuspecting lambs killed in the typical services did not know why or when they were going to die. Jesus knew. He came into our neighborhood for that purpose. At the age of 12 He gazed upon the slaughtering of the animals in the Temple and clearly understood His role as the Messiah and God's lamb of sacrifice. He fulfilled this mission—misunderstood by others, betrayed, and left alone.

One day soon He, who was resurrected and returned to the holy places above, will exit those compartments for His triumphant return to this world. In the meantime we who must live on in this present society of sin and death do so with assurance and hope that is grounded in His promise—"If I go, I will come again" (John 14:3). Then and only then will we be delivered from earth's outer court of misery and ushered (delivered) into eternal life.

The Ultimate Gift

He shall kill it on the north side of the altar before the Lord; and the priests, Aaron's sons, shall sprinkle its blood all around on the altar. Lev. 1:11.

The sacrifices died at the hands of assassins who worked with brutal efficiency. It was not a pretty sight. It was a cruel and bloody ordeal accomplished by plunging the heavy knife into the furry neck of the trusting lamb. The sharp instrument was dragged across the victim's jugular vein, producing an instant stream of warm, red, pulsating blood. The victim's eyes narrowed and closed in pain while its body contorted in the sudden and final throes of death.

Calvary too was gruesome. All crucifixions were hideous; in fact, it was the method of execution more dreaded than decapitation, burning, or stoning—the other primary capital punishment options of Christ's day.

The cross itself was a foul, odious instrument stained with the excrement of prior victims who, in the extreme agony of the final throes of death, could not control their convulsing organs.

Death on the cross came not from sudden shock or gradual loss of blood; it came from slow, tortuous suffocation as the torso of the helpless victim sank more and more heavily upon his or her weakening diaphragm. Eventually, after 72 hours of indescribable agony, even the strongest of men were unable to push up again upon the nails that fastened their feet. After a final, desperate gasp for breath, they succumbed to death.

For our true sacrifice death came much quicker than that. He died sooner because heavier than the burden of His sagging torso upon His diaphragm was the weight of our sins upon His heart; so that when because of the approaching Sabbath hours they decided to induce death by breaking the prisoners' legs, they found that He was "already dead" (John 19:33).

It has been 2,000 years since the typical lamb escaped the high priest's grasp as the antitypical lamb expired on Calvary. He is no longer spread-eagled upon the cross. He is standing politely at the door of our hearts offering His friendship and salvation. All praise to the Lamb once slain in the outer court of our evil world now risen, and fervently interceding on our behalf.

Sprinkling of the Blood

He shall kill the bull before the Lord; and the priests, Aaron's sons,
shall bring the blood and sprinkle the blood all around on the altar
that is by the door of the tabernacle of meeting. Lev. 1:5.

While Israel's relationship with their God was a corporate covenant and a mass agreement, it was also a contract between the individual and God. Israel's citizens were to personally acknowledge His sovereignty and be individually blessed or cursed.

This was seen in the fact that often the sinner, who brought the sacrifice to the altar, laid their hands upon its head, symbolically transferring their sins to the innocent animal. Additionally, there were instances that the sacrificing sinner killed the animal on their own and tearfully watched as the priest carried its blood into the holy place, where it was dabbed upon the horns of the altar of incense.

The daily transferal of blood to the holy place symbolized Christ's ministry on behalf of humanity throughout the ages. The pledge that He made at the inception of sin was fulfilled at Calvary. No longer does He ask for humans to have faith in what He will do—He has done it, His word is true, the Lamb has been slain, and the Father who gave us His only begotten Son has seen the "travail of his soul, and [is] satisfied" (Isa. 53:11). Christ's creditability with the Father is the basis of our acceptability with Him. His creditability with us is the basis of our trust that our sins are washed away and that there awaits for us in a better land the rich rewards of eternity.

During the sale of a collection of paintings by a deceased artist, the auctioneer stated that the portrait of the artist's slain soldier-son must be sold first. The confused buyers did not understand why the other portraits were connected to this one piece. After the portrait of the soldier was sold, they clearly understood when they observed all the other portraits being handed to its buyer, and the auctioneer closed the auction. Why? Because, the auctioneer explained, it was the father's plan that whoever got "the son" would be given everything.

That is an accurate reflection of our salvation. We, who receive the Son, receive not just the blood of sins forgiven, but also all the riches of eternity.

The Laver for Washing

He set the laver between the tabernacle of meeting
and the altar, and put water there for washing. Ex. 40:30.

In addition to the altar of brunt offering, the outer court also contained the laver, which was "water there for washing." By washing in the laver filled with water, the priest expressed in ritual form the principle of cleanliness to be observed by all who do service for God. This is the essence of the psalmist's questions "Who shall ascend into the hill of the Lord? or who shall stand in his holy place?" And, his apt reply: "He that hath clean hands, and a pure heart; who hath not lifted up his soul unto vanity, nor sworn deceitfully" (Ps. 24:3, 4, KJV).

Purity of motives is an unchanging requisite for God's approval. He is of course a merciful God; He does not reward us according to our sins (Ps. 103:10). He does cause the sun to shine on the just and the unjust and the rain to fall upon the evil and the good; the wicked do sometimes flourish "like a green bay tree" (Ps. 37:35, KJV). However, this does not mean that He is a God of license—a God in whose service "anything goes." He does not give lasting value to insincere motives or evil whether covertly or overly indulged.

The truly approved are those who go about their tasks in the home, in the school, in the community, and elsewhere with dedicated effort and enthusiasm. While energetic service is vital to productivity, it does not bring the lasting good that Heaven rewards unless accompanied by unselfish motives. And, what is the source of such intentionality—the Word of God. It is from this source alone that we receive both the vision and power to live and work with selfless enthusiasm.

This message was given in Paul's observation that "Christ also loved the church, and gave Himself for her, that He might sanctify and cleanse her with the washing of water by the word" (Eph. 6:25, 26) and expanded upon in His later conclusion that "not by works of righteousness which we have done, but according to His mercy He saved us through the washing of regeneration and renewing of the Holy Spirit" (Titus 3:5).

The Meaning of the Sacrifice

This is the law of the burnt offering, the grain offering,
the sin offering, the trespass offering, the consecrations, and the
sacrifice of the peace offering, which the Lord commanded Moses on Mount
Sinai, on the day when He commanded the children of Israel to offer their
offerings to the Lord in the Wilderness of Sinai. Lev. 7:37, 38.

The sacrificial system included four types of offerings that involved the individual petitioner. Two of these—burnt offerings and meat offerings—were labeled this way because of the way in which they were conducted. Burnt offerings involving animals and birds were literally consumed by fire. Meat offerings (more correctly translated meal or vegetable offerings) were sometimes combined with other types of sacrifices and usually burned as well.

The other two offering types—peace offerings and sin offerings—were referred to in this way because of the offerer's intention rather than the method of disposal. Since both of these were often burned, the distinctions are not always clear. What is clear, however, is that one common element or emphasis pervaded all types and processes of sacrifice. This key element was the Calvary event. Every dying animal or fowl, every offered branch or leaf, spoke to the death of Christ.

The methodologies varied, the substances differed, the times and occasions were not always the same. But their focus was the same—the promised Messiah. By these means, the hope of the race was kept alive—the assurance that a way out of the uncompromisingly lethal consequences of sin had been found. Grace would triumph over greed, love would triumph over lust, right would triumph over wrong, light would triumph over darkness, and good would triumph over evil. The Messiah would indeed have His heel wounded, but the dragon's head would be crushed by the selfless sacrifice of the innocent Lamb of God.

The promise first given at the scene of Eden's disaffection was fulfilled that Friday noon when the little lamb escaped the grasp of the unheeding priest as Jesus expired on the cross. The long-awaited pledge was wondrously fulfilled, and soon His long awaited promise to come again will as well—not as sacrifice, but as conquering king.

The Eternal Flame

Now this is what you shall offer on the altar: two lambs of the first year, day by day continually. One lamb you shall offer in the morning, and the other lamb you shall offer at twilight. Ex. 29:38, 39.

The most conspicuous sacrifice conducted by Israel was the daily (morning and evening) burning of the lamb. The flames that consumed the sacrifices burned slowly, but were never extinguished.

Sixteen times in Numbers 28 and 29 God reminded His people that no other offering was to supersede or replace the daily or continuous offering. Thus there was never a time that there was not a burning lamb upon the altar of burnt offerings in the outer court. The weary Israelite traveling far from home or the embattled warrior facing superior forces on some distant field of combat knew that there was upon the altar in the sanctuary a national sacrifice that he could plead to his God.

The continuous (or national) offering did not replace one's need for individual sacrifice; its presence, and those offenders against God's will, were still required to personally confess their wrongs and bring appropriate sacrifices in quest of forgiveness. The daily sacrifice was necessary because there were not enough lambs available, personal evils were not always recognized, and the needy were not always in a position to slay and burn offering.

Jesus is the Lamb slain for our iniquities. His death is our perpetual plea before the Father for forgiveness and restoration to favor. He is the sacrifice ever present before the Father that atones for all our transgressions—even our shortcomings and sins of which we are not aware.

In many countries of the world there is an eternal flame marking the resting place of a national hero—a president, a soldier general, a renowned politician. The flickering flame speaks eloquently to the admiration of the multitudes that visit there. Beneath their feet or within the burnished walls lie the remains of men and women who sacrificed heroically for the people.

The angel of resurrection told us differently; his message is "He is not here—for He is risen" (Matt. 28:6). No flames mark His resting place because no corpse is secured within the tomb where He lay. He is our living Lord, our better sacrifice, our better sanctuary, our better offering. This is why our present has so much meaning and our future such a riveting hope.

Sacrificial Praise

And you shall gird them with sashes, Aaron and his sons,
and put the hats on them. The priesthood shall be theirs for a perpetual
statute. So you shall consecrate Aaron and his sons. You shall also have
the bull brought before the tabernacle of meeting, and Aaron
and his sons shall put their hands on the head of the bull. Ex. 29:9, 10.

In addition to the standard sacrifices there were offerings specified for special individuals. These included sacrifices for the lepers (Lev. 14:19, 20), for the cleansing after childbirth (Lev. 12:6-8), for the administering of the Nazirite vow (Num. 6:13), and for the consecration of the priesthood (Ex. 29:15-35).

In each case the animal chosen by the offerer was burned upon the altar of burnt offerings in the outer court. In most cases the sacrifice was voluntarily brought; in all cases the sacrifice symbolized consecration and surrender in response to a special circumstance or event.

We would all do well to learn, from these special offerings, the lesson of conscious response to significant happenings in our lives. Too often we move from one milepost experience to another without gratitude or even recognition of their meaning to our future. Too often we fail to note life's transition events, to mark our victories, to commemorate our deliverances by reaffirmation of our covenant with God.

The occasion of acquiring a new job, a promotion or raise in salary, the birth of a child, graduation from school, the purchase of a new home or car, recovery from illness, success in a business venture, and the completion of a safe journey are all events that should be responded to in specific expressions of gratitude and rededication to God. Every recognizable accomplishment of life's goals or bestowal of special benediction whether prayed for or provided—though we had not sense to ask—is another occasion for us to express our thanks in sacrificial offerings of loving service. It is indeed, as Paul stated, our "reasonable service" (Rom. 12:1).

It was the praise and thanksgiving expressed by those He healed: the leper, the blind, the deaf, and those crippled by disease, both physical and mental, that brought such obvious joy to Jesus' heart. He is still in the blessing business and delights in the sacrificial service of all who respond to His mercy with "attitudes of gratitude" that funnel into living witness.

Stewards of Grace

When anyone offers a grain offering to the Lord, his offering shall be of fine flour. And he shall pour oil on it, and put frankincense on it. Lev. 2:1.

Meal or grain offerings, called "meat" offerings in the King James Version, consisted of a variety of flour and corn mixed with oil, wine, salt, and sometimes frankincense. Small portions of these offerings were often burned. What was left was given to the priest for their consumption.

Whereas the burnt offerings emphasized consecration and dedication, meal offerings signified submission and dependence. The offerer of the meal offerings acknowledged the sovereignty of God and his or her role as steward of temporal obligations.

This category of sacrifice was important because it had two effects upon the minds of the offerer. First, the clear reminder of God's sustaining power—dependence upon God for the material and temporal necessities of one's everyday experience. God is the author of life; every breath we breathe, every step we take is the result of energies provided by Him. We should acknowledge Him for every slice of bread, every glass of water, and every bit of income we earn or are provided.

The second important reminder surfaced by this category of sacrifice is our obligation to properly improve the opportunities that God has given us. Every right impulse, every moral urge, every spark of holiness, every spiritually enriching thought, every bit of our physical prowess and expanding mental capacity is the result of His mercy.

As good stewards of these and all other temporal blessings, we must "occupy till He comes" and, as faithful recipients of the salvation He has brought us, live and love in faithful reflection of His will.

And when does one's stewardship obligation cease? Never! As long as we are physically and mentally able to recognize His blessings, we are privileged to faithfully manage the work He has given us to do, and often with increasing productivity.

The prophet Ellen White addressed this latter point most memorably when she wrote: "The afternoon sun of . . . life may be more mellow and productive of fruit than the morning sun. It may continue to increase in size and brightness until it drops behind the western hills" (*Review and Herald,* Apr. 6, 1886).

Ready, Willing, and Able

Speak to Aaron and to his sons, saying, "This is the law
of the sin offering: In the place where the burnt offering is killed,
the sin offering shall be killed before the Lord. It is most holy." Lev. 6:25.

Sin offerings were also of a wide variety. These included the offering of a young bullock without blemish by an officiating priest; a male kid of the goats offered by a ruler; a female lamb or two turtledoves (or young pigeons) offered by a commoner. If a common citizen could not afford the usual offering, he could offer the tenth part of an ephah of fine flour (Lev. 5:11).

Sin offerings were sacrifices for sins of ignorance or sins committed without knowledge or intent. The knowledge of the transgression may have been hidden from the transgressor (verses 2-4) for some time. But when the realization came, they were to: (a) "confess that [they had] sinned in that thing" and (b) place their hand on "the sin offering, and kill it," thus symbolically transferring the sin to the innocent victim (verse 5; Lev. 4:29).

The slaying was necessitated because confession is not enough. Sin must be atoned. Each sin establishes a debt that must be paid, and we do not have the capital of holiness to do so—even our martyrdom in His name would be an inadequate payment for the least of our transgressions.

But Jesus is ready, willing, and able. He is our altogether worthy substitute. "He paid a debt He did not owe because we owed a debt we could not pay." And our sweetest thought this day and everyday should mirror the words of the song:

"I lay my sins on Jesus,
   The spotless Lamb of God;
   He bears them all,
   And frees us from the accursed load,
   From the accursed load.
   I bring my guilt to Jesus,
   To wash my crimson stains
   White in His blood most precious,
   Till not a stain remains,
   Till not a stain remains."

Offerings of Peace

When his offering is a sacrifice of a peace offering,
if he offers it of the herd, whether male or female, he shall
offer it without blemish before the Lord. Lev. 3:1.

The fourth category of sacrifice was the peace or thank offering. These were not made in hope of establishing peace with another person or group; they were expressions of peace and harmony with God. Peace offerings spoke to appreciation for harvests richly reaped, health thankfully retained, and journeys successfully completed. Peace offerings asked for no blessings or favors; they recall benedictions already bestowed.

So it was that Israel's many sacrificial types were reduced to two primary categories—sin offerings and peace offerings. Sin offerings expressed sorrow for transgression and asked for forgiveness. Peace offerings expressed gratitude for temporal and spiritual blessings. It is as if by this summary arrangement God is saying, "That's all there is, folks!" All I require is genuine contrition and heartfelt gratitude—nothing more and nothing else."

Can you think of a better formula for human response to divine benediction? Is there a more balanced state in which to approach the vagaries of life? Forgiven and grateful, we can advance with each day strengthened to obey; armed with assurance, buoyed by the evidence that "all things work together for good to them that love God, to those who are called according to His purpose" (Rom. 8:28); that "there hath no temptation taken you but such as is common to man: and God is faithful, who will . . . make a way of escape, that [we] will be able to bear it" (1 Cor. 10:13, KJV); and that He "will keep . . . in perfect peace" all "whose minds [are] stayed on [Him]" (Isa. 26:3).

As Christians we will fly through dark clouds and stormy weather. We will "walk through the valley of the shadow of death" (Ps. 23:4). Life has times and seasons when we do not feel joy or emotional exhilaration. But when the storm is passed and we look back upon the way God has led, we are constrained to give thanks not only for what happened, but also for what did not happen. We should not wait until the clouds lift or the way clears to thank Him. We must trust Him when we cannot trace Him, ever grateful for not only His provisions already received, but also for His promises yet unfulfilled.

Jesus: Strong and Beautiful

You shall also make a table of acacia wood; two cubits shall be its length, a cubit its width, and a cubit and a half its height. Ex. 25:23.

The holy place, the first of the apartments of the sanctuary enclosure, contained three pieces of furniture. In the middle, against the veil that divided the holy place from the Most Holy Place, was the altar of incense; on the left side of the entrance was the table of candlesticks, and on the right was the table of showbread.

The table of showbread was made of acacia wood—a substance that is so tightly grained that it is virtually impenetrable. Acacia wood is highly resistant to decay and very aromatic. When overlaid with gold, it was delightful to the sense of touch, smell and sight. In the holy place the table of showbread was covered with a cloth of pleasing blue, muting the glare of its golden overlay and adding to its rich but sacred appeal (Num. 4:11).

In these ways the table of showbread speaks of Christ. He is our durable, reliable, dependable, esthetically pleasing Savior, and His principles and His character have stood the ravages of time.

It was necessary that He veil His brightness. Had He come in His heavenly splendor, we could not have withstood His presence. He shrouded His glory; He dimmed His radiance. He was a prince in disguise. They did not know that the babe who cooed in the manger was the Being who "spake, and it was done; he commanded, and it stood fast" (Ps. 33:9, KJV); that the lad who played in the mud was the Lord who gave properties to the soil; that the teacher who plucked the corn was the Tetrarch who ordered the harvest; that the man who stilled the storm was the Majesty who made the elements; that the prisoner who cried, "I thirst" (John 19:28), was the Monarch who made the oceans; that the criminal who died on Calvary was the commander of angelic hosts! He was Emmanuel, "God with us," and they did not know.

However, we know Him. We know because in our hearts there glows the torch of faith lit by knowledge of His love and daily fueled by the study of His Word.

Lessons From the Showbread

And you shall set the showbread on the table before me always. Ex. 25:30.

Each loaf of showbread contained "two-tenths mills" (approximately six quarts) of fine flour. These large loaves were arranged in two stacks of six loaves each. On top of both stacks was placed a cup of fragrant incense. Because there was never a time that they were not in place upon the showbread table, the loaves were also known as the bread of presence. The bread was never allowed to spoil. Officiating priests who replaced them with fresh bread and shared them at their meals with their fellow priests removed the old stacks each Sabbath morning.

How does this tradition speak to us today? By reminding us that Jesus is the bread of life and that as bread is the source of our physical strength, so is Christ found in His Word, the source of our spiritual vitality. Even as our consumption of fruits, nuts, grains, and vegetables provides us all the ingredients necessary for muscle tone, healthy blood, and sufficient energy to do our work, so do the Holy Scriptures give us all the spiritual properties necessary for victory over sin. Jesus, Himself, highlighted this principle when He said: "I am the light" (John 8:12); "I am the good shepherd" (John 10:11); "I am the door" (verse 9); "I am the way, the truth, and the life" (John 14:6); and, most significant, "I am the living bread" (John 6:51).

Consider how rich an array of lessons the showbread provides: the twin stacks of bread upon the table reminds us that salvation history is provided in the dual testaments of Scripture—the old and the new; that the bread was not allowed to spoil tells us that Jesus' body would not suffer corruption; the priests eating the bread demonstrates our need to internalize the Word, and the fact that there was never a time that the bread was not present emphasizes our Lord's constant availability. Never, when we dial in prayer, are we put on hold, on call waiting, sent to voice mail, or told to leave a message for His later attention. Never are we left without a blessing when we prayerfully open the pages of Scripture and focus on His spoken Word in our private devotion or in public assembly. All of which gives rich meaning to our plea that must daily be:

"Break Thou the bread of life, dear Lord, to me,
  As Thou didst break the loaves beside the sea;
  Beyond the sacred page I seek Thee, Lord;
  My spirit pants for Thee, O living Word."

No Greater Sacrifice

*And you shall take fine flour and bake twelve cakes with it.
Two-tenths of an ephah shall be in each cake. You shall set them in
two rows, six in a row, on the pure gold table before the Lord. Lev. 24:5, 6.*

The flour that was mixed with oil in making showbread was "mill-grained"; this is grain that had been ground or beaten into a coarse meal. While on the stalk, the grain is a living thing—it contains the spark of life. Harvested, the grain no longer lives; however, in death it provides sustenance for those who consume it.

Jesus, the author and giver of life, was lacerated, scourged, and beaten for us. Had He continued to live, our sins could not have been forgiven. Nor could His righteous robe have been made available as the substitute holiness by which we are made acceptable to the Father. He had to die that we might live. He was ground beneath the wheels of injustice. He was crushed in Gethsemane by the enormity of our sins. Our transgressions weighed so heavily upon His humanity that they pressed Him to the earth, where He pleaded to the Father that some other way— plan B, if available—be activated to save us. So horrific was His agony that His respiratory system aborted, and He would have died there in Gethsemane (not on Calvary) had not the angel of the Lord come to encourage Him.

The angel did not reduce His pain or deliver Him from impending doom. He did not remove His agony, but He reminded our suffering Lord of the eternal covenant He had made with the Father. Even so Jesus treaded the winepress alone; He was lacerated and mauled as penalty for our sins.

In describing the throes of Christ's final passion, inspiration records: "Satan with his fierce temptations wrung the heart of Jesus. The Savior could not see through the portals of the tomb. Hope did not present to Him His coming forth from the grave a conqueror, or tell Him of the Father's acceptance of the sacrifice. He feared that sin was so offensive to God that their separation was to be eternal. Christ felt the anguish which each sinner will feel when mercy shall no longer plead for the guilty race" (*The Desire of Ages*, p. 753).

And what does He ask of us? He asks our acceptance of His sacrifices and our sharing the good news of rescue with others.

Nurtured by the Word

But He answered and said, "It is written, 'Man shall not live by bread alone, but by every word that proceeds from the mouth of God.'" Matt. 4:4.

The Word of God is our source of spiritual growth and power. We are born again by the Word; we grow by the Word; we are sustained by the Word; we are warned by the Word; we are taught by the Word; and we are saved by the Word. But none of this would be possible without the impressions of the Holy Spirit. He woos us to the Word; He clarifies its meanings; He convicts us of its teachings; and He gives us maturation and strength to live by its principals and to witness to its power.

The Holy Spirit, the third person of the Godhead, is no less in wisdom or knowledge or power or goodness than the other two members of the Trinity—God the Father and God the Son. He is equal in partnership, authority, and love. The Trinity is not aligned in a hierarchy of authority or importance.

Of course, this notion is foreign to us humans. For us there is always a first and last, a lesser and better, a major and minor—but not so with the Godhead. They relate as three equal lines in a circle, and they are indistinguishable in motive, inseparable in purpose, and indivisible in power. But they are different in function. Their roles in both our world's creation and salvation are thoroughly integrated and maximally supportive, but clearly varied. The Father, the Son, and the Holy Ghost are one; a single personality who assumes three differing forms, but one God comprised of three distinct Beings working as coauthors of our creation and redemption.

It is for our understanding that inspiration ascribes to the Godhead the names Father, Son, and Comforter. These human categories illumine for us that which the Trinity does for us, not how its members relate to one another.

When, by God's grace, we are changed to our immortal state, we will through eternity study not only the wonders of the physical universe, but also the personalities of the Godhead including the blessed third—the Holy Spirit, whose role it is to bring us convincing, conviction, and conversion by the Word.

Jesus: The Light of the World

You shall also make a lampstand of pure gold;
the lampstand shall be of hammered work. Its shaft, its branches,
its bowls, its ornamental knobs, and flowers shall be of one piece. Ex. 25:31.

There were no windows in either of the tabernacle compartments (the holy place and the Most Holy Place). The light of the seven-branched lampstand or candlestick provided its illumination. The lampstand constituted a centerpiece with six branches on either side. The stems were trimmed daily but never extinguished all at once. As there was never a time that a lamb was not burning on the altar or that fresh loaves were not on the table of showbread, so was there never a time that the lampstand was not reflecting light in all directions upon the resplendent walls and curtains of the sanctuary interior.

Just as the candlestick was the sanctuary's source of light, Jesus is the source of light for His church. John witnessed to this when he saw Him walking among the candlesticks (Rev. 2:1)—that is, personally communicating with His people, nurturing, guiding, enabling and ennobling the flock that He leads.

More broadly, Jesus is the light of the entire world. All true knowledge comes from Him. He is the wellspring of all human intellect. As attested in the superior technological prowess of Christian societies, His presence results in superior scientific and literary advance.

But it is upon His church in particular that He shines. He is the flame of truth kindled in our hearts by the breath of the Holy Spirit. His people need not look to other sources for truth. We may indeed find intellectual spoils in Egypt that we can convert into materials for kingdom building. But even those nuggets of wisdom are derived from the Christ. He is, as John, who witnessed His life-giving impact upon the darkened society into which He came, stated: "The true Light, which lighteth every man" (John 1:9).

And the light that is Christ will illumine the redeemed throughout eternity. For as Scripture records: "There shall be no night there: They need no lamp nor light of the sun, for the Lord God gives them light. And they shall reign forever and ever" (Rev. 22:5).

Jesus: Our Only Hope

You shall make an altar to burn incense on; you shall make
it of acacia wood. . . . Aaron shall burn on it sweet incense every morning;
when he tends the lamps, he shall burn incense on it. Ex. 30:1-7.

In front of the curtain that divided the holy place from the Most Holy Place was the altar of incense. The dividing veil (curtain) itself did not reach the ceiling; this allowed the aromatic clouds of burning incense to drift from the altar into the Most Holy Place, softly perfuming the inner sanctum of divine presence. The altar of incense, the candlesticks, the showbread, and the national sacrifices were never inactive. Here, "upon this altar, the priests was to burn incense every morning and evening. . . . The fire upon this altar was kindled by God Himself and was sacredly cherished. Day and night the holy incense diffused its fragrance throughout the sacred apartments, and without, far around the tabernacle" (*Patriarchs and Prophets,* p. 348).

The burning incense richly demonstrates the priestly effects of Christ's intercessory ministry. More specifically, the ascending incense represents "the merits and intercession of Christ, His perfect righteousness, which through faith is imputed to His people, and which can alone make the worship of sinful beings acceptable to God" (*ibid.,* p. 353).

As the incense ascended from the altar where the blood of animal sacrifices was freely sprinkled by obedient priests, so did the pleadings of Jesus (Himself the offerer, Himself the sacrifice) ascend to the Father as sweet satisfaction for the requirements of justice.

Scripture reminds us that "without shedding of blood there is no remission" of sin (Heb. 9:22). Unless Jesus, our complete sacrifice, had spilled His blood on our behalf, even our best efforts for forgiveness and compensation would be meaningless. This is why the prophet wrote: "The intercession of Christ in man's behalf in the sanctuary above is as essential to the plan of salvation as was His death upon the cross. By His death He began that work which after His resurrection He ascended to complete in heaven" (*The Great Controversy,* p. 489). This is why the psalmist declared, "Thy way, O God, is in the sanctuary" (Ps. 77:13), and this is why you and I can this day and every day live in happy assurance of salvation.

His Sacred Presence

And there I will meet with you, and I will speak with you
from above the mercy seat, from between the two cherubim which
are on the ark of the Testimony, about everything which I will give
you in commandment to the children of Israel. Ex. 25:22.

The focal point of the sanctuary arrangement was the ark of the covenant—the only article of furniture in the Most Holy Place. The top or cover of the ark was made of solid gold and named the mercy seat. Resting upon the mercy seat was the blue light called the Shekinah. This small cloud was the most sacred of all sanctuary locations, for here God dwelt, and from here He spoke to His people.

At either end of the mercy seat (or top of the ark) stood golden cherubim. Each angel had one wing stretched high over the ark and had the other folded to its body (Eze. 1:11). The angels faced each other with heads bowed in submissive reverence before the Creator.

Modern society's lack of awe for God was greatly augmented by the theories of the eighteenth-century philosopher Auguste Comte, who proposed that the human race had transitioned through three periods of relationship to ultimate authority. The first and most primitive was the era of belief in deities. This period, he said, was necessitated by the ancient's need to brace themselves against the ravages of nature, the cruelties of their enemies and the specter of death.

The second period he labeled as the age of metaphysics: the era of reason, when humans advanced to dependence upon philosophy rather than religion (i.e., divine beings) as a means of surviving the threatening circumstances of life.

The third era (the one in which we now live) he proposed is the age of science. No longer needing to depend upon unseen gods or speculative reason, humanity (according to Comte) is now able to solve its challenges through science and technology.

It is against this background of unbelief that God sent the angels of Revelation 14:6-12 to remind our disrespectful world that His majesty has not dimmed with time; that He is still "high and lifted up" and alone to be feared and glorified and worshipped (Rev. 15:4). By their message we are reminded that every approach to God, whether public or private, should be seen as a Shekinah privilege made possible by the intercessory work of our elder brother, Jesus Christ.

The Ministry of Angels

And you shall make two cherubim of gold; of hammered work
you shall make them at the two ends of the mercy seat.
And the cherubim shall stretch out their wings above, covering
the mercy seat with their wings, and they shall face one another;
the faces of the cherubim shall be toward the mercy seat. Ex. 25:18-20.

There are two classifications of angels mentioned in the Bible: seraphim, the six-winged creatures whose only mention is Isaiah 6:1-7; and cherubim, mentioned numerous times, the first of which is in Genesis 3:24—where they are commissioned to guard the gates of Eden which contained the tree of life from its expelled inhabitants.

All angels are beings of higher order than humans but lesser than the uncreated members of the Trinity. Angels were created as were humans to worship God and in addition to do His bidding in a wide variety of service among His created worlds.

Scripture informs us that there are more angels than earthly math can denote. Our minds are inadequate to conceive, our mathematical calculations too limited to express the total of their ranks. Nor can we adequately appreciate their transcendent powers. We know that they can divide ocean waters, move undeterred through material barriers, fly swifter than light, destroy whole armies with a touch, level the greatest of cities with a word, but we will never, this side of eternity, truly appreciate the extent of their might or their care for our needs.

One of their most critical functions in our behalf is represented by the service of the golden cherubim whose wings overspread the ark on top of which was the mercy seat—the visible presence of God. When the high priest sought divine guidance before the Shekinah presence, he looked to the covering cherub for indication of God's will. This was because: "When the Lord did not answer by a voice, He let the scared beams of light and glory rest upon the cherubim upon the right of the ark, in approbation or favor. If their requests were refused, a cloud rested upon the cherubim at the left" (*Spiritual Gifts*, vol. 4a, p. 102).

The Shekinah no longer glows between human-made cherubim on a movable ark. This is because God has arranged that we come boldly before His heavenly throne in daily praise and petition.

Our Spiritual Bread

And Moses said to Aaron, "Take a pot and put an omer
of manna in it, and lay it up before the Lord, to be kept
for your generations." As the Lord commanded Moses, so Aaron
laid it up before the Testimony, to be kept. Ex. 16:33, 34.

Manna, or small wafers of bread, rained down from heaven each morning with the exception of the seventh day. The people gathered it, ground it in mills or beat it as in a mortar, baked it in pans, and made cakes from it (Num. 11:8). Its taste was that of wafers made with honey. The psalmist called it "corn of heaven" (Ps. 78:24, KJV) and said the 40-year miracle of it falling from heaven and being gathered by the tribes was described as: "Men ate angels' food" (verse 25).

In His Word God still supplies His people "daily manna." His Word is fresh every day. Yesterday's understandings were essential to yesterday's challenges. But it is today that the Word speaks most relevantly. Our memory of yesterday's victories gives us courage for today's challenges. But today's battles cannot be fought with yesterday's strength. We need daily manna to have daily victory. We must make a sincere effort to receive God's Word.

Our methods of Bible study may differ. Some find greater satisfaction in "reading the Bible through"—examining its messages by sequentially reviewing the 66 books. Others prefer topical study and some prefer in-depth reflection upon selected books or personalities or periods. No matter what the method, the best time to gather spiritual manna is in the morning.

Of course, no opportunity is the wrong time. But again, morning is the prime time: before the pressuring events of the day begin to pound upon us; before the phone calls and family conversations; before the travel; before the turmoil of the hurried busy agenda begins to unwind, we should go to the source of our strength. Not in ritualistic or hurried surfacing, but in quiet, contemplative meditation.

We find the manna at prayer meeting, at the divine worship service on Sabbath, and in our family worship sessions. But its properties are best enjoyed and most effectively digested when we gather it and consume it in individual communion with God.

March 27

Our Physical Bread

*Therefore, whether you eat or drink, or whatever you do,
do all to the glory of God. 1 Cor. 10:31.*

In reflecting upon God's gift of manna to His people in the wilderness, Ellen White had this to say: "The same God who gave the children of Israel manna from heaven lives and reigns. He will give skill and understanding in the preparation of health foods" (*Counsels on Diet and Foods,* p. 268).

The primary lesson of the manna is that Jesus is our bread from heaven and must be sought morning by morning if we would enjoy spiritual health.

However, the miracle of the manna references our physical needs as well. Health reform, as taught by the Seventh-day Adventist Church, is an integral part of the gospel message. The skill required to provide a healthy, appetizing meal is a gift from God. Not all reach the same level of efficiency in preparation of healthy meals, but all should honor their influence upon our living.

There was a time not long ago that preaching and teaching health reform, particularly vegetarianism, was viewed as being unnecessarily conservative. Many, even in the church, often saw health reformers as overly strict if not fanatical. But this has changed. Sober minds everywhere are awakening to the relationship of diet and health—both mental and physical. The effects of large amounts of sugar in the diet, the consequences of taking liquids while eating, the burden placed upon our systems by overeating, the damage done by eating between meals, the folly of eating shortly before retiring, the effects of alcoholic drinks and drug intake, and the risks of eating animal flesh is "present truth" that we must proclaim to modern society.

While teaching the dangers of negative eating habits, we must reinforce the positive elements of health reform: rest, sunshine, fresh air, exercise, water, and trust in God. Since the best way to combat evil is to "occupy the territory with good" while decrying the unhealthy habits of our fast-paced, fast-food, and pervasively diseased society, we can and must demonstrate a better way.

Since our bodies are the temple of God, we are "bought at a price" (1 Cor. 6:19, 20). We are stewards of another's property created for His glory and, by the irrevocable principles of His kingdom, strictly accountable for the care of our bodies.

Reinforcing the Sabbath

So they gathered it every morning, every man according
to his need. And when the sun became hot, it melted. . . .
Then he said to them, "This is what the Lord has said: 'Tomorrow
is a Sabbath rest, a holy Sabbath to the Lord.'" Ex. 16:21-23.

Israel's relationship to the Sabbath is poignantly taught in the lesson of the manna: "Every week during their long sojourn in the wilderness the Israelites witnessed a threefold miracle, designed to impress their minds with the sacredness of the Sabbath: a double quantity of manna fell on the sixth day, none on the seventh, and the portion needed for the Sabbath was preserved sweet and pure, when if any were kept over at any other time it became unfit for use" (*Patriarch and Prophets*, p. 296).

Notice how the threefold miracle of the manna illumined God's gift of the Sabbath. First, the manna spoke to the sacredness of the Sabbath. No manna was gathered on the holy day. The bread fell on every day but the seventh. Six days they labored to gather food, but on the Sabbath the people rested from their activity in living demonstration of the Sabbath's special purpose.

Second, the manna spoke to preparation for the Sabbath. The manna that fell on the sixth day (Friday) was the only manna that did not sour by the next day—the holy seventh-day Sabbath.

Third, it spoke to the blessings of the Sabbath. Those blessings are memorably highlighted by Isaiah's words: "Then you shall delight yourself in the Lord; and I will cause you to ride on the high hills of the earth, and feed you with the heritage of Jacob your father. The mouth of the Lord has spoken" (Isa. 58:14). These benedictions are still provided by the God who cannot lie and who still delights in blessing the obedient.

By their dependence upon the daily provision of manna, including their enjoyment of its blessings on the day when it did not fall, Israel was reminded that their sustenance and their safety were not the result of their genius, but the goodness of God. We too must live knowing that when obedience to Him is rendered appropriately during the six days and we faithfully regard the day of "no gathering," His positive benedictions cannot—and will not fail.

A Warning Against Rebellion

And the Lord said to Moses, "Bring Aaron's rod back before
the Testimony, to be kept as a sign against the rebels, that you may
put their complaints away from Me, lest they die." Num. 17:10.

A aron's rod that budded was one of three objects placed in the golden pot inside the ark of mercy. Also placed in the pot were a supply of manna and the original writing of the Ten Commandments (Heb. 9:4).

The budding of Aaron's rod occurred in the wake of the rebellion of Korah, Dathan, and Abiram, who led a series of insurrections against Moses and Aaron (Num. 16:1-31). Conducted secretly at first, the bitter drive to discredit and unseat God's servants was finally brought to light. It was then that God publicly demonstrated His displeasure by destroying these men and their families—swallowing them up in the bowels of the earth (verses 31-33). He also destroyed 250 of their sympathizers by fire and an additional 14,000 by a deadly plague (Num. 17:35).

Then, as if to punctuate the point and to establish not only His right to choose His leaders, but also His hatred of prideful disaffection, God caused Aaron's rod, the symbol of His authority upon which were written the names of the 12 tribes, to "[produce] blossoms and [yield] ripe almonds" (Num 17:8). This the people beheld with great fear and reverence.

The lesson for us today is that the self-delusion that leads to faultfinding and criticism of God's chosen servants is not unheeded by heaven. It is true that church leaders make mistakes and that it is often tempting to become critics and correctors of these individuals. But it is also true that there are proper procedures for addressing inequities, be they real or perceived, and those who are offensive against God's church and His leaders will not escape His judgments.

It should be noted that God's punishment upon Korah and his companions was not the only negative result of their attitudes. There was a prior consequence: the loss of spiritual discernment and fervor. Criticism and censoriousness drown out cheerfulness and optimism. Suspicion and negativity cannot coexist with faith, hope, and joy.

We, as were they, may be tempted to be judgmental toward church leaders, but we are sufficiently warned by God's response to Moses' critics to avoid even the first steps toward bitterness and to cultivate kindness, openness, and optimism instead.

Law of Moses

So it was, when Moses had completed writing the words
of this law in a book, when they were finished, that Moses commanded
the Levites, who bore the ark of the covenant of the Lord, saying:
"Take this Book of the Law, and put it beside the ark of the covenant of the
Lord your God, that it may be there as a witness against you." Deut. 31:24-26.

Whereas the Ten Commandments (with Aaron's rod that budded and the manna in the golden pot) were placed inside the ark (Heb. 9:4), Moses' law, Israel's system of civic rule, was placed in a pocket on the side of the ark.

However, the difference in their placement is not the only distinction between these laws provided in Scripture. The Ten Commandments law was written with the finger of God (Ex. 31:18) and the law of Moses by his hand (Deut. 31:24). The law of God contains 10 rules, each having timeless significance—Moses' laws were given specifically for the guidance of Israel during its period of "chosenness." The law of God is an expression of His character—the laws of Moses is an expression of Israel's civic requirements. The Ten Commandments emphasize the seventh-day Sabbath—the law of Moses emphasizes various feast-day Sabbaths. The law of God was in place from the beginning of creation (Cain broke the sixth commandment when he killed his brother, Abel)—the law of Moses was inaugurated with the birth of the Israelite nation 2,000 years later. The law of God was featured and upheld by Bible characters decades past the crucifixion and resurrection of Christ (see Rev. 22:14)—the law of Moses was abolished at the cross (Col. 2:14).

In his vision of the church in the last days, John saw the woman (church) dressed in the sun with the moon under her feet. The sun that clothes the people of God today is the full gospel light that illumines its proclamation. The moon under the woman's feet represents the laws and systems of Moses. As the moon has no light of itself and shines only with the borrowed illumination of the sun, so the laws of Moses were of themselves void of salvation power. Their only benefit was their reflection of the light and glory of Jesus. God's law, however, is the genuine article—the real deal. They are eternal in nature and compared with Moses' law or any other civic set of rules regulating human conduct—clearly and everlastingly something better!

The Christx Within

*For it is God who works in you both to will
and to do for His good pleasure. Phil. 2:13.*

Jesus, who by the rituals of the sanctuary tabernacled symbolically with ancient Israel by the miracles of the virgin birth, spent 33 years in actual flesh among the human race. His dwelling among us is an act that revitalized our sagging humanity and set in motion dynamics of human progress that are still bearing cultural, scientific, and, of course, spiritual good. God's dwelling among us was the dawn of a new day for humanity. But it is God's dwelling in us that makes salvation a reality. It is His dwelling in us that captures our desires, that regulates our tastes, that controls our passions, that sanctifies our reasons, that changes our hearts and subdues the old man of sin confirming us as citizens of grace.

Christ dwelling among us resulted in raising the dead, healing the sick—the revelation of the true character of the Father and the provision of the sacrifice that atones for our sins and opens to us the possibility of eternal life. Christ's dwelling within us provides the faith to believe, the will to obey, the hope to endure, the wisdom to make good choices—the spiritual nutrients that produce the blessed fruits of righteousness and the continued infusion of power to be faithful in all of life's changes.

John is very helpful to our understanding of this. He writes: "Behold I stand at the door and knock. If anyone hears My voice and opens the door, I will come in to him and dine with him, and he with Me" (Rev. 3:20).

Holding her father's hand as they walked through the art gallery portraying the scenes of Christ's life, the little girl took it all in with silent wonder. The final scene showed Christ, freshly risen, standing at a door knocking in hopes of entering. Tugging at her father's hand as they turned to leave, the troubled child turned to her father and innocently asked, "Daddy, did He get in?"

Jesus still knocks lovingly seeking entrance into our hearts. He wishes to dwell among us today as keenly as he wished to dwell among His people then, and He still knocks patiently, persistently, pleadingly. Why not let Him in?

APRIL

A Better High Priest

Consider Him

Therefore, holy brethren, partakers of the heavenly calling, consider the Apostle and High Priest of our confession, Christ Jesus. Heb. 3:1.

Twice in the book of Hebrews we are admonished to consider our better High Priest, first in Hebrews 3:1-16, where we are urged to meditate upon His faithfulness; and then in Hebrews 12:3, where we are admonished to contemplate His saving endurance. In both instances Paul is wishing for us the fruitful benefits of rational comparison of Jesus' ministry with that of Israel's highest spiritual leadership.

Contemplation, Aristotle believed, is life's most profitable activity. In fact, for him, the highest of all human endeavors was not just "thinking" but "thinking about thinking." Unfortunately his view of contemplation contributed negatively to Western civilization's attitude toward social ills. His "thinking about thinking" translated to inactivity or passivity when "action" against evil was demanded. His philosophy greatly influenced the responses of succeeding generations to human tragedy by encouraging radical dependence upon fate as the answer to human need. Thus for many, even in contemporary society, aggression against injustice has been subordinated to deliberation and delay. Civil rights leader Martin Luther King, Jr., referred to this as "the paralysis of analysis."

Not so with our thinking about Jesus. Our contemplation of Him is not an end in itself; it is a prelude to service—to righteous activity, to godly living. By considering Him, we absorb vitality as the branch from the vine. And, that vitality produces not only the fruits of the spirit (godly traits of personality and character), but also the works of the spirit (the conversion of godly states into godly living).

It is the sure consequence of the ironclad law of "cause and effect" that makes this process not only possible, but also guaranteed. The more we study Him, the more of His graces we drink; the more we admire Him, the more of His love we absorb, and the more we prayerfully consider Him, the more in His likeness we daily grow. Since we grow in the direction of our reverences, by "beholding we become changed" (see 2 Cor. 3:18), and, since the supreme objective of our Christian vows is to be like Him, prayerful consideration of His life remains our highest privilege—our surest stimulus to godly living.

A God of Order

And Moses said to Aaron, "Go to the altar, offer your
sin offering and your burnt offering, and make atonement
for yourself and for the people. Offer the offering of the people,
and make atonement for them, as the Lord commanded." Lev. 9:7.

One of the most impressive aspects of Israel's priestly functions was the orderly manner in which they conducted their services.

This is not surprising. Their instructions came from God, and He is a being of precision and order. That is revealed in the wonders of creation, in earth's ecological balance, and in the inner workings of our physical bodies. The Creator of heaven and earth conducts His affairs with unerring regularity and consistency.

Consider the cycle of nature: The beaming sun absorbs the moisture of the ocean, creating the clouds that release their liquid treasure upon mountains and hills; from these heights water flows down in rushing streams to lands below, nourishing fields and farms then emptying at last into broadening lakes that in turn flow out into the oceans, which once again supply the moisture drawn up by the sun. Nature's predictable cycles, highlighted by her rhythmic seasons of seedtime and harvest, sunshine and rain, day and night, are all testimonies of God's orderly and purposeful ways.

We see His orderliness in the infinite species of fish and fowl that inhabit the waters below and the heavens above, in the vast variety of beasts that occupy the animal kingdom and in the lowly insect world typified by the marshaled organization of the industrious ant.

Even in heaven the angels of glory function with precise organization. Both cherubim and seraphim do His bidding in measured order. Ellen White gives clarity to this reality: "There is perfect order and harmony in the Holy City. All the angels that are commissioned to visit the earth hold a golden card, which they present to the angels at the gates of the city as they pass in and out. Heaven is a good place" (*Early Writings*, p. 39).

Yes, God is a God of order, and we who are now a nation of priests and kings serve Him best when in our personal affairs, and of course in the conduct of His business, do so in order and consistency.

A God of Holiness

You shall also make a plate of pure gold and engrave on it,
like the engraving of a signet: HOLINESS TO THE LORD. Ex. 28:36.

The golden plate with the words "holiness to the Lord" worn upon the high priest's forehead was an unmistakable reminder of the purity that is God and what He requires. How holy is God? He is holy in all aspects of His being: His works are holy (Ps. 145:17); His name is holy (Matt. 6:9); His law is holy (Rom. 7:12); His covenant is holy (Luke 1:72); His Temple is holy (Ps. 11:4); His dwelling is holy (2 Chron. 30:27); His throne is holy (Ps. 47:8); and where He dwells is "most" holy—"the Holiest of All"! (Heb. 9:3).

In fact, He is holiness personified; He is the fount of holiness; He is the origin and source of all holiness. He is where all holiness begins—this is why Hebrews 12:29 reads: "For our God is a consuming fire," which is to say that His moral purity is so intense it transforms (radiates) as physical energy.

It was for this reason that the high priest was made to wear bells around his garments as he ministered before the ark of the covenant. That is why Moses was forbidden to look upon His face. That is why the six-winged seraphim of Isaiah's vision while in His presence covered their feet and faces; and that is why latter-day believers should come into His presence with sobriety, reverence, and awe.

Revelation 15:4 explains that the reason we fear and worship and glorify God, as commanded by the three angels of Revelation 14:6-12, is that He alone is holy. The essence of the angel's warning is not commandment keeping or coming out of Babylon; it is fearing and respecting the high and holy God. The angels were sent to warn our lewd, crude, rude society that God still lives and that He is not only the best of gods, but also the only God, and that He rules the universe in holiness.

First Peter 1:15, 16 instructs us that we too must be holy. Until He shall come, we are deficient unless covered by His righteousness. At His return this mortal shall put on immortality and this corruptible incorruption, and we will be holy without fault. Even then we will be capable of unending enrichment as humans. Although redeemed, we will continue to progress in the likeness of the Creator God. Our holiness at best makes heaven happy, but it does not make heaven happen! Only Christ's holiness can do that.

Christ: Our Burden Bearer

And you shall put the two stones on the shoulders of the ephod as memorial stones for the sons of Israel. So Aaron shall bear their names before the Lord on his two shoulders as a memorial. Ex. 28:12.

The ephod, a vestlike garment worn over the robe, consisted of two pieces: one covering the chest and the other the back. It was joined together at the top by shoulder straps and at the bottom (the waist) by a skillfully woven girdle or band. "The blue, purple, scarlet, fine linen, gold, and the gems of the ephod gave it a variety and a beauty which made it the most glorious of all the priestly vestments" (*The Seventh-day Adventist Bible Commentary,* vol. 1, p. 648).

Fastened to the ephod were several objects that illumined the high priest's position. These included an onyx stone on both shoulder straps. On each stone were engraved the names of six of the 12 tribes.

The application to Christ, our high priest, could not be more forceful. When He came into the world, Jesus took upon His shoulders the cause of the entire human race. Isaiah expressed it well: "For unto us a Child is born, unto us a Son is given; and the government will be upon His shoulders" (Isa. 9:6). He bore in His body our infirmities and carried upon His shoulders not only the burden of our rescue, but also the task of vindicating His Father's character as well. From age 12 (or the time of His visit to the Temple) until His death He was fully aware of His mission.

Now He who successfully bore "our griefs and carried our sorrows" (Isa. 53:4) places upon our shoulders the responsibility of extending His kingdom throughout the world. The fact that after His resurrection Jesus met many times with His believers but never with nondisciples is evidence that the task of evangelism was bequeathed to His followers.

Our individual efforts do not have cosmic consequences; our personal contributions will never make a difference in Christ's warfare with Satan. Nevertheless, be they ever so small or seemingly unnoticed, they gladden the Savior's heart and help fulfill His commission—"Go ye into all the world" (Mark 16:15, KJV).

Christ: Our Compassionate Friend

So Aaron shall bear the names of the sons of Israel on the breastplate of judgment over his heart, when he goes into the holy place, as a memorial before the Lord continually. Ex. 28:29.

While the ephod containing the names of the 12 tribes was the most expensive apparel worn by the common priest, the most illuminating dress of the high priest was the breastplate. The breastplate was "artistically woven" into a square consisting of gold, blue, purple, and scarlet tread. On this square plate were four rows of precious stones. On each stone was written the name of one of the 12 tribes of Israel (Ex. 28:12-20).

What a forceful reminder of the absolute regard of Christ, our high priest, for His chosen people. Consider the scene: The high priest, dressed in the splendor of his holy garment made for glory and beauty (Ex. 28:2), stands in God's presence with a censer in hand and the breastplate upon his heart. Every step he takes, every gesture he makes, every beating of his heart as he stands before the altar accents his concern for the people whose names he bears upon his breast. Even while silent or motionless before the Skekinah, there is no mistaking his purpose, no missing his compassion. There, shining brightly upon his heart in sparkling colors of precious stones, was represented the entire nation of Israel.

Jesus, our high priest, our compassionate friend, the one altogether lovely, carries us upon His heart before the Father in plaintive, perpetual intercession. But He does so in ways infinitely more tender than that of the high priest. He presents us not by tribe or nation or families; He does so individually. He counts the very hairs of our heads (Matt. 10:30), and all our tears are numbered in a book (Ps. 56:8). His pleading before the altar concerns not just life in the better world, He who sees the sparrow fall sympathizes with us in our present hurts. He knows our sickness; He feels our tragedies and journeys with us "through the valley of the shadow of death" (Ps. 23:4). He does not always remove us from harm and pain, but He provides us strength to endure and even to die. So no matter what our trials or hurts, we are constantly reassured that we are prized and precious to Him and that our names are securely fastened to His kind and compassionate heart.

We Are Not Alone

And thou shall put in the breastplate of judgment the
Urim and Thummim; and they shall be upon Aaron's heart, when he
goeth in before the Lord: and Aaron shall bear the judgment of the
children of Israel upon his before the Lord continually. Ex. 28:30, KJV.

The breastplate, the most conspicuous of the ephod's attachments, also contained the Urim and Thummim whereby God was consulted and whereby He communicated His will to the people. It was through the Urim and Thummim that God indicated His pleasure or displeasure. Divine approval was signified by a halo encircling the Urim and disapproval by a cloud that shadowed the Thummim. There was no need to doubt; after consulting God in prayer for guidance, the priest would look to the left shoulder or the right one to know God's will.

Today we do not have such tangible instruments for knowing God's will. But we do have a High Priest in glory who promised that "His ear" is not "heavy, that it cannot hear" (Isa. 59:1); who told us, before He left, that if we pray "thy will be done" (Luke 11:2, KJV), He will always respond to our best benefit. David had such solicitude in mind when he said: "For this is God, our God forever and ever; He will be our guide even to death" (Ps. 48:14).

But, many ask, how do I really know His will? Does His promise to hear and answer include such practical concerns as my desires for friendship, marriage, and stock market selection, and choices of school, profession, and employment? Does it include being led in such matters as choice of city of residence, the purchase of a car, the building or buying of a house? Yes, it does.

How is His guidance given? First, by the shaping of our minds through study of His Word; reading the Bible strengthens one's reasoning powers, thus enhancing one's decision-making abilities. Second, God's people know His will because they see, in the providential arrangement of circumstances, evidence of His guiding hand. And third, we are convicted of His will by "inner illumination"—the persistent impressions given to us by the Holy Spirit.

No, we no longer have the Urim and Thummim. But we do have His promises, His providences, and His presence to guide us—we are not alone!

Our High Calling

You shall make the robe of the ephod all of blue. Ex. 28:31.

The ephod or vest upon which the breastplate hung was "of gold, blue, purple, and scarlet thread, and fine woven linen, artistically worked" (verse 6). But the robe upon which it hung was "all of blue" (verse 31).

Both the materials and the colors of the sanctuary reflected important aspects of Christ's services in our behalf. In fact, colors throughout Scripture provide special meaning and messages.

The color black frequently symbolizes judgment and affliction (Job 3:5; Rev. 6:5, 12); white often represents purity or holiness (Ps. 51:7; Isa. 1:18); red, vibrancy or vigor, and blue, as displayed in the high priest's royal robe, special place and authority.

The fact that we no longer worship the Creator under Old Testament conditions does not diminish the truth that those specifically chosen by Him to serve in spiritual matters are ambassadors—representatives of the King of the universe. The disrespect for things and people bearing the stamp of God so prevalent in contemporary society are alien to the culture of the redeemed.

Much of present-day callousness for spiritual matters is the consequence of centuries of diminishing faith and the pervasive evolution of self-seeking materialism. The "God is dead"/"me first" spirit of the twenty-first century is, in fact, manifestation of the original fault: Lucifer's jealousy and disdain for the sovereignty of God, his wish that he could be a part of the councils of the Trinity. Lucifer's plan, Ellen White observes, was to completely discredit Christ, to take His place in the Trinity, and eventually to make an effort to take the place of God the Father Himself (manuscript 37, May 1, 1903).

The tempter's effort to lure us into the camp of the disloyal has been foiled by the Savior's completely adequate arrangements for our rescue. His red blood provides forgiveness for our sins; His white robe provides covering for our creatureliness, and it is by His faithful pleading, royally reflected in the "true blue" of the high priest attire, that we are daily rendered candidates for eternal life.

Nothing Else Needed

And they made bells of pure gold, and put the
bells between the pomegranates on the hem of the robe all
around between the pomegranates. Ex. 39:25.

The blue robe beneath the ephod that the high priest wore was distinguished in a number of ways. First, it was worn not in place of but in addition to the linen dress common to lesser priests' attire. This indicated to all that the high priest's duties were not separate or apart from the work of his subordinates, but a higher type. Thus was prefigured the unique nature of the Messiah whose being was the same yet superior to ours.

Second, the robe was woven in one piece, signifying to all the seamless perfection of Jesus' ministry. His efforts on our behalf are not amenable to addition or change or further development. Not only has modern Israel no other God, but also we see in Christ's salvation ministry totality and completion beyond which lies no other need.

Third, ornaments around the hem distinguished the robe. Here were embroidered "a bell and a pomegranate, all around the hem of the robe to minister in, as the Lord had commanded Moses" (Ex. 39:26). The embroidered pomegranates were blue, purple and scarlet—signifying loyalty. The bells were colored gold—indicating royalty. Both were virtues that distinguished our true high priest's services.

In addition to the embroidered bells on the hem of his garment, there were a number of actual or live bells. On the annual Day of Atonement he ministered before the light of the Shekinah glory—the very presence of God would sound the bells, and the people knew that he was alive. If, however, because of sin in his life he had been smitten before the ark and the bells no longer rang, the saddened worshippers knew that by his own unconfessed transgressions their representative had forfeited his life.

Today we can pursue our daily tasks in absolute assurance that our Savior lives. Because He did no sin, nor was any guile found in His mouth, He is able to stand before the Father in undeterred, undiluted, unending service for the doomed occupants of this lost world.

A Two-Way Witness

So you shall put them on Aaron your brother and on his sons with him.
You shall anoint them, consecrate them, and sanctify them,
that they may minister to Me as priests. Ex. 28:41.

While a chief responsibility of the priesthood was representing the people to God, an even more solemn aspect of their duty was conveying God's will and desires to the people. In all things said and done, they were to please Him. This was not simply a case of earning His favor by meticulously following the elaborate details of their priestly prescriptions; it was first and foremost a matter conveying His righteous character and will. In other words their chief task was not speaking for the people to God, but for God to the people. Their ministry was to be shaped not by the peoples' taste and inclinations, but by God's personality and desires.

There are pastors and members today whose guiding principles of worship and lifestyle are not the holiness of God, but the feelings and goodwill of the people. The result is worship style, i.e., music and preaching and other sanctuary activity that would not be if their objective were to please Him and not "them."

We have not seen God. All of us but faintly understand His being. Nevertheless, in His Holy Word we are given glimpses of His exalted person that, if kept in mind, would inspire a level of dignity not now attained in many worship circumstances.

Structuring church services to attract the most people or to build the most excitement is not the right endeavor. Parishioners' needs should be thoroughly considered and faithfully addressed in our worship experience. However, the guiding principle of worship encounter should be God's will and way as modeled in His Word. When this is honored, no genuine human need is left unattended. This will only occur when worship leaders are dedicated to lifting the people from where they are toward where God is.

The question that should be asked at the conclusion of the worship service is not "Did we have a good time?" or "Wasn't that an outstanding display of talent and ability?" but rather "Did not our hearts burn within us as we meditated upon His majesty and were we spiritually infused by the power of His presence?"

He Couldn't Help It

Wherefore in all things it behoved him to be made like unto his brethren, that he might be a merciful and faithful high priest in things pertaining to God, to make reconciliation for the sins of the people. Heb. 2:17, KJV.

The word "behooved" is rich in its sense of moral obligation. Used here, it signifies that Jesus was "duty bound" to come into this world to save us. If so, does this conflict with the voluntary, undemanded, unrequired giving of Himself that we usually associate with the Savior's mission?

The answer is found in the fact that while He was not required to satisfy the claims of justice, His merciful heart compelled Him to do so. In these two elements, justice that demanded our immediate extinction and mercy that drove Him to seek our rescue, are the dual dynamics of our salvation.

Justice and mercy represent not a conflict of values, but a confluence of goodness. By His sacrificial ministry, nothing that concerns justice has been left unsatisfied, and nothing that embraces mercy has been left unprovided.

Jesus was not forced to come, but He could not have been happy on His celestial throne while Lucifer was ruling our world without hope of rescue. Our utter helplessness moved Him to engage a plan so humiliating and anxious that angels volunteered to come in His stead, and moved with horror, would have rescued Him from the cross had not stronger, more elevated of their number restrained them (*The Story of Redemption*, pp. 214, 215).

That is the act that inspired the prophet Isaiah to ask in stunned incredulity, "Who has believed our report?" (Isa. 53:1). Indeed, who can understand the enormity of the love that caused the King of the universe to become the babe in Bethlehem and finally the crucified of Calvary? This is an act that defies belief. We cannot plumb the depths of that love, but it is true not only that He came and died, but that He also rose and lives. It is that love that provides us meaningful living and that behooves (motivates) us to vibrant witness.

A Pledge Fulfilled

For the law appoints as high priests men who have weakness,
but the word of the oath, which came after the law,
appoints the Son who has been perfected forever. Heb. 7:28.

Because they were born into the line of priestly succession, Aaron's sons needed no formal oath as introduction into the priesthood. Their ceremonies of cleansings were acts of consecration, not "joining rites" they were assigned by birth.

This is not true concerning Jesus, our great high priest. He was not born into the lineage of the priesthood. Neither was Mary, His biological mother, nor Joseph, His adopted father, of Levite lineage. Not having the fame or credentials that make succession into the priesthood "without oath," it was necessary for Him "by oath" to assume His role as our intercessor.

This He did before the world was made, when He pledged our rescue in the event of sin. He fulfilled His vow, after 4,000 years of sin's degradation—"a body hath thou prepared for me" (Heb. 10:5, KJV). His unforced, voluntary act makes His services different from that of the regular Levitical priesthood. He qualified as our spokesperson the old-fashioned way—He earned it.

Had He not been successful, we would be without representation and recourse before the Father. Had He sworn and stumbled in His efforts to save us, we would be shorn of all hope and doomed eternally. But what He vowed He fulfilled and now "ever liveth" to make intersession for us.

What about our vows? Christ's injunction "Do not swear at all: neither by heaven, for it is God's throne; nor by the earth, for it is His footstool" (Matt. 5:34, 35) dictates that we Christians are not to invoke the authority of heaven upon our earthly dealings.

But while we do not swear by God's name, we do commit "before God," i.e., in His presence, as we utter some of life's higher obligations. These include truthfulness in courts of law and vows of marriage and baptisms—all exceedingly important, but no more important than our daily, private pledge to follow Him.

A Pledge Outstanding

For they have become priests without an oath, but He with an oath
by Him who said to Him: "The Lord has sworn and will not relent,
'You are a priest forever according to the order of Melchizedek.'" Heb. 7:21.

Jesus, who sealed the everlasting covenant by oath with the Father, has at times, sealed His promises to humans by an oath as well. He did so with Abraham (Gen. 26:3), with Isaac (Ps. 105:9), with Jeremiah (Jer. 11:5), and with others. At the end of His earthly ministry He made a similar pledge with His disciples as they partook of the Last Supper. His words were: "For I say to you, I will not drink of the fruit of the vine until the kingdom of God comes" (Luke 22:18).

Upon what better authority and with what better assurance can we believe? The Trinity has delivered upon its promises. The Father has sent the Son and accepted His sacrifice. The Son has given His life and sent the Holy Spirit. And the Holy Spirit, in fulfillment of Christ's pledge, dwells among us and instructs and empowers our individual and corporate experience.

When our first parents sinned, the Son of God solemnly swore; and after 4,000 years of strategic positioning He fulfilled His vow of entering our space and dwelling and dying among us. But before He died He pledged to come again (John 14:1-3) and, in the meantime, to be with us "even to the end of the age" (Matt. 28:20).

We cannot see the throne where Jesus functions or prove that He is coming again. But we do see His fulfillment of prior prophesy, in His handiwork in nature, in His intervention in the course of human history, and, most of all, in the changes He has produced in our own lives. These evidences are the basis of our persevering faith—the ground of our belief that this promise is sure.

There are times that dark clouds seem to veil His face and we do not understand His leading, but our experienced faith causes us to trust Him even when we cannot trace Him. And among the otherwise overwhelming circumstance of life, "walk by faith, not by sight" (2 Cor. 5:7), knowing that "He who is coming will come and will not tarry" (Heb. 10:37).

A Better Hope

Therefore, if perfection were through the Levitical priesthood
(for under it the people received the law), what further need was
there that another priest should rise according to the order of Melchizedek,
and not be called according to the order of Aaron? Heb. 7:11.

Perfection is the ultimate requirement for eternal life. This was not possible through the Levitical priesthood and its elaborate ceremonial codes. These detailed laws, recorded so carefully in Exodus and Leviticus, were guideposts pointing to the perfect priesthood of the coming Messiah.

Jesus qualified for His priestly office by dwelling among us not as a regular member of Aaron's posterity, but as a sacrificial volunteer from a higher order. His perfect contribution resulted in the death of the old order of priestly functions and the establishment of the new and better way. By His birth, life, death, and resurrection the entire priestly system, including the ceremonial laws and rights that governed its functioning, was annulled—done away (Col. 2:10-14), and the rule of grace forever ordained.

We no longer need to depend upon human priests for access to God because Jesus is now our heavenly intercessor (Heb. 7:25). Because Jesus is our perfect, pleading, personal, and present high priest, we can now individually "come boldly to the throne of grace" (Heb. 4:16). Since we can never live our lives good enough to earn a place in the glory kingdom, we desperately need the higher holiness, the richer righteousness, and the purer perfection that Jesus provides. He does so by gifting us with His sin-canceling blood that annuls our past transgressions and His "creature covering" robe of righteousness that superimposes our permanently depraved flesh. Perfection did not come by Aaron's blood-sprinkling, censer-waving descendants; it came from the blood-pleading, robe-providing ministry of Jesus.

It is true, then, as the prophet declared: "The only way in which he [the sinner] can attain to righteousness is through faith. By faith he can bring to God the merits of Christ, and the Lord places the obedience of His Son to the sinner's account. Christ's righteousness is accepted in place of man's failure" (*Selected Messages,* book 1, p. 367). It was this realization that motivated a humble-minded apostle to state in grand summary of all our salvation needs—"you are complete in Him" (Col. 2:10).

A Better Law

You shall put the mercy seat on top of the ark, and in the ark you shall put the Testimony that I will give you. Ex. 25:21.

The Testimony referred to here is the ten-commandment law. Its position within the ark was given to emphasize its sacred and eternal character.

Satan never tires of confusing God's moral law, the Ten Commandments (His permanent guide for human conduct), with the ceremonial laws of Moses that were annulled at Calvary. The law that outlined Israel's priestly succession and services was temporary. God's moral law is eternal. It was invoked long before the existence of Moses, the sanctuary and its priesthood. God's law, which is a reflection of His character, was established from the very beginning of time. The fact that the Ten Commandments were operable, though not written, long before they were recorded at Sinai is demonstrated in a number of ways.

Centuries before Moses humans encountered the first commandment's prohibition against strange gods (Gen. 35:4), the second commandment's warnings regarding worship of images (Gen. 31:19), the third commandment's declaration against taking God's name in vain (Ex. 10:16-20), the fourth commandment's establishment and observance of the Sabbath (Gen. 2:1-3), the fifth commandment's concern about honoring one's parents (Gen. 9:22), the sixth commandment's exhortation against killing (Gen. 4:8-11), the seventh commandment's instruction against moral impurity (Gen. 19:5-7), the eight commandment's urging to honesty (Gen. 31:19-32), the ninth commandment's injunction against false witness (Gen. 27:22-24), and the tenth commandment's posture regarding covetousness (Gen. 25:30-34).

The Ten Commandments were recognized as permanent by Christ during His earthly ministry. Isaiah predicted that Christ would "magnify the law, and make it honourable" (Isa. 42:21, KJV). Christ ratified that prediction with finality when He said: "Do not think that I have come to abolish the Law or the Prophets; I have not come to abolish them but to fulfill them" (Matt. 5:17, NIV).

The Ten Commandments have remained in force since the cross. We should not be surprised that James calls the Ten Commandments "the royal law" (James 2:8), and he reminds us that those who break one commandment break them all (verse 10). Paul, in an attempt to bring balance to the faith and works partnership asks, "Do we then make void the law through faith?" and replies with finality, "God forbid: yea, we establish the law" (Rom. 3:31, KJV).

In His Own Blood

Not with the blood of goats and calves, but with
His own blood He entered the Most Holy Place once for all,
having obtained eternal redemption. Heb. 9:12.

There are many ways in which Christ, our high priest, is distinguished from the earthly priests of Israel. One is His origin: He came from above. Another is His perpetuity: He continues forever. Another is His physical access to the Father: He returned to glory and is seated at His right hand. Yet another is His perfection: He alone is a holy priest, harmless and undefiled (Heb. 4:15).

As amazing as all this is, there is yet another aspect of His high-priestly ministry that is starkly superior to that of Israel's religious leaders—He is a priest who offers His own blood! All other priests offered the blood of animals and others, but not Jesus. He is both offerer and offering, sacrifice and sacrificer, bondsman and bail, redeemer and price of our redemption. In other words, he accomplishes both our sin's expiation and our case representation. He is our complete emancipator, our wholistic deliverer and the total source of our salvation.

His work on our behalf is greater, better, broader, than that of Israel's priesthood, and like the sun He is more vital and attractive than the lifeless moon. He is our unique high priest, our perfect sacrifice, our only hope of salvation.

His effectiveness with God the Father is the result of not only His familiarity with Him and His kinship with us, but also the creditability of the blood He offers.

In order for the blood of our redemption to be morally acceptable, it must be from a source or victim whose contribution was knowledgeable, willing, and innocent. The goats slain on Israel's altar were knowledgeable (they sensed impending doom) and innocent (they had not broken the moral law), but were very unwilling. The lambs were willing (they did not resist slaughter) and innocent (they too were not guilty of transgressing God's law), but not knowledgeable (they didn't have a clue).

What makes the blood of Jesus irresistibly acceptable to the Father is that its donor, our Redeemer, complied completely with all of salvation's requirements. He died as our knowledgeable, willing, and innocent sacrifice, and He now serves as our "ever-living" priest on high.

The Judge Is on Our Side

"For the Father judges no one, but has committed all
judgment to the Son," "and has given Him authority to execute
judgment also, because He is the Son of Man." John 5:22, 27.

We are awed and overwhelmed by the thought that Jesus, our sacrifice, is also our high priest—that the blood He offers before the Father is His own. But now, through the pen of the beloved disciple, Scripture informs us of another wonder of redemption—He who is our sacrifice and high priest is also our judge! The final pronouncement of eternal punishment or reward will be left to our elder brother, Jesus.

Ellen White states it this way: "Having taken human nature and in this nature having overcome the temptations of the enemy, and having divine perfection, to Him has been committed the judgment of the world. The case of each one will be brought in review before Him. He will pronounce judgment, rendering to every man according to his works" (*The Seventh-day Adventist Bible Commentary,* Ellen G. White Comments, vol. 7, p. 929).

How much does He love us? Let us count the ways: He loves us by the efficacy of His righteous blood; by the warmth of His relationship with the Father; by His firsthand knowledge of our plight; by His offering the merits of His perfect life to replace the demerits of our inherited and cultivated evil; by His forgiveness that renders all our sins inadmissible; by the promise that He, our friend and elder brother, our closest of kin, will deliver our final judgment sentence.

My brother the judge! What a fortunate circumstance, what a fortuitous development, what a favored disposition. My brother, my judge—what more privileged, more positive advantage could I, the guilty sinner, wish? My brother the judge! We are severely challenged to structure a more hopeful arrangement, and the Trinity itself, unable to save us if we refuse to accept so sure salvation.

The accuser of the brethren has met his match. The law of condemnation has met its maker, and I, fully aware of my unworthiness, can face the bar of judgment completely confident that deliverance is already assured, justice has already been served, and eternity has already begun. Why? Because my pleading High Priest is also my sentencing judge.

A Better Sacrifice

Therefore it was necessary that the copies
of the things in the heavens should be purified with these, but the
heavenly things themselves with better sacrifices than these. Heb. 9:23.

There are many ways to state the superiority of Calvary's sacrifice compared to those slain on Israel's alters. Among them are: (a) the animals of Israel's altars were not morally accountable—Jesus was; (b) the animals of Israel's altars were not conscious of their role—Jesus was; (c) the animals of Israel's altars could not have escaped death—Jesus could have; (d) the animals of the Israel's altars did not die voluntarily—Jesus did; (e) the animals of Israel's altars suffered no conspicuous self-denial—Jesus did; (f) the animals of Israel's altars did not have potential for life after death—Jesus did.

Jesus is not simply a better sacrifice. He was and is the only sacrifice capable of redeeming lost humanity. If He were not willing, our world's cause would have been eternally lost. God would have continued as sovereign of the universe, but our rightfully destroyed planet would have been forever viewed as a mistake and Satan's charges against God a matter of perpetual doubt. Calvary, however, dispelled all such arguments; Jesus' suffering is more than the gift that purchased our release, it is the act that convinced the universe of God's righteous ways.

Calvary's role in fully clarifying the contrasting characters of the principal antagonist's in the great controversy is highlighted by the fact that "not until the death of Christ was the character of Satan clearly revealed to the angels or to the unfallen worlds. Then the prevarications and accusations of him who had once been an exalted angel were seen in their true light. It was seen that his professedly spotless character was deceptive. His deeply laid scheme to exalt himself to supremacy was fully discerned. His falsehoods were apparent to all. God's authority was forever established. Truth triumphed over falsehood" (*Reflecting Christ*, p. 60).

Not only was the blood of animal sacrifices insufficient for our salvation, but also that of any other creature in the universe. His blood alone was adequate to vindicate God's law and to appease the Father's wrath against evil.

Tempted as We

For we do not have a High Priest who cannot
sympathize with our weaknesses, but was in all
points tempted as we are, yet without sin. Heb. 4:15.

Jesus was tempted as we are? But how can that be? Since "in Him all the fullness should dwell" (Col. 1:19); since beneath the human exterior He was the Lord of Creation, ruler of heaven and earth, the faultless fountain of all purity and holiness, how could He be tempted in all points such as are we?

Hebrews 5:2 explains: "he himself is also subject to weakness." That is to say, in the daily conduct of His life He functioned as human, not as God. The early Christians were correct when, at the Council of Chalcedon, A.D. 354, they attributed duality to His presence among us—He was all God and all man at the same time. When He entered the foul atmosphere of this planet, He did not shed His divinity. He veiled it; He masked His identity; He shrouded His Godhead with our humanity and lived His life in the flesh of earthlings.

One of His severest temptations was to utilize His God power to relieve His human necessities. But He never did. His God powers were used in healing the sick and calming the storms, but never for personal profit or protection. His humanity was tempted in all ways.

What are the ways in which our humanity is tempted? By "the lust of the flesh, the lust of the eyes, and the pride of life" (1 John 2:16). Jesus, our volunteer advocate, our high priest of the tabernacle not made with hands, endured the fiercest of trials in each of these areas.

And, although His temptations were "one hundred times" more intense than are ours (see *Manuscript Releases,* vol. 9, p. 231). He was absolutely victorious—He conquered completely.

Because He was faithful to His mission, we must be faithful to Him. Because He bore our sins and carried our sorrows, we must bear our crosses bravely. Because in His 30 years on earth He fully acquainted Himself with all species of our temptations, we can "come boldly to the throne of grace" and find comfort and refreshing and "obtain mercy and find grace to help in time of need" (Heb. 4:16).

A Priest Like Melchizedek

For this Melchizedek, king of Salem, priest of the Most High God, who met Abraham returning from the slaughter of the kings and blessed him. Heb. 7:1.

We see good reason for the exalted respect given Melchizedek in Hebrews 7. It was he who blessed Abraham and to whom Abraham gave tithe. It is he who the Scripture calls "king of Salem," "king of righteousness," "king of peace (verses 1, 2), and yet, the profile is incomplete; we do not know enough about his roots or his role to claim absolute confidence regarding his identity.

This much, however, we do know: He was not an angel or a member of the Trinity, because priests must be taken from among men (Heb. 5:1). On the other hand, He was not an ordinary human, because Abraham's giving tithe to him reveals a special status—in ancient Jewry the lesser always tithed to the greater (Heb. 7:7). The most logical assumption is that he was a human being with real parents who lived and died (as all persons do), but whose origins and career elevated his status and respect, exceeding that ascribed to any other member of the priesthood.

Hebrews 11 affirms that Jesus is to be honored not only more highly than the Aaronic priesthood, but also more highly than Melchizedek, whose ministry exceeded Aaron's. Thus, beyond the unique pedestal of human authority on which Melchizedek stood, we see One who is even higher—One who, while being beyond the boundaries of time, and who is the very source of life itself, found a way to take on our identity, thereby qualifying to be our spokesman before the Father. He is higher than the highest, greater than the greatest, stronger than the strongest, wiser than the wisest—our insurmountable, unsurpassable, infinitely greater high priest.

It is that essential truth that we acknowledge when we robustly sing:

"Praise Him! praise Him! Jesus, our blessed Redeemer!

Heavenly portals, loud with hosannas ring!

Jesus, Savior, reigneth forever and ever;

Crown Him! crown Him! Prophet, and Priest, and King!"

April 20/

The Greatest Sufferer of All

He then would have had to suffer often since the foundation of the world; but now, once at the end of the ages, He has appeared to put away sin by the sacrifice of Himself. Heb. 9:26.

How great was the suffering of Christ on our behalf? Greater than that endured by any other creature. His heart of love suffered the pain of disappointment when Adam sinned; He suffered the hatred of Herod upon entry into our world; He suffered the misunderstanding of family and friends as He grew to manhood; He suffered the rejection of the Jewish leaders as He pursued His ministry; He suffered the denunciations of the multitude when He made holiness and not simply happiness the burden of His teaching.

He knows our physical pain as well. He experienced the deep gouging of His flesh; the sharp, rock-hard thorns piercing His brow; the searing jolts from the steel-tipped whip cutting open His tender back; the burning sensation of rusty nails tearing through His hands and feet; the fearful agony of bursting lungs when on the cross He could no longer push up to fill them with air; and, of course, the broken heart imploded by the impact of our disobedience. Jesus knows what it means to suffer and to die.

Because of this, when we cry out in physical pain, the pain of disease or accident, or hurt of any kind—even when we "walk through the valley of the shadow of death" (Ps. 23:4), never again, in this life, to occupy space with the living—He understands. He is our sympathetic Savior, our sacrificial shepherd. He has trod the way before us; He has tested the terrain and endured all the pain we can know and so much more.

The shepherds of the Eastern world do not drive sheep as those in most other areas; they lead them. By doing so, they not only test the terrain, but also provide ultimate confidence to the sheep that follow. The sheep know that their shepherd is before them and that they can safely follow. Jesus is our true shepherd. He left glory to rescue this one lost world, and He lost His life in the rescue. But in doing so He became our example in suffering and provides us this world's only solution for happiness here and eternity beyond.

121/

The Ultimate Sacrifice

And being found in appearance as a man, He humbled Himself and became obedient to the point of death, even the death of the cross. Phil. 2:8.

Jesus died, not from a bleeding body, but from a broken heart. When He cried, "It is finished!" (John 19:30), it was not because of the punctures and lacerations of His flesh, it was because of the sadness of His soul brought about by the pressure of His mission and the knowledge of our ingratitude. It was not the thorny crown or the rusty spikes or the razor-sharp sword that killed Him. It was the unbearably heavy weight of His mission. His great suffering, His lethal pain, His terminal hurt was the thought of so many who would prefer the fleeting pleasures of this life to the enduring principles of His kingdom. He still suffers when we choose sin above salvation, the flesh above the spirit, Jericho above Jerusalem, the broad above the narrow way.

We would not think of tying His hands or slapping His face or spitting on those hallowed cheeks; we cannot imagine our holding or hammering the nails, but our sins wounded Him there. By our disobedience now and by our wayward attitudes we "crucify" Him "afresh" (Heb. 6:6, KJV). Our self-indulgent motives bring sorrow to His heart; we pain Him when we do not please Him.

I recall clearly while as a teenager of 15, coming home in the wee hours of a Sunday morning well past the Saturday night curfew directed by my mother. When she opened the door, I expected no less than a well-deserved verbal berating. But she spoke no words of condemnation; there were no threats to my liberties or my physical being. Instead, before me were the reddened eyes and swollen face of a mother whose heart was broken by my actions. I rushed to my room and fell across my bed with a stricken conscience remembering all the sacrifices she had made for me as a hardworking, self-denying single parent. I cried, prayed, and promised the Lord that I would by His grace never again bring pain to my mother.

This is exactly how it works with Jesus and us. Imparted by the unconditional love of our crucified Lord, we are compelled to yield to His will and obey His rules with unremitting resolve. No other incentive is capable of inducing such a radical response—no other love has such enduring rewards.

The Most Holy Place

For Christ has not entered the holy places made with hands,
which are copies of the true, but into heaven itself,
now to appear in the presence of God for us. Heb. 9:24.

The highlight of the services of the earthly sanctuary was the Day of Atonement. Every day for 12 months the priests had placed blood upon the horns of the altar of incense in the holy place symbolizing Christ's shedding of His blood in our behalf. Now on this day, the high priest, himself, ventured beyond the veil into the Most Holy Place to plead the blood before the glowing Shekinah presence of God.

The day of judgment was, as were all the services of the earthly system, richly figurative. As the high priest ended the annual sacrificial cycle by removing the blood that had accumulated during the year and presented himself before the presence of God, Jesus, our better high priest "once at the end of the ages" (Heb. 9:26), has gone before the Father in earnest entreaty for the human race.

The prophecies of Daniel, originally interpreted by the pioneers of Adventism as marking October 22, 1844, the time of Christ's physical return to earth, now designate that year as the beginning of His final service in the heavenly sanctuary— e.g., the cleansing that relieves the heavenly courts of the accumulated sins of earth.

At the historic Glacier View Bible Conference in August 1980 the Seventh-day Adventist Sanctuary Review Committee, comprised of more than 100 Bible scholars and church administrators, produced a consensus statement that read: "Our conviction that the end of the prophetic period of 2300 days in 1844 marks the beginning of a work of judgment in heaven is supported by the parallelism of Daniel 8 with Daniel 7, which explicitly describes such a work, and by the references to heavenly judgment in the book of Revelation."

The pre-Advent judgment, traditionally termed the "investigative judgment," remains a critical element of present truth and is basic to the first angel's warning of Revelation 14:7. This angelic witness, "the hour of His judgment has come," is a reminder of the events of Calvary in which the Lord of love was hung and died in order that humans might stand the test of judgment. Our task is to share the good news with as many people as we can, as rapidly as we can. Remember, the call to witness follows the call to surrender, and this is our primary challenge today.

Once and for All

So Christ was offered once to bear the sins of many.
To those who eagerly wait for Him He will appear a second time,
apart from sin, for salvation. Heb. 9:28.

Jesus' priestly ministry is something better, not only because He died for all, but also because He did so once and for all. So complete was the scale of His reach; so rich the value of His blood; so effective the impact of His ministry; so complete was the Father's acceptance of His travail that no further sacrifice was needed. His was a gift thoroughly adequate, completely sufficient, absolutely satisfying, and totally acceptable.

However, forgiveness offered is not forgiveness accepted; mercy deposited is not mercy claimed. The greatest of earth's tragedies is that so few among its condemned inhabitants have believed and received the generosity of our loving Lord. But the invitation still stands. Our better High Priest who once died now ever lives, ever pleads, ever offers His blood for our sins.

The "once" and "everness" of His ministry came to mind several years ago as I stood before the tomb of a young American soldier who died during a blazing battle of World War II. The simple but eloquent inscription read:

"He lived nobly, he fought bravely,
  he died willingly;
  what more could a good man do?"

This is the same with our Lord. The cosmic difference, however, is that He rose and is coming again. Our Hero lives. His services did not end with the conflict at Calvary; death was for Him but a transition point from one phase of ministry to the other:

By accommodating death, He abolished death.

By experiencing death, He exposed death.

By catering to death, He canceled death.

By submitting to death, He subdued death.

By undergoing death, He undid death.

His victory over the grave changed death from eternal nothingness to momentary sleep and validated Him as our living Lord—our eternal and better high priest.

Judgment With Love

Now when these things had been thus prepared, the priests always went into the first part of the tabernacle, performing the services. Heb. 9:6.

The daily work of the priest in the holy place was symbolic of the ministry that Christ began on our behalf when He returned from the outer court of this world to the holy place above. For the first 18 centuries after the Resurrection, the love and mercy of the Savior expressed itself in His prejudgment acts of passionate ministry for the human race.

His transition to the judgment phase of ministry that He now conducts does not indicate a lessening of His love or compassion; love itself demands that heaven bring closure to the bitter experiences of earth. Final judgment, however, cannot be meted until the facts and circumstances of each life are measured fairly. The judgment or pre-Advent investigation is both a logical sequel to His prior ministry and a proper prelude to the executive pronouncements of recompense and reward that follow.

In this phase of ministry our better High Priest pleads for us not as a conglomerate or statistical whole; He advocates for us personally, individually, and untiringly. Just accepting Him results in His blood concealing what each record reveals. For those who refuse His offerings of redemption, the second death is God's loving way of eliminating from His creation the transgression that has marred His handiwork. When His judgment work is finished, the verdict of the redeemed, "just and true are thy ways, thou King of saints" (Rev. 15:3, KJV), will resound throughout glory.

"Yes," the guilty criminal replied when asked if he had anything to say in response to his sentence of death. "Your honor, you know me. When I was a child you rescued me from certain death. I would have drowned in the heavy waters had you not pulled me from the swirling currents."

"True, I do know you," the magistrate responded, "but then I was your savior; now I am your judge."

We have been rescued and pardoned by Christ from the heavy currents of sin. His loving acts are too good to forget, too great to ignore, too gracious to refuse. We, with whom the Spirit still strides, are blessed to know His compassion, to surrender daily to His compelling love, and to be securely sheltered from the wrath of the day of judgment.

The Life That Counts

And when Aaron lights the lamps at twilight, he shall burn incense on it, a perpetual incense before the Lord throughout your generations. Ex. 30:8.

The aromatic cloud produced daily in the holy place resulted from placing sweet-smelling substances upon the fire that burned on the altar of incense. This altar, strategically positioned before the curtain that separated the holy place from the Most Holy Place, spoke eloquently to the work of salvation accomplished by our better High Priest.

God, who is a consuming fire Himself (Heb. 12:29), set the flame to burn upon the altar. The incense that was placed upon the fire represented the pure and holy life of Christ. That perfect holiness, earned during His sojourn on earth, produces an aromatic pleasure that delights the very God who gave His Son to risk all for the salvation of humanity.

Had Jesus failed, His sacrifice would have been rejected. Had the human Christ not succeeded, the God who is light and life eternal would have tragically consumed Him along with all other earthly inhabitants. But Jesus' victory negated all such logical possibilities. Through Him our redemption is fully accomplished, and the universe is forever relieved of any just concern regarding the fairness and compassion of the Godhead. The Father, who was well pleased by His Son's baptism, was completely satisfied by His Son's death.

We too are well pleased when impacted by the cost of our redemption. We can never be well pleased with ourselves. Our mistakes are too frequent, our victories too fragile, our gifts too small, our prayers too limited to allow self-satisfaction—to indulge self-approval. Beholding our spiritual progress, we are gratified but not satisfied, appreciative but not approving. Nevertheless we rest in the knowledge that when we do our best, the Father is pleased—not because our best is good enough, but because we are covered with the robe of Christ's righteousness.

How grand and glorious the assurance that "Christ looks at the spirit, and when He sees us carrying our burdens with faith, His perfect holiness atones for our shortcomings. When we do our best, He becomes our righteousness" (*Selected Messages*, book 1, p. 368).

Our Exacting God

"Then he shall make atonement for the Holy Sanctuary, and he shall make atonement for the tabernacle of meeting and for the altar, and he shall make atonement for the priests and for all the people of the assembly." Lev. 16:33.

The high priest's obligation to represent the people before the Shekinah once a year was a solemn and frightful duty. His preparation to go within the Most Holy Place began a full week ahead of time. During these days of withdrawal from the population, he engaged in prayer and deep devotion not only for his fellow priests, his family, and his followers, but also very significantly for himself. Audience before the Shekinah flame required of him complete surrender with total forgiveness of all his sins.

And God is no less holy, no less righteous, no less exacting now than then. How exacting is He? The modern-day prophet puts it this way: "The Lord requires no less of the soul now, than He required of Adam in Paradise before he fell" (*Selected Messages,* book 1, p. 373). And again: "God requires now what He required of Adam, perfect obedience, righteousness without a flaw . . . in His sight" (*ibid.,* book 2, p. 381).

In other words, anyone in whom sin is found would be cremated, incinerated, or evaporated in His presence. This is why, when He comes, we must be found in Him not having our "own righteousness" but that of Jesus Christ our Lord (Phil. 3:9). We need Him as our own great high priest, the shepherd of our souls; our living, loving advocate who intercedes before the Father on our behalf.

Hebrews 12:29 provides a clear description of the awesome persona of the Father before whom our Elder Brother pleads. It reads: "God is a consuming fire"— meaning His character is so clean, His morality so mighty, His perfection so pure, His holiness so high, His righteousness so rare that He shines. His moral nature is so radically intense that it radiates physical energy.

And we can trust Him, our Elder Brother Jesus, to deliver us safely in the Father's presence. He is a physician who has never lost a willing patient. A lawyer who has never failed a trusting client, and a friend who "sticketh closer than a brother" (Prov. 18:24, KJV). He has completed atonement for us at the cost of Calvary, and by that sacrifice we obtain "wisdom . . . and righteousness and sanctification and redemption" (1 Cor. 1:30).

Our Accepted High Priest

Who being the brightness of His glory and the express image of His person, and upholding all things by the word of His power, when He had by Himself purged our sins, sat down at the right hand of the Majesty on high. Heb. 1:3.

In Bible times the vast majority of rulers were right-handed. It was with this hand that the king extended his scepter and signed his decrees; with this hand he beckoned his servants, directed his troops, and sometimes wielded his sword in battle.

Of course, our heavenly Father is not restricted to our human patterns of functioning. He is not left-brained or right-brained. He does not have a dominant eye or hand or any one element or bodily system that overpowers the other.

Why does Scripture make repeated mention of Christ's position as being on the right hand of the Father? Because being so positioned was (is) a sign of ultimate favor in human affairs. Christ's sitting at the right hand of the Father signals His absolute approval of Jesus' earthly services.

The lesson is that Jesus is His greatly beloved; that His salvation efforts have been totally approved. That He (Jesus) not only fulfilled His earthly ministry successfully, but also has now returned to glory exalted, honored and forever praised. The Father did "see the travail of his soul" and was "satisfied" (Isa. 53:11, KJV). He who occupied the middle or highest cross on Calvary, indicating that He was guiltiest of all, now sits at the Father's right hand—honored there as worthiest of all.

Because He has honor, we have hope. He is the ultimate insider, the consummate guide, the constant friend, and the absolutely dependable kinsman upon whose influence in our behalf we can totally depend. Because He is who He is, where He is, and what He is, we can live in confident assurance of the Father's forgiveness and the fulfillment of all His promises.

In today's busy dealings the saying "it's not what you know, it's who you know that counts" speaks to favoritism and unfair advantage. However, applied to our salvation, it is a reminder that more important than acquaintance with prophetic dates or a knowledge of doctrinal details is one's personal relationship with Christ, our better high priest.

A Waiting People

And if I go and prepare a place for you, I will come again and
receive you to Myself; that where I am, there you may be also. John 14:3.

The drama connected with the high priest's ministry within the Most Holy Place was intense. As their spiritual leader ministered before God, the Israelites waited expectantly and hopefully in the outer court anticipating his emergence with the assurance of their forgiveness and the excitement of a new year in the life of the nation.

We modern Israelites are also waiting expectantly. We are poised in the outer court of earth hopefully anticipating the culmination of our High Priest's mediatorial services. We know by His own unfailing words that His intercessory efforts are not unending. Investigation and mediation will one day give way to recompense upon evildoers and reward for the righteous.

John states that He will conclude His work of patient intercession with these words: "The time is at hand. He who is unjust, let him be unjust still; he who is filthy, let him be filthy still; he who is righteous, let him be righteous still; he who is holy, let him be holy still" (Rev. 22:10, 11).

There are those who question and quibble over the meaning of "soon" as expressed in the term "the soon coming of Jesus." It is true in both heavenly and earthly understandings. It will be soon for the Godhead because "a thousand years in [God's] sight [is] like yesterday" (Ps. 90:4), and soon for humans. This is because for the deceased the space between the cession of life's brief stay on earth and eventual resurrection is chronologically nonexistent.

No matter what the actual chronology or amount of revolutions of earth have been accomplished while the dead sleep, their awakening will be soon—soon because resurrection, to be affected in a moment (1 Cor. 15:52), will for them not only be "like" but at the moment following demise.

The grand and glorious sequel is for the righteous; life when resumed will not be as it ended, but be in eminently better form and circumstance. It is thus logical and proper that we hold fast our faith—our yearning and laboring for the "soon" fulfillment of that blessed brighter, better day.

Our Unchanging Savior

But He, because He continues forever,
has an unchangeable priesthood.
Therefore He is also able to save to the uttermost
those who come to God through Him, since He always
lives to make intercession for them. Heb. 7:24, 25.

Perhaps the most memorable of all scriptural portrayals of Jesus' everlastingness is His self-presentation to Moses as "I AM THAT I AM" (Ex. 3:14, KJV).

In describing Himself in this way, God affirms that He is above, beyond, and throughout time. "I AM THAT I AM" is a claim that only He can make. Our chronological categories of past, present, and future do not adequately express His eternity. We cannot intuit everlastingness. "I AM THAT I AM" is a reminder that history cannot date Him; science cannot prove Him; philosophy cannot explain Him; and theology cannot comprehend Him. He has no beginning and no ending; He is the cause behind all causes and before all causes.

By the name "I AM THAT I AM" God warned Moses, "Do not ask Me for a résumé; even if I gave you one you couldn't understand it; My character and substance cannot be deciphered by human instrumentality. You cannot decode my essence, Moses; simply let them know that He who is the 'unbegun beginning,' the possessor of limitless eternity, the one who is eternal presence, and the source of all life and creative beings has sent you on this mission of mercy."

God's reminder to Moses is encouragement for us today. He is still the great "I AM," He is not only with respect to His limitless existence, but also in His unfailing attention to our needs. Israel's earthly priests were constantly replaced by reason of death; but His intercessory service, begun with His resurrection from the grave, has continued uninterrupted since His return to glory.

The Lord of present "truth" is also the Lord of present "tense." Consequently, the now of salvation is accompanied by the "I AM" of divined assistance. His words are "I AM the door," "I AM the vine," "I AM the bread," "I AM the way," "I AM the truth," "I AM the good shepherd," "I AM the alpha and omega," "I AM the resurrection and the life," "I AM the light of the world—one with Father," and at the same time have gone to "prepare a place for you . . . that where I am, there you may be also" (John 14:3).

Our Competent High Priest

But Christ came as High Priest of the good things to come,
with the greater and more perfect tabernacle not made
with hands, that is, not of this creation. Heb. 9:11.

The common priests in Israel occupied a pervasive role in the life of the people. They served as teachers of the law, as scribes, and as community magistrates. They sounded the trumpets in battle, gave instructions regarding tribal residence, and pronounced the lepers unclean and, if by a miracle healed, whole again.

Of course their primary responsibilities concerned the sanctuary service. They functioned in the outer court; they examined and approved the animals for sacrifice; in the holy place they maintained the candlesticks; they daily sprinkled blood upon the horns of the altar of incense, and changed the showbread each Sabbath.

The high priest had special duties. In addition to his ministry on the Day of Atonement, he chaired the sessions of the Sanhedrin, supervised the consecration of the lower priests, and led out in highly important trials, such as the one that Jesus endured.

All of the priestly functions were performed in attractive dress and coordinated pageantry. But while very scintillating and highly symbolic, their rituals had no salvation; they contained a multitude of shadows but had no substance—an abundance of types but no actuality. By them, human redemption was typified but not ratified.

Our situation demanded more than mere figures of the true; we needed the real thing, the genuine article. Our redemption required more than the incantations of saintly old men dressed in pretty robes gesturing toward God with animal blood and incense vapors. We needed someone who could speak the language of transcendence—a Royal Umpire, a God-level Lawyer, a Divine Interpreter who could tell us the truth about the Father and relate to Him the truth about us—this is why Jesus volunteered to be our better high priest.

Our need for an incarnated God is clear. What is not clear or logically explainable is the quality of love that drove Him to such a sacrifice. But this mystery will be our grand fascination as we study throughout eternity. Only then will we begin to comprehend the true depths of His compassion. What we know now is that His promises of grace far exceed the necessities of sin; and by His past and present ministry, we are saved.

MAY

A Better Temple

A Better Temple

Yet I say to you that in this place there is one
greater than the temple. Matt. 12:6.

Solomon's Temple, referred to by Christ, was so splendid in architecture and beauty, and was for centuries the wonder of admiring citizenry. The sanctuary that preceded it as God's house of worship was itself a magnificent reflection of divine glory. The Temple built by Solomon's workers over a period of seven years and six months (1 Kings 6:38) was the ultimate reflection of the grandeur of the Godhead.

The interior walls were made of aromatic timber from Lebanon; the exterior walls were fitted with costly wood from the slopes of Mount Moriah; much of the interior furniture was made of pure gold; on the exterior walls were brazen figures fashioned from the clay of Succoth and Zarethan. There never was and never will be an edifice so rich in materials, so stunning in form, so magnificent in arrangements, so strategic in placement, so pleasing in adornment.

But it did not last. It was leveled by the idolatrous armies of Nebuchadnezzar in 587-586 B.C.; rebuilt by the intrepid Zerubbabel and his loyal band in 439 B.C.; and finally destroyed by the Roman general Titus in A.D. 70, never to be replaced.

It is this history of temporary grandeur and usages that reminds us that Jesus is indeed a greater, grander temple. He is infinitively more striking in character, more superior in accomplishments, more lasting in service; He was and is the highest expression to humanity of heaven's compassionate regard.

While the materials of Solomon's garnished Temple richly reflected the divine and human encounter whereby our salvation is effected, they were but mere symbols—mute testimonials incapable of the negotiations necessary for our salvation. Not so with Jesus, our better temple. He is the one altogether lovely, the express image of the Father sent to us. Evil men also destroyed Him, but it was He who said, "Destroy this temple, and in three days I will raise it up"—and He rose again.

It is in Him, our loving, living Lord—our more glorious temple that we trust and in whom we place our confidence and strength for today's challenging journey and the unknown future ahead.

The Temple Witness

Now Solomon began to build the house of the Lord at Jerusalem on Mount Moriah, where the Lord had appeared to his father David, at the place that David had prepared on the threshing floor of Ornan the Jebusite. 2 Chron. 3:1.

Mount Moriah, also known in Jewish tradition as "the Temple hill," stood just opposite the Mount of Olives. Abraham climbed its heights with Issac; there God spoke His vows to him concerning a numerous and prosperous lineage, and it was also there that David sacrificed for himself and the nation.

It was the presence of the Temple high above the surrounding valleys that most distinguished Mount Moriah. The Temple's hilltop location was ordered by God as a way of establishing clear visibility of His power and presence among His people to the heathen who surrounded them.

Jesus, our Savior, whose ministry is pointed to all temple traffic, later said: "A city that is set on a hill cannot be hidden" (Matt. 5:14). Solomon's Temple, widely proclaimed as the most spectacular edifice ever constructed, was such a place—a citadel of glory and inspiration for the Jews and wondrous witness to the Gentile world.

The church today is called to this witness. Our proclamation of the everlasting gospel, our claim of prophetic beginnings, our counterculture lifestyle including our Sabbathkeeping, giving of tithe, and dietary and dress habits all speak loudly to the communities in which we live. When we are faithful to our trust, that testimony is indeed a light shinning amid the darkness of our postmodern society.

Sadly for Israel, apostasy, fueled by pride and greed, obscured their witness and led to God's rejection of their singularity and destruction of the magnificent meeting place that crowned Mount Moriah.

What lessons are there for us? All of God's promises are conditional: privilege with God is not a guarantee of eternal favor and "to whom much is given, . . . much is required" (Luke 12:48).

Our Lord longs to transport His people from the Mount Moriah of spiritual fellowship below to the Mount Zion of everlasting life above. This is a longing He has communicated to His people for 2,000 years; no generation has yet positioned itself to be so honored. Will ours?

Fitted by the Holy Spirit

And the temple, when it was being built, was built with
stone finished at the quarry, so that no hammer or chisel or any
iron tool was heard in the temple while it was being built. 1 Kings 6:7.

Imagine all those thousands of stones fitted together without the sound of hammer or chisel. That was a stunning, stellar accomplishment—a high tribute to the ingenuity and skill of those artisans who so carefully erected this attractive monument to God's glory.

The Holy Spirit, God's active agent of conversion, works in a similar manner. This is what Jesus meant when He said, "The wind bloweth where it listeth" (John 3:8, KJV). We do not hear or see the Spirit as He ministers, but He is constantly, quietly regulating and adjusting our hearts and building our spiritual temples.

Before we knew it He was wooing us, silently courting and pursuing us; arranging circumstances, structuring conditions, sending impulses of love to gain our attention, quietly tugging at the heartstrings of our souls. And after conversion He continues to work within us, developing and establishing more spacious and efficiently equipped rooms for Christ's dwelling.

The stones of Solomon's Temple were impressive, but they were inanimate blocks of sand hardened by time that once shaped were put in place without need of adjustment. This is not so with those fitted for God's temple. We are living personalities; creatures whose emotions are constantly affected by forces both internal and external to our being. Our fitting is not once and forever; we are distinguished by the power of choice, our use of which often requires spiritual realignment.

And we never cease maturing. Far from being a static relationship, temple status is a life of continual development. The Holy Spirit, who rescues us from the quarries of sin, never ceases the silent adjustments necessary for our spiritual development.

Do these quiet improvements suggest a quiet religion, a lifeless worship experience, or emotionless responses to the good news of the gospel? No. The silent workings of the Holy Spirit do not eventuate in muffled testimony to God's goodness. The Spirit works quietly, but the fitted believers witness to His providences in grateful song, prayer, joyful testimony, and, most of all, in visible obedience that reflects their appreciation for God's grace.

United in Christ

You also, as living stones, are being built up
a spiritual house, a holy priesthood, to offer up spiritual sacrifices,
acceptable to God through Jesus Christ. 1 Peter 2:5.

The Temple builders included 80,000 men who quarried stones and 70,000 who carried burdens (1 Kings 5:15, 16). What a workforce that was! And the stonecutters quarried from more than one mountain. They cut stones, from varied sources, ensuring for the building stones of not only different shapes but also differing textures, colors, and compositions.

So it is with the church of the living God. It is comprised of the saved from all walks of life. Even when Israel was the sole proprietor of the gospel, her "special people" status included instructions to witness to the nations about them and to adopt with special care "the stranger within their gates" (see Ex. 20:10).

Of course, the universality of God's kingdom on earth assumed special emphasis with the dawning of the Christian dispensation. Christ's instruction to "go ye into all the world" (Mark 16:15, KJV) was accompanied by His promise and His assurance—"I, if I am lifted up from the earth, will draw all peoples to myself" (John 12:32).

This power-packed mandate is being richly fulfilled today in the work of His remnant people who, in the spirit of the angel of Revelation 14:6, 7, loudly proclaim the gospel around the world. The fruitage of their witness is seen in the broad expanse of believers of differing cultures, languages, temperaments, customs, educational levels and socioeconomic status that comprise the Seventh-day Adventist Church.

How is it that the church maintains unity of doctrine and function in spite of these differences? We are cemented together by the love of Christ. His love subdues our tribalism, erases our pride of place, and melts our selfish individualism. So that while we are indeed "living stones" sometimes prone to indulge our individual or group priorities or to think our ways are better than those of others, our devotion to Him brings godly sorrow, mutual submission, and repentance.

We must confess that our demonstration of "unity in diversity" is a witness to society not yet perfectly fashioned and humbly plead for those superior graces that will fulfill Christ's plaintive prayer: "I in them, and You in Me; that they may be made perfect in one, and that the world may know that You have sent Me, and have loved them as You have loved Me" (John 17:23).

Our Able God

The stone which the builders rejected has become
the chief cornerstone. Ps. 118:22.

No aspect of the Temple construction was so significant as the choice and placement of the cornerstone. It was the most important stone of all. On it the complete structure centered; it was the weight-bearing focus of the entire edifice. As
such, it had to be not only perfectly shaped, but also capable of bearing enormous
stress and stoutly resistant to the ravages of weather.

During the long course of construction, the builders of Solomon's Temple in-
spected, rejected, and cast aside numerous stones as inadequate for this purpose—
one of which they later observed had endured many seasons of exposure without
damage. Its stability was reassessed, and that stone, which the builders had formerly
rejected, became the chief and cornerstone.

Our Lord Jesus is the cornerstone of God's spiritual temple. He too was despised and rejected of men. Exposed to the demonic elements of Satan's kingdom,
He was a man of sorrows and acquainted with grief. Denied common courtesies at
birth, misunderstood in his youth, ridiculed in manhood, abused in Pilate's judgment hall, He was crucified on Calvary with none to help or deliver Him. "He was
wounded for our transgressions; He was bruised for our iniquities; the chastisement for our peace was upon Him" (Isa. 53:5). And it was not just our sins that He
bore; He carried the burden of our entire salvation—it all rested upon Him; our
forgiveness, our righteousness, our resurrection, our eternity—our all!

But He triumphed gloriously. By His exemplary life and cruel but redeeming
death, He proved absolutely worthy to bear our weight and effect our transition
from the wastelands of transgression to temples of praise. That triumph is the cause
of the Father's satisfaction and the happy cry of the saved: "Worthy is the Lamb
who was slain, to receive power and riches and wisdom, And strength and honor
and glory and blessing!" (Rev. 5:12).

To which we say amen and ascribe eternal praise to our better temple and Elder
Brother, Jesus Christ!

Righteous Nostalgia

Then they brought up the ark, the tabernacle of meeting,
and all the holy furnishings that were in the tabernacle.
The priests and the Levites brought them up. 2 Chron. 5:5.

What would they do with the furniture of the portable tabernacle that was replaced by Solomon's stationary Temple? Would it simply be abandoned, purposely destroyed, or perhaps sold or distributed as souvenirs? No. By divine instruction they were brought to Solomon's Temple—to be used or kept in sacred memory.

Forgetting the past is a major bane of modernity. Abandoning former vows, former values, former habits, former guidelines, even former friends and beliefs under the excitement of new, more attractive circumstances often spells tragic loss.

Yes, some past deeds need to be relegated to the deep sea of unapproachable history, but not all. We need to remember former answers to prayer, former miracles for which we prayed, and those for which we had not sense to ask. We need to remember the fundamental principles of doctrine and, in the midst of all that is new and exhilarating, reflect upon "the former things of old" (Isa. 46:9).

Why? Because they remind us, they teach us; they serve as connections to ideas and ideals and even ancestors whose valor inform us and inspire us. They allow us, in the midst of the improvisations of contemporaneity, to maintain the cantus firmus—the main melody of faith and belief.

George Santayana, the modern-era philosopher, was correct when he taught that forgetting the past is tantamount to repeating its failures. This is precisely the wisdom that led Moses, when dying, to write: "Remember the days of old, consider the years of many generations" (Deut. 32:7, 8).

We who live at this critical juncture of earth's seventh millennium would do well to treasure our valued past and to observe this warning: "Thus saith the Lord, Stand ye in the ways, and see, and ask for the old paths, where is the good way, and walk therein, and ye shall find rest for your souls" (Jer. 6:16, KJV). Righteous nostalgia is incentive to present heroics and prediction of future rewards.

God's Lasting Commandments

Then the priests brought in the ark of the covenant of the Lord
to its place, into the inner sanctuary of the temple, to the
Most Holy Place, under the wings of the cherubim. 1 Kings 8:6.

While some of the furniture transferred from the portable tabernacle to Solomon's stationary Temple served simply as archival memorabilia, the ark itself did not. It was positioned as the focal point of all sacrifices, the pinnacle of priestly ministry. This had been the case for many centuries; it had sat behind the veil within the Most Holy Place, its surface adorned by sculptured cherubims whose golden wings spread protectively above its sacred surface where glowed the Shekinah light.

There was, however, one significant difference in this latter arrangement: "Nothing was in the ark except the two tablets of stone which Moses put there at Horeb" (1 Kings 8:9). In other words, the pot of manna and Aaron's rod that budded were no longer present.

Why were these two symbols of divine care and deliverance now removed from the ark and only the Decalogue retained? Evidently because in spite of His concern that Israel remember past blessings, God wished to lessen their temptations to worship these instruments of deliverance rather than the Deliverer Himself. Or perhaps their removal focused the people's attention more intensely upon the Decalogue that provided promises as complete as those symbolized by the pot and the rod, and in addition outlined the specifics of obedience required.

In either case this obvious exaltation of the law above even those two stirring reminders of their exodus miracle is strong evidence of its perpetuity and our need to soberly regard its sacred precepts.

We are God's living sanctuaries. Our hearts are His dwelling place. There, written with the pen of the Holy Spirit, is etched the moral law. It is not only a reminder of His love and our deliverance from our former slavery to sin, but it also speaks to us, as no other voice, the outline of His character and will.

Knowing His will is not the same as doing His will. Having the law enshrined in our hearts means that we not only assent to its authority but also that we yield our wills to its holy precepts.

Our Hearts: His Temple

But will God indeed dwell on the earth? Behold,
heaven and the heaven of heavens cannot contain you.
How much less this temple which I have built! 1 Kings 8:27.

When all of the building was completed and all the furniture and utensils were in place, the ark of the covenant was positioned behind the veil in the Temple, and the cloud of the Lord's presence "filled the house of the Lord" (1 Kings 8:10). It was then that King Solomon prayed the prayer of dedication. He began his prayer of earnest supplication by extolling God's goodness and greatness and claiming the promises made to David, his father. He then pled with God on his people's behalf, enunciating Israel's high prosperity if obedient and the terrible punishments if disobedient.

He then asked for forgiveness when anyone sinned (verses 31, 32); when the heavens gave no rain (verses 35, 36); when famine or pestilence or blight or sickness overtook the people (verses 37-39); and when the people went out to battle (verses 44, 45). In all these situations he essentially pleaded, "Dear Lord, do not forsake your own; hear our prayer for mercy and deliver us from our troubles."

How did God respond? Second Chronicles 7:1 states that when Solomon had finished praying, fire came down from heaven and consumed the burnt offerings and sacrifice and the glory of the Lord filled the Temple. Obviously God was pleased with the workmanship of the artisans, as well as with the attitude of the people, and He manifested His approval by a breathtaking display of His glory.

And the Lord still does that for His people. Not with literal fire, but in the inner glow of the Holy Spirit in our hearts and upon our assemblies. There are times when the divine presence is palpable, when the unseen is keenly felt, when in the hush of private devotion or the synergy of public assembly time stands still and we experience the palpable presence of God and are reenergized for our Christian journey.

As Solomon's Temple dedication remained a memorable element of Israel's history, so should our epiphanies of communion with God. Those times that heaven comes especially close and we sense God's immediate presence are not only happy moments of intellectual impulse that gladden our journey, but as Augustine the early Church Father taught—experiences of illumination that verify our faith and fortify our fidelity.

Jesus: The Way

By a new and living way which He consecrated for us,
through the veil, that is, His flesh. Heb. 10:20.

The veil that hid the ark from view was not simply an object lesson of reverence and respect, but it was a means of protecting sinful humanity from the consuming glory of God. That is because the Shekinah that glowed beneath the arching wings of the cherubs above the ark was more than symbolic; it was the radiating presence of God Himself. So sacred and special was that presence that only on the Day of Atonement could it be approached; only then would Supreme Deity accommodate face-to-face communion with earthlings; only then would the high priest dare to enter "through the veil."

Jesus is the Lamb slain whose blood was imprinted upon the horns of the altar that stood before the veil. Jesus is the high priest who carries the blood and applies it daily upon the altar. Jesus is the incense whose sweet savor wafts above the veil into the presence of the Father beyond—Jesus is the veil itself. We go to the Father's presence through Him, because of Him, by Him, in Him. There is no other path, no other door, no other way. His crucified, now-risen body is our bridge into the presence of God. Without His sacrifice we have no entrance. By His sacrifice we have sure and certain access.

The knowledge of Christ as our singular means of access to the Father structures our priorities, clarifies our vision, organizes our agendas, focuses our energies, directs our steps, humbles our pride, and captures our hearts in daily allegiance.

There are times that we are tempted to decide that it is all too impossible, that our mistake-prone lives are too confused, too sordid, too weighted with the baggage of self and sin to ever reach the high calling of righteousness required for salvation. And humanly speaking, this is true. But the good news is that Jesus has conquered; He is the way. Through Him and by Him we have access, and because of that we have victory, assurance, and joy.

The Tragedy of Pride

I have surely built you an exalted house,
and a place for you to dwell in forever. 2 Chron. 6:2.

Perhaps it is a cultural thing or maybe just the way the language translates. But isn't it striking that five times in his dedication prayer Solomon refers to the Temple as the house that "I have built" (2 Chron. 6). Maybe it was innocent, but wouldn't it have sounded better (at least to us moderns) if he had said "we" or, in addressing God, "You"? The "I" in his prayer makes it appear that the seeds of pride that reaped such a bitter harvest later in his life seem to have already been planted in his heart.

One of the more memorable demonstrations of Solomon's prideful tendency was exposing to the queen of Sheba the material beauty of the Temple while failing to mention its spiritual meaning (1 Kings 10). He preened—like a peacock—to her congratulations and reveled in her praise. Sadly, by the end of her tour, she had learned and seen all but the most important display that Solomon could have provided—the wonder and splendor of the God of the Temple.

Are we any better? Probably not! How many times have we heard our spiritual leaders say, "my church," or "my administration," or "my conference," or "my union," or "my division," or "my Sabbath school class," or "my college," or "my campus," or "my institution"? Have not we ourselves been guilty of flaunting our accomplishments, our possessions, or our positions without giving the glory to God or even sharing our successes with others?

Pride is the primeval evil—the root sin, the foundation of all other transgressions. But we cannot fake humility or manufacture childlikeness. These precious and necessary qualities are the natural consequences of connection with Christ. Daily communion with Him in prayer and study not only acquaints us with His might, but also destroys—like the laser beams of modern medical technology—the diseased masses of the soul and the debilitating cankers of self.

We will never equal the selfless quality of our model man, but by beholding Him in the dialogue of daily devotion we will come to resemble Him. Then all of our attainments, material and intellectual, will reflect His glory and our appreciation for Him.

A God of Ifs

If My people, which are called by My name will humble themselves, and pray and seek My face, and turn from their wicked ways, then I will hear from heaven, and will forgive their sin and heal their land. 2 Chron. 7:14.

God did more than grace the Temple with a modified volume of His glory. He rehearsed for Solomon the terms under which His ardent supplication would be favored. Solomon pleaded, and God replied that He would if—a stark reminder that while all of God's promises are enabling, all of His blessings are conditional.

At the beginning of his reign Solomon acknowledged, "I am a little child" (1 Kings 3:7). He began his rule with a humility inspired by reverential awe of the Creator. But the accumulation of riches, the adulation of the people, the affections of strange women, the pride of accomplishment, and the intoxication of kingly power so polluted his mind and diverted his affections that he became a stranger to the God whose covenant relation he had so eloquently invoked. His material prosperity waxed, but his spiritual life waned. The consequences were dire for him, his family, and the nation.

However, the people were no better. Attracted to the ways of the heathen around them, smug in the knowledge of their "favorite nation" status, and absorbed in prideful pursuits, they forsook the God of heaven and lusted after false gods. The Temple that had been so dramatically consecrated to Jehovah became a house of empty routine and hypercritical wrangling. Subsequently generations so desecrated its environs that over this structural gem God finally declared that the glory was departed. As a result, the soiled boots of profane Babylonian invaders polluted the precincts where for centuries only the priesthood had entry.

God still responds to His people's prayers with "if." In His fathomless mercy He does send sunshine and rain upon "the just and on the unjust" (Matt. 5:45). But true prosperity and lasting benedictions is the province of those alone who love and obey Him. That is why our prayers today and every day must be accompanied by determination to obey.

How reassuring to know that He who commands us to obedience also supplies the strength to do so and never reneges on His promised rewards.

Remembering Poor Individuals

And I became very angry when I heard their outcry
and these words. After serious thought, I rebuked the nobles
and rulers, and said to them, "Each of you is exacting usury
from his brother." So I called a great assembly against them. Neh. 5:6, 7.

One of the uses of offerings brought to the Temple was support for those who were poor. Upon his call to leadership, Nehemiah was touched by the plight of this group. They were suffering not simply because of neglect, but because of overt oppression. The Temple leaders, who should have been foremost in caring for their needs, were guilty of taking advantage of them. Prices were extorted, and heavy credit, unfair interest rates, and binding taxes were crushing the spirits and robbing large numbers of even the bare necessities of life.

Nehemiah, with a large heart, responded to their plight with energy characteristic of his labors. He angrily assembled the leaders and, after recounting for them God's counsels against unjust practices, asked how they, who had been delivered from incarceration in Persia, could now through these means oppress their own flesh and blood (Neh. 5).

Using his own example of kindness to those less fortunate, Nehemiah pleaded not only for liberality toward the poor but also for reparations or restitution—the return of the vineyards and olive groves and houses which had been unjustly taken. By this means and by properly appropriating the Temple offerings, all who had been unfairly deprived would be adequately supplied; the poor would no longer suffer depravation; justice would be meted to all.

Jesus said: "Ye have the poor always with you" (Matt. 26:11, KJV). There will always be at our temple gates (within the church family) those who, for reasons of ill health, unemployment, or other misfortunes, are in need. In fact, our prophet, Ellen White, states that we will ever have with us "the Lord's poor" to inspire our compassion and stimulate our liberality (*Testimonies for the Church,* vol. 6, p. 269).

Jesus also said: "Inasmuch as you did it to one of the least of these My brethren, you did it to Me" (Matt. 25:40). This is an incentive to witness as modern churchgoers. We can do so knowing that "the generous soul will be made rich" (Prov. 11:25), which is to say that generosity toward poor people is not just an act of Christlikeness—it is a basis of divine approbation as well.

The Need of Revival

And Hezekiah sent to all Israel and Judah, and also wrote letters to
Ephraim and Manasseh, that they should come to the house of the Lord at
Jerusalem, to keep the Passover to the Lord God of Israel. 2 Chron. 30:1.

In the long list of kings who did evil in the sight of God, there is none more flagrantly disobedient than Ahaz, king of Judah. On the other hand, in the long list
of leaders whose brave services effected revival and reform, there is no one more
impressive than Hezekiah, his son and immediate successor. Ahaz did something
no one else dared do—he stopped the Temple service. He did not suspend them for
refurbishing or repairs; he closed down the operation. He shut the church doors—
the house of God was "out of business!" Ahaz's actions were made easy because at
the time of his reign idolatry was rampant throughout the land; the people of God
had fallen into flagrant heathenism.

Hezekiah stepped into that breach of inherited evils with bold resolve. His first
act of restoration was to confer with the faithful among the priests. Next he solic-
ited the aid of any citizen willing to assist in combating the nation's evils. Years of
neglect had, as they always do, produced blindness to wrong and acceptance of evil.
But in a remarkably short time Hezekiah's band sparked revival among the people
of God. Immediately upon which he reopened the Temple doors. They washed its
walls, cleansed its vessels, polished its furniture, shined its floors, manicured the
landscape, and proclaimed God's house open again for business.

There are religious units among us today—churches, schools, clinics, and
offices—whose doors are still opened, but true effectiveness or productivity has
ceased. Could it be that the temple where we live and work, though busy with sound
and traffic, is in need of spiritual repair? Is revival or even reformation required
where you work or worship before restoration to God's favor is found?

If so, we are encouraged to know that God still honors the efforts of those who
give consecrated attention to the physical as well as the spiritual needs of His cause.
Whether it be attention to the condition of the lawns and lights, to attitudes and
attendance, to policy performance, or to doctrinal diligence, God's house must not
be left to disorder and disgrace. Each of us is a Hezekiah, called upon to assist in the
elevation and proper maintenance of God's properties and programs.

Here Am I, Send Me

So I said: "Woe is me, for I am undone! Because I am
a man of unclean lips, and I dwell in the midst of a people of unclean
lips; for my eyes have seen the King, the Lord of hosts." Isa. 6:5.

King Uzziah is another leader who directed God's people "back to basics" in a time of flagrant disregard for his law. For a time he enjoyed a well-ordered and prosperous reign. However, because of pride and ego (evils that so often afflict individuals of outstanding accomplishment) he ended his rule under the curse of God. He became so bold in transgressions that in knowing disdain for God's instructions he personally entered the sanctuary and burned sacrifices upon the altar. And, as is often the case, the paths of the people mirrored that of their leader. Idolatry, greed, gluttony, and grinding oppression of the poor were prevalent. Further-more, Judah's armed enemies, northern Israel and Assyria, who would soon wreck havoc upon them, were already scheming for invasion. Once again, because of disobedience, the people of God were poised upon the brink of disaster; once more their enemies would spoil their land destroying young and old, reducing what had been a nation of wealth and honor to a people of depravity and depression.

But they did not suffer these indignities without a warning. God raised among them Isaiah, a dedicated young man of noble birth, as His messenger to His people. Initially, however, unlike the intrepid Hezekiah, his knowledge of the people's likely refusal of God's message caused him to shrink from the challenge. Then it happened—God gave him a vision of the temple in heaven. He saw the King of the universe seated upon His throne surrounded by legions of angels who bowed low in His presence as they ascribed glory to His name. Like Moses, who was enduringly impacted by the burning bush, and Paul, whose life was forever changed by his experience on the Damascus road, Isaiah came forth from the vision changed in attitude and charged with zeal. The rest of his life was spent in witness to a rebellious people earnestly proclaiming obedience to the will of God.

We witness on a much lesser scale. But for us, as it was for him, effective service begins in a temple audience with God where appreciation for His majesty produces confession of our unworthiness, confidence in His goodness, and the zeal to witness courageously.

Listen and Live

Then, Zedekiah the king sent and took him out.
The king asked him secretly in his house, and said, "Is there
any word from the Lord?" And Jeremiah said, "There is." Then he said,
"You shall be delivered into the hand of the king of Babylon!" Jer. 37:17.

These were troublesome times for God's people. Nebuchadnezzar had already conquered the land and had taken back to Babylon many of its brightest leaders as well as the sacred utensils of the holy Temple. However, in an act of uncommon kindness, he permitted Judah to exist as a separate government and established Zedekiah, the younger brother of Josiah, as its king. Through Jeremiah, God counseled Zedekiah to submit to Babylonian rule and lead Judah to cooperate with their conquerors. Zedekiah obeyed.

However, after years of obedience false prophets caused him to alter his behavior. One of them, Hananiah, even predicted the return of the Temple vessels and complete restoration of power. When Jeremiah warned Zedekiah against this course of action, the king imprisoned him. Zedekiah did not dislike the man of God. In fact, although under pressure from evil advisors, he consigned him to captivity; he issued secret orders for his comfort and, on one occasion, fearfully inquired of the imprisoned prophet, "Is there any word from the Lord?" (Jer. 37:17). Jeremiah's response was the same as before his incarceration—repent or be destroyed! But Zedekiah delayed obedience, and shortly thereafter Jerusalem was attacked and sacked, and the Temple that had for 400 years adorned Mount Moriah was burned to the ground.

How sad that one man's lack of courage would precipitate such unspeakable loss of life and desecration of holy materials. Had he obeyed, not only would the city and Temple have been spared, but Nebuchadnezzar (who had earlier acknowledged God's power) would have also been given further evidence of the might of the Hebrews' God.

We do not rule kingdoms like Zedekiah. However, we have spheres of influence involving individuals whose impressions of God's temple depend upon our obedience even under discouraging circumstances. Is there any word from the Lord "today" for those who suffer hardships, disappointments, indignity, and confusion of any kind? Yes, there is! The Bible says: "All things work together for good to those who love God" (Rom. 8:28). And again: "Be thou faithful unto death, and I will give thee a crown of life" (Rev. 2:10, KJV).

God Is There

But many of the priests and Levites and heads
of the fathers' houses, old men who had seen the first temple,
wept with a loud voice when the foundation of this temple was
laid before their eyes. Yet many shouted aloud for joy. Ezra 3:12.

Two prophetic voices gave the enslaved Jews hope of eventual return to Jerusalem and the restoration of the Temple. One was Jeremiah, who prophesied: "For thus saith the Lord, That after seventy years be accomplished at Babylon I will visit you, and perform my good word toward you, in causing you to return to this place" (Jer. 29:10, KJV). The other was Isaiah's companion promise: "Who says of Cyrus, 'He is My shepherd, and he shall perform all My pleasure, saying to Jerusalem, "You shall be built," and to the Temple, "Your foundation shall be laid"'" (Isa. 44:28).

With the fall of Babylon to Media Persia in 328 B.C., the weary exiles experienced a more tolerant rule. It was, in fact, Cyrus, their new king, who gave them permission to return home to rebuild the Temple. A happy delegation lead by Zerubbabel was sent to accomplish the task. Utilizing some of the stones of Solomon's Temple found among the ruins and quarrying others, they succeeded in erecting a building similar to the original. When at last their task was completed, the happy exiles greatly rejoiced.

But not everyone joined in the celebration. The older ones who remembered Solomon's Temple did not celebrate—in fact, when they beheld the rebuilt foundation, they mourned sorrowfully. Thoughts of the original building and all the blessings needlessly lost during their 70 years of captivity evoked tears of sorrow, not songs of praise (Ezra 3:12).

While the second Temple's appointment did not equal Solomon's in splendor, God's presence was no less real. Were God's blessings based upon material display, the first Temple's grandeur would have guaranteed heaven's perpetual benedictions—but it did not. That is because even though God demands our choicest gifts, He honors motives, not materialism; devotion, not display; and effort, not effulgence.

He covenanted with Jacob on a stone, Moses at a bush, Elijah in a cave, the Samaritan woman at a well, the Ethiopian eunuch on a horse-drawn chariot. Wherever and whenever we pitch our tent and call upon His name in sincerity, that place becomes our Ebenezer, our Shiloh, our Mount Moriah—a temple of acceptable praise and devotion.

The Man Who Wouldn't Quit

For the children of Israel and the children of Levi shall bring the offering of the grain, of the new wine and the oil, to the storerooms where the articles of the sanctuary are, where the priests who minister and the gatekeepers and the singers are; and we will not neglect the house of our God. Neh. 10:39.

Another brave reformer was Nehemiah, whose activities impacted the rebuilding of Jerusalem. He approached his task with resolute determination, armed with permits stamped by Darius, the king who succeeded Cyrus, accompanied by a joyous, eager entourage, and fired with divine unction in consequence of earnest prayer.

When, upon arrival, he encountered the vigorous opposition of Sanballat and others who doubted his credentials and were determined to thwart his labors (Neh. 10:1-3), but Nehemiah remained undeterred. In describing his passion and dedication, Ellen White writes: "Nehemiah's whole soul was in the enterprise he had undertaken. His hope, his energy, his enthusiasm, his determination, were contagious, inspiring others with the same high courage and lofty purpose. Each man became a Nehemiah in his turn and helped to make stronger the heart and hand of his neighbor" (*Prophets and Kings*, p. 638).

Thus, in spite of the intense efforts of his faithless detractors to defeat his progress, within two short months the walls of Jerusalem were reconstructed and the people once again engaged in joyful praise to God.

What about you and your church or your family? Are you at times opposed by those who doubt your mission and motives? Are you doing your best, even though resisted by individuals and events of "Sanballat-like" character that harass and berate you? Are you ridiculed, oppressed, and inundated by circumstances that suggest you should give up, let go, give in to the pressures, and come down off the walls of endeavor? Are you sometimes given to doubting your mission or questioning your interpretation of God's directions? You are not alone; we all will at some time encounter this. The difference between those who succeed and those who fail is determination fueled by prayer and daily communion with God. Nehemiah, our hero, is our example. Why not read again the book that bears his name and be encouraged to stay on the walls and continue the battle for good?

Right Place—Wrong Reason

And I said, "Should such a man as I flee? And who is there such as I who would go into the temple to save his life? I will not go in!" Neh. 6:11.

After no less than five unsuccessful attempts to lure Nehemiah to an isolated village where they planned to take his life, his detractors (Sanballat and Tobiah) tried a different approach. They sought to disgrace him before God and the people. They attempted to do so by bribery. They influenced Shemaiah, also a false prophet, to tempt him to hide in the Temple as a means of escaping the wrath of his avowed enemies.

Nehemiah, however, blessed with a quality of perception possessed by all who hold constant communication with God, saw through their wicked scheme (Neh. 6:12). He realized that his hiding in the temple would be a serious breach of the law that allowed only priests within its precincts. He understood that the news of such an act would weaken his credibility and seriously affect the morale of his brave accomplices.

The enemy of righteousness is as inventive today as he was then in his attempts to divert, distract, and diminish those who seek to do God's will. In fact, the arch deceiver who conversed with Eve in such an appealing form, and who through the ages has successfully derailed multitudes of individuals with noble intentions but faulty sensory apparatus, is more deceptive now than ever.

The lure of riches, the pressure of peers, the quest for praise, the love of ease, the desire for revenge, the wish to dominate others are all urges that he presents in an effort to derail our spiritual journey.

A chief lesson of Nehemiah's example is that isolating ourselves in a temple for safety is not an option for gospel reformers. Nehemiah risked death rather than dessert his post. His answer to his detractor's invitation to hide was, "I will not go in!" In a similar response to pressures to retreat, he replied: "I am doing a great work, so I can't come down" (verse 3). Nehemiah was dedicated, discerning, and decisive. And we can be this way as well, if we are focused on our mission and fervent in our devotion.

The Temple Grows

In whom the whole building, being fitted together,
grows into a holy temple in the Lord. Eph. 2:21.

What is the temple to which Paul refers? It is the church of the living God. It is not a congregation or a particular group of worshippers, but the saints universal—all those anywhere of whatever physical or geographic description who love the Lord and serve Him to the best of their knowledge and ability.

God's church universal has grown from the "mustard seed" beginnings of early Christianity to the wide pervasive system that it is today. God's commandment-keeping people, a small but significant part of that system, has itself developed from its humble origins in the mid-nineteenth century to its present scale of international presence. It has grown from a small group of fasting, praying believers who gathered in barns studying prophecy by candlelight to a large and forceful people now shedding the light of truth to all but a few known people groups.

God's commandment-keeping people, comprising all of earth's major ethnic divisions, operate numerous colleges, universities, seminaries, hospitals, clinics, publishing houses, food factories, and many thousands of churches around the world. Like the proclaimed mustard seed, it has, since its beginnings, expanded exponentially in all these and other ways—and the temple still grows.

But it is not the material and statistical growth of the church universal that should occupy our minds. It is the well-being of the individual temple that each of us represent. It is not the witness of the organized body of believers that most effects and advances the kingdom, it is the witness of our individual lives. We cannot single-handedly revolutionize society or the church, but we can each and every day by our habits of devotion and dedication continue our personal progress, daily growing as holy temples of God. This reflects the wisdom of the poet who wisely opined: "Why build these [temples] glorious if man unbuilded goes? In vain we build [these temples] unless the builder also grows."

The Sure Foundation

Having been built on the foundation of the apostles and prophets,
Jesus Christ Himself being the chief cornerstone. Eph. 2:20.

Tall, sturdy buildings require a firm foundation. The bigger the building, the broader the base must be. Foundations that are inadequate for the buildings that they support are precursors to numerous structural problems and sometimes a distinct danger to life and limb.

The church, God's living temple, destined to grow from the small beginnings of the upper room to the universal presence that it now occupies, was given a foundation of no less a substantial and authentic presence than the Lord Himself. The faithful leadership of the early church, the men and women of New Testament times who, in an age of blinding superstition, rampant idolatry, and grinding persecution, kept alive the truth He handed them bravely built upon those beginnings.

Even before our Christian origins, the prophets of Judaism who prodded Israel and Judah to repent, who warned their kings and guided their armies, and who rediscovered ancient traditions performed heroically for the cause of truth. Of these, Hebrews states: "The world was not worthy." They "did not receive the promise, God having provided something better for us, that they should not be made perfect apart from us" (Heb. 11:38-40).

In other words, in spite of the sterling witness of our noble predecessors in gospel endeavor, we are advantaged. "We who are alive and remain" (1 Thess. 4:17) now experience theses events. If we are faithful, we will enjoy the culmination for which they longed—the second coming of our Lord.

Our need is to be faithful to the mission that they bequeathed to us; to run with patience the race they finished in loyal expectation. Our fervent hope is to one day soon join them; some of us revived by resurrection, and others raptured in translation to eternal praise. We will do so, not in the earthly structures that house our present dwelling, but by the grace of our gracious God, in glorious temples above.

Our Indestructible Jesus

Jesus answered and said to them, "Destroy this temple,
and in three days I will raise it up." John 2:19.

There he goes again! Destroy the Temple? Even the suggestion is sacrilegious. How could one, especially a Jew, imagine such a thing? That's worse than cursing motherhood, or burning the flag, or putting down one's family or nation. How could he? Why would he even mouth such a disrespectful suggestion?

But then, as if to heighten his sacrilege, he promises to rebuild it in three days. Did you hear that? First he conjures up the destruction of God's holy place, and then he has the nerve to say that he—single-handedly—can rebuild it in three days. What unmitigated gall! It required Solomon seven and a half years to build it and Zerubbabel four and a half years to rebuild it. And he claims he will do it in 72 hours. The man is an egomaniac, a loose cannon, an enemy of God, and a danger to the people, and a heretic like that deserves to die! This is what Christ's enemies thought.

But it was not really the Temple concerns that fueled the fires of their hatred. It was His selfless, sacrificial humility that exposed their greed and self-aggrandizement. They daily drained the people of their meager possessions, fleecing the widows, oppressing the poor, and ignoring the needs of the disadvantaged. His message and manner unmasked their ways, and they longed to rid themselves of His presence—and they did!

They crucified our God; the living embodiment of all that the earthly Temple symbolized. He was the object to which it all pointed, the subject of all its arrangements—the Paschal lamb, the fragrant incense, the candle glow, the living law, the daily bread, the protecting veil, the Shekinah presence, and they killed Him. The Temple lay destroyed, but not for long. He came forth from the grave by His own power after resting three days in the grave.

His declaration "I lay down my life, and take it up" (see John 10:17) proved not to be an empty boast, but a solemn warning to His enemies and a memorable promise to His followers; the ultimate proof of His triumph over the devil—the highest evidence that He is indeed our true and living temple.

No Need to Stumble

"And whoever falls on this stone will be broken;
but on whomever it falls, it will grind him to powder." Matt. 21:44.

To those who are disobedient, Christ is a "rock of offense" (Rom. 9:33), His kingdom principles are annoying, His peasant lifestyle is unattractive, and His persistent warnings are an irritant. The wicked refuse to fall upon the Rock and be broken; they are determined to walk in the ways of their own self-sufficiency. Though Christ intercepts their path and provides them the opportunity to surrender, they do not yield. Unbroken and unblessed by the Rock of salvation, they stumble along in godless living to a Christless grave. They refuse to fall upon the Rock; hence, the Rock falls upon them. And "on whomever it falls, it will grind him to powder" (Luke 20:18).

It is at His second coming, when the pre-Advent judgment will have ceased and punishment is fully determined, that evildoers will cry out for mercy—but then it will be too late. Christ's warning to each of us is essentially: "Fall and be broken, or stumble and be burned," consumed forever in the flames "prepared for the devil and his angels" (Matt. 25:41).

Final retribution upon the wicked is no less certain than final reward for the righteous. The God who cannot lie has promised to burn the wicked to ashes (see Mal. 4:1)—forever ridding His otherwise pure and perfect creation of the curse of sin. Membership in the church will not be enough. For in that day many will say, "Lord, did we not in Your name cast out devils, and in Your name do many wonderful things?" To which He will reply, "Depart from Me, I never knew you" (see Matt. 7:22, 23). Avowed sinners and unsaved saints will perish in the conflagration—suffering the awesome consequences of their rejection of Christ.

Please notice that it is their decision that produces their destruction. That is because Christ's love, though compelling, is not irresistible. To say it otherwise, stumbling is a choice, not a necessity.

When we decide for Jesus, we discover that He not only invites us to sweet fellowship, but also sustains us in consistent following (see Isa. 41:10). He accomplishes this by the power of His Word and the presence of His Spirit, who brings "all other blessings in its train" (*The Acts of the Apostles,* p. 50).

Depending on Him

Wherefore? Because they sought it not by faith, but as it were by the works of the law. For they stumbled at that stumblingstone. Rom. 9:32, KJV.

True encounter with Jesus comprises a full stop. Not a pause or a breather, but complete capitulation and surrender. Those who fall upon Him are those who cast away trust in personal prowess and fully depend upon Jesus. Some place their full weight upon the sturdy promises of the Rock of Ages. Their surrender is like that of the publican who prayed: "God, be merciful to me a sinner" (Luke 18:13); or like that of Isaiah, who intoned: "I am undone! Because I am a man of unclean lips" (Isa. 6:5); or like that of the thief on the cross who cried: "Remember me" (Luke 23:42); or like that of the blind men of Bethesda, who "followed Him, crying out and saying, 'Son of David, have mercy on us!'" (Matt. 9:27).

This is the only right way to respond to the Savior's invitation. We must come helpless, not halting, boldly pleading for forgiveness of sin and His righteousness covering. To fall upon the Rock means we acknowledge our incomplete, if growing, perfection and plead for His perfect, absolute holiness which alone qualifies us to live in the Father's house.

This principle is what the prophet had in mind when she wrote: "The proud heart strives to earn salvation; but both our title to heaven and our fitness for it are found in the righteousness of Christ" (*The Desire of Ages,* p. 300). Once again: "By faith in His merits I am free from the condemnation of the law. He clothes me with His righteousness, which answers all the demands of the law. I am complete in Him who brings in everlasting righteousness. He presents me to God in the spotless garment of which no thread was woven by any human agent" (*Selected Messages,* book 1, p. 396).

"How do you feel?" the children asked as their shaken grandfather stepped from the small aircraft that had taken him on his first plane ride. "It was OK," he replied, "but I didn't let my full weight down." There are many who claim Christ's name but never "let their full weight down" on His provisions and promises. Our challenge today and every day is to trust Him so completely that no other options or fidelities exist, no other obsessions remain, and no other realities control.

Connected by the Spirit

"For as the heavens are higher than the earth, so are My ways
higher than your ways, and My thoughts than your thoughts." Isa. 55:9.

God is always higher, wiser, stronger, and holier than our concepts of Him. The
name by which He introduces Himself and the temples built in His name, even
those constructed after heavenly patterns, are all incomplete portrayals of His persona. He is always greater than our representations, holier than our descriptions,
wiser than our imaginations, and more able than the sum of our theological statements about Him. He is greater because we are lesser, and the perceptual apparatus
of humanity is inadequate for grasping the categories of divinity.

There are some who dare speak of Him in absolute terms as if their grasp of His
being were complete and as if He who dwells in light eternal has, by their formulations, been adequately portrayed. Our text is a reminder that such boasts always fall
short of their billing.

All of this heightens our wonder— that one whose being and ways exceed our
thoughts "as far as the east is from the west" (Ps. 103:12) and who "we cannot by
searching" find out—the incomprehensible ruler of the universe, Himself, found
a way to tabernacle among us. Our situation demanded more than the coded representations of perishable temples—we needed the life-giving presence of the one
they represented. Buildings structured in His honor could not fill the longing of our
thirsty souls or our need for physical and mental revitalization.

That is why He personally infiltrated our humanity. And now, because He
walked our streets, ate our food, drank our water, slept in our beds, endured our
temptations, and suffered our pains, we have an Elder Brother who is "touched with
the feeling of our infirmities" (Heb. 4:15, KJV). He understands. He speaks for us
not as a third-party reporter or a secondhand witness, but as a member of our kind.

While He represents us there, He is still here—not in the flesh, but in the
person of the Holy Spirit, His primary agent of communication and care. By the
Spirit's ministry it is still true that a "greater than the temple" is here (Matt. 12:16)
and that, though His thoughts and ways are immeasurably higher than ours, we
have unfailing access to His promises and power.

Right Motive—Wrong Man

But God said to me, "You shall not build a house for My name,
because you have been a man of war and have shed blood." 1 Chron. 28:3.

David's hope of building the Temple was not ill-motivated. He wanted to do something noble for his Lord. The sanctuary, which had lasted for so many centuries, was no longer adequate in terms of size and service. A new house of God was in order. David applied for the job but was denied—right motive, wrong man! David was a warrior—a man of bloodshed and violence. A man of more docile, less pugnacious personality—Solomon, his son—would build the place of peaceable negotiation for Israel's salvation.

The services of those who surrender to God are not dictated by their own desires. The dreams and hopes of those who honestly pray "Thy will be done" are subject to a higher control than their own. When we pray that prayer, we give the one who sees the end from the beginning absolute veto power over our own strategies. He, who has our best good in mind, has our permission to direct our lives in ways that best suit His broad program—not our shortsighted ambitions.

How did David respond when told that it would be left to another to perform the feat that he longed to accomplish? His reply was: "Now, O Lord God, the word which You have spoken concerning Your servant and concerning his house, establish it forever and do as You have said" (2 Sam. 7:25).

Grateful resignation to God's will is not common among us. As moderns, we are driven by democratic impulses, particularly the spirit of independence and individualism, and are taught to suppose whatever we can imagine we can and should do, especially if the motivation is deemed right. If denied, we are prone to accuse others, blame fate or even question God's involvement in our affairs.

God's reply to David's wish reminds us that heaven functions toward us with the larger picture—the grand scheme of things in view. It is the completion of the plan of salvation (Christ's ultimate triumph in His great controversy with Satan) that dictates His sovereign will, and we are individually and institutionally better for it.

Our Bodies—His Temple

Or do you not know that your body is the temple of the Holy Spirit who is in you, whom you have from God, and you are not your own? 1 Cor. 6:19.

Christ's earthly body was verily a temple that housed "the fullness of the Godhead bodily" (Col. 2:9). Within His human frame resided divinity—"original, unborrowed, underived" (*Selected Messages,* book 1, p. 296). His world-saving, heaven-pleasing success was due to His refusal to allow any evil to taint the human temple that housed the essence of divinity. By refusing to permit entry to anything that would stain or corrupt His mind or body, He maintained the purity of His existence. By denying entrance to destructive influences, He not only protected His innocence, but also maximized His powers—never reducing His ability to discern Satan's traps and to serve the human race.

We too are temples of God. He dwells in us by the presence of the Holy Spirit. Without His strong presence, we are ineffective witnesses often, like the disciples, pleading in vain for healing power expecting miracles, but experiencing defeat (Matt. 17:14-21).

It is not without cause that we continue to sing, "Mercy drops around us are falling, but for the showers we plead." We are not yet "filled with the Spirit" (Eph. 5:18). Why? Because the lust of other things creep in, such as: dragging through life's journey the weights of nonessential, time-consuming, mission-diverting, body-debilitating habits lessens our capacity to hear the Spirit's voice and, consequently, His presence and power among us.

Our temples will never be as pure; hence, our availability to the Spirit never as open as it was with Christ's. But we can, each day, "be all that we can be," and that is all that He requires. If we will refuse all that clogs the avenues of our soul (our organs, our hearing, our seeing, our tasting, our feeling, and our smelling); if we will ban the destructive traffic that defiles the mental and physical powers and instead allow only that which is wholesome, our temples will thrive with the Spirit's power.

No, we will never match the Savior's level of influence. But, the impact of our united Spirit-filled witness will supersede in scale that which He, as a single human, exercised while on earth. And this is how we can and must fulfill His promise: "Greater works than these he will do" (John 14:12).

Surrendering to the Spirit

And suddenly there came a sound from heaven, as of a rushing mighty wind, and it filled the whole house where they were sitting. Acts 2:2.

Ellen White applies these verses as follows: "The outpouring of the Spirit in apostolic days was the 'former rain,' and glorious was the result. But the 'latter rain' will be more abundant" (*The Desire of Ages*, p. 827). "As the 'former rain' was given, in the outpouring of the Holy Spirit at the opening of the gospel, to cause the upspringing of the precious seed, so the 'latter rain' will be given at its close for the ripening of the harvest" (*The Great Controversy*, p. 611).

At Pentecost the Holy Spirit filled the house because He was able to fill their hearts. It is the way of nature that the wind seeks entry into empty space not already occupied. "The wind bloweth where it listeth" (John 3:8, KJV), but it listeth where vacuums exist, where voids invite, where vacancies beckon. So it is with the Holy Spirit. The disciples had to empty themselves of all contrary tendencies—Peter of his presumption, Thomas of his doubt, James and John of their ambition, Philip of his unbelief, Andrew of his naïveté, Simon of his resentments, etc., before they could be filled with the surging spirit.

We too, if we would be filled, must make room for His entry. We must give up our fetishes, fixations, and fascinations for the world and its events that reduce our devotion and redact our spiritual concerns.

By what process are our temples cleansed and made ready for the Spirit's infilling? We can do this by the daily surrender to His wooing voice. He is both janitor and guest of our hearts, mechanic and pilot of our souls, architect, builder and sole occupant of our spiritual temples.

This means we must take down the "occupied—no vacancy" sign that signals satisfaction with our present spirituality remembering that "all our righteousness are like filthy rags" (Isa. 64:6). Then, and then only, will our soul temples be filled and the showers of blessing for which we plead replace the mercy drops that, while helpful, are woefully inadequate for our unfinished task.

Preparing for Pentecost

When the Day of Pentecost had fully come,
they were all with one accord in one place. Acts 2:1.

The word "accord," which Luke repeats five times in the first five chapters of Acts, suggests not a group of duplicate personalities, but people of differing characteristics working with singular purpose and attitude. When tuning an organ, all keys are adjusted to the one standard pitch. The fundamental objective of our fellowship is not to agree with each other, but to key on and agree with Jesus. We can agree with each other and still be very wrong. In fact, by judging ourselves by ourselves, we guarantee ourselves failure.

So, it can be asked, with all the many differences of culture within our church and often even our local congregations, how practical is this ideal? Is it really do-able? Yes, it is if we are willing to follow in present councils the methodology that guided the early believers in their theological summits. According to Acts 15, the Jerusalem meeting of church leaders did not attempt or expect sameness. What they did attempt and achieve was unity in diversity. For them, membership in the spiritual family did not mean relinquishing one's ethnic or cultural identify. They were unified in doctrine yet diversified in social orientation. And this is how we should be. Accord does not require homogenization of personalities or cultures. But it does demand the exercise of loving humility and long-suffering tolerance. It also requires that we properly enable and empower each of our cultural parts.

Wouldn't it be wonderful if such accord existed among our families, our institutions, our conferences, our churches, and our ethnic divisions in the church today? Then, the Spirit would come in His fullness and the spaceship *Remnant Church* would be jettisoned from its usual orbit by a surge of Holy Ghost power that would boost it on toward glory.

Then, instead of pulling against each other, we would be pulling others out of Babylon; instead of arguing over theological obscurities, we would be rallying around fundamental certainties; instead of disseminating gossip, we would be spreading the gospel; instead of debating about who is the greatest of all, we would be proclaiming the one who is the standard of greatness and fairest of all—Jesus Christ Our Lord.

The Attitude of Gratitude

Now it came to pass when the king was dwelling in his house,
and the Lord had given him rest from all his enemies all around,
that the king said to Nathan the prophet, "See now, I dwell in a house
of cedar, but the ark of God dwells inside tent curtains." 2 Sam. 7:1, 2.

David's days of exile and danger were now behind him; he had been enshrined as Israel's warrior king and was now enjoying rest from rival nations without and hostile insurrectionists within his realm. But he was not at ease. Why? His place of dwelling was made of the most expensive materials available, but God's house was still a temporary tent. He was not happy dwelling in the marble hallways of his palace while God met His people in a lesser place.

David had no doubts about God's ability to meet His people in humble places. After all, he had happily conversed with Him as a shepherd boy, as hunted heir of the throne, and as exiled king in stark and barren circumstances. Under the silent, starry skies and from the dark recesses of covert caves he had often prayed and fellowshipped with his protector and God. But that has been then, and this was now. He knew that it was not appropriate that he, a mere mortal now blessed to inhabit opulence, would allow the Shekinah presence to be housed in a canvass tent.

David's desire was driven by his wish to honor not only God's majesty, but also His goodness as well. God was wondrously merciful, as He had led him from pasture to the palace and from exile to exaltation. What better way to express his gratitude than by building Him a temple worthy of His name?

It was David's spirit of praise that inspired his many songs of thanksgiving and that greatly influenced his designation as "a man after [God's] own heart" (1 Sam. 13:14).

Is the "attitude of gratitude" glowing in your soul today? If so, it will put a song in your heart, a light in your eyes, a prayer on your lips, a fire in your bosom, and a spring in your step that will, as it did with David, find expression not only in the temples where we believers meet, but also for the individualized temples that we are.

Visioning in the Temple

But when he came out, he could not speak to them;
and they perceived that he had seen a vision in the temple,
for he beckoned to them and remained speechless. Luke 1:22.

The account of Zechariah's Temple experience provides us a number of valuable lessons. First, we learn from an earlier verse that he was "blameless" (verse 6). Second, when visited by the angel, he was faithfully fulfilling his Temple duties. Third, it was in the Temple that he received the stunning news that his wife in her old age would give birth to a son.

All three elements of His experience speak meaningfully to us today. First, if we too would be used, we must be blameless before God. But being blameless does not mean being without error. Rather, being blameless means that all our sins are forgiven, that all our iniquities covered by the blood of Jesus, and that the robe of Christ's righteousness hides us. It is not our lives but His covering that makes us blameless.

Second, the true child of God is not just forgiven and covered, but also functions in faithful fulfillment of duty. We know that it is possible because He who said "Go into all the world" (Mark 16:15) and "be faithful until death" (Rev. 2:10) also promised: "I am with you always, even to the end of the age" (Matt. 28:20).

The final application of Zechariah's Temple experience is that it is often in the temple while worshipping that we receive heaven's messages regarding His will for our lives. Sometimes while seated in quiet meditation, sometimes impacted by the liberating power of the spoken Word, sometimes overwhelmed with the strains of sacred music, or sometimes while busily performing daily duties, we hear from Him warnings and encouragements directing us in willing service and godly living.

Acts reminds us that those upon whom Pentecost fell "every day . . . continued to meet together in the temple courts" (Acts 2:46, NIV). This may not be physically possible for us today. But those who forsake not "the assembling of [themselves] together" (Heb. 10:25) maximize the encounters whereby God's will is made known and minimize Satan's efforts to capture, corrupt, and contaminate the human temples that we are.

Silence Before Him

But the Lord is in His holy temple. Let all the earth
keep silence before Him. Hab. 2:20.

The creature's proper posture in worship of the Creator is that of humble reverence. True worship reverence expresses itself variously from culture to culture and even within cultures over time. But in all cultures and throughout all time, true worship reverence is required before the omnipotent, omniscient, omnipresent, omnicompetent, and eternal God.

But does Habakkuk contradicted by various scriptural examples of joyful celebration and praise enjoin not the hushed silence? Did not Miriam dance before the Lord? (Ex. 15:20). Did not David, in addition to dancing, use loud instruments of praise (2 Sam. 6:14)? And does not Scripture state that when we come before the Lord we are to lift up our voices like trumpets in the declaration of His word (Isa. 58:1)?

Yes, but there is no contradiction. Miriam's "deliverance dance" occurred on the beaches of the Red Sea, not within the precinct of God's Holy Temple. David danced in the streets of Jerusalem as he and his people rejoiced following triumph in battle, not while worshipping in the audience chamber of the revered Temple. And the voice that John heard on Patmos speaking like a trumpet was not that of a loud, shrill, emotionally charged God (Rev. 1:10); there is no scripture that loosens the reverence restraints due our God when we gather in temple worship. Isaiah's humble "woe is me, I am undone" (Isa. 6:5) posture is much more relevant to divine worship experience than are the celebration dances of Miriam and David.

Our prophet reminds us that "when the Word of God was spoken to the Hebrews . . . the command was: 'And let all the people say, Amen'"; that "there is too much formality in our religious services"; that His ministers should speak "energized by His Holy Spirit"; that in the worship experience of grateful churches will be heard "cheerful, hearty responses and words of joyful praise" (*Testimonies for the Church*, vol. 5, p. 318).

When it is remembered that the primary audience in all our worship services is God Himself and that entertainment and display have no place in the house of God, our responses will be genuine and enthusiastic while appropriate in form.

JUNE

A Better Moses

A Light in Darkness

And the Lord said: "I have surely seen the oppression
of my people who are in Egypt, and have heard their cry because
of their taskmasters, for I know their sorrows." Ex. 3:7.

The birth of Moses was at the worst of times for the Hebrew people. The rulers of Egypt had made the lot of the captives miserable in every respect. There were a few Hebrews, among them Bezalel and Aholiab, who trained in Egyptian factories "to work in gold and silver and bronze" (Ex. 35:32) and enjoyed limited privileges, but the masses were hapless field hands forced to live and labor under the heels of grinding oppression. Thus, the discovery of the baby boy by Pharaoh's daughter hidden amongst the reeds was the beginning of a new and brighter day for God's struggling people.

The socioeconomic conditions of God's people were just as bleak at the time of Jesus' birth not only for the Jews, but also for all of the world. Isaiah had prophesied that, at His appearing, "darkness shall cover the earth, and deep darkness the people" (Isa. 60:2). And indeed, society had reached its base of moral and physical debauchery. Four thousand years of sin's tyranny had contoured humans into beings who looked and acted more like the beasts of the field than the creatures formed in Eden.

When Jesus came, the light of human intellect had been nearly extinguished by the evils of idolatry, witchcraft, tribalism and intemperance. Diseases of the worst kind were spread on the wings of infectious insects driven by deadly breezes; the crude cures of physicians caused more pain and suffering than the symptoms they treated; insanity was common place and longevity a mere 30 years. Into this foul, foreboding, forlorn atmosphere Christ made His promised entry.

He too had to be hidden from the wrath of a jealous ruler. But the light that shown from His countenance in the manger was the unmistakable glory of heaven attracting the worshipful notice of men and angels. Born without stain or strain of sin, He was the very best that heaven could offer. His birth began a new day for the struggling human race. God, Himself, in pity for our enslaved planet, "so loved the world that He gave His only begotten Son" (John 3:16) as the perfect antidote for our malady, the ultimate solution for our dilemma and the only hope of our salvation.

The Goodly Child

And a man of the house of Levi went and took as wife
a daughter of Levi. So the woman conceived and bore a son. And when
she saw that he was a beautiful child, she hid him three months. Ex. 2:1, 2.

The King James Version states she saw that he was a "goodly" child. The truth is that the parents themselves were goodly. The names Amram, "kindred of the lofty one," and Jochebed, "she whose glory is Jehovah," suggest that they, unlike the majority of the captives, had not forgotten the true God. In fact, the name Jochebed provides the first known incorporation of the sacred title Jehovah. We do not know much about her. She was of the tribe of Levi, and clearly from the wise decision she made regarding the child she bore, a woman of wisdom and courage.

To this godly couple, already blessed with older children, including Miriam (the word from which is coined the name Mary), was born the baby Moses, whose name means "for he was saved out of the water."

To well-meaning parents, all babies are "goodly"—every infant is special. Parents by nature are given to high optimism about their newborn. Moses' parents, however, not only mouthed special regard for him, but also risked their lives in an effort to save him.

Moses' later heroics more than fulfilled his parents' hopes and expectations; and did so Thermuthis, the daughter of Ramses III, then Egypt's pharaoh, who looked upon the weeping babe in the floating cradle and was touched by the light of his countenance (Ex. 2:6, 7).

Later, when the adult Moses, by exile experience, became a suitable servant, God sent him back into Egypt with the message "Let My people go." Thus the beautiful babe became a dutiful deliverer—a type of "Jesus," but only in faint comparison. This is because, while Moses' mission took him from the barren desert to Pharaoh's palace, Jesus' mission took Him from the comforts of glory to the wastelands of Planet Earth.

Moses left exile; Jesus left opulence. Moses left loneliness; Jesus left loveliness. Moses left the consequences of his evil deed; Jesus left the circumstances of ultimate perfection and beauty. His act of condescension defies credulity but defines the great heart of love that makes Him infinitely our better Moses.

Patience Under Pressure

And the child grew, and she brought him to Pharaoh's daughter,
and he became her son. So she called his name Moses, saying,
"Because I drew him out of the water." Ex. 2:10.

Discovered by Pharaoh's daughter when he was 3 months old, Moses was officially the property of the princess. His mother, Jochebed, and his sister, Miriam, having cleverly arranged to be his nursemaids, exercised the greater dominance in his life until age 12. They were then obliged to deliver him to his adoptive mother for formal training in the royal palace.

During the next 28 years, or until age 40, he lived the life of an Egyptian noble prince. However, during these nearly three decades of Egyptian acculturation, he never forgot his Jewish training, and privately resented the harsh treatment that his people received.

Moses' control of his emotions and his ability to live, from all outward appearances as an Egyptian noble all those years, was remarkable. The fact that he finally exploded in an act of rash brutality is regrettable, but his decades of subdued restraint are certainly noteworthy.

Jesus, our better Moses, also had to exercise painful restraint. He was God clothed in human flesh living in our world of repulsive, revolting circumstances. He, who is the fountain and source of purity, He who is goodness incarnate, found it excruciatingly painful to coexist with human perversity.

Not for a period, but for all His life, He maintained the restraint of His powers: when observing the grinding cruelties of Romans and Jewry alike; when demons whispered retaliation for injustice that He personally suffered; when burdened with the weight of rejection by the very humanity He had come to save; when tempted to use His divine powers to escape verbal and physical torment—He was able to contain His righteous indignation, never violating the terms of His earthly sojourn.

How can we understand or adequately respond to such noble compassion? The grateful apostle, smitten by the knowledge of Heaven's gift, answers well: "I beseech you therefore brethren, by the mercies of God, that ye present your bodies a living sacrifice, holy, acceptable to God, which is your reasonable service" (Rom. 12:1).

Such dedication does not earn us salvation, but it does earn us approbation—God's pleasure for our willingness to surrender to His son, our elder brother and infinitely our better Moses.

Choosing to Suffer

By faith Moses, when he became of age, refused
to be called the son of Pharaoh's daughter, choosing rather
to suffer affliction with the people of God than to enjoy
the passing pleasures of sin. Heb. 11:24, 25.

Pharaoh's daughter, as would be expected given her high status, saw to it that her adopted son received every advantage that great and powerful Egypt afforded. Now, weaned from the trusted hands of his mother, he was quickly transformed into royalty; the son of Pharaoh's daughter—"learned in all the wisdom of the Egyptians"; schooled in the highest religious, philosophical and military education of Egypt, he became, as Stephen later observed, "mighty in words and deeds" (Acts 7:22).

But, as he walked amid the pomp and splendor of the palace, his true loyalties lay with his oppressed kin—the Hebrews whose pitiable lot he daily observed. When he "became of age," his choice was clear. He elected to suffer with the disadvantaged slaves rather than to rule and relax in the high society of the mightiest nation on earth.

Jesus, our better Moses, made such a choice when He laid down His mantle of glory and came to suffer with our lost humanity. He not only condescended, but also retained while here, a status so low that He once plaintively pled: "Foxes have holes and birds of the air have nests, but the Son of Man has nowhere to lay His head" (Matt. 8:20).

His response to the last of the three wilderness temptations says it well. When offered the world's kingdoms as glittering reward for acknowledging Lucifer's powers (powers that He the Creator had given him), He refused, opting to continue in the painful path of the cross rather than yield to ease (Matt. 4:8-11). His choice was to suffer sacrifice rather than enjoy ease, rejection rather than applause, and death with honor rather than the abandonment of His mission.

Moses left it all! Money, prestige, recognition, and servants—all the trappings of power that human hearts so readily crave. But Jesus left more—as much more as is heaven higher than the earth. This is why His sacrifice exceeds, as does the beaming sun and the flickering firefly, that of even mighty Moses.

A Better Solution

*And it came to pass that in those days, when Moses was grown,
that he went out unto his brethren, and looked on their burdens:
and he spied an Egyptian smiting an Hebrew, one of his brethren.
And he looked this way and that way, and when he saw no man,
he slew the Egyptian, and hid him in the sand. Ex. 2:11, 12, KJV.*

Moses' act of murdering and hastily burying his victim was especially abhorrent to the Egyptians. Not only did he take the life of another, but also the buried body was not embalmed. Since Egyptian religion taught that only those bodies properly prepared for burial were eligible for a future life, Moses' deed was doubly heinous. He not only took life, he also denied his victim all hope of an afterlife.

But consider Jesus, our better Moses. He was the victim, not the victimizer. He did not destroy life; He saved it. He did not remove hope of eternity; He restored it by raising the dead, by rising Himself, and by promising to return for the vast harvest of sleeping saints.

Christ's body rested in the grave not embalmed, but it revived nevertheless, springing to life again by the power that resided within Himself. Moses displayed power over physical life by taking that of another. Jesus demonstrated power over life and death by reviving His own.

The ancient Egyptian technique of embalming is still a mystery to science. Even our advanced knowledge has not allowed us to duplicate the process. The Egyptians' erroneous theories about life after death, as that of all other religions have all been exposed by the events of Calvary. The death, burial, and resurrection of Jesus substantiates that: (a) "the living know that they will die, but the dead know nothing" (Eccl. 9:5); (b) the dead sleep until the first or second resurrection (Rev. 20:5, 6); and (c) the resurrections of both the righteous and the wicked will be followed by just rewards: the righteous to everlasting life (1 Thess. 4:14-18) and the wicked to eternal destruction (Matt. 25:31-41).

The deliverer of ancient Israel took life, but couldn't give it. The deliverer of our souls laid down His life and took it up again so that we might live forever. And by this, as by so many other means, He is our better Moses.

June 6

Standing on Holy Ground

Then He said, "Do not draw near this place. Take your sandals off your feet,
for the place where you stand is holy ground." Moreover He said, "I am the
God of your father—the God of Abraham, the God of Isaac, and the God of
Jacob." And Moses hid his face, for he was afraid to look upon God. Ex. 3:5, 6.

At his official call to service, Moses was commanded to remove his shoes in the
presence of Divinity. His education in Egypt provided him superior advantages; he was, as poet, historian, philosopher, legislator, and military strategist, a
man of high and noble estate. But now, at the burning bush, he was face to face
with one greater than he, and in His presence commanded to differential reverence
and respect.

Royalty no longer rules us; we no longer bow in deference before potentates
and powers. The sovereign-subject relationship, successfully challenged and dismissed by the French Revolution, is largely a concept of fading history. We vote our
leaders into office, and, when we choose, we vote them out. We can even indict or
impeach them. Most of the nations that do retain vestiges of monarchal rule view
them more as nostalgic links to the past than relevant authorities in contemporary
affairs.

All of which makes it difficult for moderns to think of themselves as owned
and directed by a superior being. And yet there is no clearer way to express the
"creator-created" relationship. He is the ruler of the universe—He is God, our king.
He is today our sovereign and ultimate authority as when Moses stood in his bare
feet before the burning bush.

And how best, without contemporary sovereign-subject models to inform
our perceptions, do we adequately succeed and retain this imagery? We do so by
studying the Word of God by which we are impacted again and again: the "ruler-servant," "owner-slave," and "king-commoner" relationships that God sustains
with creatures in all His worlds. But more enduringly, we do so when impacted by
the unspeakable sacrifice of Him who died to save our lost world.

When that act of love captures our hearts, we will quickly take off our shoes of
self-sufficiency and receive from Him direction and wisdom and power, and humbly hear and follow His desires for our lives.

Willing and Able

"Come now, therefore, and I will send you to Pharaoh that you may bring My people, the children of Israel, out of Egypt." Ex. 3:10.

At the burning bush God arrested Moses attention and outlined his mission, and when he demurred, He reassured him repeatedly of His presence and power.

Jesus, our better Moses, needed no such prodding or urging. He gave Himself to be our Redeemer. The reality of a condemned race was motivation enough. Romans 5:7, 8 grades His sacrifice with glowing commendation, stating: "For scarcely for a righteous man will one die; yet perhaps for a good man someone would even dare to die. But God demonstrates His own love toward us, in that while we were still sinners, Christ died for us."

Moses balked at the idea of presenting himself again in Egypt. On the other hand, Jesus, the loving God, who before the foundation of the world had pledged Himself as our Redeemer, reaffirmed that commitment at the very instant of our first parents' transgression. This momentous event inspiration records: "As soon as there was sin, there was a Savior" (*The Seventh-day Adventist Bible Commentary*, Ellen G. White Comments, vol. 1, p. 1084).

Holy angels would gladly have taken His place. But since only one equal with the law could pay the cost of transgression of the law and thus deliver us from the bondage of death, He the lawgiver was alone capable. Only His redemptive efforts would be acceptable to the Father and effectively understood by the universe.

It was because Jesus had not only full capacity but also willing compassion that we are saved. Moses was made able in solitude and willing by solicitation. Jesus was found able amid the loud praises of glory and was made willing, not by urging, but by the knowledge of our dire need.

He is still willing and able—willing to forgive us and able, by the Holy Spirit, to empower us. And, further, He is eminently able to keep in perfect peace those whose minds are stayed on Him (Isa. 26:3) and to keep us "from stumbling" (Jude 24) as we journey through this wilderness of sin to the beckoning Canaan of promise.

Faith in the Future

He shall not fail nor be discouraged, till He has established justice in the earth; and the coastlands shall wait for His law. Isa. 42:4.

Throughout his years of education in Egypt and later in his schooling in the wilderness, Moses (the type) was being fitted for the role of deliverer without actually knowing it. And when at the burning bush he was made conscious of his mission, he demurred stating his inadequacies as reasons not to go.

Jesus (the prototype), from age 12 when He viewed the Temple sacrifice, clearly understood His role as our sacrificial lamb. During the 18 years between that revelation and His baptism at the hands of John, He did not quail nor become discouraged. And, during His ministry, though harried and harassed, taunted and tested by friend and foe alike, He did not flinch nor become discouraged. True, in Gethsemane He pleaded for relief and another way to accomplish the task. However, since there was no other way, He meekly yielded to the torture and death that bought our redemption. The secret of His unswerving commitment throughout childhood, youth, and His ministry from baptism in the Jordan to His surrender at Calvary was His intense relationship with His Father. Because of this life-giving connection, He was able to remain focused and faithful.

The awareness of His mission as magnifier of the law, exonerator of His Father's character, example of human obedience, and sacrifice for human sins did not discourage Him. His knowledge that His work on earth would end in martyrdom did not depress Him. His awareness that the vast majority of those He came to save would refuse His love did not deter Him. He engaged His mission with courage and confidence; He accepted His destiny as one borne to die and not to live, and was found faithful.

Ours is not the weight of earth's redemption, but we do have the sober mission of proclaiming the judgment-hour warning to the world. Individually, we have the challenge of personal faith in what are often demanding and difficult circumstances. Jesus, our better Moses, has shown us the way to steadfast loyalty. His example is our model, His suffering our inspiration, His principles our guide, and His promises our comfort and stay.

The Secret of Trust

Then Moses said to God, "Who am I that I should go to Pharaoh, and that I should bring forth the children of Israel out of Egypt?" Ex. 3:11.

Three times Moses offered frightened excuses in response to his call. The first was his lowly status (Ex. 4:1); the second was his lack of credibility with the people (verse 1); the third was his lack of eloquence—probably a reference to his loss of familiarity with the Egyptian language after 40 years of absence (verse 10).

God strengthened Moses' resolve, first of all, by turning his staff into a serpent, then by inflicting and healing his hand of leprosy, and finally by appointing his brother, Aaron, as fellow spokesperson before Pharaoh and the people.

Moses' demurring in the wilderness reminds us of Jesus' pleas in the Garden of Gethsemane. Three times He asked the Father to relieve Him of the awesome prospect of Calvary (Matt. 26:44). Jesus' demurring was not driven by fear of His persecutors or the people He had come to save, but by the cosmic enormity of His mission. He is our better Moses because each of His repeated cries—"Let this cup pass" (see verses 39-44)—was accompanied by a submissive resignation such as "Nevertheless, not as I will but as You will" (verse 39). He is our better Moses because He did not require signs and miracles to authenticate His call to Calvary. He is better because the weight of His mission involved not just that of a nation, but also that of the world. And because heaven could provide Him no partner in suffering, no accomplice in sacrifice, He had to tread the winepress alone.

There were, for the Sufferer of Gethsemane, no divine interventions, no miracles of deliverance. Though His spirits sagged under the enormous load of our sins, they did not break. His staggering faith could not see beyond the portals of the grave (*The Desire of Ages*, p. 753), but when tempted to stop He remembered the wonderful way the Father had sustained Him throughout His earthly ministry, and He was strengthened to die.

Are you challenged today by prospects that overwhelm you? Are you inundated with prospects that seem to defy your strongest capacity? Then look to Jesus. He knows the way through the wilderness of all life's trials. Acquaintance with His Word will provide the wisdom and courage to live and even, if necessary, to die in submission to His will.

Quiet Beginnings

And the Child grew and became strong in spirit,
filled with wisdom; and the grace of God was upon Him. Luke 2:40.

The childhood backgrounds of Joseph and David (both shepherd boys) and Elisha (a farmer's son) spoke eloquently to the advantages of quiet (natural) surroundings upon early character development. In reflecting upon Moses' 40-year sojourn in the wilderness, Ellen White wrote: "In the military schools of Egypt, Moses was taught the law of force, and so strong a hold did this teaching have upon his character that it required forty years of quiet and communion with God and nature to fit him for the leadership of Israel by the law of love" (*Education*, p. 65).

Jesus, our better Moses, was also prepared in obscurity. He grew and matured in the quiet town of Nazareth away from the busy traffic of city life. He could not and needed not expand His basic spiritual nature, which of course was perfect to begin with. His character, however, was subject to growth. It was necessary for Him, as He grew in physical stature, to also grow in abilities to meet the increasingly greater challenges Satan showered upon Him.

Moses is to be admired for his change of character—Jesus for the uninterrupted development of the unsoiled elements of character with which He began. Moses is to be honored for his patient endurance in wilderness exile—Jesus is to be eternally praised for His painful sojourn in the wilderness of our sinful existence.

It was Christ's human character, not His divine prowess, that was tested in His encounters with His detractors. His strength of character was not a gift. It was learned and earned. As He obeyed His Father's will, His capacity for spiritual victory grew as well as His credibility as the spotless Lamb of God.

Our level of character development will not equal that of Jesus, nor for that matter will it (prior to the close of probation) equal that of the meek but mighty Moses. Nevertheless, we should and must strive with all our energies to emulate their example knowing that in the final analysis it is not our obedience that saves, but rather the perfect righteousness of Christ, righteousness He forged and fortified amid the solitude of quiet beginnings.

Doing the Impossible

Then Moses stretched out his hand over the sea; and the Lord
caused the sea to go back by a strong east wind all that night,
and made the sea into dry land, and the waters were divided. Ex. 14:21.

The dividing of the Red Sea was a demonstration of the power of God unrivaled in all the history of Israel. In terms of sheer excitement and display of God's might, nothing in Israel's prior or later history matched their escape from Egypt's army. Even the crossing of the Jordan, which accomplished their entrance into Canaan, failed to equal its drama.

Its consequences were as final for Israel as they were fatal for Pharaoh. Final in that it marked Israel's birth into nationhood never to return to the bondage of Egypt, and fatal because it involved the slaughter of Egypt's finest—the militia that so ruthlessly oppressed them.

We are sometimes faced with Red Sea experiences as seemingly insurmountable—times when we sense oceans of difficulty before us and hostile, superior forces behind us—in other words, difficulties from which it appears impossible to escape. But if we are spiritually sensitive, we soon discover that "our extremity is God's opportunity," that "the Lord will make a way somehow," that He either removes the obstacle or, if He considers the trial for our good, gives us power to endure. Either way, by His permissive will we gain the spiritual muscle so essential for our successful engagements with the enemy of our souls, and that (humanly speaking) is doing the impossible.

More often than we know, He has answered before we called. More often than we realize, He has steered us over and around dangers of which we were not aware, and more often than we adequately thank Him, He has rolled back the voluminous waters of trouble and taken us over to dry land.

When we stand in final triumph upon the sea of glass, our greatest, grandest, most glorious rejoicing will not be in the facts of the physical, financial, and social deliverances that we have experienced; it will be in our spiritual deliverance from the kingdom of darkness through the kingdom of grace into the kingdom of glory—all accomplished by Jesus Christ, our intrepid leader, our blessed, better Moses.

The Other Side of Righteousness

But every woman shall ask of her neighbor, namely,
of her who dwells near her house, articles of silver, articles of gold,
and clothing; and you shall put them on your sons and
on your daughters. So you shall plunder the Egyptians. Ex. 3:22.

God ordained that as Israel left Egypt, they should take with them material
goods that would in some measure repay for the work they had been forced to
do. Their captors had been greatly enriched by their slave labors, and it was right
for them to claim compensation for unrewarded labor. This principle of restitution
was prominently included in the social laws that Moses later wrote. These laws
firmly incorporated throughout Israel's civic codes required fairness in matters of
material distribution not only for the Israelites themselves but also for strangers
within their gates (Ex. 22:1-15; Lev. 25).

Ours is a God of justice whose righteousness is repeatedly defined in Scripture
as compassion and concern for the disadvantaged. One of the clearest demonstrations of His social concern is the attention He gave, while on earth, to women—a
class of humanity then viewed as little more than mere chattel. He frequently made
females the subject of His parables and the object of His miracles. In fact, He even
included them in His itinerant evangelistic company (Luke 8:1-3). By these means,
so radical for His day, He eclipsed the social understandings of His time and
planted seeds of gender equality, which even now we do well to honor.

The concern of Jesus for the disadvantaged of all classifications is sharply
focused in His own words: "The Spirit of the Lord is upon me, because He has
anointed me to preach the gospel to the poor; He has sent Me to heal the brokenhearted, to proclaim liberty to the captives and recovery of sight to the blind, to
set at liberty those who are oppressed; to proclaim the acceptable year of the Lord"
(Luke 4:18, 19).

Christ's ministry addresses not only the vertical concerns of individual piety,
but also the horizontal concerns of social justice. If we are to truly reflect His character, ours will also.

A God of Order

But God led the people about, through the way
of the wilderness of the Red sea: and the children of Israel
went up harnessed out of the land of Egypt. Ex. 13:18, KJV.

The New King James Version interprets our text as: "And the children of Israel went up in orderly ranks out of the land of Egypt." The language of the Revised Standard Version is even clearer—it says: "And the people of Israel went up out of the land of Egypt equipped for battle."

What is evident from these and other translations more modern than the original King James Version is that when Moses led the people out of Egypt, they were not simply well equipped for their journey, they were well organized.

This should not surprise us. Even though he was 40 years removed from his rigorous military training, Moses remained a stickler for detailed planning and precise execution. This is seen throughout the books of Exodus, Leviticus, Numbers, and Deuteronomy. The clear directions he gave the tribes concerning their conduct in travel, the battle strategies he issued, the detailed laws for the conduct of justice, and the many rules of health and dress and family life in general that he offered all demonstrated a highly organized and disciplined mind.

God Himself is the same way: nature (with its orderly seasons) functions in predictable rhythms and by irreversible laws. And when Jesus was here on earth, He demonstrated avid attention to detail: His gathering up fragments after the miracles of feeding, His organizing for service the disciples in twos and sevens, His rising from the tomb on the third day as He had predicted, and before His exiting of the grave He carefully folded garments that had shrouded His body. Of this event, inspiration records: "The graveclothes were not thrown heedlessly aside, but carefully folded, each in a place by itself" (*The Desire of Ages*, p. 789).

Angels of glory function with such precision that as they come and go through the portals of heaven, they present a "golden card" "to the angels at the gates of the city" (*Early Writings*, pp. 37, 39). We, who expect to enter through the gates into the city at His return must prepare for our association with them then by approximating their example of orderliness now.

Lest We Forget

Then Moses stretched out his hand over the sea; and the Lord caused the sea to go back by a strong east wind all that night, and made the sea into dry land, and the waters were divided. Ex. 14:21.

Nothing establishes confidence like success. Evidences of God's leading in prior emergencies are critical to present assurance. Israel's verdict in the wake of the Red Sea miracle was that God was all-powerful, and Moses His special envoy. In the first 20 verses of Exodus chapter 15 the Bible records the people's high exhilaration and praise. But then the very next two verses prefigure the 40 years of bitter experience that ensued. Here, as Scripture records, faced with their first "post-deliverance" test, they succumbed to doubting and disenchantment, and "complained against Moses, saying, 'What shall we drink?'" (verse 24).

How soon they forgot, and, just like them, how soon do we! Like ancient Israel, we too are often guilty of "foxhole religion"—crying out for help in moments of distress, but lapsing back into our regular patterns of flagging fervor when the crisis subsides.

There are ways to combat our short-term memory of God's mercies. One is daily study of His Word. The Bible is, as much as anything else, a chronicle of God's power demonstrated in the lives of others. We are encouraged and informed by these examples.

Another is keeping a daily journal of answered prayers. Memory of God's goodness to us personally is a primary stimulus to faith.

A third means of developing and retaining faith is telling others of God's goodness. The rehearsal of His providences deepens their impressions on our minds and (very important) qualifies us for inclusion in the book especially prepared for those who speak often on His name (Mal. 3:16).

Moses survived the treachery and complaints of those he had led from slavery; Jesus did not survive the animosities of the many He had led from sickness and hopeless despair. But His faith endured and so will ours if we will read His Word, remember His goodness, and share the good news with others.

Sweetening Bitter Water

*So he cried out to the Lord, and the Lord showed him a tree.
When he cast it into the waters, the waters were made sweet. There He made
a statute and an ordinance for them, and there He tested them. Ex. 15:25.*

Marah was Israel's first test beyond the Red Sea deliverance and Moses' first trial as the leader of the newly delivered people. They had traveled three days into the wilderness of Shur happily singing and dancing as they celebrated their freedom.

But the exhilaration of deliverance soon gave way to fear and frustration—they had no water. They who had been safely conducted through the Red Sea were now dying of thirst. Were the miracles they had just witnessed all happenstance or temporary luck? Was this some cruel hoax calculated to raise their hopes and then leave them to perish of thirst? It didn't make sense—if God could divide the Red Sea, why couldn't He provide them water to drink?

Imagine their great relief when they sighted the gurgling stream of Marah and then their angry consternation upon discovering that its waters were not only very bitter, but also contaminated. And who did they blame? Moses, their visible leader who suffered what all God's leaders eventually undergo, accusation and blame for circumstances and events over which they have absolutely no control.

But while Moses had no control over these conditions, God did. He used the impasse to provide the people stark proof of His power and their need to depend upon Him. Moses was told by God to cast the branch of a chosen tree into the stream. Immediately the waters became clear and sweet and the people satisfied their thirst.

Jesus is the branch (Zech. 3:8; 6:12) whose healing virtues sweeten all the days of our otherwise bitter, valueless existence. Moses possessed no inherent virtue that could change Marah's taste. He had to use an instrument (itself a symbol of our Lord) for the purpose of bringing relief to the people.

Jesus did not cast Himself unthinkingly into our world; He volunteered—freely, gladly, and at the cost of His life. This distinguishes Him as a greater deliverer—our bountiful branch, our beautiful, beneficent better Moses.

The Danger of Criticism

So Aaron said to Moses, "Oh, my lord! Please do not lay this sin on us, in which we have done foolishly and in which we have sinned." Num. 12:11.

Miriam, Moses' sister, and Aaron, his brother, did something so often seen in our dealings with each other; they allowed frustration to turn into unkind criticism. Their surface complaint was that Moses, their Hebrew brother, had married Zipporah, an Ethiopian woman. But their more basic irritation was that of Moses' preeminence as God's spokesperson. They expressed unhappy cynicism regarding his special authority when they asked, "Has the Lord indeed spoken only through Moses? Has He not spoken through us also?" (Num. 12:2). In consequence of their evil, Miriam was afflicted by God with leprosy. Her condition reversed after seven days, but only because they confessed their error and Moses had pleaded to God for her healing.

God's punishment of Moses' closest kin should confirm for all that it was not Moses who they doubted against and whom their complaints were being lodged. Whereas the general population failed to learn from that incident, Moses and his siblings did. In fact, not long afterward as the people bitterly denounced them for not providing the food they craved, Moses included Aaron and Miriam as full partners in leadership, stating, "For the Lord hears your complaints which you make against Him. And what are we? Your complaints are not against us but against the Lord" (Ex. 16:8).

Are our leaders always right? No. In their humanity they sometimes err. Even then, however, we should be careful to respect the office to guard the reputation of the church and "to do to others as we would have them do us" (see Matt. 7:12).

There is a time and place for constructive criticism of church operations and operators, but never for murmuring and complaining. The damage done to souls by such activity is more harmful than the perceived weaknesses or mistakes addressed. Today, when tempted to murmur or complain, why not be courageous and helpful enough to speak directly with the individual(s) involved and ask God for a positive spirit? Negativism is a deadly disease, a destructive virus; optimism is a hearty, happy, healthy virtue.

Suffering for Righteousness' Sake

And all the children of Israel complained against Moses and Aaron, and the whole congregation said to them, "If only we had died in the land of Egypt! Or if only we had died in this wilderness!" Num. 14:2.

Only one who has been falsely accused and publicly ridiculed by the very persons he or she has sacrificed to help can appreciate Moses' pain. Time and time again he, the meekest of humans, found himself the object of the unmitigated wrath of an ungrateful people. Their hatred for godly discipline and lack of faith exceeded their distaste for the indignities of slavery; they regarded the rigors of Egypt as preferable to their chastening in the wilderness. Their unfair accusations and repeated discourtesies so impacted Moses that he questioned God's providence and even the value of life itself. He had done nothing to deserve such treatment.

However, the abuse that Moses experienced is but feeble compared to the virulent atrocities that Jesus suffered from those He came to save. Isaiah's prophecy that "He is despised and rejected of man" (Isa. 53:3) was starkly fulfilled in the life of sacrifice and abuse He lived. The disrespect He endured from those whom He led and fed, the insults heaped upon Him in Pilate's judgment hall, the desertion by His disciples in the crunchtime of Calvary, and the deathblows that followed Him upon the cross were unspeakably painful and degrading. The correct answer to Pilate's question ("What evil hath He done?") was "None"—nothing at all—yet they cried, "Let Him be crucified!" (Matt. 27:23).

As He fed the multitudes and healed the sick, they hailed Him King. But when He pointed them to righteousness, temperance, and judgment, they hated Him. Love was never so unrequited; never was one so maligned and rejected, and grace never so despised. Not only did He come to His own and His own received Him not, they also maimed, mauled, and mutilated Him—they took away His life.

Right doing still attracts persecution. The kingdom and its citizens still suffer "violence" (Matt. 11:12). For kingdom citizens, pain is inevitable—misery is optional. That is because of their "Thy kingdom come, Thy will be done" (Matt. 6:10, KJV) faith and firm belief in His promise—"No weapon formed against you shall prosper" (Isa. 54:17).

Jesus at His Best

Yet now, if You will forgive their sin—but if not, I pray, blot me out of Your book which You have written. Ex. 32:32.

Moses had to be a praying man. How else could he have taken it? All leadership is fraught with peril, but there has never been a group of followers more difficult, more ungrateful, more disgruntled, more forgetful, more presumptuous, and more disobedient than those that Moses led.

No doubt Moses often prayed for himself: for strength, for endurance, for patience, and for all the other virtues needed to fulfill his mission. But he also prayed constantly for the people. In spite of their mean-spirited accusations, their continuous complaining, their murmuring, their idolatrous lusting after the gods and goods of Egypt from which they had been so miraculously delivered—in spite of such obvious ingratitude, he prayed for the people.

So did Christ, our better Moses. Earnestly and frequently He prayed not just for Himself, but also for others. He did so because His heart of love was more burdened for the welfare of those He had come to save than for His own reputation and safety. He "was continually receiving from the Father that He might communicate to us" (*Christ's Object Lessons*, p. 139).

Perhaps His most tender prayer was for His disciples when just prior to His death He pled for their faith and security. His words "I do not pray for these alone, but also for those who will believe in Me through their word" (John 17:20) encompass us all.

He prayed not only for His disciples and their converts, He prayed for His enemies as well. In fact, He prayed on Calvary for the very ones who not only unjustly condemned Him but also were exulting as His life ebbed away.

His prayer while dying, "Father, forgive them, for they do not know what they do" (Luke 23:34), is the most selfless utterance ever to escape human lips. It is an unrivaled model of love and compassion. It reveals goodness that is too high for us to understand, yet absolutely necessary for us to believe. Moses' prayer for his people is stunning in its benevolence, but it does not—cannot—equal in comparison the forgiveness prayer of Jesus. Jesus was at His best when He prayed for His enemies. And, to a very real extent, so are we.

The Rock: Christ Jesus

But the Lord was angry with me on your account,
and would not listen to me: So the Lord said to me:
"Enough of that! Speak no more to me of this matter" Deut. 3:26.

There were several reasons that Moses' actions angered the Lord. The first was his ascribing human credit for bringing water from the barren stone. His words were: "Hear now, you rebels! Must we bring water for you out of this rock?" (Num. 20:10). Assuming power that belongs only to God is a cardinal error.

Moses' mistake, in that regard, was not typical of his conduct during the peoples' many years of wandering. He consistently and correctly ascribed to God the power that brought Israel its deliverance. But now, harried and harassed, he lost perspective and sadly took matters into his own hands, denying God of a powerful witness to His glory.

The second reason was that he struck the rock instead of speaking to it. His instructions were "Take the rod; you and your brother Aaron gather the congregation together. Speak to the rock before their eyes, and it will yield its water; thus you shall bring water for them out of the rock, and give drink to the congregation and their animals" (verse 8).

The fact that he struck the rock at all was an act of serious disobedience, but he struck it *twice*, thus again robbing God of glory due His name. Jesus, the Rock of Ages, from whom would flow the water of salvation, was smitten *once*. Hebrews later records it succinctly: "So Christ was offered once to bear the sins of many" (Heb. 9:28).

Moses' severe punishment (denial of entrance into Canaan) was a costly reminder to ancient Israel and to us that success in God's work requires explicit obedience to His commands and unwavering trust in His methodologies. This is true both in our personal affairs and in the institutional work that He ordains. Had Moses spoken to the rock, the water it gave would have been just as sweet and refreshing, and he would have entered Canaan with the people. Our quality of blessings and our prospects for entrance into the heavenly Canaan are no less dependent upon surrender of self and service for others.

Look and Live

So Moses made a bronze serpent, and put it on a pole;
and so it was, if a serpent had bitten anyone, when he
looked at the bronze serpent, he lived. Num. 21:9.

The wages of sin is death, and from the beginning of transgression the human race has been locked in the unyielding vise of pain, bloodshed, and all the other disastrous elements that are the souring of the good God created.

Hope? There was no hope—no earthly hope. Adam could not withstand the plague of death and destruction, nor could any of his afflicted posterity. The human race, by virtue of its fall, was utterly, everlastingly condemned. We were a race doomed to extinction. Had Christ not come into our world when He did, our physical, moral, and mental apparatus would have soon been further paralyzed and finally extinguished.

We were not a race destined to live on in bloodshed and pain; we were a people sure to die out—choked lifeless by the muscular bonds of sin's consequences. This makes for double indemnity: the first death in consequence of our natural birth and the second in consequence of our personal iniquities.

But Jesus has "the avenger stilled" (see Ps. 8:2). As Moses' serpent was the rallying point to which the snakebitten people—dying with swollen glands and failing hearts—could look and be made whole, so health and healing are provided at the cross to all who will look and live.

Moses' cross-bearing serpent was the source of salvation for only those who beheld in faith. Those who found scientific, philosophical, or other theoretical reason to doubt the efficacy of a cross bearing the symbol of the very creatures that were afflicting them died for lack of faith. Those who looked—lived! And so will we if we remain faithful and not fearful.

As the brazen serpent looked like the others but was by virtue of its metallic composition enduringly different, so was Jesus who came "in the likeness of sinful flesh" (Rom. 8:3) by His uncompromising divinity and uncontaminated humanity separate from sinners. This is why and how we can and must look to the Christ of Calvary who stands with open arms as our only source of happiness, healing, and holiness.

God in Disguise

Afterward all the children of Israel came near,
and he gave them as commandments all that the Lord
had spoken with him on Mount Sinai. And when Moses had
finished speaking with them, he put a veil on his face. Ex. 34:32, 33.

Moses was a type of Christ. As Israel's intercessor veiled his countenance, because the people could not endure to look upon its glory, so Christ, the divine Mediator, veiled His divinity with humanity when He came to earth" (*Patriarchs and Prophets*, p. 330). We shall never understand the severity of Christ's condescension from truly God to God cloaked in true humanity, or, otherwise stated, from sovereign to slave, from Creator to creature, from ruler to the rubble of sinful beings. How could it be? How could He love us so? It is implausible, incomprehensible, incredible, but true that Jesus, our better Moses, found a way to be one of us—to live with us—resuscitating our flagging spirits, rejuvenating our fading intellect, and reconstituting our connections with the Father redeeming an estranged planet.

While veiling His transcendent majesty, He unveiled the Father's transcendent mercy. While muting His shining glory, He unmasked Satan's gory schemes. While hiding His effulgence, He exposed Satan's evil. While painfully containing His celestial power, He patiently addressed the peoples' woes, courageously confronting the forces that imprisoned our doomed and dying race.

The fact that the human exterior was able to contain the God within and the God within able to restrain His absolute wrath against sin is wondrous to our eyes and salvation to our souls. Why would He risk so daringly on our behalf? Because there was no other way that our rescue could be effected; only by being vulnerable but victorious in our human sphere could He both vindicate the Father's character and provide forgiveness and covering for our lost condition.

Moses' burning bush, Noah's arching rainbow, Jacob's connecting ladder, Israel's brazen serpent, the sanctuary Shekinah presence, and the high priest's ephod lights all demonstrated that God, who after sin could no longer speak face to face with earthlings, had found a way to bridge the vast chasm created by sin and would redeem this lost creation.

Able Through Suffering

For it was fitting for Him, for whom are all things and by
whom are all things, in bringing many sons to glory, to make
the captain of their salvation perfect through sufferings. Heb. 2:10.

Another way in which Moses served as a type of Christ is by having been made "perfect through sufferings." He was disciplined "in the school of affliction and poverty" (*Patriarchs and Prophets,* p. 480) in order to prepare him for the arduous task of leading God's people from Egypt to Canaan.

Jesus, our better Moses, who is leading His people, the church universal, visible and invisible, from the Egypt of sin's bondage to the heavenly Canaan, was also disciplined by suffering. He engaged His battle with Satan not with the power of Divinity that resided within Him from eternity, but with the character developed by obedience and trials of His humanity.

We are all born with nature or bent of will that is evil; we have no choice. To be human is to have a natural gravitation toward sin. Character, on the other hand, is not what we are when we are born; it is what we become as we live. It is one's enduring pattern of response to the will of God. And the most useful and godly people through the ages are those whose character has been forged in the flames of affliction.

While pastoring in central Florida early in my ministry, I learned that the huge orange industry in the area was always happy for "cold snaps"—days when the weather was not just cold, but exceptionally cold. Why? It's the chilly atmosphere that stimulates the pulp and makes the oranges sweet. Warm winters do not produce the tastiest crop; some freeze is necessary.

Life is the same. Our uncomfortable circumstances are better teachers than our times of ease and plenty. The polishing of our character—the chiseling of the rough edges, the pruning, the scripting and chipping away of ungodly features, the discipline of sacrifice and delay, the lessons of loss and disappointment that are painful—is redemptive.

No, we are not delivered from suffering. We are shaped, sharpened, and sweetened by the pain, then prepared to live more productively in this world, and then in eternity to follow the Lamb who suffered in order to know our pain and to die a perfect sacrifice.

Compelling Love

Then Moses returned to the Lord and said, "Oh, these people
have committed a great sin, and have made for themselves
a god of gold! Yet now, if You will forgive their sin—but if not,
I pray, blot me out of Your book which You have written." Ex. 32:31, 32.

Moses' abortive strike against the injustices that he saw his people suffering was in character with the principles of force consistent with his military background. Later, after decades of reorientation in the wilderness, he came to know the laws of love that undergird divine rule and to act in harmony with their tenets. His leadership style revealed compassion for his people so strong that he chose rather to die and have them forgiven than to live and see them destroyed (Ex. 32:32).

Jesus, our better Moses, demonstrates a quality of love even more astonishing. He, who made us free moral agents, not robots wired to obey from necessity, has from our creation given to us unending evidence of His care and compassion. The diseases we suffer, the injustices that befall us, the disappointment and pain that afflict us, the disabilities of old age, and the inescapable death that descends upon us are all not His doings. None of this was a part of the Eden design. These are all consequences of our choice, our decision to disregard His rule, our straying from the safety of His presence into paths of iniquity with all their hellish consequences.

Obedience through force is contrary to His nature, but not to His rival—Satan. His intention is to subject and seduce. Christ's nature is to appeal and attract. His words "Follow me" are a joyful invitation—not a rigid command. When some such as the rich young ruler, who turn away, and others who followed only for the loaves and the fishes, desert Him in the hour of trial, His loving heart is pained.

Christ no longer walks and talks on earth as the Messiah, but through His Word we are still invited, not coerced, by the invitation "Come unto me." His appeals are "compelling, but not irresistible." We must make the conscious choice to follow Him each moment of each day. When we do, His cry on Calvary, "Father, forgive them," is accepted on our behalf, and the cash register of glory rings with overflowing mercy and forgiveness.

Jesus: Our Sin Bearer

And Moses, Eleazar the priest, and all the leaders
of the congregation, went to meet them outside the camp.
But Moses was angry with the officers of the army,
with the captains over thousands and captains over hundreds,
who had come from the battle. Num. 31:13, 14.

Moses was not one of those "safety first" officials whose wish for popularity muted his courage. He was not, as are so many leaders today, guilty of "risk avoidance." He preached obedience and commanded respect. When the people sinned, including the disobedient soldiers who against God's orders spared choice elements of their Midianite conquest, he remonstrated with them firmly. Moses' high regard for righteousness gave him a low tolerance for iniquity. As such, he prefigures the better Moses of our calling—Jesus Christ.

The truth is that our God hates sin: big sins, little sins, premeditated sins, spontaneous sins, public sins, secret sins, Sabbath sins, weekday sins, sins of omission, sins of commission. All sin is heinous in His view and contrary to His will. He loves the sinner, but He hates the sin and has promised to excise it from His otherwise pristine, pure universe.

What is absolutely surprising, amazing, and incredulous is that He who hates sin so completely was willing to condescend into its festering presence where His pure humanity was substituted for our vile perversity, thus incurring the Father's wrath and assuring our salvation.

Moses' aversion for evil and pity for his people led him to volunteer to die in their place—an offer God refused (Ex. 32:32, 33). Jesus, our better Moses, also volunteered His life in substitutionary death—an offer the Father accepted. This is the gist of Isaiah's words: "But He was wounded for our transgressions, He was bruised for our iniquities; the chastisement of our peace was upon Him, and by His stripes we are healed" (Isa. 53:5).

Christ's coming to die in our stead was the greatest risk, the highest gift, and the bravest act of mercy available to the human race. It is the wonder of the ages, the mystery of salvation and the subject, which the redeemed will pursue in unending awe throughout eternity.

A Nobler Death

So Moses the servant of the Lord died there in the land of Moab, according to the word of the Lord. Deut. 34:5.

Moses was ordered to die. God's instructions were: "Go up this mountain of the Abarim, unto mount Nebo, which is in the land of Moab, across from Jericho; view the land of Canaan, which I give to the children of Israel for a possession; and die on the mountain which you ascend" (Deut. 32:49, 50).

Moses would have died anyway. Instead of seeing 120 years, he might have seen 130 or 140 or 150. But eventually, as all of Adam's descendents, he would have fallen under the irrefutable edict of Eden: "For dust you are, and to dust you shall return" (Gen. 3:19).

Moses' mistake in substituting force for faith at Horeb was one cause for his denial of Canaan's entrance. But it was the sinful orientation of his natural birth that assured his eventual place with the rest of humanity in the silent grave. His frustration with the people precipitated his demise and changed God's exit strategy for him. But his death, like that of the rest of humanity, was inevitable.

Jesus, who is our better Moses, also died. Although longevity in His day was brief, He died much younger than a person of His perfect health. He was, as Isaiah states, "cut off from the land of the living" (Isa. 53:8). He died not having been angered by those He came to save, but having been anguished by their helpless condition. Willfully He gave His "back to those who struck" Him and His "cheeks to those who plucked out the beard" and "did not hide" His "face from shame and spitting" (Isa. 50:6). He died accused, abused, bruised, and brokenhearted because of our betrayal and not His. When He ascended Mount Calvary, He was given no stimulating view of a glorious future or promise of coming from the grave.

Moses' frustration with Israel's disobedience resulted in his mandatory death on Mount Nebo. Christ's acceptance of our sins resulted in His voluntary death on Mount Calvary. And this is how He qualifies as our better Moses.

A Better Promise

Then Moses called Joshua and said to him in the sight of all Israel,
"Be strong and of good courage, for you must go with
this people to the land which the Lord has sworn to their fathers
to give them, and you shall cause them to inherit it." Deut. 31:7.

There he stood: a regal, royal figure, now bent and gray with age but sturdy of heart and hand, told by God that it was time for him to die! What did he say in his farewell address to the people, who had full knowledge of his impending death, as they stood bowed in hush anticipation? He encouraged them by reiterating God's leading through the years of their sojourn, by urging cooperation with his successor Joshua and by reminding them of the covenant promises that would attend their obedience.

But they did not comply. They failed to obey God's instructions or trust His promises. In fact, their stubborn disobedience during Joshua's leadership years was but further foundation for the attitudes and actions that eventually led their descendants to repudiate the very Messiah they were chosen to cradle.

Jesus also gave a farewell address. It is recorded in John 14 to 17. On His way to the cross in full knowledge that His hour had come, He pronounced blessings, promised resources, exhorted to obedience, and stated that a Successor, the Holy Spirit, would be sent by the Father to work on an even grander scale than He could do.

In His final address Christ detailed for His disciples a number of promised gifts. Among them were: mansions (John 14:2), peace (verse 27), productivity (John 15:5), joy (verse 11), answers to prayer (John 14:13, 14), unity (John 17:21-23), and sanctification (verses 17-19).

Perhaps the most significant promise of this, His benedictory, is that of the Holy Spirit (John 16:7-16). Moses announced, named, and presented Joshua as his successor. Jesus, our better Moses, announced, named, and promised the Holy Spirit as His replacement. And He the Spirit now functions among us wooing, instructing, empowering, and directing us individually and collectively on our kingdom journey. The heavenly Canaan looms invitingly before us. Our entrance into its bliss is enduringly tied to our willingness to hear His voice and follow His lead.

The Goodly Land

And they spoke to all the congregation of the children of Israel,
saying: "The land we passed through to spy out is an exceedingly
good land. If the Lord delights in us, then He will bring us into this land
and give it to us, 'a land which flows with milk and honey.'" Num. 14:7.

Canaan is described in the Bible in the most appealing terms: a land flowing
with milk and honey, a land of plenty, a land where luscious vegetation grew
to grand proportions—the idyllic Land of Promise.

Egypt was not without its own charms; it was a place of highly developed com-
merce and beauty. But those benefits were denied the suffering slaves whose rescue
God had arranged by their deliverer, Moses.

Canaan, on the other hand, promised full freedom, superior nationhood,
bountiful food, attractive scenery, abundant natural resources, and vast material
possessions. There they would subdue all their enemies and, in peaceful enjoyment,
live happily ever after.

No wonder that Canaan was such an obsession. They were pushed toward
its promises by the hardships of Egypt and pulled to its presence by the vision of
its oft-mentioned bountiful benefits. God's pledge to Abraham that his posterity
would someday settle there had lost its appeal during their captivity. But events of
the Exodus now rekindled hope of its happy occupation.

Moses was divinely appointed to lead them there and driven to succeed in that
responsibility. But when, after 40 years of tension-filled administration, he stood on
Canaan's shores, he was, because of his error at Horeb, denied that lofty privilege.
His error of striking the rock disqualified him for entry.

Unlike Moses, son of Amram and Jochebed, Jesus, Son of God and Son of man,
at no point abdicated the right to lead His people home. He lived a life of perfect
conformity to the Father's will. He did "no violence, nor was any deceit in His
mouth" (Isa. 53:9).

Someday soon He will return to usher us into Canaan, where they shall "plant
vineyards and eat their fruit" (verse 21), where "the lion shall eat straw like the ox"
(verse 25), where "the eyes of the blind shall be opened" and the lame shall "leap
as an hart" (Isa. 35:5, 6), and where they shall never grow old and shall follow the
Lamb—our better Moses—wherever He shall go! (see Rev. 14:4).

Our Living Lord

Yet Michael the archangel, in contending with the devil,
when he disputed about the body of Moses, dared not bring against
him a reviling accusation, but said, "The Lord rebuke you!" Jude 9.

Both Jesus and Moses were resurrected: Moses, by the arbitrary act of the God of
the universe who wished not to let the flesh of His beloved servant waste in the
earth; Jesus, however, exited the grave by powers that were within Himself. His exit
from the tomb was not dependent upon the cry of the angel whose approach to the
earth rattled our globe, but rather authority internal to His being.

The divine Christ could not have been crucified; Divinity cannot die. It was
the human Christ that expired upon the cross; but flesh that had not sinned would
not sour. He took in death, but death could not take in Him. He died, but He never
decayed. His heart stopped beating, but His flesh never stopped being. His blood
stopped flowing, but decomposition never got going. Satan had hoped that the
lacerated, incarcerated body of Jesus would rot in the ground, but no molecular
breakdown took place—no decomposition occurred. In the truest sense, He slept!

The prison house of death could not contain the one who had boldly proclaimed deliverance to the captives; the bloodied body of Him who said He had
come to free them that are bruised would not lie long in its battered condition; the
grief stricken heart of Him who said that He had come to heal the broken-hearted
would not long remain in its ruptured condition (see Luke 4:18). Had He committed one sin during His life, death would have gripped Him forever. But He who did
no sin, would not—could not—be a permanent victim of its consequences. Having
prevailed over temptation, He prevailed over death and He rose!

And when He rose, He did so forever to retain his human identity (*Selected
Messages,* book 1, p. 258). He came into our world "divinity wrapped up in humanity"—God in human covering. And when He rose and went back to glory He
ascended, "humanity wrapped up in divinity," thus providing the human race one
of its own as representative before the Father. This is why we judge Him to be our
living Lord, our listening Lord, our loving Lord, and our truly better Moses.

Crossing Over

Moses My servant is dead. Now therefore, arise,
go over this Jordan, you and all this people, to the land
which I am giving to them—the children of Israel. Joshua 1:2.

It was in the spring of the year that Israel crossed over into Canaan. The snows from lofty Mount Hermon, whose ridges stretched 10,000 feet into the heavens, were melting, and streams of rushing water were cascading down into the Jordan below, flooding all its banks. Finding safe passage across the river at this season was virtually impossible.

Israel was commanded to cross over in the most dangerous of times and places—and so are we. Sin, cascading down upon us from its 6,000-year beginnings in Eden, has inundated our society with a "flood tide" of evil. Human history has come to the worst of times: the worst of times for viewing our public media, for dependence upon covenants and contracts, for trusting politicians, for traveling our highways, for rearing our children, for believing even the guardians of our safety, for establishing peace among the nations, for conducting gospel witness. Yet God commands us at this awesome juncture in history in this grand and awful age: "Arise—cross over!"

The prospects for Israel seemed impossible. Compounding the issue of the swollen Jordan was their dependence upon a leader far less experienced than the tried and proven Moses. But all these handicaps notwithstanding, when the priests, the spiritual guardians of the Law, in faithful obedience to God's command, placed their feet into the Jordan, its waters walled up, and they crossed safely into the Promised Land (Joshua 3).

And here again Jesus is undeniably a better Moses. He left us before we reached the heavenly Canaan, but not in the hands of a lesser. He placed us in the care of His coequal Guide—the Holy Spirit. And it is He who is now leading us through the turbulence of our sick and sordid society to the joys of the land of plenty.

When we enter there, Christ Himself will be waiting to welcome us home. We will see Him there. He will not be like Israel's leader, a hallowed memory. He will be our visible Lord of glory forever; before whom and to whom we will sing the song of Moses and the Lamb and rejoice through eternity as to how we got over!

Forlorn, but Not Forsaken

Yet in Your manifold mercies you did not forsake them
in the wilderness. The pillar of the cloud did not depart from
them by day, to lead them on the road; nor the pillar of fire by night,
to show them light, and the way they should go. Neh. 9:19.

With the exception of Caleb and Joshua, all those that left Egypt died during Israel's 40 years of desert wandering. They were, because of their faithless disobedience, a generation denied, a people unfulfilled, a nation dishonored.

Nehemiah reminds us that while they were often faithless and forlorn, they were never forsaken. Not only did Jehovah provide them shade by day and warmth by night, but He also gave them His good Spirit to instruct them and manna to feed them. As He had promised, He sustained them so that they lacked nothing. Their raiment "waxed not old" and neither did their feet "swell" (Deut. 5:8, KJV). "The Angel of His Presence saved them" (Isa. 63:9). His punishments were often bitter, but it made them better. God's wrath was not simply a matter of punitive pain, but of corrective measures that instructed the repentant.

We hear much today about the weaknesses of modern Israel, about the lack of spirituality in the church, about the fact that we, like our ancient counterparts, have wandered far too long in the wilderness. It is true that modern Israel should have reached its inheritance long ago. We too have often been frustrated in the journey. We do fit well the Laodicean description of Revelation 3. But those who are obsessed with our Laodicean characteristics can never rise above the negativity and gloom produced by inordinate focus upon the church's weakness.

We do suffer loss because of unbelief; we do acknowledge that revival, sparked by repentance and reformation, is our great and present need. However, we take heart in the fact that even with our struggles notwithstanding, we remain the "apple of [His] eye" (Ps. 17:8); and that "the church, enfeebled and defective, needing to be reproved, warned and counseled, is the only object upon earth upon which Christ bestows His supreme regard" (*Testimonies to Ministers,* p. 49). This thought generates optimism and assurance that combat the despair of those depressed by Zion's ills and spurs hopeful believers to deeper devotion.

JULY

A Better Adam

Love Found a Way

For as in Adam all die, even so in Christ all shall be made alive. 1 Cor. 15:22.

Adam is another major biblical figure whose history magnifies the superior ministry of Christ. When Adam's failure condemned our world's inhabitants to eternal destruction, there was no way for humans to escape their punishment. But love found a way!

How? In the councils of heaven there was devised a plan calculated to extricate humanity while also exonerating Divinity. This plan centered in the provision of a Second Adam. This new Adam would, if successful, prove more worthy than the first. He would be the ideal human, our perfect substitute, the new leader and champion of the race.

The superiority of the Second Adam is most clearly seen in His choosing to obey, whereas the first Adam chose to transgress. Neither Adam was deceived with regard to temptation. The first Adam did not—could not—have anticipated the unspeakably dire consequences of his transgression. But Adam did understand the specifics of God's instructions. Though adequately warned of Satan's fall and the likelihood of his approach (*Patriarchs and Prophets*, p. 52), he risked losing God's favor rather than his wife's companionship. Result? He lost them both. Not only was God's favor removed, but he was also shorn of the conditional immortality with which he had been created.

Jesus, the Second Adam, also risked a lot. He risked His reputation, He risked the creditability of the Godhead, He risked separation from His Father, and as our second Adam, He risked and lost His life. But by losing His life, He rescued ours. The consequences of His loss were the very opposite of the first Adam. The first Adam's loss brought us damnation—the second Adam's loss brought us salvation. The first Adam's loss guaranteed degradation—the second Adam's loss assured reclamation. The first Adam's loss brought condemnation—the second Adam's loss supplied liberation. By being the new head of our humanity, we have been granted access to the favor from which our first parents were banished. And that is why and how He became our praiseworthy champion, our worthy representative—our infinitely better Adam.

Our Glorious Beginning

Then God said, "Let us make man in Our image, according
to Our likeness; let them have dominion over the fish of the sea,
over the birds of the air, and over the cattle, over all the earth and
over every creeping thing that creeps on the earth. Gen. 1:26.

The original human was perfect in every way: physically, mentally, and spiritually. Adam's person reflected that of the Holy God by whose will and skill he was brought into being.

He was placed in a pure and pleasing atmosphere. Nature also demonstrated the undimmed glory of the Creator. There were no dying leaves on withering trees or poison weeds or thorny briars. There were no birds of prey or savage beasts. The climate was pleasing and the scenery storybook attractive. Earth's creatures were sinless, and earth's enfolding tapestry was unspoiled by the ugliness of death and decay.

Adam and Eve had no bias toward evil; their minds were in perfect harmony with the will of God—they felt no inward temptations to evil. They were innocent of urges to disobedience. "There were no corrupt principles in the first Adam, no corrupt propensities or tendencies to evil. Adam was as faultless as the angels before God's throne" (*The Seventh-day Adventist Bible Commentary*, Ellen G. White Comments, vol. 1, p. 1083).

However, they did possess the power of choice, and the tree of the knowledge of good and evil was a test of their obedience. Evil urges would afflict them, and their paradise on earth would be lost only, if in disobedience they ate from the tree—and tragically, they did.

Six thousand years of sin's ravages has sadly blighted earth's original beauty. Yet we still see traces of the primal attractions of Eden. These include: the captivating scenes of sunrise and sunset, the sparkling fields of iridescent flowers, the delightful colors of bright-winged birds, the orchards laden with luscious fruit, and the shining fields of golden grain. In these things we can see reflections of earth before the blight.

These are only a token of what the new earth will contain, for "eye has not seen, nor ear heard, nor have entered into the heart of man the things which God has prepared for those that love Him" (1 Cor. 2:9).

Adam, by his sin, forfeited the glorious appointments of Paradise. But Jesus, by His sacrifice, has made it possible for us to one day live in "paradise restored," where through eternity we will praise the fairest attraction of them all—our righteous Redeemer, our better Adam.

Listened and Lost

Therefore, just as through one man sin entered the world, and death through sin, and thus death spread to all men, because all sinned. Rom. 5:12.

How disastrous was Adam's failure? His disobedience brought about the worst of consequences. As sin is the diametrical opposite of holiness, its results are the very antithesis of happiness. Had Adam and Eve known that their transgression would result in the horrors that it manifested—the loss of conditional immortality, the savaging of humanity, the ravaging of nature, and the continual worsening of our condition over 6,000 years of sin's depreciation—they would not have listened and lost.

The spiritual pollution of human nature is, by all measures, the most disastrous result of our first parents' mistake. Before Adam and Eve sinned, humans had no internal compulsion to evil, no innate urge to do wrong, no inner voices urging them to disobey. We were not "created in sin and shaped in iniquity" (see Ps. 51:51); we were created in the untarnished spirituality of God, shaped in beauty of mind and a body that knew not the taste of error.

But transgression changed that for as long as the race will last. Sin did not visit our parents and leave; sin was not a hit-and-run occurrence—it struck and stuck! It took up residence with the disobedient creatures; it robbed them of the righteous glow that they were given and reversed their situation from the unsullied holiness of their origin to the unholy flesh that it produced. Sin changed their condition from "CI" (conditional immortality) to "PD" (permanent depravity). And this is why neither they nor their descendents could affect self-rescue or self-redemption. Their condition necessitated a Savior who, while one of them, was greater than they; who, while human in terms of creative order, was divine in terms of legal authority; who, while equal to Adam in ability to die, was equal to God in power over death.

Jesus became that substitute. By His ministry all that Adam lost was recovered—and more. Yes, more! The universe would have been better off if humans had not fallen, but the love of Christ showered upon this sick planet establishes, in ways never before demonstrated, the great heart of our great God and His dear Son, our obviously better Adam.

Our Volunteer Servant

Who, being in the very nature of God, did not consider
it robbery to be equal with God, but made Himself
of no reputation, taking the form of a bondservant,
and coming in the likeness of men. Phil. 2:6, 7.

One of the many ways in which Jesus' servanthood is demonstrated is in the status He assumed. Our Second Adam, in radical contrast with the original head of our race, began in the most humble of circumstances.

Servants are almost always persons whose socioeconomic status is lower than those whose houses they clean, cars they wash, yards they beautify, or errands they run. With the exception of such persons as India's formerly structured lower class who believe their lot divinely ordained, most servants would gladly trade their position for more privileged status.

Jesus, however, volunteered to be our servant. He chose to enter into our world in the lowest of social categories. Some say that His parents' inability to find accommodations the night of His birth was because of overbedded conditions in Bethlehem. But does anyone think that if Joseph had had sufficient funds a room could not have been found?

Jesus retained the servant's status that He assumed at birth throughout His life. His popularity and power did not lead Him to pursue higher social standing or to neglect the servant's work for which He had come.

Some servants work only for the money and rewards. They feel no moral obligation toward those whom they serve. In fact, many servants disdain their masters and secretly harbor ill will toward them and their class.

While here, our Lord served us with willing, undiluted dedication. And what a marvel this is. That the King would dwell with the commoner, the Creator tabernacle with the creature, the Potter mold with the clay, the Judge hang for the condemned, the One altogether lovely put on a servant's garb and live a life of selfless service is absolutely stunning to the mind, but singularly saving to the soul. His self-abnegation is eternal proof of the Trinity's love and a perpetual example for our daily interaction with one another.

Adam's Death

And Adam lived one hundred and thirty years, and begot a son
in his own likeness, after his image, and named him Seth. Gen. 5:3.

Adam lived to see nine generations of descendents. His life span was 10 times greater than ours. He was not only physically superior, but he also, as did all the antediluvians, possessed extraordinary mental powers as well. Their environment was filled with countless wonders that delighted the senses and stimulated their awe for the Creator. But over it all hung the pale of death. The dying leaves of majestic trees, the ferocity of once-docile animals, the lambs slaughtered for sacrifice, and, especially for Adam and Eve, the mutilated body of their son Abel were stark reminders of their Paradise lost.

As Adam witnessed the escalating scale of iniquity, he warned the populace of Satan's devices and told them of God's promise of a Redeemer. But his warnings were often answered with ridicule and reproach as well as bitter reminders that he, after all, was the one to blame.

So heavy was the burden of his sorrow, so cruel the taunts of those he attempted to help, that the prospect of death became, for him, anticipation of a merciful conclusion to his sad experience. His happiest thoughts were not of the wonderful days before his Fall, but the promise of resurrection and life with his Creator in the earth made new.

Death is our sad but deserved end; like Adam, we earned it. True, Adam was "patient zero" in the long list of earth's diseased, but, as Scripture affirms, "we have all sinned" (see Rom. 3:23) and are sentenced by its consequences. It is in mercy that death denies immortality to our diseased, demented species. The first Adam could only hope for an afterlife. He was powerless to demonstrate victory over the grave. But the Second Adam has triumphed—He rose from the tomb. He is our Samson who went down to Timnah and slew the lion of death; He is our David who has saved us from the powerful jaws of the beast of destruction; He is our Esther who, by His sacrificial life, gained favor with the Father, and thereby rescued us from the schemes of Satan. Christ is our mighty Redeemer, our champion in battle, the new head of our race—our blessed and better Adam.

Making Excuses

Then the man said, "The woman whom You gave
to be with me, she gave me of the tree, and I ate." Gen. 3:12.

When Adam and Eve sinned, they were not hungry. In other words, their act was illogical and unwarranted; they were not tempted by lack to doubt or disobey God's instructions, they were well fed and content in every respect. In other words, they were without excuse, need or reason.

Nevertheless, they tried to explain: Adam blamed the woman given him by God, and the woman blamed the serpent; both, by implication, blaming the Creator Himself, and both indirectly blaming each other (see *Thoughts From the Mount of Blessing,* p. 126). But their attempts to escape responsibility for their action were as inadequate in God's sight as were the leafy aprons they hastily arranged to cover their nakedness.

We, Adam's physical and spiritual clones, are also quick to try to justify our mistakes. We blame our parents, our teachers, our neighborhoods, our government, our church, and our society in general. It is true that there are some individuals and environments more influential to doing wrong than to do right. For some persons, inherited propensities to evil form an almost irresistible pattern to disobedience. God's promise is that "where sin abounded, grace abounded much more" (Rom. 5:20). And again: "No temptation has overtaken you except such as is common to man; but God is faithful, who will not allow you to be tempted beyond what you are able, but with the temptation will also make the way of escape, that you may be able to bear it" (1 Cor. 10:13).

Adam and Eve did repent. Had they not, they would have died mired in hopeless defense of their mistrust of God and misuse of their God-given powers of choice. But they laid aside their excuses, asked for forgiveness, and were accepted as candidates for eternal life (*Patriarchs and Prophets,* p. 61).

Sin is just as repulsive to God now as when He banished our first parents from Eden and when He abandoned the Second Adam at Calvary. Our only hope, our only source of forgiveness for clean conscience and for joyful fellowship with Christ, is sincere confession, prayerful devotion, and total confidence in His covering robe of righteousness.

The Thoroughly Human Jesus

Jesus wept. John 11:35.

Crying is one of the most telling of human emotions, and there are many Bible figures that cried. David wept as he pled to the Lord for mercy and deliverance (Ps. 69:10); Hannah wept as she pled for a child (1 Sam. 1:7); Nehemiah wept when struck with the full weight of Israel's apostasy (Neh. 1:4); Ezra wept as he petitioned God for revival (Ezra 10:1); and Elijah wept in contemplation of the devastation that Hazael, king of Syria, would bring upon God's disobedient people (2 Kings 8:12).

These and other instances of weeping recorded in Scripture speak factually to the poverty and pain of our human condition. We all weep when our hearts are smitten with grief so great as to overwhelm our usual composure. We weep. Some of us maintain a higher threshold of pain than others, but only those too callous to care do not weep. For those physically incapable of weeping, no tears may fall, but the hurt is just as bad.

Jesus—our Second Adam, also wept. He wept in contemplation of the sins and desolation of Jerusalem. He wept at Lazarus' tomb because of the ignorance and obstinacy of the people. He wept; not for Himself, not for the pain and rejection He would soon experience, not for the separation from His Father He must soon endure, not for His eminent betrayals and crucifixion—but for us.

His great heart, so filled with sympathy for our plight, overflowed in tears of pity and regret. He who was the essence of dignity and courage, the paragon of calm, the master of self-control and emotional stability; He, our Lord and Redeemer and our better Adam, wept even as we do. He wiped His reddened eyes and clenched His teeth and prayed for them and us.

There are other ways in which His humanity was manifested; His hunger, His thirst, and His exhaustion all reveal His humanity. But His tears for the human race demonstrated more than any other way, except His bleeding and dying upon the cross, the oneness with humanity that He had achieved and that, even now, He claims before the Father on our behalf.

He is in glory now far removed from the physical and emotional pain that He suffered while here below. But still He weeps, figuratively speaking, because His overtures of mercy are so lightly regarded and the obedient of the land so very few.

The Second Adam's Humanity

For what the law could not do in that it was weak
through the flesh, God did by sending His own Son in the likeness
of sinful flesh, on account of sin: He condemned sin in the flesh. Rom. 8:3.

The human nature that Jesus assumed had all of the physical characteristics of the generations into which He was born; He did not defy the laws of heredity by taking the flesh of the unfallen Adam or that of any generation prior to the one He entered. The human vehicle that housed the divine God contained all of the infirmities of a race depreciated by 4,000 years of sin. He did not have the original Adam's height or stamina. He did not have the original Adam's strength of organs or powers of endurance. He was "bone of our bone and flesh of our flesh" (see Gen. 2:23), and that quality was the quality of the race into which He came—not that of original humanity.

Nor was He particularly attractive in terms of His looks and physique. His appearance did not draw attention to Himself. He was slightly taller than the average man of His day (*Spiritual Gifts*, vol. 4, p. 119), but so ordinary in features that John the Baptist failed to recognize Him immediately. And when Nathaniel, the hopeful Israelite, met him, he wondered, "Could this man . . . be the Messiah?" (*The Desire of Ages*, p. 139).

The Lord of the universe entered our world as "God incognito," a prince in disguise—the King of glory wrapped in swaddling clothing. It is astonishing but true that the great Creator was here in our form possessing all our physical parts and needs; He hurt, He hungered, He thirsted, He slept, He tired, He bled, He cried, and He died.

But likeness is not sameness. His physical body was not exactly the same as Adam's or ours. It differed from Adam's created status in that it was affected by 4,000 years of sin. It differed from ours in that, though it was affected by sin, it was not infected by it.

He lived under circumstances infinitely more difficult and more treacherous than did Adam—and He was victorious. His rescue of the human race remains the marvel of the universe and the joy of our hearts, and it will be the unending object of fascination for the grateful redeemed throughout the eons of eternity.

God With Us

"Behold, the virgin shall be with child, and bear a Son, and they shall call His name Immanuel," which is translated, "God with us." Matt. 1:23.

What was the Godhead to do? Yes, they would rescue humans. Yes, they would provide us with a second chance. But how could they in mercy spare the race the second death and at the same time keep faith with the law of justice that prescribed destruction for sinners?

The race needed a righteous Adam. But more than that, it needed a Savior—someone to reveal the Father's love as well as pay our penalty of death. We needed someone capable of forgiving sins (a capacity possessed by the Godhead not humans) and at the same time capable of dying (a capacity possessed by humans but not the Godhead). In other words we not only needed someone equal with the law, but also vulnerable to its penalty.

The Godhead, it appeared, was stymied. There existed in all the universe no creature who combined these characteristics—no one in heaven or earth who possessed these traits necessary for our salvation. Satan, from all appearances, had backed God into a corner from which He could not prove His claim of balanced justice and mercy. He had succeeded, so it seemed, in forcing God to arbitrarily forgive erring humanity (and thus violate the claims of justice) or summarily destroy humanity (and violate His claims of mercy). There was, logically speaking, no way out!

And for 4,000 years, the promise of a Redeemer went unfulfilled. The long train of animal sacrifices, whose blood the people were told prefigured the true Lamb, continued day after day, year after year, decade after decade, century after century, and millennium after millennium without verification. Was it only a farce? Why wouldn't God deliver? Or, in fact, could He deliver? Was the Godhead capable of producing a being whose characteristics satisfied the seemingly irreconcilable requisites of human redemption?

Bethlehem answered all those questions. Mary's baby met the requisites totally. He was all God and all man at the same time; in Him who was fully human "dwells all the fullness of the Godhead bodily" (Col. 2:9). He was God wrapped up in human flesh, Son of God, and Son of Man, and, by that union of humanity and divinity, Satan's plans were voided, God's purposes were vindicated, and we are thereby redeemed.

Growing in Grace

"Who committed no sin, nor was deceit found in His mouth;" who, when He was reviled, did not revile in return; when He suffered, He did not threaten, but committed Himself to Him who judges righteously. 1 Peter 2:22, 23.

Christ possessed not only a spotless spiritual nature, but also a spotless spiritual character as well. Character is different from nature. By spiritual nature is meant one's moral predisposition, i.e., one's fundamental orientation with regard to good and evil. By moral character is meant one's active response to the rules of right and wrong in both thought and deed.

Thus it was necessary for Adam, though beginning with an innocent (faultless) spiritual nature, to develop and maintain a perfect (faultless) character. Whereas the first Adam sinned and thereby polluted his perfect spiritual nature, damning his posterity to be "born in sin and shaped in iniquity" (see Ps. 51:5), the Second Adam never sinned. He lived His life without a flaw. As He grew physically, His character strengthened spiritually; His perfect spiritual nature was not defected because of wrong choices. It is in this sense that "Jesus was free from all sin and error; there was not a trace of imperfection in His life or character. He maintained spotless purity under circumstances the most trying." (*The Seventh-day Adventist Bible Commentary,* Ellen G. White Comments, vol. 7, p. 929). And that "in His life on earth, Christ developed a perfect character, He rendered perfect obedience to His Father's commandments" (*Selected Messages,* book 3, p. 133).

Knowing that the consequences of Christ's life of perfect obedience would annul His victory in Eden and vindicate the Godhead before the universe, Satan harassed and harried Jesus relentlessly. From his attempt to destroy Him when He was an infant to his effort to discourage Him on the cross, he never ceased trying to derail Christ's mission. His quest was to crush Him physically and, if that failed, to cause Him to disobey by any means possible.

But the Adam born in Bethlehem succeeded where the Adam made in Eden had failed. He who was born with a righteous nature and who developed a righteous character died with both unspoiled. By that unduplicated effort our better Adam proved that God's law is just, that Adam's sin was inexcusable, that Satan is a liar and thief of true happiness, and that by God's grace we, too, may overcome.

Jesus Knows

For we do not have a High Priest
who cannot sympathize with our weaknesses, but was in
all points tempted as we are, yet without sin. Heb. 4:15.

John, the disciple whose insights and relationship to the Second Adam were the keenest of all, concludes his record of Christ's earthly sojourn by stating: "And there are also many other things that Jesus did, which if they were written one by one, I suppose that even the world itself could not contain the books that would be written. Amen" (John 21:25).

This is true not only with respect to the miracles He performed, but also regarding the temptations He endured. The gospels record for us a few of Jesus' grueling encounters with the powers of darkness. From the very beginning of His conscious being He was besieged by temptation and trial. He was "tempted by Satan in a hundredfold severer manner" than was the first Adam (*Youth's Instructor*, June 2, 1898). His entire life was a nonstop contest with the forces of evil; "wave after wave" the temptations beat upon Him. He had no vacation, holiday, or respite from His warfare with Satan. But He won! He not only survived, but He also triumphed gloriously in negotiating the destructive rapids of temptation. And there was no species of allurement that He did not face. He was "in all points tempted as we are" (Heb. 4:15).

"All points" refers to the full range of temptations given in 1 John 2:16. Ellen White states it succinctly: "He took the nature of man, with the possibility of yielding to temptation. We have nothing to bear which He has not endured" (*The Desire of Ages*, p. 117).

He suffered all the inconveniences and ills and afflictions of the human family. And He did so more intensely than any human being before Him—this is why there is no circumstance that we can experience with which He cannot sympathize. He knows every possible species of pain and temptation. He has firsthand acquaintance with all our puzzlements and problems. His experience with sinful urges was comprehensive and all-encompassing. He conquered absolutely in His bouts with "the lust of the flesh, the lust of the eyes, and the pride of life." And this is a major reason we praise Him as our elder brother and better Adam.

How Jesus Knows

Then Jesus was led up by the Spirit
into the wilderness to be tempted by the devil. Matt. 4:1.

Some ask whether Christ, like the unfallen Adam, did not possess the evil nature with which you and I are born—if He, like Adam, came into the world without the evil propensities that are innately ours—if indeed He was not "born in sin and shaped in iniquity" (see Ps. 51:5), how can He truly know my struggles and speak of them to the Father?

The answer is He can do so because His engagements with temptations were at times so intense that although He was not driven by innate urges to sin, the intensity of His hunger for legitimate bodily satisfactions (i.e., food and water) impacted Him with force that mirrors our evil cravings.

Again Ellen White is helpful: "As soon as Christ entered the wilderness of temptation, His visage changed. . . . He felt the overwhelming tide of woe that deluged the world. He realized the strength of indulged appetite and of unholy passion that controled the world, which had brought upon man inexpressible suffering" (*Selected Messages,* book 1, p. 271).

When He fasted or lost sleep because of His long hours of work and prayer, Jesus' bodily yearnings were painful and pronounced. But these desires were not sinful; they were hunger to satisfy legitimate needs. We, too, have legitimate urges. But in addition we have urges to excess of that which is good and addictive cravings for that which is evil as well.

Jesus did not have to have the alcoholic's addiction in order to know the body's painful cries for satisfaction. The legitimate need for food after 40 days of fasting was apparent. He did not have to be naturally oriented to selfishness in order to understand our leanings in that direction. His struggle with the option to "claim the crown without the cross" that Satan presented to Him in the wilderness struck at His human nature. He did not have to commit sin to know our guilt and shame. His estrangement from the Father in Gethsemane and on the cross fully acquainted Him with this condition.

Jesus outwitted and outworked the devil in real time, in real flesh, and in real circumstances, and He therefore has a real knowledge of our situation. Because of this He came to be our pure example, our perfect sacrifice, our bona fide better Adam.

The Second Adam's Unique Temptations

For in Him dwells all the fullness of the Godhead bodily. Col. 2:9.

Jesus is our better Adam because He overcame pressures and temptations that our first Adam never knew. One was the temptation to withdraw from His mission because of His repulsion for sin. The pain felt by our absolute Adam as He dwelt in the midst of wholesale evil is a trial neither the original Adam nor his descendants could possibly feel.

Christ's holy nature was repulsed and appalled by the perversity of the society in which He lived. To have lived on earth in the best of times would have been unimaginably shocking to His being, but He came when the body of human beings, made for the dwelling place of God, had become the habitation of demons. "The senses, the nerves, the passions, the organs of men, were worked by supernatural agencies in the indulgence of the vilest lust. The very stamp of demons was impressed upon the countenances of men. Human faces reflected the expression of the legions of evil with which they were possessed" (*The Desire of Ages,* p. 36).

Another unique temptation was His need to restrain His God powers from punishing His enemies. "To be surrounded by human beings under the control of Satan was revolting to Him. And he knew that in a moment, by the flashing forth of His divine power, He could lay His cruel tormentors in the dust. This made the trial harder to bear" (*ibid.,* p. 700).

Another was the temptation to use His divine strength to relieve or support Himself in times of need. But for our sakes, He "vanquished Satan in the same nature over which in Eden Satan obtained the victory. The enemy was overcome by Christ in His human nature. The power of the Savior's Godhead was hidden. He overcame in human nature, relying upon God for power" (*The Seventh-day Adventist Bible Commentary,* Ellen G. White Comments, vol. 5, p. 1108).

Yet another (and perhaps foremost) of His unique temptations was the urge to use His God powers to escape the pain and shame of His trial and subsequent death. Angels of light were watching and would have gladly rescued their suffering Lord at Calvary and at Pilate's judgment hall. But commanding angels, mightier than they, restrained them from interfering with His dying. (*The Story of Redemption,* pp. 214, 215).

Because He suffered in all points as do we (and more intensely), and because He overcame temptations and trials that no other creature could possibly know, He qualifies as the original Adam's superior—the successful Savior, the hero of universal admiration, and the worthy recipient of unending praise of the grateful redeemed.

The Second Adam's Ability to Die

And without controversy great is the mystery of godliness: God was manifested in the flesh, justified in the Spirit, seen by angels, preached among the Gentiles, believed on in the world, received up in glory. 1 Tim. 3:16.

The mystery of the Incarnation is equaled by the mystery of the Resurrection. Neither is explainable in human terms; both will be the focus of rapt investigation throughout eternity. This much, however, we now understand. At the Incarnation, the Divine God took upon His person flesh that was perishable; a body, like ours, is subject to death. At the Crucifixion, that body did truly expire. His human nature ceased to be; the form that lay in Joseph's new tomb was a lifeless corpse. The human Jesus died.

But the Divine Christ did not die. The body in which He presented Himself to humanity did. But Divinity, by definition, cannot cease to be. God is not capable of being reduced to the state of nothingness.

We are no more knowledgeable about the process by which the Divine God divorced Himself from the human Jesus on Calvary than we are the manner by which they became connected at Bethlehem. We do know, however, that Christ the Creator did not die, and Jesus the Redeemer did not stay dead. He had promised: "Destroy this temple, and in three days I will raise it up" (John 2:19). And on the third day He rose. The human Jesus swallowed death, but death could not digest in Him. He had the physical capacity to die, but not the moral guilt that makes death a "forever" reality.

Because His spiritual nature never knew sin, He did not deserve to die. He was able to die, but was innocent of death's necessity. He was capable, but not culpable—vulnerable, but not a violator. He died not because of His sin, but because of ours. "Our sins were laid on Christ, punished in Christ, put away by Christ, in order that His righteousness might be imputed to us" (*Signs of the Times,* May 30, 1895).

Upon Him who knew no sin, the guilt of all was laid. Although He knew infirmity, because He knew not iniquity, the God who was justified in slaying Him was exonerated in sparing His body from decomposition and accepting Him as our loving, living, better Adam.

Humanity Goes to Heaven

This hope we have as an anchor of the soul, both sure and steadfast, and which enters the Presence behind the veil. Heb. 6:19.

The adopted form of humanity that Jesus assumed when He came into our world was not discarded when He left. He did not rise from the grave as a ghost or aberration or, having jettisoned His humanity, fade back into eternity in His pre-earth status—His "God only" form. He came into our world "Divinity wrapped up in humanity"; He returned to glory humanity wrapped up in Divinity.

There is, of course, a major difference in the human form that He now retains. It does not contain the physical deformities borne in the body He wore on earth. The delightful form that God gave humans in Eden, so tragically marred by transgression, has been restored in the person of our Second Adam. Thus the human race is now yoked with the Father more closely than when in Eden.

"That he should carry his adopted nature to the throne of God, and there present His children to the Father, to have conferred upon them an honor exceeding that conferred upon the angels—this is the marvel of the heavenly universe, the mystery into which angels desire to look. This is love that melts the sinner's heart" (*Sons and Daughters of God,* p. 22).

There are many ways to gain the attention of those who are ignorant of God's Word. We can teach them the dates of prophecy, the rules of faith and the benefits of reform: health reform, dress reform, tithe reform, family reform, education reform, etc. We can also arrest their interest with the blessed promises of the Word and the logic and value of the unfailing principles of Scripture. But there is no truth so wondrous, so attractive or so binding to Calvary than the innocent Jesus dying for a guilty world and then returning to glory with an adopted human nature.

The thought that the blessed Son of God successfully fulfilled the "operation rescue" and returned home to pierce the veil of separation that sin erected in Eden is the essence of the gospel. It is the kernel of the Christian's hope, the primary weapon of gospel armament, and the precious summary of the sacrificial contribution of our better Adam.

Numbered With the Transgressors

For I say to you that this which is written must still be
accomplished in Me. "And He was numbered with the transgressors."
For the things concerning Me have an end. Luke 22:37.

When was the Second Adam counted as a sinner? It was not when He was an infant, for as the angel proclaimed He came a holy being (Luke 1:35). It was not when He was a youth, for He "increased in wisdom, and stature, and in favor with God and men" (Luke 2:52). And it was not when He was the itinerate teacher going about doing good—so much good that if the whole story were told, it would fill all the books in the world (see John 21:25). When, then, did He fulfill His role as the sinful one? He did so in the Garden of Gethsemane when He entered the final phase of His services on earth.

There He who had been the intercessor for others needed an intercessor. For the first time in all eternity, He became estranged from His Father. Before Gethsemane He and the Father were one; always perfectly synchronized in thought and action. But in the Garden of Gethsemane, where He took upon Himself the sins of the world, He who had been God's friend became His foe—the object of His wrath. Going into Gethsemane, He not only crossed over this Brook Kidron (John 18:1) but also crossed over the bridge of destiny from entering with God to identify with evil.

Ellen White remarks of His entry into Gethsemane "Now He seemed to be shut out from the light of God's sustaining presence. Now He was numbered with the transgressors. The guilt of fallen humanity He must bear. Upon Him who knew no sin must be laid the iniquity of us all" (*The Desire of Ages*, p. 685). And: "Christ was now standing in a different attitude from that in which He had ever stood before" (*ibid.*, p. 686).

Jesus not only stepped away from the throne of His glory to tabernacle with humanity, but also by pulling our sins over His sinless humanity He made himself absolutely vulnerable to Heaven's response to evil—He became a curse (Gal. 3:13). He who had been the "forgiver of sins" became the "bearer of sins" and was made a sacrifice for us all.

It was the pressure of our iniquities that numbered Him both with the transgressor and as the transgressor. It was the weight of our iniquities that crushed His great heart. It is the fact of His sacrifice that melts our wills and inspires our daily devotion.

The Baptism of Jesus

When He had been baptized, Jesus came up immediately from the water; and behold, the heavens were open to Him, and He saw the Spirit of God descending like a dove and alighting upon Him. Matt. 3:16.

There are two primary reasons why at Jordon Jesus presented Himself for baptism. The first was His wish as head of the race (our better Adam) to represent repentant sinners to God. Later in Gethsemane He covered Himself with our sins and literally became a curse. But the confession, repentance, and baptism He engaged at Jordan were symbolically done. Jesus had not committed any sin, and therefore He needed no repentance.

Inspiration records: "Christ honored the ordinance of baptism by submitting to this rite. In this act He identified Himself with His people as their representative and head. As their substitute, He takes upon Him their sins . . . taking the steps the sinner is required to take, and doing the work the sinner must do" (*Review and Herald*, Jan. 21, 1873).

The second reason for His baptism was His desire to give a clear example for us to follow. As Romans 6:3, 4 remind us, it is His death, burial, and resurrection that baptism commemorates. As He literally died and was buried and resurrected, so we must die to sin and rise to newness of life. All other forms of baptism fail to adequately commemorate the sacrifice of Christ. No other form of baptism, no matter how sincerely engaged, is fully obedient to His clear example.

There is a sense that the act of baptism is also symbolic for us, but its reasons are not—We are guilty! We are in need of repentance and the change of spiritual orientation that baptism expresses. Unlike our Second Adam, we do have a preconversion state that baptism establishes as null and void.

The Second Adam has shown us the way. Only by being submerged, like the eunuch who deacon Philip took "down into the water" (Acts 8:38) do we accurately follow the example of our better Adam and declare to our family and friends that we have made complete surrender to the Lord of our lives.

Jesus' Method of Victory

But He answered and said, "It is written, 'Man shall not live by bread alone, but by every word that proceeds from the mouth of God.'" Matt. 4:4.

Jesus did not utilize His Divinity to defend or deliver His humanity in the constant struggle with His adversary Satan. Within the fleshly form that the people beheld lived the one who "spoke, and it was done; . . . commanded, and it stood fast" (Ps. 33:9). He did not need the Father's help to reduce hospital census to zero, to put morticians out of business, or, as occurred, to leave whole villages without sick inhabitants. The voice that stilled the troubled lake of Galilee was the voice that spoke oceans into existence; and had He not called Lazarus by name when summoning him from the grave, all the sleeping dead would have risen. He never used the Divine powers residing within to refresh His weariness, to escape temptation, or to avenge His enemies. Had He done so, Satan would have justifiably accused Him of succeeding with advantages not afforded to Adam or any of his descendants.

Jesus engaged life on earth with fallible, earthly equipment. It was by trusting in the Father, by seeking Him in prayer, and by dependence upon the same spiritual promises and principles that are available to us that He found both the will and strength to endure.

There is an old Negro spiritual that asks, "If Jesus had to pray, what about me?" And what about us? Are we, by unbroken communion with God, finding overcoming power? Are we, as Christ encourages us to be, branches attached to the vine absorbing nourishment and nurture for godly living?

Our lives will never equal His in goodness or beauty, but we can, in our sphere and circumstance, reflect His holiness as we grow daily into His likeness. Yes, we can "grow in grace" (2 Peter 3:18); we can "love not the world, neither the things that are in the world" (1 John 2:15, KJV); we can cast all our cares upon Him (1 Peter 5:7); we can do the will of His Father which is in heaven; we can take His yoke upon us and find rest (Matt. 11:29); we can trust and obey; we can "die daily" (1 Cor. 15:31); we can be kept from falling (Ps. 56:13); we can "rejoice and be exceedingly glad" (Matt. 5:12); we can in honor, prefer one another (Rom. 12:10); we can "do all things through Christ who strengthens us" (Phil. 4:13); we can daily mature into the likeness of our Lord.

But if we are to approximate His life of dedication and service, we must imitate His habits of devotion and surrender.

Overcoming Adam's Lethal Legacy

Behold, I was brought forth in iniquity,
and in sin my mother conceived me. Ps. 51:5.

How bad is the damage to human spirituality caused by Adam's sin? Our spiritual natures are totally evil, disastrously defective, and on this side of the Second Coming nonreversible. Only when our Lord returns and "this mortal has put on immortality" and "this corruptible has put on incorruption" (1 Cor. 15:54) will humans be restored into the moral purity with which we were created. This will be the destiny of the saved alone—for the wicked, there is no change. The state of innocence will never be theirs.

Please note, however, that even the process of conversion does not bring us back to the quality of purity that we lost in Eden. True, it places Jesus upon the throne room of our hearts and controls the fallen nature so that it no longer enslaves us (Rom. 6:12), but the reason we must die daily is that the old nature, Adam's lethal legacy, has for 6,000 years poisoned the stream of human existence—though subdued by grace, it ever remains and clamors for supremacy.

Of this state of being Ellen White comments, when speaking of the apostle Paul: "That he might not run uncertainly or at random in the Christian race, Paul subjected himself to severe training. The words 'I keep under my body,' literally mean to beat back by severe discipline the desires, impulses, and passions" (*The Acts of the Apostles*, p. 314). And: "Paul was ever on the watch lest evil propensities should get the better of him. He guarded well his appetites and passions and evil propensities" (*The Seventh-day Adventist Bible Commentary*, Ellen G. White Comments, vol. 6, p. 1089). So deep is our perversity, so radical the effect of the Fall that, no matter how sincere the surrender, we remain "sin positive" as long as we live.

The triumph that is our "growth in grace" is life's greatest miracle. The Spirit of God through the Word of God, which can give us victory over evil tendencies (inherited and cultivated), is exhibit A of God's redeeming power.

How reassuring, then, to remember this day that though I may be sorely tempted, there resides with me and within me a power that "keeps me from falling" and provides me continuing spiritual success and satisfaction.

Jesus' Formula for Victory

Then Jesus was led up by the Spirit into the wilderness
to be tempted by the devil. And when He had fasted forty days
and forty nights, afterward He was hungry. Matt. 4:1, 2.

Jesus' formula for victory included the following elements. First, He did not pause to reason or rationalize with the tempter. His conclusive reply to Lucifer's repeated enticements was "Away from me, Satan!" (Matt. 4:10, NIV). He did not barter with Satan; He did not try to outwit, outflank or outtalk him. Lesson? Refusing to be lured into debate with evil is a valuable aid to obedience.

Second, He entered into the conflict with Satan thoroughly fortified by prayer. The 40 days and nights that preceded Lucifer's arrival to tempt Him were spent in deep devotion. Lesson? Praying *as* we process through our trials is necessary. But just as crucial to spiritual victory is praying *before* the storms arise.

Third, Jesus relied upon Scripture for direction and strength. His "it is written" reply to each of Satan's temptations reveals familiarity with the Word of God gained through long years of study and meditation. Lesson? Knowing God through acquaintance with Scripture is critical to spiritual victory.

It is the Word of God that undergirds all our overcoming. The written word contains the same creative powers that brought the worlds into existence when He "spoken and it was done" (Ps. 33:9). That is because as our tentacles of faith grow deeper and deeper into the soil of Scripture they absorb more and more of the rich minerals whereby we develop and produce the fruits and flowers of righteousness.

The Bible is all good: the tedious genealogical listings of Leviticus and Numbers reveal God's hand in history; the detailed laws of Leviticus speak to His fair and loving personality; the science of Job instructs us; the poetry of Psalms inspires us; the wisdom of Solomon enlightens us; the predictions of the major and minor prophets, fulfilled throughout time, reassure us. "The Old Testament is the New Testament concealed, and the New Testament is the Old Testament revealed." And they are, in entirety, calculated to awaken our love, establish our faith, and keep us in the path of obedience.

Redeeming Adam's Failure

And the angel answered and said to her,
"The Holy Spirit will come upon you, and the power of the
Highest will overshadow you: therefore, also, that Holy One
who is to be born will be called the Son of God." Luke 1:35.

A primary role of the second Adam was verification of the first Adam's ability (properly connected with God) to resist any and all temptations presented by Satan.

The second Adam succeeded gloriously in this respect. He did so by a flawless performance under circumstances a thousand times more difficult than those that the first Adam faced. The original Adam fell in Eden; the second succeeded in Nazareth—from a place from where, some stated, "no good thing could come" (see John 1:46).

As the spotless lily blooms in fragrant perfection upon the muddy, slimy pond, so Jesus, possessing our physical infirmities but not our spiritual imperfections, blossomed pure and holy in the mire of His unclean, unhealthy surroundings. The fact that He overcame, under conditions contrasting those of perfect Eden, makes His triumph all the more stunning.

Like the first Adam, it was possible for Him to sin (*Steps to Christ*, p. 62); unlike him, He never did. Like the first Adam, Jesus began "without a taint of sin" (*The Seventh-day Adventist Bible Commentary*, Ellen G. White Comments, vol. 7, p. 925); unlike him, He remained that way. Like the first Adam, He began with no "inclination" to evil (*ibid.*, vol. 5, p. 1128); unlike him He never leaned in that direction. Like the first Adam, He came into the world without the evil propensities and passions of our fallen nature (see *ibid.*); unlike him, He retained that purity and is the only person in human history so distinguished.

The richness of Christ's victory where Adam failed is graphically expressed in the words "Christ is called the second Adam. In purity and holiness, connected with God and beloved by God, He began where the first Adam began. Willingly, he passed over the ground where Adam fell, and redeemed Adam's failure" (*Youth's Instructor*, June 2, 1898).

Thus the substitute: the original, the replacement, the primary—the Adam of our salvation—the Adam of our origination. All praise and honor to Christ, the conquering Lamb.

Our Faithful Adam

And Adam was not deceived, but the woman
being deceived, fell into transgression. 1 Tim. 2:14.

Eve's initial mistake was ignoring God's instructions to stay by her husband's side. Adam's critical error was to doubt God's ability to both recompense Eve and preserve the happiness he knew. Eve's transgression began the chain of woeful events. But Adam's mistake sealed the deal that settled our fall into transgression and its consequences.

Adam is the primary culprit because God gave him primary accountability. He was chiefly responsible for the order of things. Eve, the second of created humans, the final and crowning act of God's creative genius, was in a real sense the more highly privileged. This is because Adam was tasked to care for her: to shelter and protect her, to provide for her, to guarantee her welfare and safety. But he failed. Not because he was deceived, but because he was deficient in trust of the Father's love.

However, the second Adam reversed this. By contrast, He trusted the Father absolutely. Even on the cross when His faith could not see beyond the portals of the grave, when He suffered alone and "there was none to help" (see Ps. 107:12). He was faithful unto death.

It was there that His faithfulness glowed the brightest. He suffered not just the physical pain of crucifixion, but also the most searing of all life's agonies—the hurt of repudiation by loved ones and friends. His disciples rejected Him, and even more crushing to His spirit, He was renounced by the Father Himself. His confidence bent under the load, but it did not break; His faith sagged, but it did not succumb.

You and I live 2,000 years beyond Calvary's triumph. But the same tensions of belief and doubt, trust and fear, faith and obedience that Jesus engaged impinge upon us daily. We can be victorious only as we depend upon Him who modeled on our behalf—our loving, loyal Second Adam.

Hope for the Human Race

*And I will put enmity between you and the woman,
and between your seed and her Seed; He shall bruise
your head, and you shall bruise His heel. Gen. 3:15.*

Right there on the scene of the crime, while His creatures cowered in speechless fear, God gave them (and us) the promise of a Redeemer. Our first parents clung tenaciously to that pledge. They sorely missed the peace and beauty of Eden and were anxious to reestablish their open communion with God—the invigorating face-to-face consultations of happier days. The birth of their first son (Cain) and that of each succeeding generation was greeted with the hope that the Messiah had arrived. But it was three millennia after their death, 4,000 years after sin began wreaking havoc upon the human race, that Jesus came.

When superstition had reached its broadest and ignorance its deepest, when immorality had assumed its boldest and longevity its briefest, a voice was heard in heaven saying, "A body hast thou prepared me" (Heb. 10:5, KJV). With that announcement, Jesus parachuted behind the enemy's lines and, in the midst of the kingdom of darkness, established His own dear kingdom of light. To the everlasting astonishment of loyal angels, He counted the cost and endured the loss of divine privilege that we might be restored to favor again.

Satan did "bruise His heel" (Gen. 3:15) at Calvary. He inflicted upon His person the dreadful blows of crucifixion; but its effects were not permanent. Jesus, on the other hand, through the very act of dying, inflicted upon Satan the "head wound" of eternal defeat. By paying our debt and assuring our righteousness, He has cleared the way for the Father's forgiveness of the repentant and His destruction of the disobedient.

There are some in Abraham's physical lineage who look still for the Messiah's appearing. For them, the second Adam is not yet a reality. We, however, see His grand miraculous birth, His genuine life, His generous death, His glorious resurrection, and the greatness of the promised Spirit—incontrovertible proof of His Messiahship, and for the willing and obedient, grand entrance into Paradise regained.

The Second Adam's Disadvantages

For to this you were called, because Christ also suffered for us,
leaving us an example, that you should follow His steps. 1 Peter 2:21.

Compared to the original Adam, Jesus was severely disadvantaged. When Adam ate, he was not hungry—Jesus fasted 40 days and nights when accosted by Satan in the wilderness. Adam's initial responsibility was for Eve and himself—Jesus' was that of the entire universe. Adam began with the gift of conditional immortality—Jesus with the garment of mortality.

Jesus was greatly disadvantaged in comparison to us as well. We do not, as the Second Adam, live under the burden of earth's rescue or the vindication of God's character, or the welfare of the universe as consequence of our actions.

And not to be forgotten is what must have been Christ's most gnawing temptation—utilizing His God powers to defend His honor, to relieve His pain, and even to retaliate against His enemies. At every juncture or place of trial, "He could have called ten thousand angels!" But in a manifestation of self-control too wonderful for human understanding, He refused to do so. He endured as we must endure.

We cannot equal or replicate His level of endurance. Why? Because we do not possess the powers of creation and destruction, He found it necessary to restrain while among us. Our pull to self-gratification would not permit us such self-control.

Nevertheless we must endlessly strive to reach His high standard of performance. We cannot do this by working through a list of do's and don'ts of behavior, but we can by surrendering our willful pride to Him and by keeping our eyes on Him who is our example and source of power, and not on others. And we do so by being so affected by His love that we would rather die than transgress; by remembering that when we sin, we "crucify Him afresh" (see Heb. 6:6); and by daily indulgence in meaningful prayer and study of His word.

None of this—in fact, all of this—cannot make us as absolutely perfect as is He, but it will mold us in His likeness and bring joy to His loving heart.

The Dominion Restored

And you, O tower of the flock, the stronghold
of the daughter of Zion, to you shall it come, even the former
dominion shall come, the kingdom of the daughter of Jerusalem. Micah 4:8.

When Adam sinned, he lost the dominion over earth that had been granted him. He was told when he was created that he was not only to name the animals and plants but also that he was ruler over all creation. What a splendid creation that was! Forests filled with trees that spiraled toward the cloudless sky in unbroken symmetry, vast fields of flowers that budded in charming designs, and happy streams that laced the landscape spraying clouds of misty dew that watered the earth.

The animal kingdom was no less attractive. Its colorful, docile members were a delight to see and a joy to touch and study. The same condition applied to the fish and fowl that also revealed the rich imagination of the Creator, who in love made humans for His joy and gave them a prefect, peaceful dominion of vast and varied beauty.

Sin changed all of this. By transgression, Adam forfeited his right and lost his rule. Paradise perfected became paradise polluted. Satan assumed the godship of this world. We still see God's handiwork in the interlacing immensity, regularity, variety, and beauty of nature. But the thorny rose, the snarled oaks, the toxic plants, the venomous serpents, the carnivorous animals, and the savagery of the food chain that turns creature upon creature in the skies, on the ground, and within the ocean's depths are ever-present evidences of the baleful results of the Fall.

But Satan's reign is temporary. The Second Adam, by His life and death, already regained dominion rights. What the first Adam lost because of Satan's subterfuge has been restored by Jesus' sacrifice. Satan's rule has been forever annulled, and at the Savior's second return the Adam who started the race will be restored to leadership next to the Adam who saved us. Then with the eternally redeemed, you and I, dear reader, will forever enjoy the delights of Eden regained highlighted by companionship with our Lord.

God With Us

Therefore, when Christ came into the world, he said; "Sacrifice and offering you did not desire, but a body you prepared for me." Heb. 10:5, NIV.

There were times during Christ's life when His physical exterior, though perfect in its humanity, was too weak to contain the God within. During those times divinity flashed through humanity, dazzling the company around Him.

It happened as He responded to His parents' anxiety during the Temple visit (Luke 2:41) when "on His face was a light . . . divinity was flashing through humanity" (*The Desire of Ages*, p. 81). It happened when, in the wilderness of temptation, He refused Satan's final allurements with "it is written" (Matt. 4:10). It happened when, as He cleansed the Temple, they "looking upon Christ" saw divinity flash through the garb of humanity" (*ibid.*, p. 158). It happened when, as He prayed on the Mount of Transfiguration, "Divinity from within flashes through humanity, and meets the glory coming from above" (*ibid.*, p. 421). It happened when He said, "Lazarus come forth" (John 11:43); His face was "lighted up by the glory of God," and the people saw the assurance of His power" (*ibid.*, p. 536). It happened again when, approached by the bloodthirsty mob in the Garden of Gethsemane (John 18:1-5), "a divine light illuminated the Savior's face and a dovelike form overshadowed Him. . . . Priests, elders, soldiers, and even Judas, fell as dead men to the ground" (*ibid.*, p. 694). And it happened on the final night of His life as He responded affirmatively to Caiaphas' inquiry regarding His divinity (Matt. 26:63, 64). "the divinity of Christ flashed through His guise of humanity" (*ibid.*, p. 707).

These manifestations emphasize in a dramatic way the coexistence of God and humanity in the person of our Second Adam. A primary aspect of this investigation will be the saving restraint of the God within who, while occasionally piercing the veil humanity in which He was housed, never intervened in the Savior's struggles; the divine Christ never gave Satan reason to complain that the human Jesus benefited by assistance unavailable to the rest of struggling humanity. This is a sacrifice unexplainable in human terms, an act of grace unequaled in time, and a gift of love beyond comprehension, but requisite to belief.

Alive in Jesus

For as in Adam all die, so in Christ shall all be made alive. 1 Cor. 15:22.

To be born a son or daughter of Adam is to be born spiritually as well as physically miswired. The moral materials of all infants consist of perpetual propensities to transgression. Adam's is a lasting tragedy.

The second birth reverses this otherwise helpless condition. It subdues and re-
presses the evil urges with which we are born so that they no longer have dominion
over our fallen nature. Conversion is the process whereby these are placed in remission. As Romans 6, 11, and 12 tells us where Christ abides sin no longer dominates.

There is more good news. Conversion not only subdues the evil impulses of the
sinful nature that we inherit, but it also removes the sinful propensities we acquire.
In other words the evil urges with which we are born can be subdued or repressed.
However, those that we acquire or cultivate during our journey through life can and
must be completely eliminated.

Our prophet encourages us with regard to victory over the evil drives we inherit in this way: "Our natural propensities must be controlled" (*Testimonies for
the Church,* vol. 4, p. 235), and "you must make constant effort to curb . . . evil
propensities" (*ibid.,* vol. 5, p. 335).

However, in describing victory over the evil tendencies we acquire, she states:
"Nonsense and amusement-loving propensities should be discarded, as out of
place in the life and experience of those who are living by faith in the Son of God"
(*Messages to Young People,* p. 42). And: "We must realize that through belief in
Him it is our privilege to be partakers of the divine nature, and so escape the cor-
ruption that is in the world through lust. Then we are cleansed from all sin, all
defects of character. We need not retain one sinful propensity" (*The Seventh-day
Adventist Bible Commentary,* Ellen G. White Comments, vol. 7, p. 943).

Since both our inherited (nature provided) and cultivated (character acquired)
tendencies are overcome by the Spirit's power (the former controlled and the latter
dismissed), we who are thoroughly surrendered to His will are justified in claiming
salvation—made alive in Christ Jesus, our knowing and necessary Second Adam.

The Beginning of the End

All we like sheep have gone astray; we have turned, every one, to his own way; and the Lord has laid on Him the iniquity of us all. Isa. 53:6.

Christ's sacrificial service had its ultimate fulfillment on the cross. There, He finalized His earthly ministry on our behalf. All of His service for us was critical. But it was on the cross that His substitutionary work pinnacled. There He donned our sins, paid our debt, and sealed His will so rich with righteous gifts.

The road to Calvary was led through Gethsemane. John's description of this first step of the final phase of Christ's earthly journey is given in the verse that reads: "[Jesus] went out with His disciples over the brook Kidron, where there was a garden" (John 18:1).

As He entered the garden, Jesus transitioned from the sunshine of the Father's love into the shadows of the cross. His status changed from "commandment keeper" to commandment breaker," from "friend of God" to "foe of God," from "ally" to "enemy," from intercessor to one who needed intercession, from the sunshine of God's love to the cloudy formations of His wrath. He not only crossed over the Brook Kidron, but He also crossed over "highway happiness;" He reversed roles from subject of His Father's care to object of His anger.

In Gethsemane, with "groanings which cannot be uttered," He pulled our sins upon His sinless self and thereby attracted the thunderbolts of God's anger against sin. Zechariah described this act of wondrous substitution when he wrote: "Awake, O sword, against My Shepherd, against the Man who is My companion" (Zech. 13:7). Ellen White gave it summary conclusion when she wrote: "Our sins were laid on Christ, punished in Christ, put away by Christ, in order that His righteousness might be imputed to us" (*Signs of the Times,* May 30, 1895).

In all His life Jesus had borne our weaknesses, carried our sorrows, and suffered our infirmities. But now in Gethsemane He added to the consequences of sin that His humanity already bore—sin itself. Now he was not simply numbered with the transgressors, He was numbered as a transgressor. Thus "He paid a debt He did not owe because we owed a debt we could not pay." This thought more than any other, illumines our minds, captures our hearts, and stimulates our energies to obedience and service.

The Triumph in Gethsemane

Saying, "Father, if it is Your will, take this cup away from Me; nevertheless not My will, but Yours, be done." Luke 22:42.

There are two encounters in Jesus' lifelong struggle with Lucifer that highlight most clearly His sacrificial suffering. They are the wilderness confrontation at the beginning of His ministry and the Gethsemane encounter at His journey's end.

The victory gained in the wilderness was pivotal in that it established in Lucifer's mind the great difficulty that he would have in deterring the Messiah in His mission. It also established for Jesus the intensity of engagement that was to follow. The wilderness encounter was pivotal, but Gethsemane was in some ways even more determinative—it was here that His victory was sealed.

Satan had failed to destroy Him at His birth, to deceive Him in the wilderness, or discourage or derail Him at any stage of His ministry. It was with absolute desperation that he assailed Him at Gethsemane. What he failed to accomplish throughout the Savior's ministry, he sought now to secure in the final hours of His life; he would spoil things at the end. All of Christ's prior victories would be nullified, and Calvary a sham, if in Gethsemane, he could cause Him to yield to the urge to escape the painful, shameful cross and abandon His mission of mercy.

There in Gethsemane Jesus became our sin-bearer; the weight of every sin ever committed pressed upon His frame literally crushing out His life. So severe was the pain that He would have died there in the garden had not the angel of God come to encourage Him, telling Him in essence, "Hold on Jesus, you are almost there, your mission is almost finished, you are almost home."

The Second Adam's faithful firmness under pressure in Gethsemane sharply contrasted the first Adam's faithless faltering in Eden. Eden and Gethsemane's conditions are opposites—they are polar extremes, and so are the responses of the Adams they housed. The first Adam ate in Paradise and lost his happy home; the Second Adam drank from the bitter cup of suffering and reclaimed our paradise lost; the first Adam doubted the Creator's care and yielded to temptation; the Second Adam could not see beyond the grave, but trusted His Father's love, and by this act, gloriously succeeded as our willing, wondrous, blessed, better Adam.

The Meeting of the Adams

For as in Adam all die, even so in Christ all shall be made alive. But each one in his own order: Christ the firstfruits, afterward those who are Christ's at His coming. 1 Cor. 15:22, 23.

A mong those who will rise to life everlasting will be Adam, the father of our race. He will, in his resurrected form, be taller, more robust, and more impressive in physical form than any other of the redeemed.

But as stately and attractive as He will be, there will be one even more lovely and imposing in appearance—Jesus our Redeemer. He, the prince of heaven, the one altogether lovely, the tower of the flock, the good and faithful shepherd, the diadem of glory, the lily of the valley, the Rose of Sharon, the bright and morning star, our second Adam, will be the center of universal attraction. We shall behold him close up and personal and note, with joyful appreciation, the holes in His hands and feet from whence emanate radiant diadems of love, the halo of His brow once scarred for our rescue, and the glowing from His side where the jagged spear was thrust. All these shine with iridescent beauty making Him heaven's stellar attraction.

One of the first activities of our eternal beginnings will be the meeting of the two Adams. All heaven and earth will be in breathless anticipation as the original Adam, for the first time since Eden, meets face to face with his Creator, his worthy substitute and Savior—the King who condescended to take his place; the Lord who stunned all creation by coming to redeem His failure.

While adoring angels and the redeemed behold, the Adams meet. The second reassures the first of his forgiveness and points him to his rescued posterity declaring that all was not lost, that God's love has triumphed over Satan's anger, and that "where sin abounded, grace abounded much more" (Rom. 5:20).

The Adams embrace—the Adam who mixed us up with the Adam who fixed us up; the Adam who pulled us down with the Adam who turned us around; the Adam who plunged us into sin and the Adam who brought us back again; the Adam who started the Fall and the Adam who died for us all. We will then begin an endless eternity of thanksgiving for our Second Adam's rescue from ruin.

The Adams Compared

And so it is written, "The first man Adam became a living being."
The last Adam became a life-giving spirit. 1 Cor. 15:45.

The Adam of Eden had no quickening power. He was product, not producer; actor, not author; creature, not creator. The Second Adam, however, was the self-existent Son of God; He was (and is) the source of all life and the fountain of all our universal energy. Whatever "is" began with Him. But He did not make evil; it is the souring of the good He did create.

Evil is the misuse of the power of choice that cost Lucifer his high place in glory and plunged the first family and all their descendants into the night of sin that has for so long engulfed our world. Adam had no ability to reverse that decline, and neither do we.

The prophet Jeremiah expressed our helpless plight when overcome by our sad reality. He cried: "Is there no balm in Gilead, is there no physician there?" (Jer. 8:22). David, the sweet salter of Israel, affirmatively answers: He is a God "who forgives all your iniquities, who heals all your diseases, who redeems your life from destruction, who crowns you with lovingkindness and tender mercies" (Ps. 103:3, 4); "He heals the brokenhearted and binds up their wounds" (Ps. 147:3).

The first Adam's wounds were self-inflicted—the Last Adam's wounds were selflessly accepted; the first Adam forfeited his conditional immortality—the Last Adam voluntarily surrendered His; the first Adam was brokenhearted because of his sin—the Last Adam's heart was broken because of ours; the first Adam's body remained in the ground—the Last Adam rose from the grave; the first Adam brought us eternal death—the Last Adam gave us everlasting life; the first Adam sacrificed the blood of lambs—the Last Adam sacrificed His own blood; the first Adam perpetuated the gospel by the spoken Word—the Last Adam has passed the good news to us by His written Word. By that Word we are reborn, by that Word we are spiritually sustained, and by that Word we are given faith and life and the hope of eternity.

AUGUST

A Better Witness

A Crisis of Communication

But your iniquities have separated you from your God;
and your sins have hidden His face from you. Isa. 59:2.

God is a consuming fire (Heb. 12:29). That is to say, He is so morally pure that He radiates glowing energy. Yet in the garden of our beginnings He conversed with us "one on one." He held personal conversations with us; He interfaced directly with His creatures. Because we were absolutely pure in both nature and character, we needed no one to interpret or translate for us to God or God to us. Our status permitted face-to-face, heart-to-heart communication with our Creator.

Of this original state the prophet wrote, "Graceful and symmetrical in form, regular and beautiful in feature, their countenances glowing with a tint of health and the light of joy and hope, they bore in outward resemblance the likeness of their Maker" (*Education*, p. 20). And, "Man was to bear God's image, both in outward resemblance and in character. . . . His nature was in harmony with the will of God. His mind was capable of comprehending divine things. His affections were pure; his appetites and passions were under the control of reason. He was holy and happy in bearing the image of God and in perfect obedience to His will" (*Patriarchs and Prophets*, p. 45).

In consequence of sin, the first pair forfeited both their rule and their privileged interface with their Maker. Proximity to "the burning fire" of His presence would have resulted in instant cremation. It is in mercy that our face-to-face communication was annulled.

But we were not left without hope. By visions of godly prophets, by visitations from angels, by the voice of the Holy Spirit, and by the most effective means of all, the very presence of His dear Son, we who have been saved from sin and grafted back by grace have hope.

By what instrument, we may ask, is our severed relationship sustained? It is only through the Word of God. Reading it provides audience with Him that informs, inspires, and empowers. Our sins did separate us from Him, but in the "wideness of His mercy" poured forth in His Word we are restored to life-giving fellowship and favor.

An Effective Cure

Then God saw everything that He had made, and indeed it was very good.
So the evening and the morning were the sixth day. Gen. 1:31.

After each of His acts of creation, God said, "it is good." But after His crowning work, the creation of a being in His image, His appraisal was "it [is] very good."

Everything that He had placed on earth was perfect. All of creation witnessed to the mind of the being with who originates loveliness, symmetry, harmony, fragrance, and order. But humanity was His masterpiece. Blessed with bodies nourished by blood streaming through miles of veins activated by a pump calibrated to last forever; controlled by a brain that receives sensations from five unmarred senses (sight, hearing, touch, taste, and smell); all made mobile by muscles, joints, and sinews functioning in perfect tandem with the will of their possessor—Adam and Eve were a marvel of form and function.

However, sin changed all this; it produced an infectious virus that short-circuited both our physical and spiritual processes, rendering the perfect creatures God had made defective, deranged, and doomed to extinction.

Several years ago, while lying in an emergency room in a prominent East Coast hospital, I was told that I had "third-degree heart block"; and because of swelling in the tissue around my heart, the electrical signals that told my heart to beat were being shut down. The cardiologist stated that the insertion of a pacemaker was necessary. However, not being certain that I had the luxury of waiting for that procedure, he ordered an "external pacemaker" placed on my chest "just in case." Further diagnosis revealed that I had the dreaded Lyme disease, and with proper antibiotic treatment the infection would probably be cleared and the heart blockage reversed. Gratefully, this is what happened.

This is what happened to the human race. We are all, by nature, victimized by the bite of sin. The poison of transgression has disastrously interfered with our needed spiritual impulses; our diagnosis is dire. But there is a solution—the Word of God! It is the only effective antidote for our condition. Infused by the power of the Holy Spirit, it restores us to the proper relationship with the Lord and returns us to happy, healthy, holy communion with our Maker.

All These Things

Then the Lord God took the man and put him
in the Garden of Eden to tend and keep it. Gen. 2:15.

The inspired Ellen White describes Adam's position as leader of creation as: king in Eden (*The Seventh-day Adventist Bible Commentary*, Ellen G. White Comments, vol. 1, p. 1082), head of the earthly family (*Testimonies for the Church*, vol. 6, p. 236), lord in his beautiful domain (*ibid.*, vol. 3, p. 153), father and representative of the whole human family (*Patriarchs and Prophets*, p. 48), and, very appropriately, vicegerent of the Creator (*The Desire of Ages*, p. 129).

When Satan confronted the Lord in the wilderness, he offered Him the kingdoms of the world as if they were his to give—but they were not. He had indeed wrested the keys from Adam and usurped his power. But Adam was not an independent ruler. Because "the earth is the Lord's, and the fulness thereof" (Ps. 24:1, KJV), his was delegated authority. even though he had betrayed God's trust into Satan's hands, Christ was and has ever been earth's rightful king.

Adam and Eve's delegated authority was as vast and complete as the broad planet on which they were placed. Their instructions were: "Be fruitful, and multiply, and replenish the earth, and subdue it: and have dominion over the fish of the sea, and over the fowl of the air, and over every living thing that moveth upon the earth. . . . [And] every herb bearing seed, which is upon the face of all the earth, and every tree, in the which is the fruit of a tree yielding seed" (Gen. 1:29, 30, KJV). But the totality of "all these things" was forfeited by their transgression.

Jesus, however, reclaimed the "lost dominion." He has wrested back full authority and will restore "all these things" and more to the redeemed—and not in the deteriorated condition in which they were offered by the tempter. His promise is, "Behold, I make all things new" (Rev. 21:5).

One day we who now "walk by faith and not by sight," who can "see through the glass darkly," will with all tears wiped away be restored as happy occupants of Paradise! Then we shall live and reign with Him forever, for iniquity and its separating power will not rise again to interrupt our rule. The prospects are thrilling, the promise is sure; the provider is the conquering Lamb of the tribe of Judah—our victorious, better witness.

The Test of Loyalty

But of the tree of the knowledge of good and evil you shall not eat,
but in the day that you eat of it you shall surely die. Gen. 2:17.

The first great test that God gave His creatures involved their time; one seventh of each week (the Sabbath) was to be dedicated to Him (Gen. 2:1-3). The second concerned their appetite; they were not to eat of "the tree of the knowledge of good and evil." But they did, and by doing so, unleashed all the millennia of woe that has since inundated our planet. Because of their sin, the plague of death has fallen upon all—rich and poor, Black and White, educated and uneducated, male and female, short and tall— "For the living know that they will die" (Eccl. 9:5).

There are those who question the ethics or fairness of such dire punishment for one wrong act. How could God, they ask, be so severe regarding a matter so small? That question is answered in Ellen White's statement: "Yet, in His great mercy, He appointed Adam no severe test. And the very lightness of the prohibition made sin exceedingly great. If Adam could not bear the smallest of tests, he could not have endured a greater trial had he been entrusted with higher responsibilities" (*Patriarchs and Prophets,* pp. 60, 61).

Other statements that illumine this point are: "The mildest test was given them that could be given" (*The Seventh-day Adventist Bible Commentary,* Ellen G. White Comments, vol. 1, p. 1083); "The test given to Adam and Eve was very light" *(ibid.);* "When Adam was tempted, he was not hungry" (*Signs of the Times,* Apr. 4, 1900); "Our first parents were not left without warning of the danger that threatened them. Heavenly messengers opened to them the history of Satan's fall and his plots for their destruction" (*Patriarchs and Prophets,* p. 52).

As meaningful is dual reality that sin in its slightest measure cannot abide in God's presence, and its victims once poisoned by its venom are forever afflicted. Having tasted sin, the beings created in perfection were permanently marred; their defective status demanded eradication. Their only hope (and ours) was forgiveness while yet alive and eternal life after death made possible by the selfless intervention of Christ.

It didn't have to be this way, but it is. Adam and Eve had sufficient warning and every inducement to obey. And so do we. But we have a vast advantage—their example and 6,000 years of confirmation that sin separates, while obedience brings true happiness, holiness, and unity with the Creator.

The Original Lie

Then the serpent said to the woman, "You will not surely die.
For God knows that in the day you eat of it your eyes will be opened,
and you will be like God, knowing good and evil." Gen. 3:4, 5.

Wen Adam and Eve were placed in the garden, they were instructed in good, but not evil. The knowledge of evil or the experience of sin and its results was purposely withheld from them. Had they been faithful, God would have, over time, opened their understanding to the horrors of transgression, but their act brought its knowledge and consequences summarily cascading upon them.

It was not the fruit of the tree that poisoned them; none of God's creation was toxic. It was Eve's acceptance of Satan's lie, "You will not surely die," and Adam's lack of trust in God to solve the situation without her that laced their systems with death.

As usual, Satan's observation was not totally false. His words "in the day you eat of it your eyes will be opened" were correct. But his prior comment, "you will not surely die," was not.

Evidences of the lie were immediate— their fruit-laden trees began to wither, their flowers sprouted thorns, the birds of paradise lost their plumage, the animals lost their docility, and the atmosphere lost its favoring calm. The once-innocent pair, their covering of light removed and their holy humanity gone, found themselves shut off from the most energizing of all Eden's privileges—face-to-face communion with their Maker.

No longer could they chat with God at the break of dawn, stroll with Him in the cool of the day, or leisurely ask Him about His works as they conversed beneath the starry skies of night. They were now guilty, naked, and ashamed. Their spirits were numbed by the shock of separation and the ugly reality of sin's consequences. Their mistake brought not only an end to our interface with the source of life, but it also produced a companion evil—the blight of death, with its sorrow and pain.

Sin's painful consequences are not our chief motivation to obedience; that stimulus is the love of Christ. They are, however, an effective reminder of the wisdom of obedience and the cost of the salvation wrought by Jesus, our true and better witness.

The Character of Sin

You were the anointed cherub who covers; I established you;
you were on the holy mountain of God; you walked back and forth
in the midst of fiery stones. You were perfect in your ways from the day
you were created, till iniquity was found in you. Eze. 28:14, 15.

The presence of sin explains why we were alienated from God. But how do we explain the presence of sin? The truth is, we can't. This much we do know. God did not create it; it is a foreign virus introduced to our planet by Satan, the being in whom it was first found. He is the originator of transgression. The clearest indication of what happened to the apostate angel is provided in Isaiah's description of his pre-Fall proclamation: "I will ascend . . . , I will exalt . . . , I will also sit . . . , I will be like the Most High" (Isa. 14:13, 14).

Translation? Lucifer became afflicted with himself. We do not know how or why. What is clear is that jealousy toward Christ, the Son of God, germinated in this otherwise perfect being and festered and expanded and exploded into open rebellion.

Lucifer's act, variously characterized by thoughtful theologians as selfishness, pride, ingratitude, misvaluing, willfulness, idolatry, mutiny, betrayal, rebellion, falling short, and missing the mark is, of course, the original defection. H. Richard Niebuhr, in his book *The Kingdom of God in America*, labels sin as "disloyalty to the Creator, the only trustworthy and holy, lovable reality" (p. 105). He is correct; sin is not simply the absence of loyalty to the true God, it is loyalty to someone or something else. At its core, sin is misdirected love; it is alien affection. It is bowing before other gods, an act that is possible only when, for whatever reason, we value our opinions and conclusions higher than God's Word—our personal satisfactions above His objective commands.

Sober reflection cannot explain how any creature, especially the covering cherub, could dare to demand equality with the Creator—but Lucifer did. And so do we when we knowingly disobey God's Word. The key to loyalty is trust, and the key to trust is love, not of self, but of Christ—our tried and proven witness.

The God Who Comes Looking

And they heard the sound of the Lord God
walking in the garden in the cool of the day, and Adam
and his wife hid themselves from the presence
of the Lord God among the trees of the garden. Gen. 3:8.

The law of cause and effect mandates that for every action there is a consequence. This is true in the moral as well as the physical realm. There is no inconsequential expenditure of energy; every action spawns a reaction. It provides the answer to the old-age query "Does the tree that falls in the forest, where there is no listening ear, make a noise?" The tree produces all the effects that make noise possible. No ear may have heard, no eye may have seen, but as it fell through other trees and struck the earth, it produced all the energies that constitute sound. The reality that no eyes observed its swift descent and no ears were impacted by the resulting percussion does not negate the fact that it did descend with all of nature's consequences.

In the moral as well as the spiritual realm the ironclad laws of cause and effect are inescapable. For every action there is a reaction. Nature does not function with neutral consequences—"the curse, causeless, does not come" and we do always "reap what we sow."

In the garden the first pair sowed to the wind of "selfish distrust" and reaped the whirlwind of "self-destruction." The desperate straits that befell them were the morally predestined ends of their disobedience, not the arbitrary wrath of their disappointed Creator.

What did they do when they sensed God's approach for His usual evening chat? They hid themselves. They quickly discovered, however, that they could not hide from God—and neither can we. It is true that "the eyes of the Lord run to and fro throughout the whole earth" (2 Chron. 16:9). He knows the very thoughts and intent of our hearts.

The Creator outlined for Adam and Eve the dire results of their mistake. But He also pronounced the promise of a Redeemer. If we, like they, will accept His gracious offer of forgiveness, our punishments will be no less real, but our hearts, strengthened by the presence and power of the Holy Spirit, will be filled with the joyful hope of Eden restored.

A Better Home

So He drove out the man; and He placed cherubim
at the east of the garden of Eden, and a flaming sword which
turned every way, to guard the way to the tree of life. Gen. 3:24.

Adam and Eve could not remain in the home God had given them. Having dis-
obeyed when surrounded with perfection; having committed wrong when they
had no internal drive to evil or proclivity to sin, they surely could not be trusted
now that they were infected with transgression. And besides, the tree of life was
there and, should they continue to eat from its fruit, the world would be cursed
with perpetual transgression.

Now that their natures had been rendered unholy; now that access to the garden and its life-giving properties must be uncompromisingly denied, angels with
flaming swords drove them out and prevented their reentry, ensuring the sorrowful separation their actions produced. God had created them citizens of perfection;
they made themselves strangers to Paradise.

Our pity for the plight of Adam and Eve must not deny our empathy with the
pain of God. Concerned parents always hurt when their children suffer. That is sorrow children come to understand only when, as parents themselves, they see mis-
fortunate or tragedy strike their offspring. Our wayward planet, the only foul blot,
the only discordant note in the otherwise harmonious symphony of the universe, is
a constant pain to God's great heart. But it will not always be. He has promised and
will fulfill a "better tomorrow."

The Garden of Eden was preserved for many centuries. Adam and Eve and
their sons often offered sacrifices at its gates. It was withdrawn shortly before the
flood but it will be restored to the earth made new and will appear more glorious
than in its original state (see *Patriarchs and Prophets*, p. 62).

How can there possibly be landscape more attractive than perfect Eden? We
do not know. But based upon our daily experience with our promise-keeping God,
we have full confidence that He who has gone to prepare for us a place in heaven
will, in the earth made new, give His obedient children "something better"—and so
much more. Will you be there?

God's Plan B

All who dwell on the earth will worship him,
whose names have not been written in the Book of Life
of the Lamb slain from the foundation of the world. Rev. 13:8.

With their loyalties diverted by the wily foe, our first parents found themselves gripped "in transgression's trap." Shorn of their innocence, stripped of their holiness, and starving for their prior privilege of face-to-face communion with God, they were now victims of the circumstances their acts had produced. They were, however, not without hope—they were exposed, evicted, and expelled, but mercifully not executed summarily. Their merciful Creator provided for them a second chance. While they were denied access to the pleasures of the garden, they were provided entrance into the plan of salvation.

Their reign as happy vicegerents was aborted. But right there on the scene of the crime, even before He outlined the consequences of their disobedience (painful childbearing for the woman, backbreaking labor for the man, and their inevitable return to the dust), God promised them a deliverer (Gen. 3:15).

This was no sudden decision. God's plan B, the rescue of humanity should they fall, was already in place. Christ's decision to come to our aide was not an afterthought. It was a contingency plan outlined before creation (Eph. 1:4), and "as soon as there was sin, there was a Savior" (*The Seventh-day Adventist Bible Commentary*, Ellen G. White Comments, vol. 1, p. 1084).

Transgression demanded the immediate death of the sinner. By law, Adam and Eve should have been slain on the scene of their crime. But Jesus presented Himself as their (our) substitute—His pledge to pay our debt. He affected the stay of execution until He could come into our atmosphere, and by the second death remove our fatal, final punishment.

By His ministry Jesus accomplished more than the delay of recompense for human transgression. His ministry magnified and made honorable the law. It exonerated the Father's character, it demonstrated the Trinity's compassion, it provided the blood—the legal tender whereby sin's debt is justly paid—and made possible the gift of righteousness, whereby we are qualified for entrance into the Father's house.

Living to Tell the Story

So all the days that Adam lived were
nine hundred and thirty years; and he died. Gen. 5:5.

As they lived out the centuries of their existence, Adam and Eve witnessed untiringly to their posterity regarding the promise of a coming redeemer. Inspiration puts it this way: "The knowledge of God's law, and the plan of salvation were imparted to Adam and Eve by Christ Himself. They carefully treasured the important lesson, and transmitted it by word of mouth, to their children, and children's children. Thus the knowledge of God's law was preserved" (*Selected Messages,* book 1, p. 230).

In order to keep before them the cost of redemption, God gave the first parents a sacrificial system. It was in obedience to God's instruction that Adam pulled the jagged knife across the jugular vein of the first sacrifice and watched it writhe in the throes of death while its warm, red blood ran down his garments to the ground. The shock of seeing death traumatized our first parents more than our witness to 6,000 years of sin's ravages. Death was foreign to their understanding and alien to their imagination. Watching innocent lambs expire in contortions of searing pain they had inflicted was for them a nightmare of horror.

But it also gave them hope. They knew by this symbolic act that all was not lost; that the shame and pain they had brought upon creation would one day be removed; that the blood of Jesus would atone for their sins; that as David would later declare—"weeping may endure for a night, but joy comes in the morning" (Ps. 30:5) and as Isaiah later would proclaim: "He was wounded for our transgressions, He was bruised for our iniquities; the chastisement of our peace was upon Him, and by His stripes we are healed" (Isa. 53:5).

Our time on earth is minuscule compared to Adam's nearly 1,000 years. But as he spent his years in faithful testimony, we too, impacted by the sacrifice of Calvary, are motivated and mandated to remind others that beyond this present life of sickness and seemingly unending flood of misery there lies Eden restored.

The repentant Adam will be there, all of the faithful through the ages will be there, and Jesus, the Alpha and Omega, the beginning and the end, the everlasting Lord, our gloriously better Adam, will be there. Will you?

The Legacy of Hope

And Adam knew his wife again, and she bore a son
and named him Seth, "For God has appointed another seed
for me instead of Abel, whom Cain killed." Gen. 4:25.

Seth was the beginning of a long line of antediluvian patriarchs who followed Adam as faithful witnesses to the plan of salvation. That star-stuttered succession of gospel proponents included Enoch, Methuselah, Lamech, and his son Noah. Adam lived to witness to all these men except Noah, who was born 126 years after his death. Enoch was translated before Noah was born; Lamech died five years before the Flood, and Methuselah died the very year of the Deluge. All were Adam's contemporaries and were given firsthand witness to his creation, his fall, and his contrition.

The antediluvians—those who lived in the approximate 1,600-year period before the Flood, were not only giants of size, but they were also giants of intellect. They needed no written laws. Their minds were much clearer and more retentive than ours or the intervening generations; they easily grasped the details of Adam's fall and promise to rescue—all of which they faithfully relayed to succeeding posterity. It was after the Flood, when humans added animal flesh to their diet, that the race experienced rapid degeneration of body and mind.

The weakening of humanity's mental capacity in the decades that followed the Flood presented the likelihood that the story of salvation would be polluted with myth and factual inaccuracies or even largely forgotten. That is why God commanded Moses, 2,000 years removed from Creation and 500 years removed from the Flood, to write the first five books of the Bible showing how the world began, how it became corrupted, and how and by whom it will be redeemed.

The patriarchs, the prophets that followed them, the early church that Jesus began, the martyrs of the Dark Ages, and the pioneers of the rebirth of Sabbath concern in the mid-nineteenth century, all lived nobly but died "not receiving the promise."

Will their fate be ours as well? It will, unless we, by dedication and discipline, position ourselves to be fully controlled by the Holy Spirit. Then and then only will the long line of mortal succession into which the race is locked conclude and Christ, our king, reestablish our Eden lost.

Abraham's Altars

Then Abram moved his tent, and went and dwelt by the terebinth trees of Mamre, which are in Hebron, and built an altar there to the Lord. Gen. 13:18.

Noah's oldest son, Shem, who was born 98 years before the Flood, lived 502 years beyond that, 350 years of which his father, Noah, was still alive. Thus for four and a half centuries Noah, who was alive during the last 600 years of Methuselah's life, communed with Shem regarding the hope of the Redeemer.

Abraham, perhaps the most distinguished of the long line of patriarchs, was born in the Ur of Chaldees when Shem was 450 years old. As the aging Shem declined in strength, young Abraham emerged from Ur at age 25 primed by personality and providence to "father the faithful." There is no evidence that they knew each other, but the fact that they lived contemporaneously highlights God's intention to keep unbroken the centuries-long promise of the coming Redeemer.

Of faithful Abraham, it was said that his travels were easily traceable because wherever he pitched his tent he erected and left an altar. His habit of sacrifice was his signature deed, his identifying mark the unmistakable evidence of his devotion to God and his hope of the promised Messiah. By ritual and word, he passed the good news on to his son Isaac, who in turn informed Jacob, through whose loins came the 12 tribes—one of which, Judah, was the bloodline of Jesus, the promised Messiah.

Our great shame is that we do not build altars of witness, as we should. Our highest sin is not the commission of overt acts of evil, but the omission of objective acts of good. We spend too many nights without altars, too many trackless days, too many fruitless hours in selfish pursuits. A long line of heroic witnesses for truth has passed on the witness of salvation to us. Will we, with faith like theirs, keep the flame burning in our homes, in our schools, in our churches, in our communities, and in our hearts?

The hour is late; the challenge is great; we cannot—and must not—fail.

All Scripture Is Good

All Scripture is given by inspiration of God, and is profitable for doctrine, for reproof, for correction, for instruction in righteousness. 2 Tim. 3:16.

Those who contrast the Old and New Testaments, labeling the former as no longer valid for spiritual direction, do not understand. True, many of the cultural specifics of antiquity no longer exist, but the principles of right and wrong that shaped God's commands then are still valid. In very few societies today is retaliation for being "gored" by our neighbors' ox is a concern. The Old Testament principles for adjudication regarding personal injury and property damage are just as critical to human relationships in our day as it was in theirs.

The primary good of the Old Testament, however, is not its civic and social codes. It is its promises and prophecies later fulfilled in the life of Jesus. The Messiah's New Testament fulfillment of the Old Testament predictions concerning His life is sure proof of His authenticity. The Old Testament kept hope alive with its unbroken chain of messianic predictions; the New Testament gives us a firsthand account of what it was like to be in His presence, what is was like to hear His voice and see His face, to touch the hem of His garment, to witness the light shinning in darkness, to behold "Shiloh" coming to Israel, the Lamb dying upon Calvary, and the risen Savior walking among them.

Had we not been given the Old Testament promises of the Savior's rescue of our world, His services would have been no less a reality. But it is in the comparison of type (prediction) with antitype (fulfillment) that we are provided sure verification of who He was and is and why and how He loves us so.

There are times, however, that even those who honor the Old Testament inadvertently mute its emphasis on Christ by emphasizing its symbols above its Savior. Our challenge, as we read the Old Testament, is to concentrate not upon the bricks of ancient altars or the age of the ground upon which they stood, but rather to focus upon the meaning of all its particulars, the end of all its reasoning, the subject of all its foreshadowing—Jesus Christ the Messiah, our true and faithful witness.

Blessed to Bless Others

Then He gave him the covenant of circumcision; and so Abraham
begot Isaac and circumcised him on the eighth day; and Isaac
begot Jacob, and Jacob begot the twelve patriarchs. Acts 7:8.

The patriarchs most often mentioned in Scripture were firstborn males who
inherited not only birthright privileges, but also responsibility for preserving
expectations of the promised Messiah. In Jacob, Abraham's grandson, this principle
took a new and dramatic turn. Not one, but each of his 12 sons was given patriar-
chal status; each son became a progenitor of a tribe that would constitute the nation
of Israel.

God's vow to Abraham was: "I will make you a great nation; I will bless you and
make your name great; and you shall be a blessing. I will bless those who bless you,
and I will curse him who curses you; and in you all the families of the earth shall be
blessed" (Gen. 12:2, 3). This covenant, twice repeated at Mamre (Gen. 18:18) and
again at Mount Moriah (Gen. 22:18), was not given for Abraham's personal fame or
prosperity. Through his lineage "the light of heaven" was to shine to all the world,
appealing to the nations to turn from their idols to serve the true and living God
(*Testimonies for the Church*, vol. 5, p. 454).

Israel was to be the depository of God's law. They were to be the showcase of
His mercy—the vehicle by which the promise given to Adam and later espoused by
Seth, Enoch, Methuselah, Lamech, Noah, and Shem and Abraham and his descen-
dents would be taken to the world.

The physical nation that Abraham sired through Jacob and his sons is a type of
who we are today. We are spiritual Israel called to reveal His love by our preaching
and teaching by institutional functions and by the rightness of our lives. As ancient
Israel's primary task was to warn and prepare the world for Christ's first advent, we
are called into being to warn and prepare humanity for His second appearing. For
that purpose "the church in this generation has been endowed by God with great
privileges and blessings, and He expects corresponding returns" (*Christ's Object
Lessons*, p. 296).

We can and should, this very day, be alert to all opportunities to fulfill this high
and holy mission.

Reaching the Next Level

*After he begot Methuselah, Enoch walked with God
three hundred years, and had sons and daughters. Gen. 5:22.*

The individual history of the patriarchs reveals that many times God's most memorable evidences of favor were followed by His servants' most disappointing failures. Noah's drunken folly after he exited the ark, and Elijah's fleeing Jezebel after the Mount Carmel experience, illustrate this negative pattern. The experience of Enoch, on the other hand, demonstrates the reverse of this phenomenon. After the birth of his son, a highly anticipated and treasured event, his life, already one of dedication, reached an even higher level. How great and marvelous it would be for our families, for our children, for our communities, and for us personally if, rather than suffering emotional letdown following significant manifestations of God's power, we, like Enoch, would use those occasions as impetus for renewed dedication.

Each day we experience countless manifestations of divine care. Every morning we awaken, every breath we breathe, is reason for thanksgiving and surrender. But then there are the special moments—the high times, the anniversaries, the promotions, the graduations, the contracts secured, and birthdays that keep coming that speak loudly to answered prayers—all these and other such events should serve as calls to higher levels of praise and surrender.

That dedication must go beyond special diets and punctilious Sabbathkeeping. These are not the "end-all" responses to God's goodness. Scripture does not detail for us the specific ways in which Enoch's renewed righteousness was demonstrated. But this much we can be sure: since he "walked with God," he was in tune with His will and that will includes "practical godliness" in the everyday crucible of life. Why was Enoch missed or "found not" by the evil society in which he lived (Heb. 11:5)? Because his deeds, as well as his words, provided a positive, cheerful influence upon the degraded humanity about him. Everyone did not love him, but all respected him, and his removal from their presence created a vacuum of righteousness in their communities. Our faithful witness is no less needed, our fruitful service no less valued, our loving God no less deserving—no less able.

From Rags to Riches

*All these are the twelve tribes of Israel, and this is what
their father spoke to them. And he blessed them; he blessed
each one according to his own blessing. Gen. 49:28.*

Jacob's predictions about his sons in Genesis 49 is one of the more remarkable insights into human nature found in Scripture. The father's knowledge of his children's personality and character, augmented by the wisdom of the Holy Spirit, allowed him amazing insights into the future of each son and his posterity. Jacob's predictions were not all positive. While stating the ways in which his son's good qualities would bring them success, he also identified the faults that would contribute to their many sufferings and eventual downfall.

The troubled witness of the tribes and their subsequent rejection as God's special people was largely because of the fact that evil tendencies, often unchecked, were passed on and sometimes enlarged in succeeding generations. However, in spite of their repeated stumbling, in spite of their checkered and often tragic history, we note with interest that each of their names, with the exception of Dan, is inscribed upon one of the 12 gates of the Holy City (Rev. 21:12; 7:5-8).

How could that be? It is because each of the individual sons (again with the exception of Dan) was an overcomer. Each eventually found God's grace and forgiveness. And although succeeding generations were often guilty of abusing God's love and laws, many, having repented, died in the hope of the promised Messiah.

Israel's witness provides many lessons for us today. Among them are: (1) our destinies and those of our children are not the result of happenstance or blind luck or misfortune—we reap, in personality and productivity, what we sow in character and choice; (2) God's mercy is greater than our misery. The truly repentant all experience the truth that "where sin abounded, grace abounded much more" (Rom. 5:20); (3) we are chosen not simply for our salvation but for the salvation of others—and as God uses us to "tell the story," He continues in us the work of grace whereby we are ripened for life in the kingdom above.

The 12 Tribes

Now all these things happened to them as examples, and they were written for our admonition, upon whom the ends of the ages have come. 1 Cor. 10:11.

The history of Jacob's 12 sons and their descendents demonstrates the tragic effect that parental weaknesses, untamed, have upon succeeding generations. This principle is seen in each tribal history: the tribe of Reuben's failure to produce leadership talent commensurate to its size is traceable to its instability (Gen. 49:4); the lack of growth seen in the tribes of Simeon and Levi was a natural cause of their culture of cruelty (Gen. 34); the tribe of Judah's history of tumult and treachery was a consequence of their lack of self-control (Gen. 38:12-30); Zebulun's stubbornness with regard to worldly alliances was the root cause of their crippling secularity (Judges 1:30); Issachar's subservient posture to the other tribes was caused by its material greed (Gen. 49:15); Dan's removal from the roster of the saved is traceable to their judgmentalism and idolatry (verse 17); Gad's lack of popularity to their warlike disposition (verse 19); Asher's withdrawal from national affairs to that tribe's lackadaisical spirit (Judges 5:17); the "attitude of ingratitude" displayed in Naphtali's descendants, even in Christ's day (Matt. 11:20, 21), was a logical result of their presuming upon the blessings of God (Judges 1:33); Joseph's failure to produce children of note cannot be traced to any obvious weakness, however, his repeated weeping (Gen. 42:24; 43:30; 45:14, 15; 46:29; 50:17) does paint him as a man of soft, if not exaggerated, sentimentalism; Benjamin's reduction to near extinction (Judges 20:1-14) is logically associated with their leaders' radical individualism (Gen. 42:36-38).

God's purpose for the church today is the same as it was for these ancient tribes—the preparation of society for the coming of the Messiah. And His promise is: "That which God proposed to do for the world through Israel, the chosen nation, He will finally accomplish through His church on earth today" (*Prophets and Kings*, p. 713).

Our measure of efficiency in this high and holy endeavor is, in no small means, proportionate to our willingness to heed the lessons of these—our spiritual predecessors. By avoiding their mistakes and benefiting from their triumphs, our witness can and will succeed.

A Prophet Among Us

Surely the Lord God does nothing, unless He reveals
His secrets to His servants the prophets. Amos 3:7.

Whereas the tribes were called to witness to the nations about them, the prophets in their midst were called to witness primarily to the chosen ones themselves.

The prophets were instructed by angels, by visions, by audible communication from God, and by intuitive feelings regarding His will. The prophets not only witnessed by oral utterances and symbolic acts, but also produced much of the written word that we now treasure.

Some writers, such as Isaiah, Jeremiah, and Ezekiel, are classified as "major" prophets. Others, mainly Hosea, Joel, Amos, Obadiah, Jonah, Micah, Nahum, Habakkuk, Zephaniah, Haggai, Zechariah, and Malachi, are called "minor" prophets. Their designation is not because their witness was less, but because their messages are not as lengthy. In the case of all the prophets, the core of their ministry (from Samuel, the last of the judges and the first of the prophets) was the preparation of the people for the coming of the Messiah.

The prophets performed a number of valuable functions. They warned of danger from enemies, they championed social justice, they instituted revival, and they addressed events of the future and past in ways that edified the nation.

The remnant church has a prophet—Ellen G. White. Her demise in 1915 removed her from us physically. However, her words and her influence remain vital for our living by them, she "being dead yet speaketh" (Heb. 11:4, KJV). The church is correct not to utilize her words as a basis of doctrine. She is, by her own self-description, "a lesser light" compared to the "greater light" of the Bible (*Evangelism*, p. 257). Nevertheless, we cannot forget that the same Christ who spoke to the prophets of old inspired her. Her writings illumined our understandings of doctrine and provide a sense of urgency with regard to obedience of God's Word.

For many reasons we are wise to familiarize ourselves with the substance of this wonderful gift. The most meaningful of all is its portrayal of the ministry of Jesus. There is no doubt as to why God encourages us to "believe in the Lord your God, and you shall be established; believe in His prophets, and you shall prosper" (2 Chron. 20:20).

Judah: A Type of Jesus

The scepter shall not depart from Judah,
nor a lawgiver from between his feet, until Shiloh comes;
and to Him shall be the obedience of the people. Gen. 49:10.

The long line of judges, kings, and stalwart warriors produced by the tribe of Judah accurately fulfilled Jacob's lofty prophecy concerning their prominence in national affairs. Caleb, David, Solomon, Jehoshaphat, Samuel, and Hezekiah are but a few of the many outstanding leaders who came from Judah's lineage. The root element of the generations of military and civic leadership provided in Judah's posterity was the wholesome character of the patriarch himself. He was "ground zero" for the long line of descendants that Jacob had in mind when he predicted, "The scepter shall not depart from Judah, nor a lawgiver from between his feet, until Shiloh come" (Gen. 49:10).

What were the character traits that made Judah have such a rich source of leadership personnel? First, he was a man of deep sympathy. It was Reuben, the eldest son, who averted Joseph's certain assassination, urging that he not be slain but thrown into the pit. It was Judah who ensured his survival by insisting he be sold to the Ishmaelites (Gen. 37:18-28). Second, he was a man of personal sacrifice. Reuben offered the lives of his two sons as security against Benjamin's return to Egypt, but Judah offered his own life as security for the youngest brother (Gen. 43:8, 9). And third, he was a man of passionate persuasion. It was Judah who, when Joseph's silver chalice was found in Benjamin's sack, successfully pleaded for his younger brother's life and that of the others (Gen. 44:14-34).

Sadly, in spite of these sterling qualities, Judah, like all the other tribes, failed to accomplish its spiritual destiny. Shiloh, the rest giver, did come through the tribe of Judah (Heb. 7:14). But the people through whom and to whom He came rejected Him. They rejoiced at His healing and feeding, but they resented His condemnation of their sins, and they crucified Him as a common thief.

The lesson for us is threefold: (1) individual generosity is a precursor to personal blessings; (2) no amount of sacrifice, however dear, substitutes for obedience; and (3) there are in every tribe and nation, the honest in heart whom God uses to fulfill His will on earth.

Faithful, but Fallible

For prophecy never came by the will of man,
but holy men of God spoke as they
were moved by the Holy Spirit. 2 Peter 1:21.

In spite of their nearness to God, the prophets were not perfect. Speaking of their fallibility, Ellen White wrote: "Though some of these men wrote under the inspiration of the Spirit of God, yet when not under its direct influence they sometimes erred. It will be remembered that on one occasion Paul withstood Peter to the face because he was acting a double part" (*The Seventh-day Adventist Bible Commentary*, Ellen G. White Comments, vol. 6, p. 1065). "We see how they [the patriarchs and prophets] struggled through discouragements like our own, how they fell under temptation as we have done, and yet took heart again and conquered through the grace of God" (*Steps to Christ*, p. 87). "None of the apostles and prophets ever claimed to be without sin. Men who have lived nearest to God, men who would sacrifice life itself rather than knowingly commit a wrong act, men whom God has honored with divine light and power, have confessed the sinfulness of their nature" (*The Acts of the Apostles*, p. 561).

All of them, as Ellen White stated, were fallible and flawed. We do not have full details of their spiritual struggles, but this much we know: Noah got drunk, Abraham lied, Moses lost his patience, Jacob was a deceiver as a youth and exercised favoritism in his old age, Eli did not parent very well, David murdered, Solomon was a philanderer, Samson was seduced, and, of course, the list goes on.

What do we learn from this record of flawed witnesses? First, that ours is a forgiving God and that "if we confess our sins, He is faithful and just to forgive our sins and to cleanse us from all unrighteousness" (1 John 2:9). Second, we learn that perfection is a matter of direction and maturity, not absolute freedom from evil urges. Third, we learn that God judges us not by occasional good deeds or misdeeds, but by the tendency of our words and acts (*Steps to Christ*, pp. 57, 58). Fourth, we learn why humanity so desperately needed a better witness than Israel had known. They needed Him to sweep away the debris that had been piled upon the law of God, to disclose the Father's character fairly and accurately, to prove that God's law could be kept, and to provide for them and us the perfect, unsullied righteousness that is the unyielding requisite for eternal life.

In the Fullness of Time

But when the fullness of the time had come,
God sent forth His Son, born of a woman, born under the law. Gal. 4:4.

Adam and Eve expected rapid fulfillment of the promise of a redeemer, but it was not to be; it would take 4,000 years for the effects of sin to condition humanity for the Messiah's coming. So century after century the story was repeated. "In every sacrifice Christ's death was shown. In every cloud of incense His righteousness ascended. By every jubilee trumpet His name was sounded. In the awful mystery of the holy of holies His glory dwelt" (*The Desire of Ages*, p. 212).

And then at last He came—when the lamp of human intellect was flickering at its lowest and longevity was at its briefest; when blindness was rampant and mental illness epidemic; when infant mortality was commonplace and deadly plagues, spread by infectious insects and foul breezes, victimized hapless communities, decimating whole towns and villages; when, because of lack of effective treatment, people's teeth rotted painfully in their mouths; when wickedness was so dense that earth's inhabitants looked more like the creatures of the forest than the God in whose likeness they were made; when Isaiah's prophecy of "gross" moral darkness was being tragically fulfilled and the weary populace desperately needed "something better" than the vacuous promises of heathen mythology, a voice was heard in heaven saying, "a body You have prepared for Me"(Heb. 10:5). Jesus came!

His coming, said John, was like the sudden appearance of a light shining in darkness. And how could it be otherwise? For He is the source of all light: physical, intellectual, and moral. And though He masked His glory in the flesh of the generation in which He appeared, from the very beginning He was Immanuel—"God with us."

The shepherds whom the angel's visited that glorious night were actually conversing about the Messiah's advent when the angel told them of His birth (*The Desire of Ages*, p. 47). Could it be that a more intense longing for His return would in our day hasten the flight of the angelic entourage that will accompany His second advent; that one day soon we will hear the welcome cry "behold the bridegroom cometh!" In the "fullness of time" it will happen! Our prayer should be "even so, come, Lord Jesus!"

Christ: Our Knowledgeable Witness

For it is the God who commanded light to shine out of darkness,
who has shone in our hearts to give the light of the knowledge
of the glory of God in the face of Jesus Christ. 2 Cor. 4:6.

There are many ways in which Jesus qualifies as our better witness. One is His intrinsic knowledge of the Father, whose character for 4,000 years had been so maligned by Satan. His is not third-party testimony or information gained by hearsay or even circumstantial evidence. He was with the Father from before the beginning. He was there when the foundations of the earth were laid and when "the morning stars sang together" (Job 38:7). He knows the Father not as a historian knows history or as a biographer writes life stories or as an archaeologist explains past cultures. He knows as the best of friends know one another and as family members are personally acquainted with characteristics of each other.

The German language has two words for knowledge: *wissen,* meaning to know as in learning or memorizing facts; and *erkennen,* meaning to know as in a personal relationship. It is revealing to note that when Martin Luther translated the word "knowledge" in our text, he opted for the latter use, and rightly so. John wrote, concerning the Father-Son relationship: "In the beginning was the Word, and the Word was with God, and the Word was God. He was in the beginning with God" (John 1:1, 2). Jesus is the Father's thought made visible; the bond is so close that He could say, "He who has seen Me has seen the Father" (John 14:9). The babe of Bethlehem was not a copy or a "look-alike." He was " the preexistent, self-existent Son of God" (*Evangelism,* p. 615). And in comparison to the long chain of human witnesses who preceded Him, he was not simply unparalleled, but a far superior order.

Sadly, however, the world loved darkness more than light and consummated its rejection of His offerings by crucifying Him. But that was then, some say, and this is now—it's different now. But it isn't! The Son of God still stands at the door of human hearts offering witness to the Father's love and life everlasting, only to be rejected by multitudes that see and choose the seductive lights of society rather than the saving light of salvation.

Our Lord's promise is: "My Spirit shall not strive with men forever" (Gen. 6:3)—there will be "payday" someday! Gratefully, you and I, guided by the better witness of the Word, can live in full assurance of shelter from present evil and complete confidence in His guidance through whatever days the future may bring.

It Behooved Him

Wherefore it behooved him in all things to be made like unto his brethren, that he might become a merciful and faithful high priest in things pertaining to God, to make propitiation for the sins of the people. Heb. 2:17, ASV.

High on the list of the admirable qualities of Jesus, our true witness, is His sacrificial spirit. It "behooved" Him to come into our world and suffer. That is, His coming was morally necessitated. There was no legal, physical, or political pressure that made Him come and then die. He did so because His great heart of love would not allow Him happiness in glory while we agonized on earth.

The call to service is heard in many ways: by the flow of genealogical succession, as with the Levitical priesthood; by dramatic intervention, as with Moses and Paul; by convictions stimulated by the example of others, as with Elisha in his association with Elijah; or simply by the voice of duty, as heard by Abraham.

But Jesus' emergence to witness was the most memorable of all. He was not arrested, startled, prevailed upon, urged, paid, induced, or genealogically determined to witness. He came into our realm because it "behooved" Him! He wanted to come—our need was His motive, our plight was His inducement, and our salvation was His ample persuasion.

There are those who say that not having an earthly father disqualified Him as a bona fide witness; and that to be a truly legitimate witness He must have had, as do we, both earthly parents and that His representation is invalidated by the unique circumstances of His birth.

This objection is undone by a number of facts. Among them are: (1) He redeemed Adam's failure under circumstances that were "one hundred times more difficult than Adam knew"; (2) He never utilized His God nature to avoid, escape, or overcome the impulses and trials of His human flesh; (3) as our Second Adam, His birth was actually more akin to ours than it was to that of the original Adam, who had neither earthly parent; and (4) He "was tempted in all points" as are we (i.e., on all three of sin's classifications—the lust of the flesh, the lust of the eyes, and the pride of life) without sinning (Heb. 4:15).

It behooved Him to come to our planet and suffer that we might live. This act of infallible sacrifice is what behooves us to respond in total surrender to Him.

Our Logical Witness

Whoever therefore breaks one of the least
of these commandments, and teaches men so, shall be called
least in the kingdom of heaven; but whoever does and teaches
them, he shall be called great in the kingdom of heaven. Matt. 5:19.

Satan's campaign to distort God's image causes him to portray the Father on one hand as a being of harshness, and on the other hand a being of permissiveness.

Jesus came to witness against both false claims regarding God's character. First, He openly attacked the Jewish leaders' penchant for making God's commandments oppressive. He exposed the punctilious regulations that they piled upon the law for what they were—rules created to extract the servitude of the people for personal advantage. Jesus taught a better obedience: one based upon love and not slavish adherence to tradition or superstitious regard for custom. He taught that hatred was murder, that lust was adultery, and that the Father was far more concerned with what was in the heart than what was seen in outward appearance.

He also witnessed against the opposite evil that Satan had promoted—the idea that God was soft on sin and not really concerned about the details of obedience. Jesus countered that distortion by making it clear that He had come to fulfill and uphold all aspects of the law—not to destroy or take away "one jot or one tittle" of its force (Matt. 5:17-20)—by reminding us that we must "be perfect" as the Father in heaven is perfect (verse 48) and by teaching that only by entering the straight gate is salvation possible (Matt. 7:13).

Why is God so particular? Because even the smallest deviation from His will has negative effect upon us and upon His created handiwork. He is particular because He knows that evil is contagious and must be excised from His holy universe. He is particular because He is perfect, and imperfection is foreign to His holy nature.

Our generation is no less blinded and confused with respect to obedience than were the hearers in Palestine. There are those who live fanatically, blindly responding to the letter of the law, and there are those who regard loosely, believing God too gracious to grade critically, too merciful to author hellfire. Jesus' death is the ultimate proof that God means exactly what He says—and this includes the promise that while "the wages of sin is death, . . . the gift of God is eternal life" (John 3:16).

A Compassionate Witness

*And he arose and came to his father. But when he was
still a great way off, his father saw him and had compassion,
and ran and fell on his neck and kissed him. Luke 15:20.*

When Jesus was born, the false views of the Father as being either severely harsh or leniently loose had been advanced by Satan for 4,000 years. But it was the former view that dominated. Given the wretched state of humanity at the time of His birth, the fact that disease and suffering, most usually brought about by dissipation and idolatry, was so pervasive, it is not surprising that the Creator was seen as lacking in compassion.

For 4,000 years the sacrifices had declared the coming of the Messiah without fulfillment of the promise. Rivers of blood had flowed, forests of wood had been consumed, mountains of stony altars had been erected, and generation after generation had died in hope of deliverance that did not arrive. But then, when in the fullness of time, He did come—He, the Father's verbal, tangible expression to humanity, gave full proof of His true character.

He demonstrated by His acts of mercy, His words of comfort, His sacrificial living, that He, the human, visible teacher of Galilee, the son of Mary and Joseph, friend of humanity and healer of hearts, was God's true witness. He repeatedly reminded the people that He and the Father were one. He illustrated this truth by many parables. One concerned the absent landowner who, after sending several servants to inquire of his property, finally sent his son, whom the evil stewards slew (Matt. 21:37-40). Another featured the prodigal son whose father, upon his return, "had compassion" and welcomed him home; still another, the good Samaritan who had mercy upon the wounded traveler (Luke 10:33).

He also highlighted the Father's love by the model prayer in which He taught them, and us, to petition Him as a loving benefactor. His most eloquent expression, however, was dying—not just deserted by His earthly followers, but estranged from His Father as well.

He, our risen witness, is still the same—"His compassions fail not" (Lam. 3:22). He is no longer with us physically, but by His angels and Holy Spirit He speaks peace to our hearts, confirming that "earth has no sorrow that heaven cannot heal," encouraging that above "the dim unknown" sits the "divine watcher" directing in ways best for His children, reminding them "that all things work together for good for those who love God" (Rom. 8:28).

Immanuel: God With Us

"Behold, the virgin shall be with child, and bear a Son, and they shall call His name Immanuel," which is translated, "God with us." Matt. 1:23.

Christ was with us before the Bethlehem event. He came in the cloud that cooled His people by day and the fire that warmed them by night. He was in the Shekinah that covered the ark of the covenant, and in the Urim and Thummim that stood upon the breastplate of Israel's high priests.

But these were veiled visitations—muted manifestations and significant but sheltered encounters with divinity. In the living Jesus we are provided the ultimate witness; He was Immanuel—God with us! "God, who at sundry times and in divers manners spake in time past unto the fathers by the prophets," now spoke to us by the Son (Heb. 1:1, KJV).

He was here! He ate our bread, drank our water, bathed in our streams, breathed our air, felt our pain, and faced our temptations. He was here in person; in our flesh, we saw Him, we heard Him, we touched Him, and we crucified Him. He was born into our world; He was buried in the very ground that He brought into existence.

But before He died, He said, "He who has seen Me has seen the Father" (John 14:9). His life and death are ultimate proof that the Father is not a passive potentate of distant worlds, physically removed from our daily concerns. He is not a deity "who [haunts] the lucid interspace of [worlds above], where never creeps a cloud, or moves a wind, nor ever falls the least white star of mow, nor ever lowest roll of thunder moans, nor sound of human sorrow mounts to mar their sacred everlasting calm" (Alfred, Lord Tennyson, "Lucretius"). He has not removed Himself from the calamity of humanity: no, He is Christ—God with us!

It was one thing for Him to dispatch patriarchs and prophets and angels to assist us, or to Himself occasionally appear, as to Moses at the bush, and dazzle us with muffled displays of His glory. But it was an entirely different thing for Him to bypass all intermediate orders of being and dwell within our doomed and dying race. He did not come to stay, but He promised: "I go to prepare a place for you . . . that where I am, there you may be also" (John 14:2, 3). Before He left, He taught us to pray, and promised that whatever we ask in His name, believing, He would provide according to His will.

Justice Exonerated

Behold! My servant whom I have chosen,
My Beloved in whom My soul is well pleased! I will put My Spirit
upon Him, and He will declare justice to the Gentiles. Matt. 12:18.

The sins of Adam and Eve boldly challenged the relationship between God's mercy and His justice. Why? Because the law required death, and had God slain the pair as deserved, Satan would have charged Him as lacking mercy. On the other hand, had He summarily forgiven them, He would have charged Him as lacking in justice.

From Eden to Bethlehem, the universe waited as promised reconciliation of these principles was delayed. Promises of both destruction and redemption were continuously provided through the patriarchs and prophets. But for four long millennia, humans lived and died without seeing their fulfillment.

Knowing that through a Messiah, God had pledged to vindicate the offerings of justice and mercy, Satan sought continuously to frustrate His purposes. His highest energies were utilized in portraying God as unsympathetic and unkind. He pointed to the dire consequences of sin as evidence of God's harshness. By intensifying over time the misery of humanity, Satan characterized God as an aloof, elitist, unsympathetic, unfeeling bystander and, at worst, the heartless perpetrator of human suffering.

For all who would and will listen, Satan's disinformation campaign is a failure. For them, Jesus' ministry provides perfect balance of law and grace. His witness is the highest possible rationale for clear compatibility of justice and mercy.

And while He was here He told us that only those who willingly neglect the free gift of mercy will be lost; that it is not His will that any should perish, but that all might have everlasting life; that flaming justice will be the lot of those that purposely hide their talent, who intentionally hoard their resource, who consciously reject His invitation to discipleship.

The cross, of course, was His ultimate statement. There, justice was satisfied—its character fully exonerated, its claims upon the human race fully met, its penalty everlastingly fulfilled, its principle shown as completely reasonable, and His mercy always available.

Mercy Exalted

The Spirit of the Lord is upon Me, because He has anointed
Me to preach the gospel to the poor; He has sent Me to heal the
brokenhearted. To proclaim liberty to the captives and recovery
of sight to the blind, to set at liberty those who are oppressed. Luke 4:18.

In addition to vindicating God's justice, Christ's witness gave ringing endorsement to the Father's mercy. During the 4,000 years that intervened between the first Adam's failure and the Second Adam's favor, the Godhead conveyed many evidences of its love. The rainbow that arched the heavens following the Flood, the Shekinah that illumined the surface of the ark, Aaron's rod that budded and the pot of manna kept within the ark's bosom were only a few of Israel's visible reminders of God's protection and care.

From our sinful fall in Eden to the sinless fountain shed on Calvary, it was mainly God's justice that we saw. The Old Testament record of salvation history is filled with accounts that bear the truth that "righteousness exalts a nation, but sin is a reproach to any people" (Prov. 14:34), that we do indeed "reap what they sow" (see Gal. 6:7). It was as if mercy hid herself in celestial repose while justice ruled unbridled in the affairs of earth.

With the advent of Jesus the scenario altered radically; now it appeared that the sterner rules of justice were replaced by the softened tenets of mercy. This "changing of the guard" was repeatedly characterized in Jesus' reversals of prior instructions regarding human conduct. His words "Ye have heard that it hath been said, . . . but I say unto you" replaced the "eye for an eye" of Old Testament justice with the "love your enemies" emphasis of New Testament mercy (Matt. 5:38-48).

Christ did not ignore the claims of justice. But His overriding thrust was mercy. It was mercy to the demoniacs, whose dementia was the consequence of dissipation; mercy to the woman found in adultery; mercy to the paralytic whose sins He forgave; mercy to the man let down as He taught in the home of Peter's mother-in-law; mercy to the man born blind; mercy to the widow of Nain; mercy to the desperate petitioner that touched the hem of His garment—He was mercy incarnate. And while His death was justice's strongest claim, it was also mercy's highest cry. Further, it is the sinner's greatest appeal and the believer's strongest incentive to faithful devotion and service.

Christ's Balanced Witness

Mercy and truth have met together; righteousness
and peace have kissed. Ps. 85:10.

Where and when did righteousness and peace (justice and mercy) meet and reconcile? At Calvary! Prior to that time the universe was left to wonder regarding Satan's charge that God could not be both just and merciful at the same time (*The Desire of Ages*, p. 761).

The role of Christ in establishing the link between justice and mercy is seen in the fact that at Christ's first advent "Justice and Mercy stood apart, in opposition to each other, separated by a wide gulf" (*The Seventh-day Adventist Bible Commentary*, Ellen G. White Comments, vol. 7, p. 936). "His [Christ's] object was to reconcile the prerogatives of Justice and Mercy, and let each stand separate in its dignity, yet united" (*ibid.*, p. 935).

Christ's sacrifice upon Calvary settled the question forever. There, "Justice moved from its exalted throne, and with all the armies of heaven approached the cross. There it saw One equal with God bearing the penalty for all injustice and sin. With perfect satisfaction Justice bowed in reverence at the cross, saying, It is enough" (*ibid.*, p. 936).

Thus to Christ's cry "It is finished" was added heaven's evaluation "It is enough!" No further proof was needed, no added justification required. Christ had given enough—enough sacrifice, enough service, enough love, enough blood to show to all that justice and mercy were not mutually exclusive, but were, in fact, compatible principles perfectly blended in the Father's heart.

What does this mean for us? It means that no sin can be committed for which satisfaction (justice) has not been met; that God can forgive the obedient and punish the disobedient without violating His quality of mercy; that you and I have an example to follow in our homes, in our congregations, and in all our other relationships.

The answer to the question "Which is greater: justice or mercy?" is neither—each exceeds the other. Justice is the foundation of God's throne, and mercy is the law of His universe. As the Lord of justice, Jesus is typified as the Lion of Judah; as the Lord of mercy, He is represented as the Lamb of Calvary. We cannot ascribe superiority to either quality. But this much we know: when we pray, we pray for mercy, and when He returns, we will "follow the Lamb wherever He goes" (Rev. 14:4).

The Kingdom Witness

From that time Jesus began to preach and to say,
"Repent, for the kingdom of heaven is at hand." Matt. 4:17.

As Jesus went forth preaching "The kingdom is at hand," the people interpreted this as a "glory" kingdom of earthly rule. They envisioned the overthrow of Rome and their return to the splendor and authority of Solomon's days. Even the disciples who touched Him in intimate association, who heard His parables and witnessed His miracles, expected Him to restore the former glory. Their heartbreak at His failure to do so is reflected in the sorrow of the less intimate, but equally distraught, travelers to Emmaus, who pined, "We had been hoping that he was the man to liberate Israel" (Luke 24:21, NEB).

True, Christ came to provide us access to a physical kingdom—the future kingdom of glory. But His immediate purpose was to explain and demonstrate the principles of the "now" kingdom—the kingdom of grace.

So He urged us to be childlike, to forgive our enemies, to avoid Phariseeism. He told us that to serve and not to rule is the substance of greatness and that we should cherish the sacred above the secular. He spoke of the transitoriness of the material and the endurance of the spiritual. He talked of the rewards of sacrifice in contrast to the recompense of greed; the joys of sharing versus the folly of hoarding; the error of judging by the external rather than the internal; the wisdom of "deferred gratification" in contrast to the waste of self-aggrandizement, and that motives, not consequences, are the proper index of action.

But the people did not want truth and correction. They wanted safety—not salvation; riches—not redemption; deliverance from their captors—not deliverance from their sins; so they rejected and destroyed Him!

Satan understood well that the Prince of heaven would attempt to establish the kingdom of grace—a kingdom of light amidst the kingdom of darkness he had built. That is why he fought so bitterly to mute His influence and why, eventually, he led the mob in crucifixion of the Father's star witness. But in doing so, he sealed his own doom. For the death of Christ is the clearest of all testimonies of the validity of God's rule and the superiority of the kingdom of grace that He brought us.

His Lasting Witness

But you shall receive power when the Holy Spirit has
come upon you; and you shall be witnesses to Me in Jerusalem,
and in all Judea and Samaria, and to the end of the earth. Acts 1:8.

Every social revolution has its charter proponents and protagonists, its foundational advocates and apologists, and its true founders and followers. In most cases, however, with the demise of its leader and the passage of time, even the most fervent cause fades into history.

Not so with Christianity. The cause of Christ has not only endured with time, but it also has enhanced. Like the anvil that has worn out many hammers, the gospel of Jesus has survived the ensuing centuries overcoming and outliving all its critics along the way. There are other religions that have lasted over time, Buddhism and Hinduism, for example. But none has conquered more grandly than the peaceable kingdom established by the lowly Nazarene. None approximate the 800 languages into which the Bible is now translated; none has produced as many libraries and universities or inventive minds and technological societies. Christ is a lasting revolution. His primer, the Bible, is a perennial best seller. His cross, the most telling witness of His life, has adorned more homes, hospitals, and hearts than any other symbol.

There have been since His advent times and stages, as in the Dark Ages, when the torch that He lit in our darkened world flickered low. But even then, dedicated advocates such as the Waldenses witnessed faithfully, often at the cost of their lives. The light of truth that Jesus passed on to His disciples and they to their successors has, at times, been obscured, but it has never died.

The torch of truth is now in our hands. Through us He desires to perpetuate and heighten His testimony to the goodness of the Father. Doing that faithfully is a consequence of being so radically impacted by the love of God that we simply must tell the "good news." Not as reporters who chronicle a rescue at sea, but as ourselves, the saved—plucked from the angry waves by one who loves us eternally and who sacrificed beyond human comprehension that we might have something better!

SEPTEMBER

A Better Priority

I Am the Way

Jesus said to him, "I am the way, the truth, and the life.
No one comes to the Father accept through Me." John 14:6.

Priorities are inevitable. Consciously and subconsciously, we choose hundreds of times a day. Our decisions are ordered not by random happenstance, but by magnitudes of importance. Unexpected events, some welcome and some threatening, often force us to alter our plans and change our priorities. In the end, however, the quality of each day's journey is not so much the result of accidents or luck, but of our choosing.

We choose to study or not to study, to exercise or not to exercise, and to eat correctly or incorrectly. There may be very persuasive circumstances that limit our options to choose, but we do choose. We choose from fear or for reward; we choose because of others (parents, children, teachers, friends, etc.) or because of want of self-satisfaction. The most important of all motivations, however, is fulfillment of the will of God. And with this comes clear directions, right understandings, and determined wills. These are precisely what Christ promises in His words "I am the way, the truth, and the life" (John 14:16).

But the Bible is not an encyclopedia of obedience; it is not a lexicon of right and wrong detailing for us each of life's specific events. We cannot flip its pages and find an alphabetized listing with coded answers for our moment-by-moment choosing. It is a book of precepts and principles and examples given to guide and empower us. It is exhaustless in that it addresses all of life's categories of living. Its broad and comprehensive instruction assures that we are not left without counsel or comfortless in our chaotically pluralistic world of choices.

Christ's principles of choice shine through in both the greater light of Scripture and in the lesser light of the writings of Ellen G. White. It too does not specifically reference many of the options encountered in today's society, but it does give us clear guidelines for reasoning and potent patterns to guide.

Jesus qualifies as our better spokesman, but not primarily because of the superior priorities He has given us. He qualifies because He Himself is a better priority. Our fixation on Him is occasion not so much by the excellence of His precepts and principles (e.g., "Do unto others" and "It is better to give" dictums), but by the excellence of His example and the undimmed, unequaled, undeniable beauty of His person.

Prioritized Choosing

I beseech you therefore, brethren, by the mercies of God,
that you present your bodies a living sacrifice, holy,
acceptable to God, which is your reasonable service. Rom. 12:1.

Conscious choosing is the better kind. Individuals whose agendas are driven by the drift of circumstances or the whims of others seldom reach a destination that approximates their potential. They may be content or even happy, but they can never be as effective or as productive as God desires or their abilities and opportunities suggest.

Intentionality with respect to goals is critical to success. Prioritized choosing results in correctness with respect to options; concentration with respect to energies; confidence with respect to outcomes; and clarity with respect to evaluation and review.

Jesus made our salvation His conscious priority. He weighed carefully the alternatives and chose, in spite of the personal sacrifices involved, to affect our redemption. His choice drove Him to abdicate His heavenly throne, be placed in Mary's womb, and be born in the likeness of sinful flesh. It structured His activities while He was here: His devotional life, His social life, and His role as preacher, teacher, healer, prophet, priest, and king.

And the Father approved of His actions with the most complete evaluation possible. His words were "This is My beloved Son, in whom I am well pleased" (Matt. 3:17). It was that reassurance, so dramatically pronounced at His baptism and indeed evidenced throughout His ministry, that gave Him strength to endure in the face of rejection and abuse. His choice (our redemption) was His "magnificent obsession," His all-consuming passion, the mission and mandate of His sacrifice for this lost creation. His confidence regarding the outcome of His sacrifice was severely tested by our ingratitude, but He persevered and thereby qualified as our perfect sacrifice.

We can never, in our earthly sphere, fully understand that selfless choosing or fully express our appreciation. But we can and should respond to His love by total surrender to Him. This choice will bring life, not death; blessings, not curses (Deut. 30:19).

Since such surrender brings light to the mind, strength to the will, happiness to the heart, cleansing to the soul—in summary, since it is absolutely critical to our individual salvation, it is the most rational and reasonable of all life's choices.

The Giants Keep Coming

Yet again there was war at Gath, where there was a man of great stature, who had six fingers on each hand and six toes on each foot, twenty-four in number; and he also was born to the giant. 2 Sam. 21:20.

Each of us is daily challenged by our personal giants—the imposing impulses of our inner selves. We arrive in the world bent to evil, proclaimed to wrong—oriented toward sinful priorities. The state of desiring that nature provides us is seen in the actions and attitudes of every child. Selfishness, pride, and jealousy are the enduring legacy we inherit from Adam. It is against this inbred perversity or natural animosity toward right that the Holy Spirit must war. This is why it is impossible to rightly prioritize without divine assistance.

The unconverted are sometimes capable of profitable priorities—choices that produce effective results. But unless their motive for deciding is godly, even their fruitful decisions will lack heaven's stamp of approval. Dietrich Bonhoeffer, the saintly German martyr, labeled positives accomplishments without divine motivation "stolen goodness"; Augustine called it "accidental right"; and Ellen White speaks of such as "scaffold morality." All of which reminds us that only that good accomplished in response to God's Word merits heaven's approval.

Paul's daily struggle to subdue the ungodly flesh with which nature equips us is described by Ellen White: "That he might not run uncertainly or at random in the Christian race, Paul subjected himself to severe training. These words, 'I keep under my body,' literally mean to beat back by severe discipline the desires, impulses, and passions" (*The Acts of the Apostles,* p. 314).

All the more reason we must begin each day with surrender to God's will. Only as we attach to Him as the vine to the branch will we have nourishment and strength adequate for each day's testing choices.

David, the intrepid warrior, slew not only the giant Goliath, but also many others. It is possible to say that in his warfare against the Philistines, the giants kept coming! That is also true in our lives. But Christ has provided us the Holy Spirit, by whose power we can slay them. And those victories will be ours if, in the battle, we depend upon His wisdom and strength and not our own.

Creatures of Habit

Now His betrayer had given them a signal, saying, "Whomever I kiss, He is the One; seize Him and lead Him away safely." Mark 14:44.

Many think that choice is an activity of the moment: that we choose as we go along and that decision is the response to present stimuli or current circumstances. But that is not so. We choose according to the way we have chosen thousands of times before. We are creatures of pattern, purveyors of custom, and instruments of sameness. Our tastes are cultivated by indulgence. They are predispositions, not decisions of the moment. Each choice (good or bad) is a step that makes continued journeying in that direction easier and more likely. We choose, not at the moment of response, but as we have been conditioned by responses over time.

Ananias and Sapphira did not choose to withhold from the Lord because of a sudden impulse to selfishness. Their decision to hoard was formed by many prior acts of grasping and greed. Joseph did not decide on chastity nor did Daniel prioritize prayer based on suddenly assumed devotion. They had, through the years, built patterns of righteous response. And Judas did not betray his Lord all at once. His fatal decision was fueled, forged, and fixed by years of smaller, less dramatic or visible decisions that established his will and way above that of his leader. And so it is with all of us. Our future, to a great extent, lies behind us.

Do you have habits that you long to break? Are you, today, struggling with patterns of lifestyle or evil thoughts from which you long to be delivered? The good news is that no matter how large the cable of habit that binds us in some undesirable vice, Jesus can free us. He is not only a way maker, he is also a habit breaker—the Great Physician by whom our tendencies to evil are excised and our thoughts and decisions controlled.

By proper and consistent deciding, we will eventually become so habituated to right decision-making that we will, in temptation, turn as naturally to God for guidance as does the sunflower to the sun (*Sons and Daughters of God,* p. 151). This is a promise of power that we must all choose to believe, and the habit of believing is the most essential of all.

September 5

Overcoming Bad Habits

I can do all things through Christ who strengthens me. Phil. 4:13.

The sinful tendencies we inherit are not our only barrier to right choice; we are also plagued by the sinful tendencies we acquire—the bad habits we accrue after conception. These cultivated tendencies to evil (laziness, tardiness, forgetfulness, etc.) differ from the inherited kind in that they are removable, not just simply resisted, and totally excised—eradicated altogether!

On the other hand, the inbred clamors of the flesh with which we are born (selfishness, pride, greed, etc.) are not removable. They can and must be subdued, but, as the building blocks of our unholy flesh, they cannot be eradicated. It is our constant war against these ever-present (even if dormant) urges that is depicted in the prophet's words: "So long as Satan reigns, we shall have self to subdue, besetting sins to overcome; so long as life shall last, there will be no stopping place, no point where we can reach and say, I have fully obtained. Sanctification is the result of lifelong obedience" (*The Acts of the Apostles,* pp. 560, 561). It is also inspiration for Ellen White's statement that "at every stage of development our life may be perfect; yet if God's purpose for us is fulfilled, there will be continual advancement. Sanctification is the work of a lifetime. As our opportunities multiply, our experience will enlarge, and our knowledge increase. We shall become strong to bear responsibility, and our maturity will be in proportion to our privileges" (*Christ's Object Lessons,* p. 65).

Has heaven provided any help for our continuous overcoming? The direction of the Holy Spirit (John 16:13); the enlightenment of Scripture (Ps. 119:11); the invigorating influence of personal witness (Rev. 12:13); and the power of prayer and fasting (Matt. 17:21).

This is not to suggest that we are able to achieve the absolute overcoming that gains heaven. We do not. But "Christ looks at the spirit, and when he sees us carrying our burden with faith, His perfect holiness atones for our shortcomings. When we do our best, He becomes our righteousness" (*Selected Messages,* book 1, p. 368), and "it is the righteousness and perfection of His Son, who takes upon Himself our sins, our defects, our weaknesses, which God accepts. . . . Christ's righteousness becomes our righteousness, if we sustain a living connection with Him" (*Review and Herald,* Dec. 18, 1888).

Our Moral Machinery

And do not be conformed to this world, but be transformed
by the renewing of your mind, that you may prove what
is that good and acceptable and perfect will of God. Rom. 12:2.

Our choosing is the work of interconnected mechanisms of the mind. Ellen White calls these related parts our "moral machinery" (*Testimonies for the Church*, vol. 4, p. 84). Just as our automobile or television or the watches we wear have engines or internal parts that connect and relate making the mechanism work, so are our choices driven by very specific moral components. The three primary ones are our appetite (Gal. 5:16, 17), our reason (Isa. 1:18), and our will (Rom. 7:18).

Our fundamental quandary is that, at birth, all these elements are faulty. Morally speaking, we are "DOA" (dead on arrival). Our appetites are distorted, our reasoning skewed, and our wills flabby. There is only one true solution available—we must take our miswired machinery to the One who made us, the One from whom our first parents strayed; the One who says, "Come unto me, all ye that labour and are heavily laden, and I will give you rest" (Matt. 11:28, KJV). He alone can fix our broken parts.

How does He do it? He does it through the agency of the Holy Spirit—the conversion specialist. He takes us to the Word, where He functions with the tools of redemption, the Old and New Testament. There He exposes us to the healing, changing, life-giving power of God, and we are remade in His image. That change involves not only our basic desire to obey, but also our ability to perform—this is to produce fruits and works of righteousness.

But the moral machinery of our hearts is not fixed "once and for all." We must constantly rededicate it to God for His care and keeping. We must "die daily" or surely revert to the times of weaker control. This is because, even though we have been changed or elevated to new more noble tastes, our appetites, reasons and wills remain lodged in sinful flesh and can rightly function only when under the control of God's Word. That is the most satisfying relationship of all, the happiest experience of the human heart and the only prescription for decision-making that will stand the test of eternity.

Our Appetites

I say then: Walk in the Spirit, and you shall not fulfill
the lust of the flesh. For the flesh lusts against the Spirit,
and the Spirit against the flesh; and these are contrary to one another,
so that you do not do the things that you wish. Gal. 5:16, 17.

Our appetite is the most elemental component of our moral being, and we have two kinds: legitimate and illegitimate. The legitimate kind is our normal cravings; the logical drives to satisfy the needs of the body. The fact that our bodies crave water and food and sexual satisfaction is quite normal and not sinful. That is the way we are made.

Then there are our illegitimate cravings—the wish to indulge in excesses that which is good and the desire to indulge in that, which is basically harmful. It is against these evil urges that the Christian is at war each day of our lives. Since "In our own strength it is impossible for us to deny the clamors of our fallen nature" (*The Desire of Ages*, p. 122), that is no easy task. In fact, it is impossible to control our appetites without "the love of Christ [that] constraineth us" (2 Cor. 5:14, KJV).

In this manner it can be said as it was of Paul, he "was ever on the watch less evil propensities should get the better of him. He guarded well his appetites and passions and evil propensities" (*The Seventh-day Adventist Bible Commentary*, Ellen G. White Comments, vol. 6, p. 1089); and "there are hereditary and cultivated tendencies to evil that must be overcome. Appetite and passion must be brought under the control of the Holy Spirit. There is no end to the warfare this side of eternity" (*Counsels to Parents, Teachers, and Students*, p. 20).

Add to the above the fact that "as long as life shall last, there is need of guarding the affections and the passions with a firm purpose. There is inward corruption, there are outward temptations" (E. G. White letter 8b, 1891). And we are driven to rejoice with the victorious apostle who reassures: "There hath no temptation taken you but such as is common to man; but God is faithful, who will not suffer you to be tempted above that ye are able" (1 Cor. 10:13, KJV).

Our prayer today and everyday should be "Lord, I confess that my appetites often conflict with Your will and even my desire to do Your will. I admit, dear God, that my urges are often selfish and unholy. Please cleanse me from my evil desires and give me strength to indulge legitimate urges in balance and to absolutely abstain from evil ones." Amen.

Our Reason

"Come now, and let us reason together," says the Lord,
"though your sins are like scarlet, they shall be as white as snow;
though they are red like crimson, they shall be as wool." Isa.1:18.

The second element of our moral machinery is reason. Appetite is the part of our moral apparatus that desires. The reason is the element that deliberates (calculates) about the wisdom of following our appetites and desires. What one's passions wish, the rational powers must ponder. To this end Ellen White writes: "It was God's design that reason should rule the appetites, and that they should minister to our happiness. And when they are regulated and controlled by a sanctified reason, they are holiness unto the Lord" (*Child Guidance*, p. 378). Also, "the kingly power of reason, sanctified by divine grace, is to bear sway in our lives" (*Messages to Young People*, p. 238). And, "every emotion and desire must be held in subjection to reason and conscience" (*Testimonies for the Church*, vol. 5, p. 177).

Proper reasoning is an essential element of proper choosing. The greatest aid to our proper reasoning is the study of the Word of God. That is because "the testimony of the Lord is sure, making wise the simple; the statues of the Lord are right, rejoicing the heart; the fear of the Lord is clean, enduring forever; the judgments of the Lord are true and righteous altogether" (Ps. 19:7-9).

Do you have decisions, large or small, for which you need a clear mind and discerning eye? Do you wish God's leading in matters of marriage, lifework, school, or neighborhood in which to live? Are you faced with choices regarding finance, selection of personnel, the challenges of some relationship or finding a job? The Bible is the answer; its study strengthens our intellect, sharpens our analytical power, develops our abilities to discriminate, it enhances our decision-making capacity and, as no other source, develops our faculty of discernment. A marvel of Scripture is that it not only subdues evil appetites, but it also elevates our powers of apprehension, our abilities to differentiate the good from the evil, the false from the genuine, and the lesser from the greater good.

David said it very convincingly: "I have more understanding than all my teachers, for Your testimonies are my meditation" (Ps. 119:99).

Esau's Example

And Jacob gave Esau bread and stew of lentils; then he ate and drank, arose, and went his way. Thus Esau despised his birthright. Gen. 25:34.

Esau is a classic example of an individual whose unsanctified reason failed to properly control his appetite. Sell the precious birthright for a mess of pottage? No one in his right mind would have made such a deal. The pottage could have waited—or could it? It should have, but when reason, already skewed by nature and indulgence, has been neglected by a lack of communion with God, or even worse, inflamed by constant contemplation of the tawdry imagery of society, it never does. Unsanctified reasons do not correct ungodly appetites—they approve them; they are partners in crime.

And make no mistake, sanctified reason is necessary for avoidance of the misuse of our conversion birthright and all its intended blessings. And what are the privileges that accompany our new birth? Confidence in God's leading, a clear, clean conscious, the joys of Christian service, an upright character, a good reputation, and the promise of His presence even in the "valley of the shadow of death."

But unlike Esau, whose birthright came as a matter of heredity, our spiritual birthright must be sought. We must ask God—we must seek and find the Lord. True, the Holy Spirit woos us long before we are aware of His pleading, but we too have a work to do—that of desiring fellowship with Christ.

The problem, of course, is the constituent condition of our carnal nature described in Luther's words: "The material itself is faulty, the clay, so to speak, out of which this vessel began to be formed, is damnable. What more do you want? This is how I am; this is how all men are. Our very conception: this very growth of the fetus in the womb is sin, even before we were born, and begin to be human beings" (*Luther's Works*, vol. 12, p. 348).

Conversion does not destroy the faulty material, but it does reorient our appetites and reason, allowing us to present to our wills the other element of moral being, the materials of proper choice.

Our Will

For I know that in me (that is, in my flesh) nothing good dwells; for to will is present with me, but how to perform what is good I do not find. Rom. 7:18.

The third component of our moral machine is the will. "The will is the governing power in the nature of man, the power of decision, or choice. Every human being possessed of reason has power to choose the right" (*Education,* p. 289).

Whereas the appetite desires and the reason debates, the will decides. It is the trigger element of choice; the buttons we press when reason has settled upon the means to fulfill the desires of appetites.

The moral philosophers of Greece and Rome knew about appetite and reason. Most of their formulas for good citizenship included helpful concepts for enhancing human desiring (i.e., our appetites and reason). However, it was left to Christianity to complete the picture by identifying the will as the deciding element of moral agency.

It was left to the apostle Paul to bring us the clearest of understandings. One such presentation is in Romans 7:18. Here he highlights the role of the will in decision-making as follows: "I can will, but I cannot do, what is right" (Goodspeed); "For the wish to do right is there but not the power" (Weymouth); "No matter which way I turn, I can't make myself do right. I want to, but I can't" (TLB); "For I have the desire to do what is good, but I cannot carry it out" (NIV); "I can will what is right, but I cannot do it" (RSV); "The wish is there, but not the power of doing what is right" (Moffatt) and, "For the willing is present with me, but the doing of the good is not" (NASB).

Concerning Paul's personal experience, our modern-day prophet wrote, "his will and his desires every day conflicted with duty and the will of God" (*The Ministry of Healing,* pp. 452, 453). All of which resonates with the testimony of the contrite Augustine who later confessed, "I will to sin even though I will not to will to sin."

The secret of victory is yielding our wills to Christ. By doing so, we become one with Him in purpose and desire. Only when Jesus comes and these mortals put on immortality and these corruptible incorruption, will we be free from the battle with evil. Meanwhile, our daily surrender gives results in overcoming by the power of Him who, in total surrender, said, "Father, . . . not my will, but thine, be done" (Luke 22:42, KJV).

Dealing With the Unenforceable

Therefore, whether you eat or drink, or whatever you do,
do all to the glory of God. 1 Cor. 10:31.

The three functional realms of obedience in which the Christian operates are: (1) the realm of church stipulations, (2) the realm of government statutes, and (3) the realm of personal standards. Disobedience to the doctrines of the church makes one vulnerable to church discipline. Disobedience to the laws of the land subjects one to civic or civil sanctions. And, for the healthy minded, disobedience to standards of personal ethics (laws of conscience) results in individual discomfort and condemnation.

Yet it is in this third arena, often referred to as "the realm of the unenforceable," that the vast majority of our daily decisions are made. Our most common choices are not about breaking the Sabbath, or paying taxes, but about what we read, how we spend our money, and how we utilize our time.

Because such choices are not ordinarily subject to the judgments of church or state, many regard them as inconsequential or "nobody's business" but our own. However, knowing that "no man is an island," the truly ethical are sensitive to the impact of actions upon others. Even when no personal sanctions apply, they act with respect for the good of others. Those bold souls who exercise their freedoms without regard for lateral damage are slaves to the very independence they espouse!

There are many helpful sources for guidance to sound ethical decision-making: nature, history, philosophy, sociology, and often the positive preachments of family and society itself. The best source, however, is the Word of God. Because the specifics of lifestyle today are vastly different from that of Bible times or even the pioneer days of our church's history, we cannot always mimic the individual actions of Bible heroes. Rather, we must mine from the Word its timeless principles of moral agency and apply them to our daily challenges.

The truly converted will strive to be in harmony with the rules of the church and government. But just as surely, and perhaps even more important, he or she will seek godly peace where external sanctions do not fall. Sincere study of God's Word makes such obedience not only possible or probable but, by the immutable councils of inspiration, inevitable.

Rules Versus Principles

I am the Lord, I do not change; therefore you
are not consumed, O sons of Jacob. Mal. 3:6.

There are those whose Christian journey is unnecessarily complicated because they equate standards (rules) with the higher orders of values and principles. These individuals often charge their fellow believers with apostasy because certain rules have changed since they first believed and were baptized. The more extreme are seen wearing clothes just like those worn in the pioneer days of Adventism, stoutly declaring, "God doesn't change!" We forget that while the principle of modesty, born of our belief in God, does not change, the standards that relate to it do. No, principles never yield; they are everlasting. Rules, however, are not eternal; they adapt to time and circumstance. Our challenge is to understand and apply principle when and where we live. We cannot recapture and then, literally, copy the deeds of Joseph or Jesus. However, we can and must act with like intentions.

The process whereby we determine right actions involves several identifiable steps. The first references our attitude or beliefs about God. Who God is or whether or not He is—that's the starting point of all our choices. Second, from our beliefs about God are born our values or convictions regarding the relative importance of life and living. These values, in turn, give birth to principles or underlying assumptions about our proper relationship to life's values. Principles, in turn, spawn coded (specific) standards or rules that regulate our activities.

Believers who stoutly proclaim fidelity to the unchanging character of God are correct in doing so. But that understanding is incomplete without the realization that while God's character and personality do not change, His methodologies do, as seen in the biblical record and His dealings with individuals and groups. They vary from generation to generation and sometimes within them.

Holding to the unchanging melody of God's will amid the improvisations of time is not easy. However, the child of God whose ear is tuned to the Master's voice in daily devotion is empowered to do so. This posture includes not only awareness of the difference between eternal principles and relative rules, but also the discipline to obey. Like the lily that blossoms fresh and fragrant upon the muddy, scummy pond, true believers grounded in the Word of God will produce, amid the distortions of society, lives that reflect the undimmed loveliness of their Lord.

The Efficient Cause

And you He made alive, who were dead in trespasses and sins. Eph. 2:1.

The basic reason that the philosophy of the ancients does not satisfy humanity's need for salvation is that the wise men of Greece and Rome lacked knowledge of the true God. It is interesting to note, however, that among their many prescriptions for better living are some that, while nonsalvific, are helpful.

One such formula is Aristotle's theory of the four causes—his proposition that all objects may be regarded for: (1) their formal cause—the appearance of a thing; (2) their material cause—the substance of which an object consists; (3) the final cause—the reason for the object's existence; and (4) the efficient cause—that which makes the object function properly. When he applied this theory to moral agency or activity, Aristotle identified the formal cause as the individual or acting agent; the material cause as the moral apparatus (one's appetite and reason); the final cause as good citizenship; and the efficient cause as habit or repetition whereby conduct is ingrained.

Other philosophers identified the efficient cause of conduct as education, meditation, imitation, etc. Jesus, the greatest teacher of them all, taught that the efficient cause of good behavior is the Holy Spirit. From His teachings we learn that He is the active agent of conversion, that He sustains us in daily growth and obedience, that He motivates and instructs us to proper choices, and that He and He alone provides us the will that enables us to do God's biding no matter how contrary to our will. Good habits, good education, good example—all identified in ancient philosophy as aids to proper behavior—are helpful indeed.

Because the Holy Spirit alone guarantees sustained obedience to the moral law, it is not too much to say that His presence is the key to our proper choosing—the critical element of all right actions. He is the activator of our faith; He is the sustainer of our belief; He is the instructor of our growth; He is the strength and might of our daily walk with God—the only efficient force for profitable choice. And He brings "all other blessings in [His] train" (*The Acts of the Apostles*, p. 50).

The Grandest Goal

Brethren, I do not count myself to have apprehended;
but one thing I do, forgetting those things which are behind
and reaching forward to those things which are ahead, I press toward the
goal for the prize of the upward call of God in Christ Jesus. Phil. 3:13, 14.

Paul's grandest goal—the likeness of Christ—should be that of every believer. Christlikeness must be at the top of our list of things to do. It is when we make this our goal (that which will be done if nothing else is accomplished) that we properly proportion our time, expend our energies, and allocate our mental, emotional, and physical resources.

It is by beholding that we become changed into His image. Our constant focus upon His life and love molds us into His likeness. The transformation is not completed in a day, a year, a decade, or even, for that matter, a lifetime. We never cease growing into His image. He is so pure and holy that a millennium of living would be insufficient to equal His loveliness.

But we do grow; we advance. We see His dear face in nature, we trace His steps in history, we view His compassion and character throughout Scripture, we sense His love in our lives, and we are cleansed, converted, and changed into His image.

There are many men and women with admirable characteristics and personalities: heroes, saints, martyrs, intrepid warriors, and brave apologists for truth whose lives we would do well to study and emulate. But there is no life or example like that of Jesus. In addition to being the only sinless human, His life is the only one the study of which provides the reader power to overcome. In Him is not only light, but also life; not only divine inspiration, but also divine infusion.

The prayerful study of Christ's life erodes old habits and establishes, by the power of the Holy Spirit, new tastes and patterns for living. Since the quality of our spiritual growth is the surest sign of our commitment to God, all other priorities are secondary; all other aims are less; all other hopes are inferior; all other goals must yield to this, the grandest goal of all.

Newness of life in Christ should be evidenced before baptism or formal entry into the body of believers. However, "sanctification is the work of a lifetime," and we Christians who never count ourselves "to have apprehended" or to have arrived at the end of perfection must journey in faith, ever onward, ever upward, to the goal of godliness.

The Goal Versus the Gift

And be found in Him, not having my own righteousness,
which is from the law, but that which is through faith in Christ,
the righteousness which is from God by faith. Phil. 3:9.

Paul's objective was the goal of Christ's likeness; his obsession was the gift of Christ's righteousness. His hope was the gift of Christ's righteousness. He did not expect, nor should we, that our personal conduct, even at its best, qualifies us for heaven. Our highest obedience is superseded by His dearest gift—the substitution of His life for ours.

In his letter to the church in Rome Paul contends that in Christ we are "more than conquerors" (Rom. 8:37). He knew well the Olympic games of his day and was fond of making spiritual application of athletic events. He uses the sacrificial dedication of those who compete as runners (1 Cor. 9:24, 25), boxers (verses 26, 27), and wrestlers (Eph. 6:12) as examples of the painful sacrifice we Christians must make in our quest for eternal life. He urges that we "work out [our] salvation with fear and trembling" (Phil. 2:12). In all these thoughts he is consistent with the counsel of our Lord Himself, who said that heaven is available only to those who try violently" (see Matt. 11:12).

But are we more than conquerors? What could be more honorable, more desirable, more satisfying than conquering in the spiritual life? The answer—being made heirs! (Rom. 8:16). Conquerors work for their laurels and are awarded prizes that will taint and tarnish with time, and finally one day will perish in the fires that will purify this sinful world. But those who are heirs—those who are recipients of favor not because of labor, but because of merciful regard or a fond relationship—are infinitely more blessed, and their rewards, in Paul's spiritual analogy, eternally secure.

God motivates our good works, and He has a book of remembrance in which all our obedience is cataloged and will be remembered in the better world (Mal. 3:16). But these good works do not save us; the gift of Jesus' life does that. This is why our striving for the likeness of Christ is secondary to our praying for the righteousness of Christ. When the later becomes our ardent obsession, the former will be our happy obsession.

September 16

A Working Faith

*For as the body without the spirit is dead, so faith
without works is dead also. James 2:26.*

A definition of faith that deserves more notice than is usually given is that which
describes it as doing "the right thing at the right time" (*Testimonies for the
Church,* vol. 6, p. 24). What Martin Luther King, Jr., often referred to as "the paralysis of analysis" has sunk more ships, torpedoed more careers, lost more battles,
canceled more victories, wasted more energies, and cost more lives than any other
character weakness. Indecision is indeed the bane of success. It is true that "on the
plains of hesitation bleach the bones of countless millions who, at the dawn of victory, sat down to wait, and [in] waiting—died" (George W. Cecil), and that often
"it is better to try and fail than to do nothing and succeed."

There are, of course, those who decide precipitously—rushing in "where angels
fear to tread," not counting the cost or charting the consequences of their actions.
That is the opposite weakness and just as damaging to individual and the corporate
good. Even more disastrous to the welfare of family, church, and society is the inability to decide. Greed (wanting it all), radical possessiveness (unwillingness to
share), fear (unhealthy dread of negative consequences), perfectionism (inability
to act without absolute assurance), and laziness (lack of motivation) all contribute
to this condition.

Fortunately providence (some would say fate) sometimes provides us a second
chance. Time in its kindness sometimes gives us moments of redemption, which
if seized allow us recovery of lost advantages. While most lost opportunities cannot be revisited, they can be helpful if their painful memory informs our future
choices. Meanwhile, the steady hand of time moves relentlessly on, never retreating
or retiring to the station it has passed. Even when we do correct past mistakes, the
interest in blessings we should have earned (had we made the right choices in the
first place) are lost.

Our prayer today: "Lord, help me to recognize and seize all the golden opportunities this day shall bring for the good of others, for the growth of Your kingdom,
and for my own personal welfare. In Jesus' name, amen."

God or Mammon

And if it seems evil to you to serve the Lord, choose for yourselves this day whom you will serve, whether the gods which your fathers served that were on the other side of the River, or the gods of the Amorites, in whose land you dwell. But as for me and my house, we will serve the Lord. Joshua 24:15.

Joshua was an old man now. He had come to the end of his illustrious career and was about to die. His farewell sermon was a stirring review of God's deliverance from Egypt and their 40-year journey to Canaan. Historical reminiscing, however, was not his primary objective. What he wished more than anything else was to inspire God's people to renewed dedication to Him. So he demanded, "Choose you this day whom ye will serve, Jehovah God, who has manifested himself to you these many years, or the icon gods of your former captivity."

Joshua's challenge is relevant for every generation. We must all choose in this regard. There is no escaping. Every person must decide, and our alternatives are as well defined now as they were then. We will choose the Creator God or we will choose the false gods of material and sensual satisfaction. Not choosing is to choose nonetheless—there is no neutral ground; we either choose Him who made us and has redeemed us, or we align ourselves with one of the many gods of Satan's creation.

Joshua's plea to choose "this day" does not suggest a "once and for all" brand of salvation. We must choose every day. Each day's challenge is different. The gods of selfishness, lust, and pride reinvent themselves each day in ways that threaten our covenant with the true God. But by placing our wills on the side of God's will, and by daily renewal through study of His Word, we will find their appeal less and less compelling and our responses to the true God more and more natural and rewarding.

A great need for today is more Joshuas in our pulpits, classrooms, conference offices, campus dormitories, hospitals, family kitchens, and church pews, willing to declare for Jehovah as stoutly as the departing patriarch. When that happens, revival and reformation will follow, and the promises of the latter rain will be gloriously fulfilled.

Choosing Bravely

"Curse Meroz," said the angel of the Lord, "curse its
inhabitants bitterly, because they did not come to the help of the Lord,
to the help of the Lord against the mighty." Judges 5:23.

Sisera, proud general of Jabin, king of Canaan, had been soundly defeated by the
Israelites. Along with the remnants of his troops, he sought retreat back to his
home that led through the very territories he had conquered. Despite the dangers
involved, the families of Israel joined in a heroic effort to prevent his escape and
probable return to further ravage their lands. But there was one group that refused
to assist in preventing his escape: the people of Meroz. The refusal of the inhabitants of Meroz to assist in this time of crisis did not alter the final outcome (in terms
of the will of God), but their doing nothing during the emergency earned for them
the bitter denunciation of today's scripture. Our text is also background of one of
Scripture's most heroic acts—the slaying of this proud warrior, Sisera, by Jael, the
wife of Heber, as he lay exhausted in her tent (Judges 5:22-27).

A woman is assaulted on a city street in clear view of the passing crowd, and
no one comes to her rescue. A shrill cry for help pierces the night, alerting adjacent
apartment dwellers of a brutal attack in their complex, but no one dares to inter-
vene. Thousands of children in war-torn and food-deprived countries die daily,
while knowing citizens in lands of wealthy consumption and conspicuous waste do
nothing—say nothing. In the United States of America, more than 10,000 people
die annually at the hands of drunken drivers and more than 1,000 women die annually at the hands of enraged husbands and boyfriends—and most people of this
proud land simply go about their business as usual.

"Doing nothing" in a crises is a universal disease of unspeakably dire consequences. The prophet Ellen White referenced God's attitude about such neglect
when she wrote, "If God abhors one sin above another, . . . it is doing nothing in
. . . an emergency" (*Testimonies for the Church*, vol. 3, p. 280).

In the emergency of being lost, Jesus made our redemption His personal priority. He chose to risk all for us. His act is both our means of salvation and our
shining example.

The Sacred Versus the Secular

But whoever drinks of the water that I shall give him
will never thirst. But the water that I shall give him will become in
him a fountain of water springing up into everlasting life. John 4:14.

Everything about her spoke to the fact that she was a Samaritan—her features, her dress, her speech. Christ saw her and immediately recognized the diamond in the rough: the fruitful witness she would be if only He could reorient her priorities and render her amenable to the Holy Spirit.

She did not really see Him. Well, she did, but she didn't. She knew by His features and dress that a Jewish man was sitting there beside the well. But she, as a Samaritan, had no inclination to give Him notice and was absolutely startled when He interrupted her routine by asking her for a drink of water from the cup she was carrying.

Her reply of disbelief was "How is it that You, being a Jew, ask a drink from me, a Samaritan woman?" (John 4:9). His calm but penetrating answer was "If you knew who it is that ask you for a drink, you would [ask] him" (verse 10, NIV).

What a masterful way to begin His evangelistic endeavor! He asked her for a favor and, by doing so, got her attention. When she protested her ethnicity and her gender, He gently and firmly pointed her to a higher level of concern—her salvation. Not that Jesus was soft on the social issues that she raised; His work among those who were poor, His focus on women provided in so many of His parables and miracles, and His emphasis upon nondiscriminatory neighborliness (i.e., parable of the good Samaritan) clearly reveal His concern for the socially disadvantaged.

However, He pressed to bring her salvation. He did not stop to discuss her gender or ethnicity. He sympathized with the real needs that the water would supply. But, undeterred, He bore forward with even more essential revelations regarding the spiritual water she needed.

Lesson? Our social and secular concerns, be they ever so legitimate, are always superseded by the sacred. We can and should, like the Master Evangelist, utilize the common circumstances of life as a means of gaining the confidence of others. The main goal of our witness addresses not the temporary needs of this life, but the infinitely more important requirements of life everlasting.

Christ's Loving Manner

The woman said to Him, "Sir, give me this water,
that I may not thirst, nor come here to draw." John 4:15.

The condition of the woman who Christ saw approach the well is mirrored by the general populace of today. Her life had been punctuated by a series of fleeting thrills and short-term relationships. She had no abiding happiness or emotional security. Our sin-sick society is filled with such pleasure seekers—people of shallow satisfactions, surface summations, ancillary answers, temporary triumphs, finite fixes, and vaporous victories, who routinely gather at the well of short-term solutions.

The longer our time on earth the more difficult it is to arrest their attention and attract them to Jesus. But we must try. And we must do so knowing that Christ's methodology still works; kindness and love expressed in demeanor and deeds are far more effective in leading to Christ than debate and denunciation.

Our modern-day prophet wrote: "It is of little use to try to reform others by attacking what we may regard as bad habits. Such effort often result in more harm than good. In His talk with the Samaritan woman, . . . Christ . . . [offered her] something better than she possessed. . . . This is an illustration of the way in which we are to work" (*The Ministry of Healing*, pp. 156, 157). Once again: "The less we criticize others, the greater will be our influence over them for good. To many, frequent, positive admonitions will do more harm than good. Let Christlike kindness be enjoined upon all" (*Medical Ministry*, p. 209).

That advice of course is good not only as it relates to evangelism of neighbors and friends, but also with respect to our households and especially our children. "Too many frequent positive admonitions?" Yes, it is possible that in our zeal to steer our children in the right direction we are guilty of "gospel overload"! By ill-timed "good advice" we sometimes create tensions that defeat our purposes. Does this suggest tolerance of evil or passive regard for wrongdoing? No, but it does suggest positive attitudes and a lean toward mercy in our training methodologies. Most of all, it suggests keeping open the lines of communication and our dependence upon the impulse and imprint of the Holy Spirit as the key operative in the processes of witness and nurture.

God Is a Spirit

But the hour is coming, and now is, when the true
worshipers will worship the Father in spirit and truth; for the Father
is seeking such to worship Him. God is Spirit, and those who
worship Him must worship in spirit and truth. John 4:23, 24.

The well by which they conversed was noted by the woman as Jacob's gift to the people of Samaria. It was a legacy of their birth: the most visible symbol of their connection with history and history's God. She would have the Jewish traveler know that this well, this ground, this water, and their provider, Jacob, were all part of the heritage that was uniquely Samaritan and superior to any claim that He and His people might have.

The gentle Jesus understood. Without debating or berating, without depreciating or denigrating the value of her first birth, He pressed ahead with His promises of the better possession of the second birth He now offered. And it worked! Her transition was complete—she was born again with undeniably better consequences.

The first birth gave her the roses of Shechem.

The second provided her the Lily of the Valley.

The first birth gave her the fruits of Sychar.

The second birth gave her the fruits of the Spirit.

The first birth gave her water from a well.

The second birth gave her the Water of Life.

The first birth gave her claim to Mount Gerizim.

The second birth gave her access to Mount Zion.

The first birth afforded her Samaritan dress.

The second birth gave her the robe of Christ's righteousness.

The first birth gave her pride in ethnicity.

The second birth gave her place in eternity.

The first birth gave her Jacob's well.

The second birth gave her Jacob's God.

No wonder the prophet wrote: "Something better is . . . the law of all true living. Whatever Christ asks us to renounce, He offers in its stead something better" (*Education,* p. 297).

An Unavoidable Witness

And many of the Samaritans of that city believed in Him because of the word of the woman who testified, "He told me all that I ever did." John 4:39.

For the woman at the well, the encounter with Jesus meant not only new direction, but also unavoidable motivation to share the Jesus she had found. Her joy was so great she could not do otherwise. When she realized that this was indeed the Messiah with whom she had been conversing, she burst forth in uninhibited witness to His power and person.

We can see her—throwing back her hair, abandoning her half-filled water pot, kicking off her sandals, lifting up the hem of her garment so as to move unimpeded; the once-curious listener now a converted disciple running with excited enthusiasm back to town to tell the good news.

Many of the Samaritans of the city "believed in Him" (verse 39), and, after He (Jesus) had abode with them there two days, "many more believed because of His own word," saying, "Now we believe . . . for we ourselves have heard Him and we know that this is indeed the Christ, the Savior of the world" (verses 41, 42).

An unavoidable result of choosing Jesus, of being freed from harmful vices and hurtful traditions and of finding forgiveness and hope in everlasting life, is dynamic witness. We simply can't remain silent about our new friend, Jesus. He becomes our sweetest thought, our dearest possession, the highest value in our lives, and a happiness that cannot be hidden. When we come to the realization of His voluntary choice to come and die, the Creator for the creature, the King for the servant, the Judge for the condemned, we are fueled and fired to witness to that love.

It is the knowledge of His giving us "something better"—His holiness for our sins; His sacrifice for our selfishness; His seamless robe for our garment of guilt; His gift of purity for our works of righteousness; His perfect holiness for our relative perfection—that makes us animated disciples.

Not all communities will respond like the unnamed Samaritan village. There are places that, when warned, are deserving of our "shaking the dust from our feet." Thank God, however, that there are many other places containing "sheep not yet of the fold," who will gladly embrace the "something better" of His Word.

September 23

A Better Offer

Jesus answered and said to her, "If you knew the gift of God,
and who it is who says to you, 'Give Me a drink,' you would
have asked Him, and He would have given you living water." John 4:10.

Jesus' offering of "something better" to the Samaritan woman contained no less
than five distinctive promises. By His mention of a "gift of God" (verse 10), He
promised her a better priority; by His pointing to a well of "water springing up"
(verse 14), He promised her a better prospect; by His decrying her affiliation with
several husbands (verses 16-18), He promised her a better performance; by coun-
tering her views about superior mountain worship (verses 21-24), He promised
her a better prospective; and by replying to her cautious reference to the coming
Messiah (verse 25) with the statement "I . . . am He" (verse 26), He promised her a
better possession.

These promises constitute the "something better" that we Christians offer the
world. They highlight "something better" than the quickly evaporated excitement
of commercialized sports; "something better" than endlessly routinized labor;
"something better" than living out our days to the slavish conformity of marching
through life as helpless victims in the mortal succession of passing generations;
"something better" than the morbid philosophy of the intellectuals who define life
as "the cruel eruption of the peaceful state of nonexistence"; "something better"
than wasted talents and the Christless graves of those who reject His love.

Believers need not enter into debate or consume their energies in disputes designed to criticize and denigrate the teachings of others. The positive gospel of Jesus
is convincing enough; it stands out in bold relief against all other formulations. It's
most legitimate, appealing, and convincing claim—something better.

The woman at the well accepted and was transformed. She arrived consumed
with pride of place, but left convinced by the hope of the race; she arrived besieged
with selfish tradition, but left believing in the Great Physician; she arrived trans-
fixed with Jacob's sod, but left transformed by Jacob's God; she arrived to work in
her daily vocation, but left immersed in a brand-new relation; she arrived bound
by sin's cruel wages, but left broken by the Rock of Ages; she arrived full of lust
and strife, but left filled with the Water of Life. And so it is with all who choose
Him—the "better way."

Risky Choosing

Abram dwelt in the land of Canaan, and Lot dwelt in the cities
of the plain and pitched his tent even as far as Sodom. Gen. 13:12.

Lot made the wrong choice. The well-watered plains, the greener pastures, the
lake view, the mountain vistas, and all the other physical advantages were al-
luring, but because of their proximity to Sodom, Lot was dangerously positioned.
When God destroyed that wicked citadel, Lot escaped, but his family did not.

No, Lot did not choose Sodom, but he risked wrongly by pitching toward it. To
his deep regret, and as a stark warning to all, his choice resulted in the corruption of
the lives of those he loved most. Not only was his wife, who looked back longingly
at the city and turned into a pillar of salt, but also most of his children, the supreme
object of his and every good parents heart, were lost as well.

In describing the ruins of Sodom and Gomorrah, George Adam Smith wrote:
"The grave of Sodom and Gomorrah is flung down the whole length of scriptural
history. It is the popular and standard judgment of sin. The story is told in Genesis;
it was applied in Deuteronomy, referred to by Amos, by Isaiah, by Jeremiah, by
Ezekiel and Zephaniah and in Lamentations. Our Lord employs it more than once
as figures of judgment. He threatens upon cities where the word is preached in vain,
and we feel the flame scorch our cheeks. . . . Paul, Peter, Jude make mention of it.
In Revelation the city of sin is spiritually called Sodom" (*The Archaeological Bible
Supplement,* Thompson Chain-Reference Bible, p. 360).

While the ruins of Sodom have disappeared, the glare of its destructive fires
still blaze upon the pages of the Written Word, urging us to pray as Christ taught:
"Lead us not into temptation."

Sodom is the Christian's undimmed reminder that it is better to risk auster-
ity, privation, discomfort, and second-rate circumstances where God's goodness is
proclaimed, than to enjoy material and social advantages where godlessness reigns.
But since spiritual things are spiritually discerned (1 Cor. 1:14), that is a posture
that can be made and sustained only by daily communion with Christ. It is that
relationship alone that attaches and binds us to Jesus, our city of refuge, our protecting, providing, productive something better.

Deferred Gratification

And everyone who competes for the prize is
temperate in all things. Now they do it to obtain a perishable crown,
but we for an imperishable crown. 1 Cor. 9:25.

Deferred gratification—the willingness to suffer present pain for future gain, to sacrifice immediate enjoyment for later, greater rewards—has been a difficult choice for humans. However, it is made all the more difficult for moderns because of the "instant" craze that influences our deciding. Ours is a society of immediate gratifications; a generation strongly influenced by such sayings as "If it looks good, buy it"; "If it taste good, eat it"; "If it feels good, do it"—we have difficulty waiting.

Our generation has become accustomed to instant news, instant cash, instant communications, instant foods, instant marriages, instant divorces, instant diplomas, and instant contracts. We are happiest when we receive instant services at banks, airports, and the checkout lanes of megamarkets.

During most of my 14 years of presidency at Oakwood College in Huntsville, Alabama, I was enrolled in doctoral studies at Vanderbilt University in Nashville, Tennessee, about 100 miles away. The program requirements involved acquaintance with a number of theorists, ancient and modern, plus a reading knowledge of German and Spanish, and of course, a dissertation that eventually took two years to complete. There were times I was tempted to opt for a lesser degree; to leave the lengthy, arduous program the university structured and enroll in one of the more easily managed "degree mills" I saw advertised in various journals.

One warm spring afternoon, while wearily rehearsing German grammatical structure, I raised this possibility with my tutor, Prof. Robert Buyck. His response was "Brother Rock—you want to earn a serious degree." Yes, I certainly did. And sacrifices not withstanding, I plodded on for 10 full years. The results have far exceeded what might have been otherwise achieved or what I could have imagined.

What is the "serious degree" of your dreams? What is it that you dare hope to do in your professional career, in your educational attainments, in your family affairs? Our text reminds us that if you would "go for the gold"—temporal or eternal—present sacrifice for future reward is a necessary choice.

The Ultimate Choice

And he said to Him, "All these things I will
give You if You will fall down and worship me." Matt. 4:9.

The hero of France's struggle with England during the Hundred Years' War was Joan of Arc. When England besieged Orléans in the fall of 1428, young Joan announced that she had orders from God to direct in the defense of the nation. Twice she pleaded unsuccessfully with French leadership for authority to organize resistance. It was only after the populace became excited by rumors of a prophecy concerning a teenage virgin who would lead the country to victory that they agreed.

After months of tutoring in matters of warfare, Joan declared herself battle-ready. When asked by the authorities if she were really serious, she replied, "Rather now than tomorrow. And tomorrow than the day after!" (William Track, *Joan of Arc in Her Own Words*).

What followed is the stuff of which legends are made. Recovering from arrow shots and masquerading as a man in order not to risk attention and capture, she rallied the flagging energies of her people. After freeing Orléans in 1429, she led her troops in successful battles in a number of key locations. She was captured in May 1430. While on trial, she was questioned by crafty English judges as to whether or not she was in a state of grace. Her answer, avoiding the political trap that had been set, was "If I am not, may God put me there, and if I am, may God keep me there!" And when urged to recant, she said, "I would rather die than do what I know to be sin."

In 1431, at the age of 19, she was burned at the stake for heresy. But her death galvanized the French populace in even greater resistance. By the end of the war in 1453, all of their territories except Calais had been recaptured, and Joan had become a household legend.

We see in Joan's actions a parallel to our deliverance through Jesus. Touched by our mistreatments at Satan's hands, Jesus chose to leave heaven, and at a young age engaged the enemy. Satan often pressed Him to abandon His mission. But He refused to be distracted, diverted, or deterred. Nothing, from the loneliness of childhood to the insults of Calvary, could stop Him. All praise to our blessed Lord, our worthy Redeemer—our champion of grace.

September 27

Ultimate Priorities

His mother said to the servants, "Whatever He says to you, do it." John 2:5.

All biblical injunctions are valuable in that "all Scripture is given by inspiration of God, and is profitable for doctrine, for reproof, for correction, for instruction in righteousness, that the man of God may be complete, thoroughly equipped for every good work" (2 Tim. 3:16, 17). However, there are some injunctions, some statements, some counsels, some declarations that stand out as not simply sound advice, but as absolutes of behavior. Paul's writings are a rich source of such instruction. Illustrations are: his urging to act one's age (1 Cor. 13:11); his advice to sow generously (2 Cor. 9:6); his counsel to cultivate faith above all (Eph. 6:16); his warning to abstain from evil appearance (1 Thess. 5:22); and his encouragement to cultivate the mind of Jesus (Phil. 2:5).

Jesus Himself uttered directives that stood out as beacons of obedience. Among them: "Seek first the kingdom of God and His righteousness" (Matt. 6:33); "Do to others what you would have them do to you" (Matt. 7:12, NIV); Forgive as you wish to be forgiven (see Matt. 6:12); "Take up [your] cross and follow Me" (Mark 8:34); "Go ye therefore, and teach all nations" (Matt. 28:19, KJV); "Whosoever will be chief among you, let him be your servant" (Matt. 20:27, KJV); and the most fundamental of them all: the premiere priority of Christian discipleship, "Ye must be born again" (John 3:7, KJV).

These are all ultimate spiritual and social success. Living by such principles guarantees the very best of returns that life can offer. They constitute the operations manual handed us by the Creator by whose wisdom we are made. He who knows us best has not left us without appropriate guides to happiness and productivity. We need not structure for ourselves outlines or syllabi for optimum choosing—we couldn't if we tried. Life's most productive guides for personal enhancement and appropriate relations with others are already provided in the Word of God who made us.

In order to know the Word, we must hear the Word. We do this in our private, our family, and our public devotions. In these ways we drink from the fountain of ultimate wisdom and are informed, encouraged, and empowered to identify and achieve ultimate priorities.

Proximate Priorities

The law of the Lord is perfect, converting the soul;
The testimony of the Lord is sure, making wise the simple. Ps. 19:7.

In addition to the ultimate or absolute principles of behavior that the Bible provides, we also find in it a wealth of proximate or everyday rules for living. Among Solomon's many memorable counsels are: "Go to the ant, you sluggard! Consider her ways and be wise" (Prov. 6:6); "A little sleep, a little slumber, a little folding of the hands to sleep—so shall your poverty come on you like a prowler, and your need like an armed man" (Prov. 6:10, 11); "A merry heart does good, like medicine, but a broken spirit dries the bones" (Prov. 17:22); and "Wine is a mocker, strong drink is a brawler, and whoever is led astray by it is not wise" (Prov. 20:1).

Among Paul's more memorable rules for practical living are: "Let him who stole steal no longer" (Eph. 4:28); "Prove all things" (1 Thess. 5:21, KJV); "In honour preferring one another" (Rom. 12:10, KJV); and "Be ye not unequally yoked together with unbelievers" (2 Cor. 6:14, KJV).

Ellen White's writings, while never to be regarded as equal with the Bible, are a gold mine of proximate counsels. Among them: (1) in most cases, two meals a day are better than three; (2) meat eating is not good for the body or mind; (3) guard well the edges of the Holy Sabbath day; (4) our homes should be generously blessed with sunlight and music; and (5) parents should never dispute or disagree in the presence of their children.

Times have drastically changed since Bible days and even the era of Ellen White. But basic human nature has not changed. The gods of this world have different names and faces, but the temptations are still "the lust of the flesh," "the lust of the eye," and "the pride of life" (see 1 John 2:16).

Thank God He has provided us not only the general absolutes of behavior, but also a wealth of practical (proximate) guidance as well. Those who take time to listen and obey are constrained to sing with the psalmist: "More to be desired are they than gold, yea, than much fine gold; sweeter also than honey and the honeycomb. Moreover by them Your servant is warned, and in keeping them there is great reward" (Ps. 19:10, 11).

An Individual Matter

"If these three men, Noah, Daniel, and Job, were in it, they would deliver only themselves by their righteousness," says the Lord God. Eze. 14:14.

The prognosis had not been good. Already Ezekiel had, in no uncertain terms, proclaimed frightful judgments upon the remaining citizens of Jerusalem. Their refusal to follow God's commands, he had predicted, would soon result in severe punishment from heaven. So his visitors, a group of returning elders, were not surprised when he repeated doom upon Israel's disobedient citizenry.

What must have struck them, however, was the unusual force with which he punctuated his warnings, stating that even the presence of Noah, Daniel, and Job, three primary icons of Israelite history, could not avert pending disaster. The prophet brought ironclad closure to any hope of deliverance for the doomed inhabitants of the city. He invoked the names of those stalwarts not once but four times during their brief conversation, as proof of God's intention to thoroughly recompense Israel's evil.

It is revealing to note that Noah, Daniel, and Job had each been instruments of heroic rescue: Noah, his whole family (Gen. 6:18); Daniel, his companions (Dan. 2:18); and Job, his friends (Job 42:7, 8). Ezekiel's warning was that even if all three heroes were now in Jerusalem at the same time, rescue for its wicked inhabitants could not be accomplished. This is a clear reminder that salvation is an individual matter: we cannot be saved by one another, no matter how right or righteous, and there is a limit to God's patience and pardon.

While salvation is indeed an individual matter, individual salvation is enhanced by the influence of others who are godly. It is by God's grace only that anyone is saved. However, by their righteous example, their wise counsel, and their intercessory prayers, godly individuals often inspire to godly living.

In a broader sense, there is hope the presence of godly persons inspires God to tolerance for the erring. His agreement to spare Sodom and Gomorrah if only "ten [righteous could] be found" (Gen. 18:32), and His merciful response to Moses' plea to blot him out but spare the people (Ex. 32:32), illustrate this grace.

The ultimate demonstration of the Father's willingness to be influenced by the intercession of the good for the bad is His acceptance of Jesus' righteous life and death in place of ours. To that end, Jesus, our representative, now intercedes, and we His people choose to live for Him in trusting assurance.

Contrasting Priorities

I call heaven and earth as witnesses today against you,
that I have set before you life and death, blessing and cursing; therefore
choose life, that both you and your descendants may live. Deut. 30:19.

Prideful indulgence lies at the root of every destructive choice detailed in the Word of God. For Cain, it was indulgence of jealousy; for Lot's family, it was indulgence of excitement; for Dinah's brothers, it was indulgence of revenge; for Saul, it was indulgence of popularity; for Absalom, it was indulgence of power; for Amon, it was indulgence of lust; for Gehazi, it was indulgence of greed; for the rich young ruler, it was indulgence of riches; for Judas, it was indulgence of personal opinion; for Pilate, it was indulgence of fear; for Herod, it was indulgence of ego; and for Ananias and Sapphira, it was indulgence of selfishness.

On the other hand, humble surrender to God and the willingness to abandon one's natural urges to follow His will lies at the root of every productive priority chronicled in Scripture. For Joseph, it was a surrender to God's principles; for Moses, it was surrender to His presence; for Esther, it was surrender to His providence; for Daniel, it was surrender to His power; for David, it was surrender to His power; for Isaiah, it was surrender to His purity; for Peter, it was surrender to His person; for the Ethiopian eunuch, it was surrender to His passion; for Paul, it was surrender to His priestly function; and for John, it was surrender to His perfect love.

The lessons are clear: priorities that are rooted in self always lead to sorrow, and priorities that are ordered by divine wisdom always lead to salvation. Self-pleasing priorities may not immediately evidence their baleful harvest, but the incontrovertible laws of the moral universe ensure their negative consequences. God-pleasing priorities do not always show immediate benefits, but their blessings are as unalterable as are the purposes of God.

God has promised to honor right choices. It is our duty to obey, and His business to affect the laws of wholesome reaping—He will show "mercy [to] thousands of them that love [Him] and keep [His] commandments" (Ex. 20:5, KJV).

OCTOBER

A Better Righteousness

A Higher Holiness

But we are all like an unclean thing, and all our righteousnesses
are like filthy rags; we all fade as a leaf, and our iniquities,
like the wind, have taken us away. Isa. 64:6.

Righteousness is being right and doing right. It is not what people think we are,
it is what God knows we are. It is the sum total of one's relationship to God
expressed in both thought and action. Righteousness references not the committing
of individual acts, but the overall state or quality of one's spiritual health. Further,
in order to qualify for eternal life, one's righteousness must be absolutely spotless—
immaculately sinless. Imperfect righteousness disqualifies one for life everlasting,
and that is our inescapable problem. Our righteousness is ever inadequate. Our
state of being and doing is always deficient.

Paul had this dilemma in mind when he wrote, "For all have sinned and fall
short of the glory of God" (Rom. 3:23). Notice the comprehensiveness of his words:
they cover our past "have sinned" as well as our present—"and fall short." Ellen
White drives home the point that the future, as well, will find us deficient. She says
that "the closer [we] come to Jesus, the more faulty [we] will appear in [our] own
eyes; for [our] vision will be clearer and [our] imperfections will be seen in broad
and distinct contrast to His perfection nature" (*Steps to Christ*, p. 64).

This is our unhappy state. The righteousness that qualifies for glory can have
no flaws; it cannot be "relative" or still progressing—it must be absolute or finished.
We, on the other hand, are not righteous—"no, not one" (Rom. 3:10). Clearly, we
need something better . . . a purer perfection, a greater goodness—a higher holiness if we would be saved. And what is this? It is the righteousness of Jesus. This is
exactly what Paul had in mind when he pleaded, "And be found in Him, not having
my own righteousness, which is from the law, but that which is through faith in
Christ, the righteousness which is from God by faith" (Phil. 3:9).

Yes! His righteousness is better and more precious than that of any other in
the history of the broad universe of created beings. Better because it was earned
under circumstances unimaginably difficult; better because it was fueled by a love
unthinkably magnanimous; better because it was secured by the precious blood of
the innocent Lamb of Calvary; better because He did not (as do many formally poor
upon reaching prosperity) abandon His lowly kin; and better because He "ever
liveth" to make intercession on behalf of those He came to redeem.

How We Got This Way

Behold, I was brought forth in iniquity, and in sin my mother conceived me. Ps. 51:5.

Imagine living without a negative—nothing sordid, nothing scary, nothing sinful—life in an atmosphere of unmarred health and happiness! Think of what joy that would be. This was the case with Adam and Eve. They were (before sin) totally free from evil desires, evil deeds, and evil designs. In mind and character they were perfectly pure; the sinful suggestions to which they yielded were not native to their being; they were tempted by external stimuli—inducements that were foreign to their holy natures. But when they sinned, their status changed; evil did not visit them and leave, it took up residence in their system. They were permanently corrupted; from then on urges to wrong sprang from within their beings.

There was (is) no natural reversal from sin's disastrous effects. Adam and Eve could not regain their former state of innocence. Satan had won. He had succeeded in disastrously damaging the beings God created in faultless purity; creatures made to replace Satan and his fallen angels (see *Prophet and Kings,* pp. 588, 589). But it was not only the first pair whose beings were ruined, but those of succeeding generations as well. The disease that they brought upon themselves is the baleful birthright we all inherit, and it is this condition that more than anything else disqualifies us for the kingdom of heaven. It is our unalterably, unholy flesh that types us as sinners *even when we are not sinning!*

Ellen White helps detail our dilemma thusly: "It was possible for Adam, before the fall, to form a righteous character by obedience to God's law. But he failed . . . , and because of his sin our natures have fallen, and we cannot make ourselves righteous" (*Steps to Christ,* p. 62).

Because even our good deeds pour forth from unclean vessels (unholy flesh); they can never be "the providing factor" of salvation. At best they constitute soiled sacrifices, ragged righteousness and damaged devotion. This is why His righteous life is needed and thus is what He freely provides. The apostle had it right: "For if, by the trespass of one man, death reigned through that one man, how much more will those who receive God's abundant provision of grace and of the gift of righteousness reign in life through the one man, Jesus Christ" (Rom. 5:17, NIV).

Our rags for His righteousness! Our incomplete holiness for His purity! Our misery for His majesty! What a bargain, what a blessing! What a God!

Our Spotless Gift

For as by one man's disobedience many were made sinners,
so also by one Man's obedience many will be made righteous. Rom. 5:19.

There are many mysteries surrounding Christ's entry into our world. We will never fully understand how God became flesh and dwelt among us, how He was all God and all human at the same time and how He healed as God but faced and overcame temptation as a human. We know *that* He did, but we do not know *how* He did it. We can never fully explain how He could function as all God and all man without ethical conflict or mismanagement.

There is even mystery about the quality or depth of humanity He assumed. We have difficulty and disagreement in deciding whether He faced temptation with the uncorrupted spiritual nature of Adam before the fall or that which he (Adam) had following his transgression.

What is not mysterious, however, and what is very clear, is that "He had done no violence, nor was any deceit in his mouth" (Isa. 53:9), that "when He was reviled, did not revile in return; when He suffered, He did not threaten, but committed Himself to Him who judges righteously" (1 Peter 2:23). And that when He completed His spotless performance in human flesh, He arranged with the Father to apply His hard-earned credit to our impossibly deficient accounts.

For many this gift is too good to be true, and they spend their time seeking to prove worthy of Christ's priceless endowment. But we cannot earn Christ's goodness. No amount of trying or doing will merit His mercy or produce characters that qualify us for eternal life. The process whereby we are, through Christ, made acceptable contains many mysteries. But the consequence is clear—we are saved! Once we were lost, but now we are found—were blind but now we see. We are now redeemed and can rejoice with the prophet and say: "Thank God that we are not dealing with impossibilities. . . . We are not to be anxious about what Christ and God think of us, but about what God thinks of Christ, our Substitute" (*Selected Messages,* book 2, pp. 32, 33). "The life which Christ offers us is more perfect, more full, and more complete than was the life which Adam forfeited by transgression" (*Signs of the Times,* June 17, 1897). This is our highest rejoicing, our richest inheritance, our grandest, most glorious hope.

Our Greatest Gift

Yet in all these things we are more than conquerors
through Him who loved us. Rom. 8:37.

The provisions of wills increase greatly the material possessions of heirs. No ethical individual knowledgeable of inclusion in another's will would wish that person's demise, but the sure prospect of death, especially of aged benefactors, often produces high, if guarded, expectation.

Jesus is our benefactor; He left a rich will for His people. It was uttered a few hours before His death and is recorded in John 14-17. He introduced His will by saying, in language both sorrowful and sublime, "Let not your heart be troubled: you believe in God, believe also in Me. In My Father's house are many mansions; if it were not so, I would have told you. I go to prepare a place for you . . . that where I am, there you may be also" (John 14:1-3).

Many of the provisions He promises His followers are earthly, not heavenly. Yes, we will have heavenly mansions. We know from 1 Corinthians 2:9 that there in our eternity of "much more," we will enjoy untold wonders in glory. But this is not the primary substance of His will. The main emphasis of His will is that which He plans for His waiting people while on earth.

That array of pronounced benefits includes His peace (John 14:27), His joy (John 15:11), His successor, the Holy Spirit (John 16:7-13), His power (verse 26), His unity (John 17:21), and yet another absolutely crucial provision—His perfect sanctification or holiness (verses 17-19).

Why Christ's righteousness? As Scripture states, we must be "more than conquerors" (Rom. 8:37) in the struggle with sin. It is true that in our daily experience we do conquer, we grow, we progress, and we overcome. But since our sinful natures remain with us, since what we overcome are the evil urges of the unholy flesh we inhabit, we must be more than conquerors—we must be heirs.

Our righteousness cost Christ His life. Were it not for His death, His will would be unavailable and we irretrievable—eternally lost. On Calvary He signed in blood the benefits of His will, and all who accept are happy heirs of the "righteousness which is of faith" (Rom. 10:6, KJV).

A Ready Gift

When evening fell, the owner of the vineyard said to his steward,
"Call the labourers and give them their pay, beginning with those who
came last and ending with the first." Those who had started work an hour
before sunset came forward, and were paid the full day's wage. When it was
the turn of the men who had come first, they expected something extra,
but were paid the same amount as the others. Matt. 20:8-10, NEB.

We know *why* we need the righteousness of Christ—our righteousness is never sufficient; we know *how* we receive the righteousness of Christ—it is a gift from Jesus provided in his will. But the question is often asked, *when* do we receive the precious promise? The answer is provided in the following statement: "The moment the sinner believes in Christ, he stands in the sight of God uncondemned; for the righteousness of Christ is his: Christ's perfect obedience is imputed to him" (*Fundamentals of Christian Education*, p. 429).

The why and how and when of salvation are all demonstrated in the experience of the thief on the cross. He had no time to do good works or to neglect obvious duties. Prior to being nailed there, he was a criminal—a thief and robber, harmful to himself and society. But when impacted by the love of Jesus, he sincerely repented. He was, right then and there, without possibility of good deeds, declared righteous. He was in that instant transformed from enemy to friend, sinner to saint, lost to found, both justified and sanctified by Christ's saving robe of righteousness.

The bad news is that even when deathbed confessions are sincere, the repentant leave undone a myriad of good works that might have been accomplished had confession come sooner. The good news, however, is that there will be among the redeemed many whose "late in life" conversion provided them little or no opportunity for good works, but whose salvation will be as complete as if they had accomplished them. This is because, as the lesson of the "last-hour laborers" in the parable of Matthew 20:1-16 reminds us, it is not the length or strength of our works that saves, but rather the purity and perfection of the life that Christ substitutes on our behalf.

The Free Gift

But the free gift is not like the offense.
For if by the one man's offense many died,
much more the grace of God and the gift by the grace
of the one Man, Jesus Christ, abounded to many. Rom. 5:15.

The righteousness of Christ is a gift. We cannot earn it, buy it, create it, procure it, or deserve it. Christ gives it, bestows it, donates it, imputes it, and imparts it at great cost to Himself, but no cost to us.

As humans we are programmed to attach self-worth and societal approval to positive accomplishments. We are taught from childhood that reward follows good deeds and merit comes by effort; that nice things happen when we earn them, and we get what we deserve and deserve what we get. So it is hard to believe that our salvation is a result of Jesus' obedience, not ours; that His spotless life is provided not because of anything we do, but simply because He loves us. We find it difficult to accept that "both our title to heaven and our fitness for it are found in the righteousness of Christ" (*The Desire of Ages,* p. 300).

Yet it is true—our salvation is a matter of Jesus' love "plus nothing" on our part but acceptance of His free gift. That gift is better than a lifetime of labor that we can fashion; it is ours when we "let go and let God!" It is ours when we fall at the foot of the cross pleading "nothing in my hands I bring, simply to the cross I cling." It is ours when we realize that no matter how learned we are, how rich we are, how talented we are, how connected we are, how high in society we are, or how long we've been in the church, nothing we hold or do counts for our redemption—the gift of salvation was completed on Calvary and is deposited in our name in heaven's bank and awaits our acceptance.

Some things advertised as free are not free at all. They are the ploy of crafty manufacturers and super salespersons. The offer of Christ's free gift is neither ruse nor reward; it is neither matched nor manufactured by our good works. It is the undeserved, unearned, unencumbered bestowal upon the sinner who, under the conviction of the Holy Spirit, recognizes Christ's offer—believes it, receives it, and by it is transplanted from the kingdom of darkness to the kingdom of light.

A Fragrant Gift

"You shall make of these an incense,
a compound according to the art of the perfumer,
salted, pure, and holy. And you shall beat some
of it very fine, and put some of it before the Testimony
in the tabernacle of meeting where I will meet with you.
It shall be most holy to you." Ex. 30:35, 36.

The righteousness of Christ is symbolized in Scripture in many graphic ways. One is the fragrant cloud that ascended from the altar of incense at the holy place wafting its way over the veil that shielded the Most Holy Place. As the priest performed his duties facing (but not seeing) the ark of the covenant on the other side of the veil, so must we now direct our prayers to the unseen throne of God on high—ever flavored with the righteousness of Christ.

I love the way the prophet puts it. "As the inner veil of the sanctuary did not extend to the top of the building, the glory of God, which was manifested above the mercy seat, was partially visible from the first apartment. When the priest offered incense before the Lord, he looked toward the ark; and as the cloud of incense arose, the divine glory ascended upon the mercy seat and filled the Most Holy Place, and often so filled both apartments that the priest was obliged to retire to the door of the tabernacle. . . . The incense, ascending with the prayers of Israel, represents the merits and intercession of Christ, His perfect righteousness, which through faith is imputed to his people, and which can alone make the worship of sinful beings acceptable to God" (*Patriarchs and Prophets*, p. 353).

What makes Christ's righteousness so fragrant to the Father? It is His willingness, the purity of His motives, and the perfection of His performance. Viewed otherwise, that which makes Christ's life a saving favor to humanity is precisely what makes it a fragrant savor to the Father.

It is that righteousness that stimulates the sinner's love, awakens the sinner's will, and fastens the follower's faith; it assuages the Father's wrath, assures the Father's approval, and rejuvenates the church below while rejoicing the church above. It is a grand and glorious provision, a priceless transaction—a life-giving gift that is ours for the asking.

October 8

A Seasoned Gift

"For everyone will be seasoned with fire, and every sacrifice will be seasoned with salt. Salt is good, but if the salt loses its flavor, how will you season it? Have salt in yourselves, and have peace with one another." Mark 9:49, 50.

Salt is another one of the scriptural representations of Christ's righteousness. In instructing His people regarding the sacrifices of animal flesh, God commanded, "And every offering of your grain offering you shall season with salt; you shall not allow the salt of the covenant of your God to be lacking from your grain offering. With all your offerings you shall offer salt" (Lev. 2:13).

Ellen White is clear about this meaning, "In the ritual service, the salt was added to every sacrifice. This, like the offering of incense, signified that only the righteousness of Christ could make the service acceptable to God" (*The Desire of Ages*, p. 439).

We are intrinsically flawed. Our sacrifices and good works are ever deficient and, unless salted with the righteousness of Christ, our works remain unpalatable, untenable, and unacceptable, no matter how long or loud our praises and good deeds. His "value added" life alone transforms our deficient offerings into fully acceptable service. His perfection superimposed upon our faulty performances makes the difference. His success atones for our failures. His merits applied to our needy account are complete payment for our debt. His provisions of holiness and happiness are greater than our needs and necessities. His gift is something better than we could have dreamed or imagined. It transforms flesh "dead in sin" to lively beings happily oriented to the Father's glory. His touch makes blind eyes open, dense minds clear, empty hearts full, dry bones live, and tasteless sacrifices acceptable.

It should be remembered that the salt of Christ's righteousness is given not just for our personal, prioritized holiness; it is bestowed in order that we may flavor those around us. We are to be the salt of the earth—God's agents of preservation in the home, on the job, in the school, or wherever we go.

Our text reminds us that our effectiveness in enhancing others and expanding Christ's kingdom on earth depends not upon our talent and creativity, but upon the Holy Spirit's activating presence within us. By His power we become not only seekers of holiness, but also depositors of power, and thereby, agents of change in a doomed and dying world.

A Precious Gift

Again, the kingdom of heaven is like a merchant seeking beautiful pearls, who, when he had found one pearl of great price, went and sold all that he had and bought it. Matt. 13:45, 46.

He was a businessman like thousands of others of his time—a risk-taker who found enjoyment in the art of the deal— one of which was buying and selling pearls. Finding and admiring these gems of the ocean was in some ways as pleasurable to him as selling them. And while he never saw a pearl he didn't like, he never had one he wouldn't sell.

Then one day it happened—most likely in a small, unpretentious shop at the edge of one of the busy coastal cities he often frequented—he encountered the largest, brightest gem he had ever seen. It was love at first sight! Its luscious purity dazzled his senses and delighted his desires; it was the pearl of his dreams. This one was too gorgeous to sell; he must have it as his own; but at what price? That was the problem! It cost more than he had or could afford. He had prepared to make the kind of ordinary purchases such trips usually demanded, but this one required more—far more funds on hand or even in the bank. In fact, its price exceeded the sum of all his liquid assets. Purchasing this pearl would require the total of all his assets—the sum of his entire net worth. But for him there was no question. Completely obsessed, he hastened home and sold all that he had in order to purchase the object of his affection.

Jesus is the pearl of great price. The businessman is every confessing sinner whose eyes have been opened to His righteousness; who, having lived a life engaged in lesser joys, encounters the wondrous truth that salvation is made available not because of our works, but because of the life that Jesus has already lived—He is our ultimate attraction, our highest quest, our magnificent obsession.

The only logical response, the only right reply, the only wholesome reaction for the sinner when this glorious truth appears is total surrender; the complete divesting of self in absolute trust and obedience to Him. No sacrifice is too dear, no surrender too painful, no self-abnegation too costly. Christ's righteousness, the superimposition of His holiness upon our helpless frailty, is the transaction of a lifetime—the sum and substance of our hope for eternity.

The Necessary Gift

But when the king came in to see the guests,
he saw a man there who did not have on a wedding garment.
So he said to him, "Friend, how did you come in here without
a wedding garment?" And he was speechless. Matt. 22:11, 12.

While world cultures differ in ways that weddings are celebrated, all demonstrate high value for this significant event. A wedding symbolizes not simply a change of status for the couple involved, but the making of society's most meaningful units—the home.

Sober-minded citizens understand that it is no easy task for "the twain to become one"; that after the euphoria of the event comes the personal adjusting required for true bonding; that "leaving and cleaving" necessitates sacrificial submission; and that, in the words of Edgar Guest, "It takes a heap o' livin' in a house t' make it home." Nevertheless, weddings are universally happily celebrated occasions.

One way in which the specialness of the wedding event is noted is in the dress of the bride and groom. In Christ's day special dress was also required of those who attended. In fact, a person without the proper attire was refused entry, and if necessary, embarrassingly removed from the ceremony.

Jesus is the bridegroom, the redeemed His holy bride; the wedding event is the second coming of Christ. This is why John wrote, "Let us be glad and rejoice and give Him glory, for the marriage of the Lamb has come, and His wife has made herself ready. And to her it was granted to be arrayed in fine linen, clean and bright, for the fine linen is the righteous acts of the saints" (Rev. 19:7, 8). And this is the crux of Paul's ardent desire to be found (at Christ's return) not having his own righteousness, but that of his Lord (see Phil. 3:9).

Jane Lauber said it well,
"You have your work clothes on, my dear,
 That simply will not do.
 The wedding is near,
 Please will you wear
 The garments bought for you?"

A Costly Gift

Christ has redeemed us from the curse of the law, having become a curse for us (for it is written, "Cursed is everyone who hangs on a tree"). Gal. 3:13.

Satan's attempts to derail Christ's mission were never-ending. He failed in his attempt to slaughter Him at birth and thus, physically abort His mission. But he pummeled and harassed Him relentlessly throughout His life and harbored more than just retaliation for his expulsion from heaven. His primary objective was Christ's disqualification as our substitute. He realized that the success of Christ's service was dependent upon His dying a perfect sacrifice. He knew that just one mistake, one little error, one evil thought on the part of Jesus would invalidate His ministry. He left no stone unturned, no trick unused, no opportunity wasted to defeat the Savior's purposes.

He realized that if Christ succeeded in living a life of perfect obedience, He would not only expose Satan's claims against the Creator as lies, but Christ would also die a perfect sacrifice. He harassed Him relentlessly. He sent lawyers to trap Him, women to tempt Him, Pharisees to taunt Him, Sadducees to trip Him, demons to terrorize Him, and Roman soldiers to tear at His innocent flesh. But in all of this, Jesus did not sin.

How severe were His trials? "Christ alone had experience in all of the sorrows and temptations that befall human beings. Never another of woman born was so fiercely beset by temptation; never another bore so heavy a burden of the world's sin and pain" (*Education*, p. 78). He was "tempted by Satan in a hundredfold severer manner than was Adam" (*Youth's Instructor*, June 2, 1898). "Could one sin have been found in Christ, had He in one particular yielded to Satan to escape the terrible torture, the enemy of God and man would have triumphed" (*The Desire of Ages*, p. 761).

How did Jesus overcome? By unswerving surrender to His Father's voice and will. He overcame by relying upon the "it is written" of the Word of God and by the power of the Holy Spirit, who strengthened Him in every temptation.

That victory—the only complete perfect triumph of humanity over temptation—He offers to you and me. He applies His life to our need, and by His "better righteousness" we, though otherwise unacceptable, are made acceptable to the Father.

The Best Gift

But the father said to his servants, "Bring out the best robe and put it on him, and put a ring on his hand and sandals on his feet." Luke 15:22.

It was a sight for sore eyes. After all those years, he was back. Back from a life of reveling, from sowing fields of wild oats, from wasting his strength on fickle, fair-weathered friends, from squandering all his considerable inheritance on events that left him drained, depleted, and discouraged. But now as he returned, familiar territory greeted his eyes: the rich fields of grain, the freshly painted barns, the grazing cattle, and the sturdy backdrop of majestic mountains. It was a warm, welcome sight. However, the glow in his heart was no match for the hollow in his stomach. He was happy, but he was afraid. What would his father do? Would he order him away, have him banished to the servant's quarters, read him the riot act, and refuse him forgiveness?

Perhaps there was a better way of doing this. Maybe he should ask one of the servants, who might recognize him, to warn his father and ask if it were all right to come back and thus avoid the embarrassment of rejection. But before his fears could overcome his hopes, there he was—his father, with his servants behind him, running his way with arms opened wide! When he reached him, he grasped him in a warm, tearful embrace—he was indeed forgiven, wanted, and welcomed.

He was received, but he was not ready for entrance into the father's house. His clothes were rumpled, his hair was matted, and he had the distinct smell of pigs on him. He was pardoned, but not prepared; forgiven, but not fit—his reentry must be preceded by his being properly cleaned and clothed. This is why the father ordered fresh clothing be given him before the welcome party.

And like the prodigal son we are not ready. Though repentant and forgiven, this does not qualify us for life in the glory kingdom—we must be appropriately cleansed and clothed.

The covering we receive is the very best heaven can provide: the robe of Christ's righteousness. That is what inspired the prophet to write: "By His perfect obedience He has satisfied the claims of the law, and my only hope is found in looking to Him as my substitute, . . . who obeyed the law perfectly for me" (*Selected Messages,* book 1, p. 396).

A Priceless Gift

For what profit is it to a man if he gains the whole world, and loses his own soul? Or what will a man give in exchange for his soul? Matt. 16:26.

We've all had the experience of losing something valuable: a watch, a purse or wallet, a credit card, a cell phone, our eyeglasses, etc. Losing such valuable objects can be an annoying and even painful experience—not just because of the inconvenience involved, but because of personal blame and shame in the light of our admitted forgetfulness or carelessness; the realization that we were in too much of a hurry or not as vigilant as we should have been.

Then there are those losses we incur for which we are not directly responsible. Consider the financial pain occurred because of depreciation of real estate or a drop in the stock market or underachieving savings accounts, all caused by failed government policies.

There are also other devastating kinds of losses: the loss of health, the loss of a friendship, the loss of a loved one. Happiness in life is, as much as anything, a matter of adjusting to loss: rebounding physically and psychologically from the hurt of being permanently or even temporarily separated from something or someone of value.

Christ's righteousness, provided at the moment of conversion, can also be lost. Like the conditional immortality given to Adam and Eve, it is operable only as long as we are obedient. The good news, however, is that it is not removed each time we sin. In fact, inspiration records: "We are accepted in the beloved. The sinner's defects are covered by the perfection and fullness of the Lord our righteousness" (*Our High Calling*, p. 51). "Christ looks at the spirit, and when He sees us carrying our burden with faith, His perfect holiness atones for our shortcomings. When we do our best, He becomes our righteousness" (*Selected Messages*, book 1, p. 368).

Christ's robe of righteousness is not easily lost; continued premeditated rebellion is the only cause for its removal. And if lost, there is no substitute replacement. Time cannot reduce the penalty of its absence; its value is inestimable, it's virtue unachievable, and there is no possible substitute or solace for its saving presence.

Our prayer today and every day should be, "Heavenly Father, keep me by Your grace, close to Your heart of love—ever covered by the Savior's robe."

An Exalted Gift

Go through, go through the gates; prepare ye
the way of the people; cast up, cast up the highway;
gather out the stones; lift up a standard for the people. Isa. 62:10, KJV.

A standard is a banner or flag by which a people or cause is identified. Each of Israel's tribes had such an identifying banner mounted high above their individual encampments and, in warfare, carried in the forefront of their fighting troops. The tribe of Judah had on its fluttering banner the image of a lion. Benjamin was identified by a wolf, Dan an eagle, Naphtali a deer, Ephraim an ox, Reuben the face of a man, etc.

Israel's standards served many purposes. They not only identified individual tribes and served as rallying points in battle, but also inspired to dedicated devotion in religious activities and were a constant reminder of God's presence among them.

We modern-day believers also have a standard: a banner that inspires us to sacrifice, a flag we are to lift for all to see, a sign that identifies us as God's special people. It is the standard of righteousness.

Concerning this standard, inspiration records: "God calls upon all who claim to be Christians to elevate the standard of righteousness, and to purify themselves even as He is pure" (*Medical Ministry*, p. 147). And again: "The standard of holiness is the same today as in the day of the apostles. Neither the promises nor requirements of God have lost aught of their force" (*Testimonies for the Church*, vol. 5, p. 240); "The church on earth is to be the representative of heavenly principles. Amid the awful confederacy of injustice, deception, robbery, and crime she is to shine with light from on high. In the righteousness of Christ she is to stand against prevailing apostasy" (*Medical Ministry*, pp. 132, 133).

The standard is then both a goal and a gift. Concerning the goal, the aged Paul wrote, "I have fought the good fight, I have finished the race. I have kept the faith. . . . There is laid up for me the crown of righteousness" (2 Tim. 4:7, 8).

Concerning the gift, he had confessed with even calmer conviction at an earlier time that he had already "become one with him, no longer counting on being saved by being good enough or by obeying God's laws, but by trusting Christ to save me" (Phil. 3:9, TLB).

The apostle's quest for both the goal and the gift as mirrored by us individually and lifted high by us collectively is what our world needs and our God requires.

Our Qualifying Gift

For if by the one man's offense death reigned through the one,
much more those who receive abundance of grace and of the gift of
righteousness will reign in life through the One, Jesus Christ. Rom. 5:17.

Simply saying yes to Jesus is not enough. We must seek (Luke 12:31), strive (Luke 13:24), and resist in the fight for the kingdom (James 4:7). Paul puts it clearly: "I don't mean to say I am perfect. I haven't learned all I should even yet, but I keep working toward that day when I will finally be all that Christ saved me for and wants me to be. No, dear brothers, I am still not all I should be, but I am bringing all my energies to bear on this one thing: Forgetting the past and looking forward to what lies ahead, I strain to reach the end of the race and receive the prize for which God is calling us up to heaven because of what Christ Jesus did for us" (Phil. 3:12-14, TLB).

Jesus Himself said, "Until now the kingdom of heaven suffers violence, and the violent take it by force" (Matt. 11:12). Ellen White, in commenting upon this statement, writes: "This violence takes in the whole heart. To be double minded is to be unstable. Resolution, self-denial, and consecrated effort are required for the work of preparation. . . . Every faculty and feeling must be engaged. Ardent and earnest prayer must take the place of listlessness and indifference. Only by earnest, determined effort and faith in the merits of Christ can we overcome and gain the kingdom of heaven" (*Youth's Instructor,* May 24, 1900).

How do we gain the motivation and strength to exert such strenuous effort? Simply by beholding Christ we can gain the strength and motivation. It is in the study of His sacrificial ministry on our behalf that we receive both the desire and the drive to obey. Each day's consecration brings us another impartation of His grace; each day's surrender positions us for further units of blessings.

But does this daily impartation of righteousness, born of the Spirit's working in our hearts, qualify us for glory? No. Only the gift of Christ's righteousness does this. The daily impartation of His righteousness produces the growth that distinguishes our discipleship, and it is the imputed gift of His righteousness received at conversion that guarantees our acceptance and decides our eternal destiny.

Our Permanent Gift

Therefore He is also able to save to the uttermost those who come to God through Him, since He always lives to make intercession for them. Heb. 7:25.

The growing Christian is grateful not only for the covering robe and the growth experience that accompanies it, but also the tenacious love of Christ that engulfs us even when we err. Christ's robe is not fitted upon us lightly or temporarily, but rather, it is ours to keep. True, we can lose it through premeditated sins and conscious exercise of evil; Christ's robe does not cover insincere profession of faith. Those who claim His name, but whose love for Him does not express itself in good works, gradually move from under His covering canopy. His robe is not for sale or hire or sham. It is available only to those whose surrender is complete.

It is a covering of hope and ultimate assurance. Those for whom the covering of Christ is a firm reality live each day knowing that although "we shall often have to bow down and weep at the feet of Jesus because of our shortcomings and mistakes, but we are not to be discouraged. Even if we are overcome by the enemy, we are not cast off, not forsaken and rejected of God" (*Steps to Christ*, p. 64). The redeemed have the assurance that when Satan tells us that we are beyond the limits of grace, we can answer: "Jesus gave His life for me. He suffered a cruel death that He might enable me to resist temptation. I know that He loves me, notwithstanding my imperfection. I will rest in His love. God has accepted His perfection in my behalf" (*Signs of the Times*, Aug. 13, 1902).

He loves us with an everlasting love. His provisions for our pardon far exceed sin's demands for our punishment. But His love, while supremely compelling, is not irresistible. His love is uncompromising, all-powerful, all-encompassing, all-knowing, and urged upon us by the Holy Spirit, but it is not forced upon us. When we accept that unimaginably gracious provision, we begin a new life of joy and productivity—He is ours and we are His. Our loudest praise will be the joy of salvation; we will live out our days as glad citizens of grace, permanent prisoners of hope, covered and completed by His righteousness, yoked with the Father by cords of love, that while we trust, cannot be broken.

A Coveted Gift

Blessed are those who hunger and thirst
for righteousness, for they shall be filled. Matt. 5:6.

Christ's righteousness is given only to those who desire it with uncommon desire; those who are desperate to have it; those who seek it with the craving expressed so graphically in the words of Psalm 42:1: "As the hart panteth after the water brooks, so panteth my soul for thee, O God" (KJV). That is how the hungry crave for food or the lover for the companionship of his or her mate.

And how is this affected in the heart? When by the wooing of the Holy Spirit we are brought to see the fallacy of sin, the temporariness of riches, the fleetingness of fame, the folly of intemperance, the brevity of life, the nature of eternity, and most of all, the beauty of salvation; when "the things of earth grow strangely dim, in the light of His glory and grace," then we will thirstily ask, seek, and find the love of God and the gift of His righteousness.

Once we experienced this we will not only want more of His righteousness, but also our capacity to receive it in greater measure will increase. Experiencing His righteousness is an energizing, enabling, soul-enhancing transaction. Its affects are so powerful and pervasive that we want nothing more than to be in league with Him; nothing more than to be covered by His life, sheltered from the storm of our sinfulness—by the sinlessness of His perfect being.

His covering symbolized in Scripture by Aaron's robe (Ex. 28:4), Joshua's garments (Zech. 3:1-5), Esther's apparel (Esther 5:1-3), the wedding guests' attire (Matt. 22:11, 12), the prodigal son's robe (Luke 15:22), the white garments granted Laodiceans (Rev. 3:18), the celestial robes of the redeemed (Rev. 7:9-15), and in the very genesis of our fall, the "tunic of animal's skin" with which God replaced the "fig-leaf apron" the first parents hastily created (Gen. 3:21) is the most precious commodity in heaven's treasure-house of goods. It is ours to be coveted, claimed, and kept.

His Ethical Gift

Therefore, all things He had to be made like His brethren,
that He might be a merciful and faithful High Priest in things pertaining
to God, to make propitiation for the sins of the people. Heb. 2:17.

One of Satan's means of seeking to discredit Christ's saving grace is to portray His intervention for our salvation as unfair or unethical. How could it be, he proposes, that the sacrifice of the Creator could alone atone for the sins of the created? It is not right that the blood and robe of Christ should be accepted in the place of human's disobedience and uncleanness. Of course, Satan would be right were it not for several unassailable facts.

The first is that Christ came into our world as redeemer not because He was compelled, but as a free moral agent. The second is that He really did take on human flesh upon His divine nature; in reality, He became our second Adam. Third, He really did die on Calvary; the divine Jesus was willing to die, but unable to do so; the human Jesus did die, though undeservedly so. Fourth, the plan was a genuine risk—if Jesus had failed to endure the "test and trial which the first Adam had failed to endure . . . the world would have been lost" (*The Seventh-day Adventist Bible Commentary*, Ellen G. White Comments, vol. 5, pp. 1082, 1083).

The plan for our rescue was weighted in terms very perilous for the human Christ. The risks involved were fraught with universal and eternal consequences. Jesus, the human being, could have failed. Satan's access to Him was just as immediate as it was to Adam and Eve, and more intense than they or we could ever know.

God's acceptance of His Son's offer to fight the angel of evil in humanities armor of innocence was not unfair. What was unfair were the relentlessly evil harassments Satan pressed upon Christ all of His life, and finally, the savage abuse he led in afflicting Him upon the cross.

Satan had every opportunity to discourage and trap and defeat our Lord, but Jesus won. His victory cannot be discredited, disavowed, disparaged, disregarded, disallowed, duplicated, or even dually explained. This much we do know: the Father "saw His sacrifice and was satisfied" (see Isa. 53:11). And so are we, the trusting beneficiaries of His love.

Covered, but Climbing

For by one offering He has perfected forever those
who are being sanctified. Heb. 10:14.

Christ's righteousness does not negate the need for our growth; that is, our personal, spiritual development. His holiness covers distance unattained, but never forgiveness unclaimed or a life that is mired in sin. His righteousness is our only saving factor, but it is not the only factor operable in our salvation experience; continued growth is also necessary. In the same way that a husband and wife are formally married the moment they exchange vows as they will be 70 years later should the union survive, we are saved from the moment of surrender as we will be at the end of life's journey.

But while surrender renders us completely covered, it does not render us completely grown. We are by conversion totally accepted, but not totally accomplished. We are newborn babes, with desires for the "sincere milk of the Word," eager to imbibe and grow (see 1 Peter 2:2). Thus, while covered, we are still climbing; while saved, still striving; while righteous, still reaching; while perfected, still progressing; and while assured, still ascending toward the high mark in Christ Jesus.

When Christ returns and provides mortals immortality, when our corruption is replaced by incorruption, we will no longer need the covering of His righteousness. This is because, after returning to the absolute perfection that our parents lost, we will be without need of substitute holiness. Fully restored in His image, we will no longer require covering for the faulty nature provided at birth.

Clad in the garb of conditional immortality, no longer badgered by the internal braying of Satan's hellish hounds—the internal tendencies for evil with which we were born and in this life never to escape—we will joyfully exclaim, "Free at last, free at last, thank God Almighty, I am free at last!"

And how is all this accomplished? By the gracious gift of His precious robe, that while making us already acceptable, inspires us to deeper devotion, and consequently loving obedience.

True Righteousness

For I say to you, that unless your righteousness
exceeds the righteousness of the scribes and Pharisees,
you will by no means enter into the kingdom of heaven. Matt. 5:20.

Y ou can see them, can't you—priestly dignitaries with neatly trimmed beards and long flowing robes moving with practiced dignity about their temple duties? They were well dressed, well organized, well regarded, but they were not well motivated. Their service was a performance. They were strict about the letter of their obedience and the legal details of what others should or should not do, but it was all a farce—they were fakes. They feigned devotion, but they craved adoration; they pretended consecration while they sought applause. They were not nice people, and Jesus let them have it—he unmasked their subterfuge. He pulled the blanket from their rotten intentions and exposed them for all to see, labeling them what they truly were—"blind guides," "whited sepulchers," and "hypocrites" (Matt. 23:16, 27, KJV).

They were punctilious about minor forms and ceremonies, but oblivious to the majors of human kindness and the sanctity of life. They tithed mint, anise, and cumin—the small plants of their gardens—and they were right in doing so: "these [they] ought to have done" (Luke 11:42). But doing so while ignoring the plight of the poor and the needy demonstrated their lack of understanding not just of God's Word, but also of God's character and the true meaning of righteousness.

Their brand of goodness would never do, and ours will not either, if like theirs it is cursed with the error of valuing policy above practicality, ends above means—the letter above the spirit of the law. If like theirs, our obedience is self-seeking and people-pleasing, our condemnation is just as certain, our recompense as baleful and deserved.

Returning a double tithe, readiness for the Sabbath 30 minutes before the sun sets, a vegan diet, etc., will not suffice. Righteous living is righteous doing. It is more than privatized devotion; it is a loving regard toward others. When His saving robe covers us, our regard for others, especially the "least of these," will be evident. Those good deeds that form the "works of righteousness" will not save us; they do not purchase our salvation—the blood of Jesus has done this. But they do reveal the true state of grace shared by all those who see realistically and surrender fully to His love.

More Than This

For it is God who works in you both to will
and to do for His good pleasure. Phil. 2:13.

The "imputed" holiness given us at surrender is what saves us. It is the abiding protection of all who remain in Christ, and it is what qualifies us for life in the Father's house. But it is not the only component of Christ's righteous gift. The repentant sinner also receives "imparted" holiness—the day-to-day, ever-developing sanctification of the soul.

Imputed righteousness qualifies us; imparted righteousness quantifies us. It is what people see; it manifests itself in the character we exhibit in our deeds—our daily doings.

In this sense imparted righteousness is external evidence of internal transformation; it is the "more than outward covering" that Christ's righteousness provides and what is meant by the quote: "More than this, Christ changes the heart. . . . Then with Christ working in you, you will manifest the same spirit and do the same good works—of righteousness, obedience" (*Steps to Christ*, p. 62).

Unfortunately, there are some whose righteousness by faith emphasis mutes obedience; whose accent on our rich gift devalues our right goal—holiness character. But this is a tragically misguided approach. Jesus demands uncompromising obedience. The gift of Christ's robe always includes and, in fact, unfailingly demands and sustains the desire to attain perfection, i.e., complete compliance to God's holy will. The "more" consequences of sanctification is an inevitable sign of conversion, the surest evidence that one's life is "under the robe."

A. G. Daniells, in his enlightening book *Christ Our Righteousness,* makes the point with clarity: "Righteousness by faith is an experience, a reality. It involves a complete transformation of the life. He who enters into this new life has experienced deep contrition and has made sincere, heartfelt confession and repudiation of sin. With his divine Lord, he has come to love righteousness and hate inequity. And being justified—accounted righteous by faith—he has peace with God. . . . All things have become a new" (p. 75).

The bottom line is that righteousness by faith is not a theory; it is a living, working experience whereby the child of God, covered by His robe of perfection, continuously develops in the graces of the Spirit.

True Sanctification

For I say to you, that unless your righteousness
exceeds the righteousness of the scribes and Pharisees,
you will by no means enter the kingdom of heaven. Matt. 5:20.

Continued sanctification of those covered by Christ's righteous robe is not simply required, it is inevitable. It is impossible to remain covered by His righteous robe and not grow in grace. It is God's good pleasure and our good fortune that righteousness imparted accompanies righteousness imputed and that those who have this gift continuously develop in His likeness.

We cannot see the robe of Christ's righteousness that we wear. This is a credit to our account cared for in the courts of glory. What we can and should see, however, are the evidences of continual growth, a certain sign of which is kindheartedness toward others. This is because: "Righteousness within is testified to by righteousness without. He who is righteous within is not hard-hearted and unsympathetic, but day by day he grows into the image of Christ, going on from strength to strength. He who is being sanctified by the truth will be self-controlled, and will follow into the footsteps of Christ until grace is lost in glory" (*Review and Herald*, June 4, 1895).

We who are being sanctified continuously develop in the direction of the one who sanctifies (Heb. 2:11). He who sanctifies is Jesus Christ. He is both our sanctifier and our sanctification. His example of good deeds is our model, and our performance in this regard is a more certain index of His covering than punctilious tithing, strictness of diet, or conservatism of dress.

Love expressed to fellow believers remains our most critical mirror of His grace. As James reminds us, "Pure and undefiled religion before God and the Father is this: to visit orphans and widows in their trouble, and to keep oneself unspotted from the world" (James 1:27). He further alerts that this capacity begins at home and that those who deny their own are worse than infidels.

But the charity of the redeemed is not provincial or exclusive; it includes all whose wants we can supply and whose oppression we can relieve. In fact, Jesus Himself warned us that if we love or show respect to only those who love us, we are no better than the unconverted Pharisees, whose religion had deteriorated to worthless form and fashion. The antidote for such selfish neglect is the impartation of His covering robe—His infinitely better righteousness.

God's Merciful "As If"

For what does the Scripture say? "Abraham believed God,
and it was accounted to him for righteousness." Now to him
who works, the wages are not counted as grace but as debt.
But to him who does not work but believes on Him who justifies
the ungodly, his faith is accounted for righteousness. Rom. 4:3-5.

Imputed righteousness is righteousness that is externally bestowed. It is companion to, yet different from, righteousness that is earned or developed within. The latter is accomplished with the believer's participation. The former is accomplished without the believer's help. It is purely and simply the work of Christ. It is all of His doing and none of ours, and by it alone we are accounted (reckoned) as absolutely righteous, completed and qualified for the Father's house.

How radically divorced from our personal efforts is the righteousness that Jesus earned—the righteousness that saves us? Ellen White states it this way:

1. "This robe, woven in the loom of heaven, has in it not one thread of human devising. Christ in His humanity wrought out a perfect character, and this character He offers to impart to us" (*Christ's Object Lessons*, p. 311).

2. "All that man can possibly do toward his own salvation is to accept the invitation, 'Whosoever will, let him take the water of life freely'" (*The Seventh-day Adventist Bible Commentary*, Ellen G. White Comments, p. 1071).

3. "The proud heart strives to earn salvation; but both the title to heaven and our fitness for it are found in the righteousness of Christ" (*The Desire of Ages*, p. 300).

The righteousness of Christ does not make us absolutely perfect, but it does make us absolutely acceptable. We are not, upon conversion, removed from our unholy flesh, but when covered by His robe, are looked upon by the Father "as if" we were. As admonished in Romans 6:11: we now live "reckoning" the old man of sin as dead; that is to say, not only knowing that he no longer dominates our doings (verse 14) but functioning as if he no longer lurks within us. Meanwhile, the Father sees our surrender and because of Christ's covering regards us "as if" we have never sinned (*Steps to Christ*, p. 62).

Our holiness is made possible by Jesus' substitution. In this sense, our own worthiness is never literal or real. What is real is the pain that He suffered, the blood that He shed, the death that he died, and the glorious resurrection that followed Calvary—all of which stimulate and sustain our daily devotion.

Imparted Righteousness

Blessed are those whose lawless deeds are forgiven,
and whose sins are covered; Blessed is the man to whom
the Lord shall not impute sin. Rom. 4:7, 8.

The word "imputeds" speaks most enduringly to the reality of how Jesus places His righteousness "upon" us. The word "imparts," however, speaks most practically to the daily work of sanctification that the Holy Spirit accomplishes "within" us. Imparted righteousness emphasizes our spiritual growth, our internal progress, our practical moment-by-moment, day-by-day responses to the commands of God.

It is this distinction that Ellen White had in mind when she wrote, "The righteousness by which we are justified is imputed; the righteousness by which we are sanctified is imparted. The first is our title to heaven, the second is our fitness for heaven" (*Messages to Young People,* p. 35).

The impartation of Christ's righteousness results in our steady growth in the likeness of Jesus and is demonstrated by the transformation of our natures (*The Desire of Ages,* p. 172), the overcoming of inherited and cultivated tendencies to evil (*ibid.,* p. 671), the presence of Christlike attributes in our lives (*ibid.,* p. 805), our death to self and sin (*ibid.,* p. 172), the sanctification of the soul (*Christ's Object Lessons,* p. 384)—all accomplished by the in-working of the Holy Spirit (*Selected Messages,* book 1, p. 395).

The fitness or "better righteousness" that Christ imparts references not so much our record of goodness, but our attitude—our orientation toward obedience. It is not the volume of work that we do or the frequency of the good we accomplish or the pain and sacrifice we make that fit us for glory. We are qualified by having been born again and given hearts that reject the urgings of our unholy flesh and yearns for fellowship with Christ.

Destined to live in unholy flesh until we mortals put on immortality (1 Cor. 15:53), our personal fitness, no matter how rich and full, will never do. Christ's perfectly immaculate life is our only hope of salvation. This gift, made available to us by His death on Calvary, entitles us to all of the promises of the redeemed; promises that we do not deserve, but which are ours nevertheless.

Our text in the NIV reads: "Blessed is the one whose sin the Lord will never count against them" (verse 8). The glorious truth is that He who imputes His righteousness to cover us imparts His righteousness to sanctify us. And by that equation, we are redeemed.

Righteousness at Work

The Lord is exalted, for He dwells on high; He has filled
Zion with justice and righteousness. Isa. 33:5.

Righteousness and justice are often coupled in biblical expression. Job said, "I put on righteousness, and it clothed me; my justice was like a robe and turban" (Job 29:14); Jeremiah said, "A King shall reign and prosper, and execute judgment and righteousness in the earth" (Jer. 23:5); Amos said, "But let justice run down like water, and righteousness like a mighty stream (Amos 5:24); Solomon said, "Better is little with righteousness, than vast revenues without justice" (Prov. 16:8); and God Himself, through Isaiah, proclaimed, "I will make justice the measuring line, and righteousness the plummet" (Isa. 28:17).

The view of righteousness as a privatized devotional relationship with God divorced from social justice was born in the writings of the early Church Fathers; it is not the Bible way. Aristotle, whose writings emphasized meditation or "thinking" as a superior activity to "doing," was a chief architect of this misconception. The early century Stoics, who held suffering to be a divine virtue, and the Ascetics of the same historical period who made withdrawal from earthly pleasures and comforts a religious form, also contributed mightily to this trend.

As a consequence of these and kindred influences, Christ's injunction to "not let [the] left hand know what [the] right hand is doing" (Matt. 6:3) was disassociated from its true meaning (the command not to trumpet one's good works) and was used to sanction secrecy and avoidance of observable social action.

This is another one of Satan's efforts to suppress a vital aspect of Christianity. It is as true now as it was when the Bible authors scathingly rebuked those who oppressed the poor and needy, that justice and righteousness are inextricably interwoven.

God's righteousness is most clearly defined by His just dealings with humanity. The most persuasive evidence of our likeness to Him is our fairness in dealing with one another.

Character and Nature

For the wages of sin is death, but the gift of God
is eternal life in Christ Jesus our Lord. Rom. 6:23.

Christians, although continuously growing under the perfecting cloak of Christ's righteousness, never achieve the absolute Godlike, heaven-required holiness needed for salvation. The Holy Spirit's working within means that we experience daily growth, but by both the "nature of our character" and the "character of our nature" we are prevented from attaining the quality of perfection required for heaven's entrance.

The nature of our character is deficient in that we all "have" sinned (that is past tense). On the other hand, we also "come short" (that is present tense), meaning we are now currently deficient. True, when we realize our errors, we ask forgiveness, and by God's grace, we rise to overcome or to continue our never fully realized quest for absolute righteousness. This is why, when we pray, we are careful to ask for mercy, not justice and forgiveness, not rightful recompense.

The character of our nature, on the other hand, is defined not by performance, but by the very substance of our being. The psalmist's observation that we are "born in sin and shaped in inequity" (see Ps. 51:5) is accurately echoed in Luther's observation: "The material itself is faulty. The clay, so to speak, out of which this vessel began to be formed, is damnable. What more do you want? This is how I am; this is how all men are. Our very conception; this very growth of the fetus in the womb is sin, even before we are born and begin to be human beings" (*Luther's Works,* vol. 12, p. 348). We come into the world with proclivities (tendencies) to evil, and our fallen human flesh never ceases to suggest or crave toward wrong. True, "the love of Christ constraineth us" (2 Cor. 5:13, KJV), and by His power we continue to resist and overcome, but because our flesh ever remains a source of evil impulses, it is ever—this side of translation or resurrection—irreversibly stained.

So what is the solution for our dual dilemma? The robe of Christ's righteousness! It cares for the problems produced by the "nature of our character" in that "Christ's righteousness is accepted in the place of man's failure" (*Selected Messages,* book 1, p. 367) and "His perfect holiness atones for our shortcomings" (*ibid.,* p. 368). It also cares for the problems produced by the "character of our nature" in that "Jesus makes up for our unavoidable deficiencies," i.e., the innate sinfulness, which makes unacceptable even our well-meaning deeds (*ibid.,* book 3, p. 196).

No wonder the apostle, in summarizing our elevation from base to better righteousness, conclusively declared, "You are complete in Him" (Col. 2:10).

Our Double Assurance

Behold what manner of love the Father has bestowed on us,
that we should be called children of God! Therefore the world
does not know us, because it did not know Him. 1 John 3:1.

Want a statement to brighten your day—one that is guaranteed to bring you hope and encouragement? Try this one: "The character is revealed, not by occasional good deeds and occasional misdeeds, but by the tendency of habitual words and acts" (*Steps to Christ*, pp. 57, 58). And why is this so wonderful? Because it speaks to the "double" protection connected with conversion. First, we are given (imputed) Christ's character and, by that act, accounted as acceptable to the Father. Second, the quality of our lifestyle, the obedience we render, is judged not by the stumbling and bumbling that we are so often guilty of, but by our dominant patterns of behavior.

What are our occasional misdeeds? Eating too much or too fast, working too hard or too long, judging others, jealousy, pride, forgetfulness, gossiping, listening to and spreading rumors, failure to stand up in moments of crisis, love of display, wasting time and money, lustful desires, prideful display, "little white lies," wrongful Sabbath thoughts, selfish hoarding of our means, doing good in hope of acclaim, and overlooking the plight of the poor and needy. These are the ways in which we often err. God's indefatigable agents— the holy angels by whose watch "He sees all we do and hears all we say"—record them all.

The good news, however, is that if we continue to fervently pray and trustingly obey, we are not, by our confessed errors, excommunicated from the family of God. The fact that He understands our frames and knows that we are but dust and judges our "never-completed" development in the light of Christ's covering holiness (not a list of our deeds and misdeeds) is as stimulating as it is stunning.

Though he arduously tried, John the Beloved could not find adequate words for such compassion. Frustrated in the attempt, he abandoned his search for superlatives and exclaimed in resigned but rapturous awe, "Behold what manner of love the Father has bestowed" (1 John 3:1).

He (John), who saw Christ's love more clearly than any other, could not find satisfactory language for God's grace—and neither can we. We can, however, as Scripture admonishes, "by beholding become changed" (see 2 Cor. 3:18). This fixation is a journey of a lifetime, our mandate and assurance for this and every day.

From Now On

I counsel you to buy from Me gold refined in the fire,
that you may be rich; and white garments, that you may be clothed,
that the shame of your nakedness may not be revealed;
and anoint your eyes with eye salve, that you may see. Rev. 3:18.

Christ's better righteousness, now largely undervalued, will one day be the ral-lying cry of the entire body of Christ—the church. This is confirmed by the promise that in the final hour of Pentecostal power, "one interest will prevail, one subject will swallow up every other—Christ our righteousness" (*Review and Herald,* Dec. 23, 1890).

Other statements that highlight the critical role this doctrine will have in latter-day spirituality are: "There is not a point that needs to be dwelt upon more earnestly, repeated more frequently, or established more firmly in the minds of all than the impossibility of fallen man meriting anything by his own best good works. Salvation is through faith in Jesus Christ alone" (*Faith and Works,* p. 19); "Our churches are dying for the want of teaching on the subject of righteousness by faith in Christ, and on kindred truths" (*Gospel Workers,* p. 301); "When the free gift of Christ's righteousness is not presented, the discourses are dry and spirit-less; the sheep and lambs are not fed" (*Selected Messages,* book 1, p. 158); "Christ and His righteousness—let this be our platform, the very life of our faith" (*Review and Herald,* Aug. 31, 1905); and "The present message—justification by faith—is a message from God; it bears the divine credentials, for its fruit is holiness" (*Selected Messages,* book 1, p. 359).

You and I cannot affect the revolution of thought our worldwide body of be-lievers needs in this regard. But we can, by living demonstration of the principles of righteousness, inspire right religion in our homes, our offices, our neighborhoods, our classrooms, and our congregations.

And now that we know, now that the Holy Spirit has opened our eyes to this, the only source of our salvation, now that we realize that it is not our goodness (what we have done and are doing), but Christ's goodness (what He has done, is doing, and will do) that saves us, we can face today and all our tomorrows enlight-ened, encouraged, and empowered.

The Role of Faith

And be found in Him, not having my own righteousness,
which is from the law, but that which is through faith in Christ,
the righteousness which is from God by faith. Phil. 3:9.

Faith is the vehicle by which we receive and sustain the merits of Christ's righteousness. What is faith? It is belief that God is real; that He is not only all-powerful, but also completely faithful and that even when we cannot trace Him, we can trust Him.

Our actions—our good works are visible indications of the transformation that takes place when this belief is a reality. Our good deeds do not count for salvation; they do count, however, as salvation's evidence. They are secondary elements of our faith relationship with Christ. The primary element of this relationship is the Father's acceptance of Jesus' merits. We do not physically see that transfer, but we accept it by faith, firmly believing that the Son's credits are good enough and that the Father's love is broad enough to save us.

The lack of faith that characterizes our postmodern society is previewed in Jesus' rhetorical question: "When the Son of man cometh, will he find faith on the earth?" (Luke 18:8, KJV). The answer, of course, is yes, but very little. Ours is an antifaith age; an age dominated by demands for proof and demonstration, an age of human failures so prolific and so public as to discourage trust, an age of increasing dependence upon hardwired technology and decreasing dependence upon invisible otherworldly forces; ours is an age and atmosphere unfriendly to faith.

How then do we in this age of "faith's de-emphasis" receive and retain it? Primarily by the study of God's Word (Rom. 10:17). The Bible alone contains the re-creative powers that germinate faith and prosper growth allowing us to appropriate His better righteousness.

Amid all the other voices that bombard our senses—the voices of pleasure, excitement, and national, family, and personal crisis—we must stay keenly tuned to the voice of God. The voice that spoke life to our unadorned world can and will speak assurance to our otherwise fretful hearts. His Word, sincerely sought, is the antidote to cynicism and lack of faith. Since "without faith it is impossible to please Him" (Heb. 11:6), and since "faith cometh by hearing, and hearing by the word of God" (Rom. 10:17, KJV), both the role and path to faith is compellingly clear.

The Giants Keep Coming

Yet again there was war at Gath, where there was a man of great stature, who had six fingers on each hand and six toes on each foot, twenty-four in number; and he also was born to the giant. 2 Sam. 21:20.

It seemed that it would never end, this protracted war between Israel and the Philistines. True, David had embarrassed the foe in his battle with Goliath, but here they were again, one giant after another. First, Ishbi-Benob (verse 16), then Saph (verse 18), then the unnamed brother of Goliath (verse 19), and now this unnamed warrior so huge that he had six fingers on each hand and six toes on each foot (verse 20). Yes, the giants "kept coming."

David's long battle with the giants of Philistia is reflective of our battle with the demons of our own unholy flesh. These are the giants of our inherited tendencies to evil—as well as the giants of our cultivated tendencies to wrong—those we add to the evil predispositions with which we are born. These latter cultivated and acquired tendencies to wrong are the tastes and habits that are disposable, e.g., evils of nonsense and amusement (*Messages to Young People*, p. 42)—these can and must be eliminated.

But the inherited ones, those fleshly clamors that are a part of the evil nature with which we are born, are nondisposable—never discarded. After conversion they do not control us, but they continue to pester and prod toward evil because they are basic to our nature. Their eradication will come only when this corruptible shall have put on incorruption and this mortal shall have put on immortality (1 Cor. 15:54). However, while not eradicable, they can and must be overcome (*Christ's Object Lessons*, p. 354), curtailed (*Testimonies for the Church*, vol. 5, p. 335), subdued (*ibid.*, p. 648), controlled (*ibid.*, vol. 4, p. 235), subjected (*The Adventist Home*, p. 128), and repressed (*Gospel Workers*, pp. 127, 128). And this is "the work of a lifetime"—the never-ending battle against the forces of our unholy flesh.

The victories of David, the intrepid warrior, encourage us. He not only slew the giant, Goliath, but he also slew many others. It is possible to say that in his warfare against the Philistines, that though the giants kept coming, David kept winning! This may also be true in our lives. As Heaven provided the future King of Israel wisdom and courage and strength to be victorious over superior odds, our God and His potent Word provide us continuous victory over the giants of self and, at His coming, eternal reward.

The Struggle Ended

For this corruptible must put on incorruption,
and this mortal must put on immortality. 1 Cor. 15:53.

The caterpillar, so the story goes, tried to cross the broad, busy highway and stuck its head out from among the leaves and began the slow process of inching its way across the pavement. But the heavy vibrations of rumbling traffic in the distance forced it back into its leafy hiding place. The process was repeated again and again until finally, the pitiable creature crawled under a pile of muddy debris and gave up the struggle. When it did, nature, in an act of mercy, wrapped a cocoon about it to protect it from the elements. Soon the summer sun waned, the autumn winds blew, the snows fell, and the creature, now buried, rested securely in its covering. There it stayed until the spring winds came and blew away the leaves, exposing its encasement to the piercing rays of the sun. Those rays warmed the covering of the tiny creature until it dried, cracked, and then opened. And when it unfolded sufficiently, it was not the ugly caterpillar, but a beautiful multicolored butterfly that flitted happily across the once impassible highway onto attractive fields beyond.

I see another drama today—the whole human race bound and restricted by sin. I see us ever struggling for perfection and realizing at last that ultimate purity is always beyond our grasp. Finally, Father Time and Mother Nature affect our demise, and we lie down in death, hounded to the end by the braying of the flesh; locked into our mortal beings and left out of immortal life if not for the wondrous saving gift of Jesus' blood and robe.

God's promise is that one day He will abort earth's spiral of sin; the trumpet will sound, and the Son of Righteousness will speak words that shall pierce the cocoons of our graves. What will emerge will not be the sin-scarred creatures of this mortal world, but the glorious bodies of the saved, now freed from the curse, invited to join the transformed, translated, transported redeemed in perpetual peace and harmony—world without end! Amen.

NOVEMBER

A Better Resurrection

Why Death?

For the living know that they shall die; But the dead know nothing, and they have no more reward, for the memory of them is forgotten. Eccl. 9:5.

Death was unknown to the universe before sin. At no time or place in all God's chartless universe had matter decayed or life ceased to be.

There are those who chide the Creator concerning death; those who say death is too ponderous, too absolute, too gross and gruesome a consequence for the minor mistake of the first pair—that they were, in fact, unwitting victims of a superior foe—blindsided and overcome by curiosity.

But such reasoning overlooks two controlling facts. The first is that the tree of knowledge of good and evil was given as a test of their loyalty and not a temptation to disobedience. The first pair was provided with the power of choice—they were not created as robots, mechanically performing the Creator's will with no possibility to err. In simple language—they blew it! And in doing so, became partners in the rebellion conducted by fallen angels. This rebellion is not innocent neutrality or harmless curiosity; it is intentional defiance. Now, as then, sin is choosing darkness over light, self-will above God's will; it is the insurrection of created beings against their Maker.

The second fact is that sin in any form, no matter how slight, is ultimately destructive. All sin is contagious, expansive opposition to God and, therefore, calamitous. Death was necessitated as sin's consequence because it is a lethally infective, terminally defective, and finally fatal disease. Not to recompense sin with death would be to immortalize evil—to perpetuate disorder in the universe.

By sinning (a choice they did not have to make), the first pair forced God to a choice He wished not to make—the sentence of death. That is the bad news. The good news is that death was not His final decision; He made another choice—one so generous that it defies understanding or explanation—the sending of His Son to redeem our error and restore our lost immortality.

Not God's Fault

And the woman said to the serpent, "We may eat the fruit of the trees of the garden; but of the fruit of the tree which is in the midst of the garden, God has said, 'You shall not eat it, nor shall you touch it, lest you die.'" Gen. 3:2, 3.

Ellen White illumines our first parents' mistake very graphically in a number of seldom read but highly revealing statements. Consider the following: "Our first parents were not left without a warning of the danger that threatened them. Heavenly messengers opened to them the history of Satan's fall and his plots for their destruction, unfolding more fully the nature of divine government which the prince of evil was trying to overthrow" (*Patriarchs and Prophets*, p. 52). And again, "The angels cautioned Eve not to separate from her husband in her employment, for she might be brought in contact with this fallen foe. . . . The angels charged them to closely follow the instructions God had given them in reference to the tree of knowledge, for in perfect obedience they were safe [from] this fallen foe" (*The Story of Redemption*, p. 31).

Compounding their mistake is the fact that not only were they adequately warned, but they were also minimally tested. Consider the following: "The test given to Adam and Eve was very light" (*The Seventh-day Adventist Bible Commentary*, Ellen G. White Comments, vol. 1, p. 1083); "The mildest test was given them that could be given; . . . there was no need of eating of the forbidden tree; everything that [was] required had been provided" *(ibid.)*; "Yet, in His great mercy, He appointed Adam no severe test. And the very lightness of the prohibition made the sin exceedingly great" (*Patriarchs and Prophets*, pp. 60, 61); "When Adam was tempted, he was not hungry" (*Signs of the Times*, Apr. 4, 1900).

We are reminded by these comments that: (a) heaven has sent us sufficient warnings; and that (b) there is no such thing as an irresistible temptation (1 Cor. 10:13). What staggers the imagination is not the magnitude of the punishment versus that of the crime, but the unspeakable cost of the salvation that has been wrought through Jesus Christ. Salvation does not deliver us from the first death—the natural consequence of sin—it does, however, through the sacrificial intervention of our Lord, deliver us from the permanent nothingness of the second death and guarantee us life everlasting.

The Christian Advantage

O Death, where is your sting? O Hades, where is your victory? 1 Cor. 15:55.

Our sure mortality is the one absolute of life. We know that death will come to every human being. One man of obvious wit is quoted to have said, "If I only knew where I was going to die and when I was going to die, I just wouldn't go near that place at that time!"

Job had it right when he said, "My days are swifter than a weaver's shuttle" (Job 7:6). The psalmist was also on point when, in characterizing the human condition, he wrote: "For a thousand years in thy sight are but as yesterday when it is past and as a watch in the night. Thou carriest them away as a flood; they are as a sleep: in the morning they are like grass which groweth up. In the morning it flourisheth, and groweth up; in the evening it is cut down, and withereth" (Ps. 90:4-6, KJV); as was James, when musing: "For what is your life? It is even a vapor that appears for a little time and then vanishes away" (James 4:14).

Just where do we go when we vanish in death? Back to the dust! We were made of the earth, and whether our bodies are placed in vaults, mummified, cremated, buried at sea, or, as in some cultures, exposed to rooftops for birds and insects to consume, they eventually return to the dust. In all cases the forms that remain when breath has left the flesh go back to the nothingness from which we were made.

Satan's original lie, "You will not surely die" (Gen. 3:4), since Eden has been perpetuated by multitudes who, blinded to the realities of Scripture, have lived out their days praying profitless prayers to the deceased. Multiplied billions of Adam's descendants are yet tragically deceived, pleading to decayed and decaying heroes for material gain and for guidance in decision-making for protection against enemies, for appeasement of unruly nature, and even the forgiveness of sin. Some, in what must be regarded as Satan's most masterful delusion, gladly sacrificed their lives and those of others in hopes of entrance into a nonexistent utopia.

The true Christian advantage in all this is scriptural enlightenment regarding life on our planet as created by God, forfeited by sin, and redeemed by the blood of our crucified and risen Christ—the architect of our being, the author of a blessed, better resurrection.

November 4

Hope Springs Eternal

*If in this life only we have hope in Christ,
we are of all men the most pitiable. 1 Cor. 15:19.*

Not only is death inherent to fallen humanity, but fear of death is also. There are many ways that we humans rationalize with respect to death and dying. One view of the inevitable cessation of life is the return to silent nothingness in the Epicurean teaching that death is the eternal, painless loss of consciousness. "Death is nothing to me," Epicurus said. "It does not concern either the living or the dead, since the former is not, and the latter are no more."

A second view is that of the Stoics, who taught that overcoming the dread of death required one's thinking about it constantly—not in fear, but rather by viewing life as a banquet from which it is an obligation to graciously retire back into nonexistence. The philosopher Spinosa held just the opposite view. He felt that overcoming the fear of death necessitated our thinking about it as little as possible or not at all. Leonardo da Vinci championed the idea of our living life to the fullest and then, at death, being ushered happily into eternal abyss as one who would lie down at night after a hard day's labor.

There are other views of course, but singularly or in concert, they do not provide the meaning or hope of the scriptural view—that death is but a temporary sleep and that faith in Jesus is the only escape from dread of eternal demise.

"You go in!" one of the two lads standing in front of the abandoned mine said to the other. "No!" the second lad said. "I am afraid." "Oh, go ahead," the first boy replied. "Don't be afraid, you're not the first one, look— I see tracks going in." "That's the problem!" the second boy answered. "I see those tracks going in, but I don't see any tracks coming out."

The yawning grave awaits us all, and all who enter in remain. We see no tracks coming out—none, that is, except those of the risen Galilean. In conclusive demonstration of His power over the grave, He exited triumphantly from the darkness of death, thus thwarting Satan's designs. He spoiled the devil's plan; He broke the bonds of the tomb; He loosed the race from the curse of eternal extinction. His victory is our assurance of the restoration of the race to its original state. By it we are drawn to believe, delighted to obey, driven to hope of a glad resurrection.

Our Living Lord

But the angel answered and said to the women, "Do not be afraid,
for I know that you seek Jesus who was crucified. He is not here; for He is
risen, as He said. Come, see the place where the Lord lay." Matt. 28:5, 6.

It was the human Jesus who died upon the cross, and it was the human Jesus who
rose up from the grave. "Deity did not die," it did not sink under the agonizing
tortures of Calvary—deity cannot die. The man Christ Jesus died, and when he was
laid in the grave, "all that comprised the life and intelligence of Jesus remained with
His body in the sepulcher; and when He came forth it was as a whole being; He
did not have to summon His spirit from heaven" (*The Seventh-day Adventist Bible
Commentary,* Ellen G. White Comments, vol. 5, pp. 1113, 1151).

The Second Adam's body is more like ours than the first Adam's in that it was
developed in a sinful woman's womb, now lay beaten and scarred—His visage having been more marred above that of any other man (Isa. 52:14). It was restful sleep
that engulfed our battered elder brother in the cold and silent bowels of the very
earth He spoke into existence.

Satan understood well what was at stake. He had seen Moses resurrected and a
host of sleeping saints poised to exit their graves as Jesus cried, "It is finished!" He
knew that if Jesus did rise, and they with Him, their testimony would be irrefutable, Christ's intercessory services unstoppable, and his kingdom forever lost. He
had failed to foil Him at Bethlehem, failed to fool Him in the wilderness, failed to
frighten Him in Gethsemane, failed to force Him in Pilate's judgment hall. Now,
having felled Him at Calvary, he sought victory at last by preventing Him from exiting the tomb. To that end, he commissioned the most trusted leaders of his rebel
army to obstruct His coming forth.

But they could not! As surely as must the darkness of night give way to the
rising sun and the icy fingers of winter release their grip upon the resurgent life of
spring, death and hell gave way to victory—releasing our risen Lord. He swallowed
death, but death could not swallow Him; He took in death, but death could not take
in Him. The Pharisees could not discourage Him; the mob could not depress Him;
Herod could not destroy Him; death could not demolish Him; and the grave could
not detain Him. He rose as He had predicted and is today our living, loving Lord.

"Daddy, the Pain"

*And about the ninth hour Jesus cried out with a loud voice,
saying, "Eli, Eli, lama sabachthani?" that is, "My God,
My God, why have You forsaken Me?" Matt. 27:46.*

The Father's suffering during the death throes of the Son was forcefully brought to mind during the birth of our last and only female grandchild. Her mother, the oldest of our three daughters, had tried several times to give birth, and each time nature aborted the attempt. The third and last time was especially painful because the fetus' age, by law, necessitated a funeral. On the fourth try, she and her husband went to greater lengths than ever to guarantee, as much as humanly possible, a live delivery. There was, of course, trepidation in all our hearts. So fearful was she that, early in her pregnancy, she requested her pastor-father be with her during the delivery, should birth occur—and that is what happened. At the end of eight months of cautious preparation, the physician decided to induce labor, and I was ushered into the delivery room, scrubbed and garbed, to provide moral support to a very frightened young woman.

But her pain was so great that she forgot I was there. "Push, Cheryl," they kept urging her as the birth process proceeded. The veins in her neck, arms, back, and legs all registered the superhuman effort that she was making to cooperate. I ached for her—I ached with her. I wanted to help alleviate the pain, to relieve her of the bloodletting and agony, but I could not. Suddenly she remembered that I was there, and, turning in my direction, she blurted out, "Daddy, Daddy, the pain, oh, Daddy, the pain!"

My heart nearly burst. I would have done anything to help her, but all I could do was a mechanical thumbs-up. She said later that she saw that and it helped. But suppose I had turned my back on her? Suppose if at the height of her ordeal she had reached out for support and I had turned my back in a "suffer no better for you" attitude? Unimaginable! But that is exactly what the Father did at Calvary. When Jesus took upon His sinless body our sins, He became the object of the Father's wrath and suffered our punishment. The Father, who hates sin, could not save His Son and save us, so He sacrificed Him for us.

How can we not love a brother so precious and a father so true?

He Lives

And He said to them, "Why are you troubled?
And why do doubts arise in your hearts?" Luke 24:38.

Christ's promise, "Destroy this temple, and in three days I will raise it up" (John 2:19), infuriated the Sanhedrin council, puzzled the disciples, and energized Satan to acts of desperation. His statement, "I will raise it up," promised "self-resurrection"—overcoming death by returning to life by His own innate powers. This was more than startling; it was unbelievable! But that is exactly what He did. "When He came forth it was as a whole being; He did not have to summon His spirit from heaven" (*The Seventh-day Adventist Bible Commentary,* Ellen G. White Comments, vol. 5, p. 1151).

The theories that Jesus had fainted but not expired or that His followers had removed His body to a safer place are more than countered by the testimony of the Roman guard (Matt. 28:4), the announcement of the angel (verses 5-7), the appearance of those resurrected with Him (Matt. 27:52, 53), and the 10 post-Resurrection appearances that He made to His followers.

Christ's resurrection is a historical fact; the jury is in, the verdict is clear—and final! And this is why His followers so often proclaim in confident praise:

"I serve a risen Savior, He's in the world today;

I know that He is living, whatever men may say;

I see His hand of mercy, I hear His voice of cheer,

And just the time I need Him, He's always near.

He lives, He lives, Christ Jesus lives today!

He walks with me and talks with me along life's narrow way.

He lives, He lives, salvation to impart!

You ask me how I know He lives?

He lives within my heart."

Christ's living within our hearts is best testified not by our lusty congregational singing. It is best revealed by our actions; by our responses to both the everyday tragedies and triumphs of life. It is in the consistency of our patience, our humility, our compassion and forgiveness that His resurrection reality is most clearly declared. By these qualities we testify that "He lives within our hearts" and that our old man of sin has been crucified and that now, "just as Christ was raised from the dead," we also "walk in newness of life" (Rom. 6:4).

The Promise Fulfilled

Now it came to pass, while He blessed them, that He was
parted from them and carried up into heaven. And they worshiped Him,
and returned to Jerusalem with great joy. Luke 24:51, 52.

Reunion with their risen Lord transformed the frightened disciples into a happy band of flaming witnesses. Christ's death, burial, and resurrection became the centerpiece of their existence, the motivation of their service, the catalyst of the movement for which they willingly sacrificed their lives.

But it was not only the disciples who were revived. Unfallen angels and worlds above were also joyfully enthused. The tension that gripped the universe while Jesus lay in the grave, and their joy at His subsequent resurrection, is mirrored in the case of Stanley Ketchell, world-class lightweight fighter who, in the early 1920s, achieved fame by often winning bouts after having been knocked down in apparent defeat. The word was, no matter how badly he was hurt, Ketchell was sure to "beat the count"—he would always get up!

Tragically, one night in a dark alley in an unsavory Philadelphia neighborhood, while yet at the height of his career, Ketchell was robbed and killed. His manager, in England at the time, left the wireless station reading the tragic news and was overcome with disbelief and grief. But he quickly collected his thoughts and went back to the desk of the message clerk with this terse reply to his fallen fighter's family and friends—"Start counting; he'll get up!"

Christ's silence in the grave prompted dread and doubt throughout the broad expanse of creation. However, the Father's serene demeanor declared, "Start counting, He'll get up!" The prophetic clock struck one on Friday evening and the universe wondered; on Saturday, the second day of His incarceration, the count reached two and there was still silence in the grave. At sunset Saturday the clock struck three and still only quiet in the tomb. Unfallen worlds and angels waited with bated breath—could He do it? Would He keep His word? Then, as dawn approached on the first day of the week, it happened! The Savior awoke and exited the tomb in triumphant splendor. He had kept His word! But then, He always keeps His word. He did so then, He does so now, and He will do so yet again when He returns to claim His own.

A Better Resurrection

Women received their dead raised to life again. Others were tortured, not accepting deliverance, that they might obtain a better resurrection. Heb. 11:35.

Jesus is not just a better resurrection, He is the only resurrection. Satan, for all his considerable powers, cannot create life. He can imitate it, simulate it, and copy it, but he cannot bring it into existence. He cannot raise the dead. He can mimic resurrection, he can develop apparitions as with Saul and the witch of Endor, he can form ghostlike approximations and frighten and fool humans, but he can neither create life nor resurrect it once it has expired. Had he the power to create, he would no doubt add liberally to his army in hopes of a greater surge in his warfare against Christ. If he could resurrect, our planet would be inundated with the unrepentant since Eden.

He is not a "life-giver"; he is the "life-taker." His promises always lead to death. He is the lord of lethal wars, the fount of every deadly "ism," every false good, every road that leads from everlasting life. He exults on all occasions of death.

All humans must die, and the sadder the death, the happier he is. To that end he has sent floods and fires, earthquakes and avalanches, tornados, tidal waves, and tsunamis to sweep away millions in untimely, tragic demise. God's people are not exempt in this regard. We too are sometimes victimized by accidents and natural disasters, and if not one of these, eventually felled by our sin-cursed genealogy.

What shall we do in the face of the surety of death? First, we would do well to heed the wise man's counsel: "Whatsoever thy hand findeth to do, do it with thy might; for there is no work, nor device, nor knowledge . . . whither thou goest" (Eccl. 9:10, KJV).

Second, we are wise to place our confidence in Christ's promise to return to claim His own, firmly convinced that "he that shall come will come" (Heb. 10:37, KJV) and that those who die "in Him" will be resurrected from the temporary nothingness of death to experience life everlasting amid fadeless joys of eternity.

Dying to Live Again

Do not marvel at this; for the hour is coming in which all who are in the graves will hear His voice and come forth—those who have done good, to the resurrection of life, and those who have done evil, to the resurrection of condemnation. John 5:28, 29.

The two resurrections taught in the Bible are exactly 1,000 years apart and very different in character. The first occurs at the second coming of Jesus and will involve the righteous dead. It is called the resurrection of the just (Luke 14:14) and takes place in connection with the second coming of Christ (1 Cor. 15:51). Those who have part in the first resurrection will die no more. Upon them God will restore the conditional immortality forfeited in Eden (Luke 20:36). Their characters and personality, already perfected through trials, and the bestowal of Christ's righteousness will not be changed, but their bodies will be changed into the likeness of His glorious body (Phil. 3:21). As His followers recognized the resurrected Jesus, so will the personal identity of the redeemed be preserved in this, their new and glorious form (*The Seventh-day Adventist Bible Commentary,* Ellen G. White Comments, vol. 6, p. 1093). Heaven and "the new earth" will not be a gathering place of substanceless spirits, but real, live people who have had their corruptible bodies replaced by incorruptible ones.

"Pastor, tell me how to die; I know how to live, but I don't know how to die," she said as her sunken eyes peered at me from beneath the blanket that covered the skeleton of what was once a handsome, robust form. Now, ravaged by cancer and knowing that death was imminent, Anne was pleading for understanding.

"I have no personal knowledge of death," I replied, "but I do know one who was alive and died and now is alive again. His Word supplies the answer."

What is His formula for dying revealed in Scripture? It is absolute trust in the Father's love, total commitment to the Father's providence, complete surrender to the Father's will. Jesus taught us that death is a sleep from which the righteous awaken to everlasting life. That is possible only because He rose. His death was not the beginning of the end; it was the end of the beginning for all trusting, believing disciples.

A few weeks later I eulogized my friend Anne with heavy heart but joyful anticipation of a better resurrection.

Baptism: A Sign of Resurrection

Therefore we were buried with Him through baptism into death,
that just as Christ was raised from the dead by the glory of the Father,
even so we also should walk in newness of life. Rom. 6:4.

The longstanding, widely pervasive view that the apostles instituted Sunday as a memorial of the Resurrection is not scriptural. The truth is that He who rested on the seventh day, when He had completed His work of creation, also rested on that day when He had completed His services of redemption. Furthermore, by resting in the grave on the day between His death and His resurrection, Jesus exalted that day to even holier heights than it had known.

Does an event so momentous, so pivotal for Christian faith, as the Resurrection deserve special commemoration? Yes, it does. And it has been given that recognition in the rite of baptism by immersion. This mode of baptism incorporates all three major elements of Christ's return to life: His dying, His resting, and His rising.

By submitting to water baptism, we declare publicly our death to our former life of sin: when plunged beneath the water, we symbolize the burial of our sinful past; when raised from the watery grave, we attest that we have, indeed, left our former ways to walk in newness of life. Baptism by sprinkling, pouring, or any other method falls short of accomplishing these sacred expressions and are therefore inadequate.

A memorable model of the correct baptismal form is given in Acts 8:38, 39: "So he commanded the chariots to stand still. And both Philip and the eunuch went down into the water, and he baptized him. Now when they came up out of the water, the Spirit of the Lord caught Philip away, so that the eunuch saw him no more; and he went on his way rejoicing." Add to that example the experience of Jesus Himself, who "when He had been baptized, . . . came up immediately from the water" (Matt. 3:16), and scriptural emphasis becomes very clear.

Baptism itself does not impart special grace. It does, however, signal to the church, to society, and to heaven itself, that we have staked all our hopes and energies on the powers and promises provided by the death, burial, and resurrection of Christ.

He Is Able

*For the death that He died, He died to sin once for all;
but the life that He lives, He lives to God. Likewise you also,
reckon yourselves to be dead indeed to sin, but alive
to God in Christ Jesus our Lord. Rom. 6:10, 11.*

We all come into this world, in a spiritual sense, DOA: dead on arrival. This faultiness of the flesh that is a consequence of the original sin is what Augustine had in mind when he said, "Sin is also the punishment of sin." It is what Paul had in mind when he said, "Sin . . . wrought in me all manner of concupiscence" (Rom. 7:8, KJV).

We all carry in our flesh the physical properties that will eventuate in our demise. In a very real sense we are all terminally ill. Humanly speaking, there is no other exit, no other way out! The poet Longfellow had it right: "Life is real, life is earnest . . . and our hearts, though stout and brave, still, like muffled drums, are beating funeral marches to the grave." And unless Christ returns in the immediate future, our physical decline—our death march to nothingness—is unalterable and irreversible.

But our spiritual decline is reversible. For this otherwise terminal condition there is a balm in Gilead, a sure physician, a healing force. Our natural tendencies to evil, our innate distaste for holy things, the miss-wiring of our reasons and wills, our love of the world, in short, all the binding evils of our first birth, can be arrested. We can be made to "stay alive" in Jesus; by His creative word dry bones can and do live again.

We who were dead in sin, indifferent to righteousness, insensitive to the law, unmoved by grace, unaffected by the lure of God's love, are living testimonies to God's resurrection powers. As the sun shines through the sod warming dormant seed that, already softened by dew and rain, springs to productive life, so the Son of Righteousness, when warming hard hearts, prepped by the Holy Spirit, produces vibrant, valiant, victorious Christians.

We can no more explain the dynamics of this miracle than could the blind man his healing. But with him we can testify that "once we were blind but now we see" (see John 9:25); once we were bound in the kingdom of darkness, but by His grace and power our eyes have been opened, our ears have been unstopped, our dungeons have been shaken, our chains removed, and we are freed from sin and its baleful penalty.

It Is Finished

So when Jesus had received the sour wine, He said, "It is finished!"
And bowing His head, He gave up His spirit. John 19:30.

Christ's shouting "It is finished" when dying upon the cross was heard differently by those who beheld it. The Jewish leaders thought it meant that He was confessing defeat; the Roman soldiers thought that their gruesome task was done; the callous mob thought that His mission had failed; His suffering mother that her son's life was over; the cringing disciples that their dreams were ended. But none of that was true. What the dying Lord meant was that His work on earth had been successfully completed; that He had successfully negotiated the rapids of sin and could now die the perfect sacrifice.

In truth, His death and imminent resurrection were the finishing of one dispensation and the beginning of another. This is because in His dying, "type met antitype" (*Review and Herald*, Oct. 10, 1899). The real Lamb died fulfilling four millennia of redemption expectations. Now at last, the promissory notes of many centuries were finally fulfilled. It was finished! The Lord Himself had come; humanity had been eyewitness to His sinless life. His followers had seen the glory of the Father reflected in His personage; the Father had now seen the travail of His soul and was satisfied.

When He was risen, He ascended on high to dispense gifts to His people, to plead His blood and robe before the Father, and to make final preparation that where He is, there we may be also. The promised new earth has not yet been consummated, but it has been verified by the wave sheath of the resurrected that Christ took with Him upon His return to glory and by the thunderous outpouring of the Holy Spirit at Pentecost.

He who shouted "It is finished!" at Calvary will one day shout "It is finished!" to all sin and its consequences. Then the saints will be translated, the millennium will be inaugurated, heaven will be populated, sin will be eradicated, wickedness will be terminated, sorrow will be obliterated, wars will be terminated, disease will be annihilated, injustice will be prostrated, death will be eliminated, evildoers will be humiliated, sinners will be consternated, the devil will be subjugated, humanity will be fumigated, the earth will be renovated, redemption will be consummated, peace will be perpetuated, God's love will be vindicated, the church will be elevated, and our Lord Jesus Christ—our "something better"—will be congratulated by all of creation.

The Choice Is Ours

*Blessed and holy is he who has part in the first resurrection.
Over such the second death has no power, but they shall be priests
of God and of Christ, and shall reign with Him a thousand years. Rev. 20:6.*

The first resurrection occurs when the righteous are raised at Christ's second coming. "The rest of the dead," the wicked, do not "live again" or are not raised (resurrected) until a thousand years later (Rev. 20:5). The period between the resurrection of the righteous and the wicked is commonly called the millennium. This, in divinity's reckoning, is a space as brief as yesterday (Ps. 90:4). In human chronology, however, it is 10 centuries or 100 decades or 365,000 days or, more personally, 40 successive generations.

And how will the righteous be occupied during this lengthy period while the wicked continue to sleep? They will be judging the books—the records of glory (Rev. 20:4): comparing the law of God with the licentiousness of the wicked, examining the records that condemn the disobedient—viewing uncontestable evidence that God is just and merciful, seeing that heaven could have done no more in its efforts to save; that indeed, it was not God's will that any should perish, but that all should have "everlasting life" (John 3:16).

And what are Satan and his angels doing? They are on "administrative leave" or, better stated, forced vacation—and a very unhappy vacation at that. Why? The resurrected and translated righteous are all in heaven; the wicked are all dead; Satan and his imps, who have only themselves with whom to commiserate, will coexist in a state of constant dissension and unrest.

But then it happens: the 1,000 years expire and the wicked are raised, thus loosing Satan from the lonely circumstances that bound him. This is the second resurrection, and it is prelude to the second death, which occurs shortly thereafter when hellfire descends and destroys Lucifer, his fallen angels, and all his resurrected followers (Rev. 20:7-10).

Jesus has already died the second death for us. By accepting His gracious offer of love, we are guaranteed a life of joyous satisfaction here. The choice is ours.

The Final Solution

They went up on the breadth of the earth and surrounded
the camp of the saints and the beloved city. And fire came down
from God out of heaven and devoured them. Rev. 20:9.

Have you ever thought about the condition of those brought from the dead at the second resurrection? What a sordid, motley bunch! All who come up at the first resurrection are brought up in immortal bloom. All who come up in the second resurrection come forth to eternal doom. The righteous will be raised with no sign of the curse; no evidence of the physical and mental deterioration time and circumstances had etched upon their forms before and at the moment of death.

But not the wicked; they come up as they went down into their graves—diseased, deformed, demented, deranged, determined to defy God's will and defend their profligate leader. They constitute a vast army of fanatically angry, evil rebels. Their forms reveal varied degrees of degeneration brought about by debaucheries of their choice. They differ in marks of degeneracy, and they have one thing in common—their hatred of God and His people.

Theirs is a state that cannot be allowed to exist in God's otherwise pure universe; sin must now be completely excised. "When God finally purifies the earth, it will appear like a boundless lake of fire. As God preserved the ark amid the commotions of the Flood, because it contained eight righteous persons, He will preserve the New Jerusalem, containing the faithful of all ages, from righteous Abel down to the last saint which lived. Although the whole earth, with the exception of that portion where the city rests, will be wrapped in a sea of liquid fire, yet the city is preserved as was the ark, by a miracle of Almighty power. It stands unharmed amid the devouring elements" (*The Seventh-day Adventist Bible Commentary*, Ellen G. White Comments, vol. 7, p. 986).

When the fire has completely purified this world and God has spoken the re-creative words and Planet Earth is restored to its Edenic state, the saints will exit the city and inhabit the earth made new. What a delight! What a deliverance! What a privilege! What a salvation!

Groaning for Heaven

For in this we groan, earnestly desiring to be clothed
with our habitation which is from heaven, if indeed,
having been clothed, we shall not be found naked. 2 Cor. 5:2, 3.

Is there anywhere that shows a graphic description of the believer's longing? In 2 Corinthians 5:1-9, Paul visions eloquently beyond his death to the state of his resurrected body. Our earthly, temporary tabernacle will be dissolved, he reasons, but God will give us a better body—one that will gloriously replace the mortal home in which we now reside (verse 4). And for this future state we earnestly groan.

Groaning is longing at its deepest and most earnest level. Groanings are mournful, painful sounds forced from the depths of our burdened souls. Our groaning is unmistakable evidence of irrepressible pain and agony. What Paul is saying is precisely how we as Christians long for heaven.

While our deepest groaning is for heaven, as Christians, ever sensitive to the tragedies of this present life, we also groan because of the human condition. We groan because of civic injustice; we groan because of the horrific accidents and natural disasters that sweep away hapless multitudes. We groan because of wars and serial murders and ethnic cleansing. We groan when friends and loved ones are taken away by disease and or old age. We groan when our children suffer physically or emotionally, when our relationships with relatives or friends are severed by turbulent misunderstandings or even the stealthy passage of time. We groan because the insatiate grave never ceases its thirsty quest and because "we who are alive and remain" are so quickly robbed of our strength, reduced to slivers of the once robust and energetic creatures we were. We groan at the ambulance's shrill wail, the fire trucks labored rumbling, and the litany of lust, looting, and loss displayed on every evening newscast.

But again, our groaning is beyond all that. It is groaning not simply because of human disaster, but for heaven's attractions. We groan to see Jesus our Savior. We groan to be with Him and each other in our glorified bodies, then to cast our crowns at His feet and His dear name in love repeat. We must wait, perhaps beyond our lifetime, but until then, we earnestly groan for that better day.

Not Ashamed

For both He who sanctifies and those who are being sanctified are all of one, for which reason He is not ashamed to call them brethren. Heb. 2:11.

Through the miracle of the incarnation the divine God took up residence on earth, and through the miracle of the Resurrection the human Jesus now has residence in glory. Two of Ellen White's illumining statements on Christ's continuing humanity are: (a) "Christ . . . ascended to heaven in the form of humanity" (*The Desire of Ages,* p. 832) and (b) "He took this humanity with Him into the heavenly courts, and through the eternal ages He bears it as the One who has redeemed human being in the city of God" (*The Seventh-day Adventist Bible Commentary,* Ellen G. White Comments, vol. 5, p. 1125).

Christ did not return to heaven just to tell what it is like on earth; He did not return simply to report regarding our condition. That would have been gracious, indeed, but He went beyond—He went as one of us. He kept His human identity; He did not go to talk about us as a race apart, but as a part of our race. On earth He was "God with us," and now He is "us with God." On earth He was innocent humanity numbered as a transgressor; in heaven He is representative humanity numbered with the Godhead.

Most people of high honor distance themselves from their misbehaving relatives; few persons of national or international fame freely connect with unsavory kin. Celebrities do not usually own ties to criminal elements. Luminaries are prone to soon forget the hidden hamlets of their birth—the lowlands of their lesser beginnings. But not so with Jesus, He has, before heaven and the universe of unfallen worlds, retained His human identity. The sad reality is that, though He is not ashamed to be called our brother, we so often succumb to the pressures of the world and, by word and action, mute our relationship with Him.

Recently I took my cell phone back to the store where it was purchased for repairs. I had damaged it rather harshly, and while it would vibrate softly, it would not ring. The clerk explained it carefully before handing it back with this conclusion: "Your phone," he said, "is stuck on silence!" And so are many of us who claim His name. We vibrate softly at times, but damaged by worldly interference, fear, and the world's allurements, we remain "stuck on silence." The solution? Reverential appreciation for the sacrifices past and present of the One who ever liveth to intercede for His kin below.

"He Is Not Here!"

He is not here, but is risen! Remember how
He spoke to you when He was still in Galilee? Luke 24:6.

Epitaphs can be very revealing—particularly the self-made kind. One example is that of early American statesman Thomas Jefferson, who left these proud words etched in granite on his tomb at Monticello: "Here was buried Thomas Jefferson, author of the Declaration of American Independence, the Statute of Virginia for religious freedom and father of the University of Virginia." Another is the inscription of the television host Merv Griffin: "I will not be back after this message."

Epitaphs designed by others (family and friends) who wish the deceased remembered in a special way can be just as revealing of one's life experience. Such is the one I read some time ago in a highly decorated cemetery for U.S. soldiers of World War II at Guadalcanal. There, row after row of pearly plates marked the graves of American soldiers who gave their lives on that distant shore for the cause of freedom. The inscriptions vary, but one that caught my attention read simply:

"Here lies soldier Allan Simpson,

He lived briefly,

He fought bravely,

He gave completely,

What more can a good man do?"

And how might the sorrowing disciples have worded Jesus' epitaph? Perhaps something like this: "Here lies the Good Shepherd—Man of Miracles, Ambassador of a Better Life." That description would have been true had He stayed in the grave, but He did not. Because He rose! Buddha, Confucius, Zoroaster, Muhammad, and all the other founders of religious orders still rest in their dusty beds. Their hollow skeletons remain in the place of their entombment marked with words of shining accomplishment. Not so with Jesus. Above the place where He was laid, there glows the simple caption: "He is not here!" No, He is not there in the darkened tomb—He has risen. But His works continue for us in glory and through us on earth. In that sense He indeed "is here" in us. And that is how His work on earth continues.

The Honest Heathen

Indeed, when Gentiles, who do not know the law,
do by nature things required by the law, they are a law for themselves,
even though they do not have the law. Rom. 2:14, NIV.

There will be in the first resurrection several classes of people whose presence will give added evidence of God's great mercy. One such group is children and infants who died before the age of accountability. Of this group Ellen White writes: "As the little infants come forth immortal from their dusty beds, they immediately wing their way to their mothers' arms. They meet again nevermore to part. But many of the little ones have no mother there. We listen in vain for the rapturous song of triumph from the mother. The angels receive the motherless infants and conduct them to the tree of life" (*Selected Messages,* book 2, p. 260).

A second group whose presence confirms the wideness of God's grace is those adults who, in the midst of heathen culture, heard God's voice in nature and in their consciousness responded, though ignorant of the Decalogue to the Holy Spirit's leading. Of this group our prophet writes: "Among the heathens are those who worship God ignorantly, those to whom the light is never brought by human instrumentality, yet they will not perish. Though ignorant of the written law of God, they have heard His voice speaking to them in nature, and have done the things that the law required. Their works are evidence that the Holy Spirit has touched their hearts, and they are recognized as the children of God" (*The Desire of Ages,* p. 638).

And a third group whose presence evidences the unfathomable love of God is the well-meaning slaves, who though denied social and political freedoms exercised their powers of spiritual choice on the side of right. Ellen White's words regarding the victims of American slavery are: "Then commenced the jubilee, when the land should rest. I saw the pious slave rise in victory and triumph, and shake off the chains that bound him, while his wicked master was in confusion and knew not what to do; for the wicked could not understand the words of the voice of God" (*Early Writings,* p. 286).

The obedient of all ages will be there and with them the innocent infants, the honest heathen, the pious slave—and we must be there as well.

Jesus: The Firstfruits

*For as in Adam all die, even so in Christ all shall be made alive.
But each one in his own order: Christ the firstfruits,
afterward those who are Christ's at His coming. 1 Cor. 15:22, 23.*

In Christ's time the Jews celebrated three major feasts dictated by the Mosaic Law. They were: (1) the Passover, which fell on the fifteenth day of the first month (Nissan) of the year; (2) the Feast of Weeks or Pentecost (also called the Feast of Harvest or Firstfruits), which fell exactly 50 days after the Passover season began; and (3) the Feast of Tabernacles or Booths (called Ingathering) that came at the full moon of Tishri, the seventh month, and marked the final reaping.

Each of the feasts had major implications for harvesting. For instance, it was only after the priest waved the sheath of barley grain before the altar on the second day of the Passover that the "early harvest" could begin.

Jesus, the antitypical lamb, on the day of His resurrection, returned to glory for preliminary approval of the Father. But he did not, at that time, take with Him the wave sheath—the earnest of the obedient that rose with Him. Their presentation to the Father would wait until His formal return from the Mount of Olives weeks later. However, on the day of His resurrection, He went alone for a quiet, private, personal reunion with the Father.

In this manner, He, the firstborn of God, was Himself the firstfruits of the resurrection harvest. Rightly appreciated, He is not only first with the Father, but also the first in all His trusting believers' priorities. And should time last and we too be laid in the tomb, when we awaken, His will be the first voice we hear, the first face we see—our first welcome to an eternity in which death and dying shall be no more.

Since "affliction will not rise up a second time" (Nahum 1:9), its presence in our world will be seen as its first and only appearance in the universe—a tragic aberration then completely excised by the death of Christ, destined never again to disturb in all God's vast and peaceful domain.

Living Proof

And the graves were opened; and many bodies of the saints
who had fallen asleep were raised; and coming out of the graves after His
resurrection, they went into the city and appeared to many. Matt. 27:52, 53.

The earthquake that occurred on the Friday when Christ died opened many graves from which exited on the Sunday of His resurrection a large company of sleeping saints. These were people of all classes and periods from the beginning of time who had borne testimony for truth at the cost of their lives (*The Desire of Ages*, p. 786).

How did the risen saints spend their time between their resurrection and their ascension with Christ? They went about the streets of Jerusalem appearing unto many triumphantly declaring, "Christ [is] risen . . . and we be risen with him" (*ibid.*). In this manner they bore witness to Jesus' power over the grave and fulfilled Isaiah's prophecy: "Your dead shall live; together with my dead body they shall arise. Awake and sing, you who dwell in the dust; for your dew is like the dew of herbs, and the earth shall cast out the dead" (Isa. 26:19).

The resurrected believers interfaced boldly with the general population, witnessing gladly and gratefully to His triumph over death. Their testimony was living demonstration of Christ's power over the grave; conclusive evidence that all the prophets had said about the coming Messiah was fulfilled in Jesus.

We, who were once dead in sin and have now risen to newness of life, bare that same testimony today. Our miraculous transformation from lives of sin to living for Him speaks loudly to those about us. We are His epistles; His grand display and His primary advertisement to the nations. During the 40 days between His crucifixion and His final ascension, He appeared 10 times to His crestfallen followers. Never once during that period did the resurrected Savior witness to unbelievers—the common citizens of society. This obligation He left to His followers both then and now. This is a calling we happily accept, an honor we gladly wear, a responsibility we, enthused by His gracious acts of salvation, dutifully and sacrificially fulfill.

Oh, Happy Day

Behold, He is coming with clouds, and every eye will see Him, even they who pierced Him. And all tribes of the earth will mourn because of Him. Even so, Amen. Rev. 1:7.

In addition to the general host of righteous who will be resurrected at Christ's coming, there are two special categories of the dead who will be raised to witness this glorious event. One group will be "all who have died in the faith of the third angel's message" (*The Great Controversy*, p. 637). That is to say, all who in the last days of earth's history treasured God's Word in spite of prevailing trends and philosophies. These are they who remained faithful in spite of society's teachings against creationism, the Ten Commandments, the nonimmortality of the soul, and the holy seventh-day Sabbath.

Then there is another special group that will be raised to witness His return—those "who pierced Him" (Rev. 1:7). Christ had warned, "Hereafter shall ye see the Son of man sitting on the right hand of power, and coming in the clouds of heaven" (Matt. 26:64). In other words, those whose tongues falsified at His trial; whose arms propelled the whip that lacerated His tender back; whose mouths spewed saliva upon His sorrowing face; whose hands jammed the garland of thorns into His sensitive brow; and whose gnarled fists drove the spikes through His tender feet and hands and then jammed the heavy cross into the rocky ground—they will be raised to witness His glorious return.

Pilate who feared, Herod who leered, the multitude who jeered, and the soldier who thrust the sword into His side will be there. The Sadducees who regarded the afterlife as an illogical belief and the Pharisees who made the present life an unwholesome burden will be there. Those who led the people in shouting "Crucify him, crucify him" will now join in the baleful declaration, "He is indeed the Son of God, the Messiah!"

How will the waiting redeemed respond as the wicked quail in the presence of heaven's majesty? Their joyous cry will be, "Lo, this is our God, we have waited for Him, and He will save us." Oh, happy, happy day!

The Mystery Solved

And without controversy great is the mystery of godliness: God was manifested in the flesh, justified in the Spirit, seen by angels, preached among the Gentiles, believed on in the world, received up in glory. 1 Tim. 3:16.

One of my favorite illustrations of Christian belief and trust in God is mirrored in the story of the chauffeur who told the scientist he drove from convention to convention that he had heard his lecture so often he could give it himself. Understandably reluctant at first, the good-natured professor finally acquiesced to his driver's request. At the very next appointment the professor took a seat in the balcony wearing his chauffeur's uniform, while his driver, dressed as the professor, delivered a flawless recitation of the speech he had come to memorize.

When the chauffeur finished, there was loud applause, but a huge problem. The moderator informed him that, in this particular forum, it was customary that the speaker responds to audience questions regarding the subject matter. Not surprisingly, the very first inquiry addressed issues about which the terrified impostor knew absolutely nothing. He was about to confess the ruse when a marvelous idea changed his downcast demeanor. Turning to the moderator, he said, "Sir, that is a very easy question. In fact, it is so very simple (now pointing to the balcony), I'm going to ask my chauffeur to stand up and give you the answer!"

This is how we should be with Jesus. We can and must, in our daily lives, follow His example, but Satan knows that we do not really have the answers. So when he challenges us to explain the mysteries of the incarnation, the crucifixion, and the resurrection, we are without scientific explanation. We can no more explain the mysteries of redemption than Job the patriarch explain the marvels of creation. As humans we are as close to binding "the sweet influences of Pleiades" and loosing "the bands of Orion" as we are unraveling the secrets of salvation (Job 38:31, KJV).

How can it be that God can also be human? Where was the divine Jesus when the human Jesus died? And how, in our case, can rotted flesh and dried bones revert back to warm and vibrant beings? We cannot explain, but Jesus can. He, who has taken on our human garb and clothed us in His righteousness, not only has the answers—He is the answer: the alpha and omega, the beginning and the end, our promise and pledge of a better resurrection.

The Blessed Hope

But I do not want you to be ignorant, brethren, concerning those who have fallen asleep, lest you sorrow as others who have no hope. 1 Thess. 4:13.

The hope of the soon return of Jesus is a major element of Christian joy and endurance. Paul's words were addressed to the Thessalonians, who unfortunately were losing hope. They had begun their journey as a happy, thriving congregation. They had heard Paul preach the commandments, the cross, and the coming, and a large number had joined the church. They were baptized together; they attended Sabbath school, prayer meetings, and camp meetings together and fully expected (not just hoped) to be translated together. Baptism was for them not only the symbol of Christ's death, burial, and resurrection, but it was also a promise of immunity from death, and they drank their communion wine as the medicine of immortality.

But then as months lengthened into years and one member after another was taken by death, they became disillusioned, despondent, and depressed. What had been a blessed hope became a broken hope; so that they "with anguish . . . looked for the last time upon the faces of their dead, hardly daring to hope to meet them in a future life" (*The Acts of the Apostles,* p. 258).

Theirs was not simply a broken hope, it was a bogus hope fueled by misunderstandings and selfish desire. Paul had not intended absolute assurance of Christ's return in their day; it was clear from his portrayal of Christ having "died for us, that whether we wake or sleep, we should live together with Him" (1 Thess. 5:10). What then was the problem? The Thessalonians had become so enthralled by the "goodies" of salvation that they had lost trust in the God of salvation and His will for their lives.

So how is it with you and me? Are we so centered upon heavenly rewards that we project His return in our lifetime with undisputed certainty? Or do we trust His divine will so completely that, even if we must sleep, we will lie down in sure confidence of His powers of resurrection and firm belief that heaven, no matter what its provisions or when it's appearing, is worth the waiting?

If it is the latter, we have achieved the ultimate faith and can plan wisely for tomorrow while conducting ourselves as if each day may be the last.

First Things First

For if we believe that Jesus died and rose again, even so God
will bring with Him those who sleep in Jesus. 1 Thess. 4:14.

Notice that the apostle based his corrections of the Thessalonians' error concerning the state of the dead on the resurrection of the Life-giver Himself. The implication is that their hopes were not to be grounded in future personal reward so much as an appreciation for the sacrificial services (past and present) of the living Lord. It is true that Second Coming emphasis distinguishes Adventism within the family of Christianity, but it is also true that unless grounded in the ministry of Jesus, that flagship doctrine is inevitably skewed and distorted.

Preaching the clouds before the cross makes ill-formed Christians. It makes for "fanatical" Christians—those who try to hasten the time of trouble and Christ's return by radical pronouncements. It makes for "fretful" Christians—those who do not understand that our strivings will never bring peace or salvation; that our good works make heaven happy, but only Christ's righteousness can make heaven happen. It makes for "faithless" Christians—those who have long since lost their fervor; who have become immune to "cross-less" cries of "Jesus is coming!" It makes for "fraudulent" Christians, whose mechanical "Happy Sabbath"s mask a faded, formless expectation. And it makes for "fearful" Christians—those who are more focused on Sunday blue laws than on the red blood and white robe of Jesus Christ.

Maximizing the clouds while minimizing the cross is the source of hard-hearted, critical, merciless, sour-disposition members, whose conduct gives proof to the cynical definition of a saint as "somebody who has to live with one."

Believers whose hopes are anchored upon Calvary have a trust that cannot be dissipated by trial, diminished by time, or dimmed by the growing list of dying faithful or even the steady approach of their own demise. They are the brave soldiers of the cross who know, themselves, not to be greater than the Lord who *Himself* tasted death. All their hopes rest upon His dying to save, His rising to intercede, and His pledging to come again that where He is, "there [we] may be also" (John 14:3).

Prime-time Preeminence

For this we say to you by the word of the Lord,
that we who are alive and remain until the coming of the Lord
will by no means precede those who are asleep. 1 Thess. 4:15.

By these words Paul boldly addresses two crucial errors produced by the Thessalonians' flawed understandings. The first was their unjustified certainty of the Lord's return in their lifetime. The unhappy consequence of their misguided notion was that the more apparent it became that they might not be a part of the "we who are alive and remain," the more confused and despondent they became.

The second problem was that they regarded the death of their friends not as the natural consequence of the human condition, but as divine displeasure upon the deceased individual. Aversion for death, even for Christians, is natural, but the Thessalonians went too far. Their misunderstanding spawned for them selfish superiority over those who had died. In other words, theirs was not just a broken and bogus hope; it was a biased hope as well.

Paul, their teacher and friend, sought to correct their thinking by reminding them of not only the possibility of their death (1 Thess. 5:10), but also that at Christ's return preeminence will be given to the sleeping saints in that they will be resurrected to greet the Lord before the living are called to meet Him. They will be transformed before the "remaining" are translated, resurrected before the "remaining" are raptured and "brought up" before the "remaining" are "caught up." His words were perfectly calculated to correct their negative views and to establish clearly that those who rest from their labors, not the living saints, will be given prime-time billing at the Lord's return.

To which we, who are now alive and remain, continuously cry, "How long, O Lord, how long?" And while doing so, resolve that no one and nothing shall separate us from the lively hope that we have in Christ Jesus. Also, we do so knowing that what is important is not our rank or position at the Second Advent or in the environs of glory, but our being included in that number "when the saints go marching."

One of a Kind

*For the Lord Himself will descend from heaven with a shout,
with the voice of an archangel, and with the trumpet of God.
And the dead in Christ will rise first. 1 Thess. 4:16.*

Each element of this description is arresting: the Lord will descend—not an emissary, but the Lord Himself. And the Lord will shout! He has, of course, shouted before. He shouted on the cross when He had finished His painfully sacrificial journey in our midst, and He shouted at the tomb when He exited the darkness of death. The first was a shout of relief, the second the shout of rejoicing, and when He returns, it will be the shout of final restoration as He physically reclaims the redeemed.

Our text states that He will speak with the voice of an archangel. The only other mention in Scripture of an archangel speaking is in Jude 9, where Michael (Jesus), the archangel, rebuked Lucifer with stern authority while contending over the body of Moses. It is with the same unmistakably authoritative voice that He will call as He approaches earth to resurrect the righteous dead and translate the living faithful.

As the text continues, there is heard the trumpet of God. Trumpets in Bible days were used to announce the arrival of important personages—to celebrate the beginning of the feasts. This trumpet also announces the arrival of an important figure—the King of the universe. It also heralds the commencement of a feast—the grand and glorious festival of eternity. And it likewise declares victory; the complete and final triumph of the Lamb over the dragon—the consummation of the great controversy.

But the trumpet that will sound at Christ's return has one characteristic for which there is no historical precedent or likeness. All other trumpets have depended upon the faculty of hearing. This trumpet, however, supplies (not assumes) auditory capacity; it produces the faculty of sound. And the dead in Christ shall rise first—not banged up, broken up, burned up, bloated up, or bound up as they died, but caught up fully restored in the image of God.

This is a promise worth waiting for and a hope worth dying for given by a God worth living for—today, tomorrow, and every day the rest of our lives.

Caught Up With Jesus

*Then we who are alive and remain shall be caught up
together with them in the clouds to meet the Lord in the air.
And thus we shall always be with the Lord. 1 Thess. 4:17.*

The Greek meaning of the expression "caught up" is "magnetized." It conveys a sense of being unshackled, unfettered, freed, extricated, or cut loose. All of which is very accurate. For 6,000 years earthlings have been bound to this globe, held fast by the ironclad laws of gravity. But at His coming, the world will have lost it charms; sin will have lost its grasp; gravity will have lost its pull; the flesh will have lost its propensities; death will have lost its hold; the grave will have released its grip; and the redeemed will then be drawn to the presence of the glorified Savior.

But in order to be physically loosed from the earth then, we must be spiritually freed from sin now. Those who dare hope for life in the kingdom of glory must follow His will in the kingdom of grace. It does not matter whether we are alive and remain or we must sleep and await the resurrection, heaven's ultimate concern is not our personal longevity, but the proper conduct and conclusion of the plan of salvation. God is vitally concerned about both the quality and quantity of our life on earth. But He orders the universe with the larger picture in mind. He, for whom tomorrow is as clear as yesterday, for whom 1,000 years is but as "a watch in the night" (Ps. 90:4), for whom the end is as clear as the beginning orders, and allows for us, individually, what is best for us, eternally.

"Are you ready?" the doctor asked me as he and his associates prepared to put me to sleep prior to a delicate and somewhat painful procedure. I smiled and said, "Yes"—and that was all I knew for approximately an hour. The time between hearing his voice and hearing my wife's at the bedside in the recovery room simply did not exist. For my conscious chronology, "Are you ready?" was followed immediately by her voice, "Can you hear me?"

So it is with the sleeping saints—the final events of this brief and troubled life will be followed immediately by the "welcome home" of our returning Lord. The question for each today and every day is "Are you ready?"

The Final Triumph

Then we who are alive and remain shall be caught up
together with them in the clouds to meet the Lord in the air.
And thus we shall always be with the Lord. 1 Thess. 4:17.

When Adam and Eve sinned, they were given rulership over all three realms of our planet: the surface of the earth, the regions below earth's surface, and the heavens that surround our globe. However, when Satan triumphed in Eden, their authority in each of these realms was abdicated to the evil one.

When Jesus came, He demonstrated unquestioned ownership in two of the three spheres claimed by Satan. He showed superiority over things upon the earth by cursing the fig tree and by healing disease. He showed superiority of things under the earth by raising the dead and Himself exiting the grave. While it is true that in calming the storm upon the Galilean Sea He also demonstrated authority over the winds above the earth, His rulership in the higher region was not as starkly seen as His authority in the other two. Thus, Satan was able to boldly posture as "prince of the power of the air" (Eph. 2:2).

For 6,000 years Satan has rained down destruction upon the human race. He has from the air rained down windstorms, tidal waves, hailstones, mudslides, hurricanes, cyclones, dust storms, tornadoes, and tsunamis. From the air he has poured out lethal gases and deadly plagues and crippling epidemics. It is in the midst of this, his cherished stronghold, his workshop of evil, the very arena from which he has for so long badgered and bothered earth's suffering citizens, that the returning Christ will assemble the saved.

Having now lost his final staging ground, Satan will be deprived not only of his kingdom, but also its citizens as well. The earth will be empty, the righteous dead will have been resurrected, the righteous living will have been translated, the wicked living will be slain, and the wicked dead remain dead. Thus begins the millennium of Satan's pain and the ongoing eternity of the universe—void of evil.

Faith Unshakable

Therefore comfort one another with these words. 1 Thess. 4:18.

"But," I hear the skeptics say, "how long can you people believe all this? The disciples hoped, the early church hoped, the church of the Dark Ages hoped, the pioneers hoped, your parents hoped, and you have hoped. You hoped when you were a youth, you hoped when you were middle-aged; now you are hoping in advanced years—how long can you hope?" How long? The response of the faithful is "We will hope till He comes, and if He does not come in our generation, we will hope till we die."

"But," the skeptic asks, "how can you preach what you cannot prove? You cannot give incontrovertible demonstration of your belief."

"You are right," we believers reply. "We cannot prove it, but we can substantiate it." We see it in the cycles of nature, in the fulfillment of prophesy, and, as important, in our sanctified reason. We cannot prove it, but we have decided that we would "rather die in an endless hope than live with a hopeless end."

"But," the skeptic continues, "this is the twenty-first century. Can't you see it is all a hoax, an apparition, a dream?" "Believe that if you will," faith responds, "but this dream has given us meaning while living and hope beyond dying. It has given us an accurate worldview. It has unwrapped prophecies and allowed us to see more on our knees than the philosopher on their tiptoes—if we are dreaming, let us dream on!"

This is the sum of our position, the statement of our faith. Because of our appreciation for the cross of Jesus Christ and for all the gifts of life and learning and living that are provided in His Holy Word, we can approach even the open grave knowing that we are not alone in our trek through "the valley of the shadow of death." He is with us. He too drank from the cup of personal demise—we, therefore, do so knowing that on the other side of the mountain whose peaks darken the valley through which all humanity must pass there is a heavenly home made secure by the sacrifice of Jesus. We do so knowing that in the tribunal where all great cases are being decided the judge is on our side and that beyond this life of toil and tears there is—"something better"—a land of uninterrupted, unfettered, unending joy.

DECEMBER

A Better Reward

The Payoff

Then Peter answered and said to Him, "See, we have left all
and followed You. Therefore what shall we have?" Matt. 19:27.

Peter, whose curiosity and candor often sparked memorable responses from the
Lord, was at it again! This time he wanted to know what the payoff for discipleship would be. His question was, "What do we get out of this? We have left our jobs,
our families and friends to follow you. What is in it for us?" Jesus' answer was "A
hundredfold greater satisfaction in this life and, in addition, life everlasting in the
world to come" (see Matt. 19:28-30). Was Peter wrong to wonder about the rewards
of discipleship? No, he was in fact expressing a legitimate human hope for positive
consequences in response to sacrifice and service.

As seen in Scripture, God Himself often used the principal of cause and effect to motivate toward doing good. Ancient Israel was told repeatedly that their
prosperity was directly tied to their responses to God's commands: that the welfare
of their families, the quality of their nationhood, even the successes of succeeding
generations was dependent upon their acquiescence to His will. "Obey and live,
disobey and die" was their unmistakable command.

It is the same with us today. We too live in relational contract with our God of
unconditional love, but conditional rewards. The great payoff of course is that of
eternal life—unaltered joy and peace in the better world to come.

The Canaan that Israel finally entered was plush with beauty, but it was not
free from danger and death. There they encountered not only giant ecological challenges, but also the giant warriors of hostile nations. Not so with the Canaan toward
which we are journeying. It is a land of perfect safety and plenty. There are no
dangerous rivers to ford, no dark valleys to traverse, no rough mountains to cross,
no evil occupants to combat. We can be there; we must be there; we will, by God's
grace, be there to shout, as we plant our feet on territories deeded in our name by
the blood of Jesus—glory, glory, home at last!

More Beyond

"And everyone who has left houses or brothers or sisters
or father or mother or wife or children or lands, for My name's sake,
shall receive a hundredfold, and inherit eternal life." Matt. 19:29.

Until Columbus' journey led him to the sprawling Americas, the world was thought of as consisting of only the known continents of Africa, Asia, and Europe. In commemoration of his discovery of new lands, Spain minted a coin with his picture—the back of which proudly proclaimed "plus ultra" or more beyond!

This proclamation aptly describes the Christian's perspective. The unbeliever looks at death's dark door and sees only the rotting flesh and bleaching bones of a silent eternity—nothing else! For such, life is but a biological happenstance: the miracle of breath, the inevitability of death, and then, nothing more. But this not so for the Christian. We have hope of something better: the belief that there is more—much more beyond.

Our rewards for serving God are not relegated to the future world; they begin in this life. As a result of our enlightened obedience, life in this present world is enhanced with benefits not known to unbelievers. The rewards of liberality toward the poor (Isa. 58:6-9), of conscientious tithing (Mal. 3:8, 9), of faithful Sabbathkeeping (Isa. 58:12-14), of proper diet, dress, and, of course, daily devotions are real and tangible for the obedient child of God. Serving Jesus pays not only in psychological benefits (clear conscience and emotional calm in the storms of life), but it also pays in physiological benefits (optimum health and longevity) as well. Serving Christ does not prevent illness and pain, but it does enhance whatever lifespan we are willed by God and produces the courage to face our unavoidable surrender to death.

God's tomorrow is sure. Though it tarry beyond our time to die, it is as certain as every reborn morning; as inevitable as were His fulfillment of Isaiah's glowing predictions of His virgin birth (Isa. 7:14); His death upon Calvary (Isa. 53:7); and David's cheering promise of His resurrection from the grave (Ps. 16:10). The New Testament fulfillment of Old Testament prophecies concerning His ministry are undeniable evidences of His veracity and the ultimate basis of our unfaltering hope.

Imagine That!

While we do not look at the things which are seen, but at the things which are not seen. For the things which are seen are temporary, but the things which are not seen are eternal. 2 Cor. 4:18.

All that this world contains will someday cease to exist. It will either decay with time or be destroyed at the second coming of Christ. All that our physical eyes behold is, by the authority of God's Word, destined to be no more. In other words, everything visible to our sight will someday return to nothingness.

On the other hand, all the materials of heaven are eternal. They are not afflicted with the virus of decay and death—they are unending.

Seen in this light, the apostle is telling us to look away from the visible nothingness of this world to the invisible "somethingness" of the world to come. And this is after all, the challenge of faith—is it not? From "visible nothingness" to "invisible somethingness" is really the believer's challenge—the leap of faith all Christians must make. As we follow Christ we must place our confidence not upon tangibles destined to secede from existence, but from never fading intangibles of glory.

Is this easy to do? No. It is against the grain of human nature; it is contrary to reason and hostile to our vaunted scientific methodologies. But it is the surrender without which we "cannot please God"—that is, have a wholesome relationship with Him.

What are the positive consequences of placing our hopes in the invisible appointments of glory? Strength to endure the trials of our temporary existence in this world; accurate evaluation of events in our lives and the society around us; assurance that when we cooperate with His will, it is His will that will guide our lives; confidence that should the grave claim our bodies, they will burst forth at His call to everlasting life, or should He come in our lifetime, knowledge that we will be transformed to a state in which death has no part.

Today as we go about our duties, we can do so knowing that no matter what tragedies or troubles may come our way, they are but temporary pain someday soon to be replaced by a wondrous eternity in the presence of our precious Lord. Imagine that!

The Half Has Never Been Told

But as it is written: "Eye has not seen, nor ear heard,
nor have entered into the heart of man the things which
God has prepared for those who love Him." 1 Cor. 2:9.

Our brains receive, decipher, organize, and appropriate information delivered to it by our five senses: the capacities of touch, taste, hearing, smell, and sight. The impressions conveyed by these means are processed as thought in categories of size, shape, color, weight, density, and direction. The brain then compares the data presented it with prior information and organizes those impressions as functional reality. This is how we know and understand.

As much as we try, we will never interpret or process the data of heaven. The categories of glory exceed the capacity of our senses. Divinity cannot be comprehended by humanity. Infinity is an order of being that finite creatures are incapable of knowing. Our reality is not the same as God's; the constituent elements of His being, i.e., omnipotence, omnipresence, omnicompetence, omniscience, and everlastingness, are higher than our comprehension. Our senses, structured to appropriate elements of this present world, cannot decipher those of heaven; the computer that is the human mind is not able to know transcendence.

This makes heaven all the more attractive. The quest to revel one day in the storehouse of heaven's "something better" is an effective stimulus for our desiring to be there. For there we will dwell in the dream world of eternal discovery; there we will, from one eon to another, find new and more glorious realities to relish; there, with mortality overcome by immortality and corruption replaced by incorruption, our apparatus for knowing will be compatible with heaven's glorious appointments; there our glorified senses will forever vibrate with the onslaught of fresh discoveries of universal love and wonder; there, on that higher plane of being, we will continuously thrill to the discovery of "something better" and proclaim abroad as did Sheba's queen, when impacted by Solomon's glory—"the half has never been told!"

Delighting Our Senses

Set your mind on things above, not on things on the earth. Col. 3:2.

Negative imaginations are those that are prideful, vengeful, fearful, and lewd. Healthy imaginations are gratified, hopeful, cheerful, constructive, uplifting, encouraging, and pure. The former cripple our powers of reasoning and ability to cope with reality; the latter strengthen our rational powers and enhance our capacity to negotiate life's challenges. It is this kind of imagining, especially that of "the glorious future to come," that the remnant prophet encourages us to engage (*The Great Controversy*, p. 488).

There are numerous benefits for doing so. One is the crowding out or the displacing of evil imaginations. Another is the strengthening by exercise of what Ellen White terms as our "sanctified imagination." Still another is the development of faith that increases with such contemplation. And yet another is the benefit upon our physical self that accrues from positive thinking.

This is why we are admonished, "As your senses delight in the attractive loveliness of the earth, think of the world that is to come, that shall never know the blight of sin and death; where the face of nature will no more wear the shadow of the curse. Let your imagination picture the home of the saved, and remember that it will be more glorious than your brightest imagination can portray" (*Steps to Christ*, p. 86).

Today and every day there will be ample opportunity—while driving our cars, waiting in lines, lounging at lunchtime, participating in devotions, etc., when we can engage in wholesome imagining. This capacity, so often utilized in the parables by Christ to drive home eternal truths, should be a pleasant exercise frequently engaged by the Christian.

Imagine living in a world of perfect peace, total justice, unmarred health, and absolute righteousness. Imagine walking on a street and realizing it to be a street of gold; gazing upon a sea and knowing it to be a sea of glass; eating from a tree and knowing it to be the tree of life; breathing air and realizing it is the atmosphere of eternity; hearing a voice and recognizing that it is a long-lost friend or loved one. Imagine shaking a hand and finding it to be the nail-pierced hand of our loving Lord— imagine that!

A World of Peace

The work of righteousness will be peace, and the effect
of righteousness, quietness and assurance forever. Isa. 32:17.

Let's see! How many ways can we describe it—these tumultuous wars that affect our globe? We have conventional wars and nuclear wars, hot wars and cold war, religious wars and race wars, regional wars and rice wars, class wars and civil wars, guerrilla wars and gang wars, sea wars and sky wars. We have star wars, jungle wars, drug wars, ethnic wars, territorial wars, and world wars. So constant is the revelation of mayhem and madness that we have become accustomed to it all. Ours is a world boiling and bubbling in the white-hot heat of global conflict, and sadly, society has come to expect and accept it all.

The violence of war is not the only brand of conflict that mars our peace. There is the escalating volume of family abuse: spousal abuse, child abuse, and the growing epidemic of elderly abuse. Add to this violence in the workplace, road rage, police brutality, the alarming increase of mass murderers, the searing horror of international terrorism and the dismal picture of our troubled society is clear.

Now with that background of disquiet in mind, imagine if you will, a world without conflict; a world of perfect peace. True, Jesus gives His people peace of mind in midst of present troubles. However, living peaceably in a turbulent world is not the same as living amid peace in a trouble-free world. We hopeful pilgrims are still inundated by the sights and sounds of "the curse" and, at times, are physically, psychologically, emotionally, and economically victimized by the evils that surround us. While trusting in the eventual outcome of the war between good and evil, we are not immune to the hits and hurts that are the consequences of sin.

But in that better world we will be safe from the chilling blights of violence. There we will have peace in the valley: "the lion shall lie down with the lamb and a little child shall lead them." No troublesome elements or troubling citizens will enter there; only those who have believed, received, and experienced the promise: "These things I have spoken to you, that in Me you may have peace. In the world you will have tribulation; but be of good cheer, I have overcome the world" (John 16:33).

Perfect Health

And the inhabitant will not say, "I am sick";
the people who dwell in it will be forgiven their iniquity. Isa. 33:24.

Imagine living in such a world: a world untouched by sickness and death. True, modern science has delivered us from most of the diseases that beleaguered the citizens of past centuries. Nevertheless, for every disease now conquered, a new strain of untreatable virus is discovered. "The earth . . . waxes old like a garment" (Isa. 51:6, KJV), and with age, the protecting elements of creation recede before the advancing onslaught of global pollution.

We are choking on the very by-products of our industrialized society. Millions of tons of raw sewage are pumped into our waterways each year; our cars and aircraft are belching clouds of poisonous gases into our smog-infected skies; our nuclear factories are depositing mountains of toxic waste in the bosom of the earth. We walk on polluted ground; we breathe polluted air; we drink polluted water; we eat polluted food; we are bombarded with polluted noises. No wonder that, in spite of the stimulating advances of modern science, our hospitals are overflowing and our graveyards are full. We are suffocating on the fumes of industrialization and crippled by the consequences of our technological advance.

There is an even more basic cause of our physical woes: the inevitability of our demise in consequence of sin. It is a fact that "as soon as we are born we begin to die." The cynic who defined life as a sexually transmitted disease with 100 percent mortality is not all wrong. Sickness and death are the unavoidable, inescapable realities of our sin-cursed world.

But not in the world to come! There will never be a tear nor tare, an itch or a twitch, a snarl or a sniffle. There, matter will not decay, substance will not sour, time will not erode. There's no 9-1-1 or code blues or wailing ambulances or shrieking, screaming sirens to be heard. There in that cloudless, crimeless, fadeless day, we shall never grow old, and inhabitants shall not say "I am sick!" There we shall have escaped the ironclad laws of nature that now condemn us to death and decay—and "the leaves of the tree [will be] for the healing of the nations" (Rev. 22:2).

A Land of Justice

Behold, a king will reign in righteousness,
and princes will rule with justice. A man will be as a hiding
place from the wind, and a cover from the tempest, as rivers of water
in a dry place, as the shadow of a great rock in a weary land. Isa. 32:1, 2.

Imagine living in a land of perfect justice; a world without favoritism or nepotism or sexism or racism; without discrimination based on height, color, weight, gender, accent, age, education, demography, or any such factor; a world that is fair—absolutely fair—where no hint of advantage accrues because of perceived or real superiority.

In our world of swollen pride and sweltering egos, our world of selfish desires and diseased wills, we are aflame with all manner of discrimination. It is not fair that some children are born to conspicuous consumption while others die of starvation. It is not fair that females are neglected in matters of hiring, promotion, and pay; that girl babies in some cultures are destroyed because they are not as economically valued as males and that in other cultures just the opposite is true. It is not fair that so many thousands of wives and sweethearts are murdered in the United States each year by their more physically dominating companions; that longevity is less for the economically deprived; that education, health care, housing, and general access to the nation's resources are lesser for minorities; that the decisions of so many guardians of justice (police, judges, etc.) are driven by vice and votes rather than virtue.

But there is light at the end of the tunnel. When He comes, our righteous God will establish a rule of justice: a regime where fairness will reign unimpeded, where no courts will be necessary to adjudicate the claims of the oppressed, where no suffering citizen will cry for relief because of want. In the kingdom to come there will be no appeal regarding rights denied or wrongs endured because the Lamb is a just ruler and all His subjects will be absolutely entitled, completed fulfilled, equally connected with the Giver of life and richly rewarded throughout an untarnished eternity—imagine that!

Growth in Glory

*Beloved, now we are children of God; and it has not yet been
revealed what we shall be, but we know that when He is revealed,
we shall be like Him, for we shall see Him as He is. 1 John 3:2.*

There will be no favoritism or injustice in the kingdom of glory. However, this does not mean that all will be the same. There will be noticeable differences in heaven's inhabitants. There will be a difference in height because those raised from the grave will be the same height as when they died (*The Great Controversy*, p. 644). There will be differences in knowledge because we shall come forth from the grave with the same stock of information with which we ended our earthly life (*This Day With God*, p. 350).

We will not remain at either entry level. Malachi's promise is that "ye shall go forth, and grown up as calves of the stall" (Mal. 4:2). Ellen White, in commenting upon the intellectual development that shall be there, states, "There every power will be developed, every capacity increased. The grandest enterprises will be carried forward, the loftiest aspirations will be reached, the highest ambitions realized. And still there will arise new heights to surmount, new wonders to admire, new truths to comprehend, fresh objects to call forth the powers of body and mind and soul" (*Education*, p. 307).

And there are other differences to be noted. Our starry crowns will vary in their content. This is because each star represents someone saved by our endeavors (*The Seventh-day Adventist Bible Commentary*, Ellen G. White Comments, vol. 6, p. 1104). Also, some saved will be awarded closer proximity to Jesus than the rest of the redeemed; these are the martyrs who died for His cause (*The Great Controversy*, p. 665; *Testimonies for the Church*, vol. 1, pp. 68, 69).

In glory, our ego-driven categories of prideful place will have vanished. We will not preen or pout about our status. Our joy of being redeemed will have erased all thoughts of being bigger, better, faster, richer, prettier, or in any other way more advantaged than another. Our happiness will accrue from inheriting a utopia without myopia, a society without psychiatry, a paradise without parasites, an eternity without infirmity, a glad, everlasting tomorrow without tears or sorrow, unending life without pain and strife; to which we longing pilgrims cry, "Even so, come, Lord Jesus!"

A Land of Holiness

A highway shall be there, and a road, and it shall be called the Highway of Holiness. The unclean shall not pass over it, but it shall be for others. Whoever walks the road, although a fool, shall not go astray. Isa. 35:8.

One of the primary rewards of the world to come will be life without the ever-present urges of our sinful flesh. At no time since the fall of Adam and Eve has any human, except Jesus, come into the world without natural tendencies to evil. We are born with these tendencies and cannot, as long as we live, escape them; they are a permanent part of our being. The love of Christ daily absorbed from His Word controls, subdues, and overcomes them, but unlike the "cultivated" tendencies (those we acquire after birth that can be totally eradicated), these fatal flaws with which we are born remain as long as we live.

When Christ is in the heart, they do not "rule" our activities as before conversion (Rom. 6:11, 12), but they are always with us. Emaciated by lack of fueling, debilitated by lack of indulgence, they are, after our surrender to Christ, incapacitated and consequently controlled by the superior forces of God's Word. After conversion, these powers of the flesh no longer dominate, but they are never done trying. In consequence of our continuous devotion, they are neutralized and, although dormant, living components of our moral machinery.

What is it that we Christians must overcome? Not simply external incentives, but the internal urges of our sickly heritage bequeathed by Adam and Eve. It is because these urges never cease their clamoring that their conquest is "the work of a . . . lifetime" (*The Acts of the Apostles,* p. 560).

However, when Jesus comes, our glorified bodies will be free from all urges to evil. Robed in immortality, we will no longer be captive to sinful desires or hounded by the beasts of our carnality. Extricated from our faulty nature, we will no longer grapple with the demons of the past—we will indeed be free at last!

"There," states Isaiah, will be a "highway of holiness" and, I suggest, a boulevard of happiness, a road called peace, and an avenue named amazing grace leading to the holy throne, where is the royal seat of our righteous, ruling God.

Seeing Jesus

And there shall be no more curse, but the throne of God
and of the Lamb shall be in it, and His servants shall serve Him. They shall
see His face, and His name shall be on their foreheads." Rev. 22:3, 4.

During the 14 years of my presidency at Oakwood College in Huntsville, Alabama, I was privileged to meet (usually at banquets arranged by prestigious higher education organizations) a long list of prominent individuals. They include Henry Kissinger, Ronald Reagan, George and Barbara Bush, Edward Kennedy, Jane Fonda, Muhammad Ali, Nat King Cole, Leontyne Price, Henry Aaron, Martin Luther King, Jr., Ben Carson, Leonard Bailey, Sammy Davis, Jr., Jesse Jackson, Johnnie Cochran, Judge Mathis, and others.

One of the more memorable encounters was my brief contact with then senator from Massachusetts, John F. Kennedy. I was among a large number of persons at the Miami, Florida airport who welcomed the dashing, young politician to that state shortly before the presidential election of 1960. I struggled through the jostling mass, hoping to get close enough to shake the senator's hand as he leaned from the slowly moving convertible. But the crowd was too large. I finally gave up—satisfying myself with the thought that, if he became president, at least I had had the privilege of personally seeing, if not touching, him.

Then it happened! Suddenly, as if on cue, the limo reversed directions and moved directly toward my position. As the thick wall of humanity parted at the insistence of the agents trotting beside the car, I was soon within easy reach and then absolutely delighted when, as he passed by, he grasped my hand and said, "thank you very much." Soon thereafter he became the leader of an admiring nation and the hope of the entire free world. His assassination at the peak of his popularity remains one of the most shocking episodes in our country's history. What we have left is only his memory and his buried remains.

How different with our hero, Jesus. He, too, brought hope to an admiring public. He, too, inspired multitudes by His personal appeal. He, too, was struck down in His youth, but He rose and has gone "to prepare a place for us." Seeing Him in person is our highest motivation for being there.

The Gaze That Counts

But we all, with unveiled face, beholding as in a mirror
the glory of the Lord, are being transformed into the same image
from glory to glory, just as by the Spirit of the Lord. 2 Cor. 3:18.

There is a wise adage that says, "We grow in the direction of our reverences." In other words, that which we cherish most determines the contours of our development. Like the tendrils of the vine that stretch toward the sun or the sprigs of grass that move toward the pond or the roots of trees that stretch toward moist areas of soil, we grow toward our affections. This is "the bottom line" message of our text. It is also the gist of Paul's other encouragement: "Set your affection on things above, not on things on the earth" (Col. 3:2, KJV).

On what do we set are our gazes? Is it the violence portrayed in the media? Is it the excitement and brutality of some professional sports? Is it pornographic print? Or is it the mercurial ways of the stock market or even the health of our bank accounts? Is it a life of ease or the hopes and plans of a luxurious retirement? Or perhaps it is our education, our family and its welfare. Or is it our employment that has become more important than the condition of our souls? God's promises of the bright and beautiful world to come should supersede even the legitimate quests that occupy our lives. When that is not the case, when our primary affections have been diverted to secondary goods, we have, in fact, made gods of lesser deities and will inevitably suffer the consequences of our alien affections.

When our dearest desires are the offerings of God, we will focus above the muck and mire of contemporary society: the hay and stubble of every day successes, the sights and sighs of daily disappointments, the grief and groans of life's unending tragedies, even the fleeting rewards we occasionally gain to the enduring gifts that our Lord will provide. These gifts are not just wondrously superior, but they differ in nature and kind from all that vies for our attention now. So much so, that no matter what our sacrifice of time, talent, and treasure; no matter how dear the cost to our pride or place, there engulfed in the opulence of transcendence, we will joyfully proclaim, "Heaven is cheap enough!" (*Life Sketches of Ellen G. White*, p. 67).

Keeping the Sabbath

"And it shall come to pass that from one New Moon
to another, and from one Sabbath to another, all flesh shall
come to worship before Me," says the Lord. Isa. 66:23.

The Sabbath is an oasis in the desert of life. At the end of each week of toil, it posits itself in glad relief from secular activities. The Sabbath is a resting place for the weary; a day of renewal and revitalization—no other day has such an impact because no other day has been blessed, hallowed, and sanctified. Worship on any other day cannot provide its benefits; its spiritual, emotional, and physical consequences are singular.

But what about life in the world to come? Will we keep the Sabbath there? Yes, we are promised Sabbaths in heaven, not because we tire or need physical rest, but because even there, where all is made right and bright by the divine presence of God, its observance will remain a reminder of Christ's acts of creation and redemption.

Sabbaths in heaven will not be times for zoning out the secular and focusing on the holy as is the case in this life. All activity there will be holy. But while every day in glory will conform to heaven's holiness, each seventh day will provide occasion for special praise to the Lamb by whose sacrifices our presence has been granted.

When the earth is made new and it is far removed from the violence of this present existence, the redeemed will lay final claim to their promised rewards. Here, we shall plant vineyards and eat the fruit of them; we will till the responsive soil and train the obedient vines and direct the docile beasts in fields clothed in effulgent verdure. We will build our dream houses and inhabit them; reveling and rejoicing in that land of peaceful habitation. Here in Eden restored, the Sabbath will once again provide rest from labor; not the backbreaking, nerve-racking, heart-weakening toil we suffer in this tyrannical rule of sin, but the wholesome expenditure of energy in satisfying, nonintrusive labor.

The Sabbath is now a joy, and in the ages to come it will remain a special gift to humankind—a central delight of our better world.

Education in Heaven

But to you who fear My name, the Sun of Righteousness
shall arise with healing in His wings; and you shall go out
and grow fat like stall-fed calves. Mal. 4:2.

A h, the joy of learning—the sheer delight of mind-expanding, eye-opening, vision-clearing acquirement of knowledge. The possession of riches is an exciting state. While it provides leverage for living, riches themselves do not improve one's intellect. Marriage is another one of life's special experiences, but while it provides joys of companionship and the completion of one's social self, it does not of itself expand one's mental capacity.

So it is with all of life's best and brightest activities. Other than conversion—the decision and acceptance of Christ as Lord—there is no experience that can compare to learning.

All education, whether formal and informal, expands one's understanding of human nature, human history and the universe around us. True education, however, not only adds to one's stock of knowledge, but it also enhances our ability to cope with life's problems and brings us ever closer to God, who is the source of all true knowing and the totality of all knowledge.

In both heaven and the new earth, our learning will go on eternally. Our minds will be capable of limitless expansion, and in that pure environment, capture and catalog endless wonders of science and grace. Every day and in every way we will be impacted by fresh data that will satisfy our curiosity and thrill our souls.

All of this is made appealing in the statement that reads: "Heaven is a school; its field of study, the universe; its teacher, the Infinite One." "There, when the veil that darkens our vision will be removed, and our eyes shall behold [the] beauty of which we now catch glimpses through the microscope; when we look on the glories of the heavens, now scanned afar through the telescope; . . . with the blight of sin removed, the whole earth shall appear in the 'beauty of the Lord our God!'"

In that grand and glorious day of final reward, we shall "in the vast universe behold 'God's name writ large,' and not in earth or sea or sky one sign of ill remaining" (*Education*, pp. 301, 303).

Christ: The Center of Attraction

And every creature which is in heaven and on earth
and under the earth and such as are in the sea, and all that are in them,
I heard saying: "Blessing and honor and glory and power be to Him who
sits on the throne, and to the Lamb, forever and ever!" Rev. 5:13.

It is Jesus who leads the angelic host in triumphant descent to claim His own; it is Jesus who calls forth the sleeping faithful. It is Jesus who leads the host of innumerable redeemed to heaven's gates; it is Jesus who opens the gates and says, "Come you blessed of My Father, inherit the kingdom prepared for you" (Matt. 25:34). It is Jesus who presents us to the Father as the full harvest He prefigured when He ascended on high; it is Jesus who, in triumphant gladness, reinstates our first parents, Adam and Eve, to their original status; and it will be Jesus who will sing with the redeemed in sheer delight (Zeph. 3:17).

Jesus will be the subject of every conversation; the object of glad, eternal study; the Leader Lamb whose righteous redeemed will follow Him wherever He goes. He will be the object of everlasting praises of the saints who will never tire of singing, "Worthy is the lamb, worthy is the lamb to receive honor and glory and power."

Jesus will personally pilot the New Jerusalem in its descent from glory to earth. He will personally requisition hellfire upon the devil, his angels, and all those who harden their hearts in disobedience to His Word, and He will Himself speak the re-creative words that will restore the world to its pre-sin condition. And then this planet, purged of evil and rid of both sin's root (Satan) and its branches (his followers), will shine in the effervescent glow of its original beauty. Throughout the universe:

Jesus will reign
Where 'er the sun
Does its successive journeys run;
His kingdom stretch
From shore to shore,
Till moons shall wax and wane no more.

Real Life in Glory

They shall build houses and inhabit them; they shall plant vineyards and eat their fruit. They shall not build and another inhabit; they shall not plant and another eat; for as the days of a tree, so shall be the days of My people, and My elect shall long enjoy the work of their hands. Isa. 65:21, 22.

When resurrected, we will not be formless spirits dwelling in blissful silence interrupted only by dinner calls and the lyrical fluttering of angels' wings. We will be real people in heaven dwelling in the flesh of conditional immortality; flesh no longer limited by the creaturely weaknesses of our present state. We will inhabit visible, vibrant bodies; the redeemed will not be the translucent, transparent, substanceless souls of everlasting leisure often portrayed by well-meaning but ill-informed instructors.

How do we know? We know because those were discernable people who were transfigured on the mount with Jesus; Elijah and Moses did not appear as apparitions (Matt. 17:2, 3). We know because the resurrected Jesus who walked toward Emmaus was, to His surprised companions, a personage of form and substance (Luke 24:13-15). We know because Mary recognized His voice when He greeted her; because His wounded side was available to the touch of doubting Thomas; because He dined with His disciples on the shore of Galilee; and when He was taken up from the earth, the angel promised, "This same Jesus who was taken up from you into heaven, will so come in like manner as you saw Him go into heaven" (Acts 1:11).

We pilgrims of this lesser existence, now bound by the chains of time, locked in the prison house of sin, doomed to dwell in earthly tents so soon to fade and decay, are incapable of self-salvation. Our rescue is wholly dependent upon Christ, who at His return will "change our vile body, that it may be fashioned like unto his glorious body, according to the working whereby he is able even to subdue all things unto himself" (Phil. 3:21, KJV).

And what body is that? It is the human body that He assumed while here and that He now maintains as our elder brother, our sure defender, our constant guide—the "something better" of the kingdom to come.

The Role of Rewards

"And behold, I am coming quickly, and My reward is with Me,
to give to everyone according to his work." Rev. 22:12.

We do well to remember that "good works can never purchase salvation, but they are an evidence of the faith that acts by love and purifies the soul. And though the eternal reward is not bestowed because of our merit, yet it will be in proportion to the work that has been done through the grace of Christ" (*The Desire of Ages*, p. 314).

We can never be good enough to earn or merit eternity. However, the extent of the reward (the volume of recognition given in the better world) will correspond to our efforts in the present world. True, those accomplishments are made possible by the presence of Christ. It is His love that motivates the saved to serve; His energies that sustain the believers in ministry; His gift of the Holy Spirit's power that makes our witness effective. We who are redeemed are conduits of mercy, channels of grace, and instruments of His love.

Our great motivation to Christian labor is not to acquire promissory notes or to collect redeemable IOUs in the better world. It is Christ's love that motivates us, and while some crowns will be heavier with stars than others (indicating greater witness), being there with one star will be cause for inexhaustible joy. In glory there will be no pecking order inspired by pride, desire for domination, or even the need for authority, all will be content with the size of the crown, the home, the lawn, and the land we will be given. There we will have gradations of reward, but not gradations of joy. Ours' will be an experience of unimprovable absolutes: we will have absolute reconciliation, absolute redemption, absolute restoration, absolute satisfaction with the rewards bestowed.

His promise is that this state will come quickly. How quickly? Not as quickly as we hope, but as quickly as divine wisdom determines that its promise for earth's redemption is accomplished. We cannot single-handedly bring on the apocalypse, but we can help "keep hope alive" and bring joy to the heart of our loving Lord, who wishes for the day of His return with infinitely more ardent desire than His yearning people.

The Earth Made New

Now I saw a new heaven and a new earth, for the first heaven and
the first earth had passed away. Also there was no more sea. Rev. 21:1.

Ellen White, commenting upon our text states, "The sea divides friends. It is a
barrier between us and those whom we love. Our associations are broken up by
the broad, fathomless ocean. . . . Thank God, in the earth made new there will be no
fierce torrents, no engulfing ocean, no restless, murmuring waves" (*The Seventh-
day Adventist Bible Commentary,* Ellen G. White Comments, vol. 7, p. 988).

In that land of never-fading nature illumined by the presence of Christ, we will
eat the fruit of trees bowed with the weight of their luxurious offerings; we will revel
in the beauty of flowers without protesting thorns. There majestic fields of waving
foliage will softly bend in gentle breezes, and the redeemed, unfettered by mortality, will joy with "unutterable delight in the perfect state of creation restored." The
poet put it well.

"There is a land of pure delight,
  Where bliss eternal reigns,
  Infinite day excludes the night,
  And pleasures banish pain. . . .
  Could we but stand where Moses stood,
  And view the landscape o'er,
  Not all this world's pretended good,
  Could ever charm us more."

The new earth: the eternal abode of the redeemed; newly crowned capital of
joy and rejoicing; the planet where will be housed the New Jerusalem; the city be-
decked, bejeweled, and bestowed by God Himself, will not be available to those for
whom the old nature survived until judgment.

The new earth will be inhabited by those who have experienced the new birth;
who have been given a new heart and a new spirit; who walk in newness of life and
who, affirmed by the blood of the New Testament and given a new name, will sing
a new song: "Thou art worthy to take the book, and to open the seals thereof; for
thou wast slain, and hast redeemed us to God by thy blood out of every kindred,
and tongue, and people, and nation" (Rev. 5:9, KJV).

Worth It All

When He had called the people to Himself, with His disciples also, He said to them, "Whoever desires to come after Me, let him deny himself, and take up his cross, and follow Me." Mark 8:34.

> "Must I be carried to the skies
> On flowery beds of ease,
> Whilst others fought to win the prize,
> And sailed through bloody seas?"

This question eventually faced by every follower of Christ is a reminder that suffering is inevitable for those who seek the kingdom of glory. But this is not a surprise; did not Christ command, "Take up your cross and follow Me?"

What kind of marketing strategy is that? The cross was the most despised, vilified, and degrading instrument of ancient society. To the Romans it was a statement of weakness; to the Greeks, a sign of barbarity; and to the Jews, a symbol of subjugation and oppression. And yet Jesus' invitation to discipleship begins with this calling card—what Dietrich Bonhoeffer, the Christian martyr, labeled as Christ's call to "come and die."

Christ, making the cross the symbol of His kingdom movement, is tantamount to our beginning an organization today and using the electric chair or hangman's noose as our logo. Imagine the effect of such an advertisement upon the recruitment of friends and new members.

Why the cross? First, it reminds us of the cost of our salvation: the sacrifices of Christ. Second, it unmasks Satan for the murderous tyrant that he is. And third, it warns us that "the servant is no greater than his Lord" (see John 13:16); that if Jesus perfected holiness through suffering, so must we.

"It hurts!" said the stone as the sparks flew from the grinding wheel that sought to change its appearance and destiny. "But I must do what I must do to make you the diamond you want to be," the wheel replied. "If that is the case," the suffering stone exclaimed through bitter tears, "grind on, big wheel, grind on!"

Heaven will, indeed, "be worth it all." There is no earthly satisfaction compared to it; no worldly joy equals it. There is no problem or pain great enough to deter or derail one whose heart is fixed on it—our better reward.

The Portals of Paradise

Also she had a great and high wall with twelve gates, and twelve angels at the gates, and names written on them, which are the names of the twelve tribes of the children of Israel. Rev. 21:12.

Why would God adorn the gates of heaven with the names of Israel's tribes; the very nation used by Satan to arrange the crucifixion of His Son? Because in doing so, He signals to us that His love is abundantly available; that amid the seemingly wholesale evil of nations, He has those who honor Him; that bad beginnings need not lead to bad endings; that where sin abounds, grace hath much more abounded; that heaven's "grace provisions" exceed earth's "forgiveness necessities"; that God can save from the "guttermost" to the "uttermost"—from the ridiculous to the sublime—from rags to riches; that no matter what our weakness, His grace is sufficient.

We who comprise modern Israel are no better than our ancient counterparts. They were rebellious and obstinate—so are we; they fraternized with unbelievers to their detriment—so do we; they ignored and neglected the prophets—so do we; they wandered in deserts outside the promised land and delayed their entrance into Canaan—so have we; they disputed against each other—so do we; they distrusted the plain "thus saith the Lord"—so do we. That their names are inscribed upon the heavenly gates is undeniable proof that the church is not "a deep freeze for the saints, but a hospital for sinners." And that God judges the converted, covered by the robe of Christ's righteousness, is deemed acceptable.

It is noteworthy, of course, that hospitals are for making people well—and so is the church. Our fellowship of struggling sinners, bound together by the promises and principles of God's Word, must never relax its efforts for spiritual growth and capacity for service. God's grace is sufficient, but it doesn't excuse or cover those whose will, should they be transported to glory, would find existence foreign to their desires. Those who would enjoy the "something better" of God's blessed tomorrow must accept the richer something of His plans and principles today.

Plenty Good Room

*The city is laid out as a square; its length is as great as its breadth.
And he measured the city with the reed: twelve thousand furlongs.
Its length, breadth, and height are equal. Rev. 21:16.*

In ancient times the distance around the walls, or the circumference, was used to measure cities. The greater the circumferences and the larger the population, the more famous the city became. For instance, Gibeon was referred to as a great city (Joshua 10:2) and so was Nineveh (Jonah 1:1), meaning that they both comprised large areas and housed dense populations.

Other centers of the ancient world, such as Babylon, Gath, Corinth, Athens, and Jerusalem, were also famous for their circumference and their burgeoning populations. But the New Jerusalem dwarfs them all in size and beauty.

John saw the Holy City as measuring 12,000 furlongs in total circumference. A furlong is an eighth of a mile; 12,000 furlongs equals 1,500 miles. This means that each of the equal sides of the New Jerusalem is 375 miles long. The city contains 140,625 square miles of living space!

As earth's inhabitants advance even deeper into the twenty-first century, more and more cities of expansive geography and population are recognizable. The New York City metropolitan area contains approximately 20 million people; Mexico City also 20 million; Tokyo exceeds 37 million; and Seoul houses 22 million plus. Singularly or together, however, all the major cities of our time are not to be compared in population or grandeur to the city built by God. Its walls of jasper (144 cubits, or 213 feet, tall), its streets of transparent gold, its sea of glass, its foundations of precious stones, and its 12 pearly gates (Rev. 21:17-21) render it something vastly more impressive than earthlings can conceive.

The best news, of course, is captured in the rhythmic lyrics of the Negro spiritual that remind us that in the New Jerusalem there is:

"Plenty good room, plenty good room
Plenty good room in my Father's kingdom.
Plenty good room, plenty good room
Just choose your seat and sit down."

Our Happy Home

Then I, John, saw the holy city, New Jerusalem, coming down
out of heaven from God, prepared as a bride adorned for her husband.
And I heard a loud voice from heaven saying, "Behold, the tabernacle
of God is with men, and He will dwell with them, and they shall be
His people. God Himself will be with them and be their God." Rev. 21:2, 3.

What will be the residence capacity of the New Jerusalem? Scripture does not give us a census prediction. However, John the revelator was inspired to write: "After this I looked, and there before me was a great multitude that no one could count, from every nation, tribe, people and language, standing before the throne and before the Lamb" (Rev. 7:9, NIV).

The New Jerusalem—the showplace of all creation will not be the home of the multitude of the redeemed. It is the vehicle that transports us from heaven back to earth's atmosphere from where we will observe God's fiery cleansing of this polluted planet. Then, after the world has been purified by devouring fire, the righteous will stream forth from the city's gates to inhabit their paradise regained.

The New Jerusalem will remain to accommodate the redeemed in gatherings of praise, but the entire planet will constitute our rule. From the vast outreaches of our world, restored and renewed, the saved will go up to the Holy City to worship, and that worship will be highlighted by the presence of Christ, our Savior and Lord.

Seeing Christ will be our greatest reward; thanking Him will be our greatest joy; following Him will be our grandest pleasure, and this enjoyment will be perpetual. Ours will be an eternity of uninterrupted, untainted, untarnished, unsullied, unmitigated, undiluted, unending happiness.

That anticipation is the stimulus of our joyous expression:

"In His glory, I shall see the King,
And forever endless praises sing;
'Twas on Calvary Jesus died for me;
I shall see the King some day."

We Need Each Other

And the Lord spoke to Moses and Aaron, saying:
"Everyone of the children of Israel shall camp by his own standard,
beside the emblems of his father's house; they shall camp
some distance from the tabernacle of meeting." Num. 2:1, 2.

God carefully prescribed the living arrangements of the twelve tribes. On each of the four sides of the tabernacle there were three tribes strategically positioned. On the east side of the tabernacle were the tribes of Judah, Issachar, and Zebulun; on the south side were Reuben, Simeon, and Gad; on the west side were Ephraim, Manasseh, and Benjamin; and on the north side Dan, Asher, and Naphtali.

By this configuration the more industrious tribes were yoked with the more sedentary, the more warlike with the more peaceful, the more resolute with the more fickle; the worldly with the more spiritual; and the more aggressive with the more timid. Clearly, God intended that each tribe's character and personality traits would be balanced by the virtues of others.

This interdependence was essential to their survival as they faced the rigors of nature and the superior power of military foes. But it was also crucial for their moral and spiritual development—each tribe's weakness being balanced by the strength of another, and each tribe's strength shared in support of another.

This principal of mutuality is expressed in the benedictory hymn below:
"Blest be the tie that binds
Our hearts in Christian love!
The fellowship of kindred minds
Is like to that above. . . .
We share our mutual woes,
Our mutual burdens bear,
And often for each other flows
The sympathizing tear."

In the kingdom to come there will be no need for the counterbalancing required by our sinful states. Nevertheless, as demonstrated by the interlocking personalities of the triune God, even there the redeemed will enjoy the blessings of mutually enhancing associations.

The Wideness of God's Mercy

And I heard the number of those who were sealed. One hundred and forty-four thousand of all the tribes of the children of Israel were sealed. Rev. 7:4.

Some Bible students view our scripture as providing the exact number of individuals who will be found faithful on the earth at the second coming of Jesus. Others understand the number to be symbolic of the various personality types exhibited by the 12 sons of Jacob. We cannot with ultimate confidence substantiate either position. However, the fact that each of the 12 gates of the Holy City will bear the name of one of the twelve tribes lends credence to the latter view and provides hope to the entire spectrum of human types and personalities.

This wide human variety is seen in our individual differences of temperament and outlook. It is also seen in the identifiable characteristics of family, races, and nations. The saved at Christ's coming will encompass them all. Christ's invitation to "whosoever will" and the cry of the first angel of Revelation 14 (verses 6, 7) to every nation, kindred, tongue, and people guarantees that the harvest of the living redeemed will include the entire array of earth's population groups.

It is not critical to our salvation that we have precise knowledge regarding the number of the living faithful at His coming or the exact percentages of population groups that will be saved. What is absolutely essential is that we live each day so that in Paul's hopeful observation, whether we "wake or sleep" (1 Thess. 5:9, 10), we will be among those who will happily welcome His return.

A major requirement for participation in the unified family in heaven is love and respect for God's family here on earth. Christianity does not ask that we surrender our individuality or root personality. It does require, however, that we understand that with God no group has "favorite nation" status; that He loves all groups alike, and so should we.

No, unerring certainty regarding the identity of the 144,000 is not vital to salvation. What is vital and what our text assumes is that

"There's a wideness in God's mercy, like the wideness of the sea;
   There's a kindness in His justice, which is more than liberty."

And that He is willing that none should perish, but all should come to the knowledge and obedience of His will.

Judah, Reuben, and Gad

Of the tribe of Judah twelve thousand were sealed;
of the tribe of Reuben twelve thousand were sealed;
of the tribe of Gad twelve thousand were sealed. Rev. 7:5.

The first of the tribes seen by John entering the heavenly Canaan is Jacob's fourth son. Judah had many noble characteristics. It was he who saved Joseph from the pit, and it was he who offered to be surety for Benjamin. But Judah was plagued by a weakness common to so many of his day and ours—the lust of the flesh. A memorable instance of his indulgence of this tendency was his adulterous involvement with Tamar, his daughter-in-law (Gen. 38:6). Centuries later this evil surfaced with tragic consequences in the lives of two of his more famous descendants: David, who coveted and corralled Bathsheba, and Solomon, whose many wives "turned his heart" (1 Kings 11:4) away from God.

The second of the tribes mentioned is Jacob's first son, Reuben. His character defects were also pronounced and, like that of his younger brother, Judah, bore bitter consequences in later generations. His weakness? Instability. In giving blessings and warnings to his sons, the dying Jacob said, "Reuben, you are my firstborn, my might and the beginning of my strength, the excellency of dignity and the excellency of power. Unstable as water, you shall not excel" (Gen. 49:3, 4).

The third of the tribes identified as contributing to the host of the redeemed is Gad—the warrior tribe. Quarrelsome and pugnacious, Gad and his descendents exhibited fierce independence and an all too eager willingness for combat. Of Gad, Jacob predicted, "Gad will be attacked by a band of raiders, but he will attack them at their heels" (verse 19, NIV).

The weakness of each of these tribes is recognized in contemporary society. Judah's sensuality, Reuben's instability, and Gad's pugnacity are in abundant evidence all about us. What our text suggests is that if these three faulty patriarchs and their equally guilty brothers were redeemed, so can we. It also suggests that as we enter glory we will go through the gate bearing the name of the patriarch that we closely resemble.

Its citizens once proudly proclaimed, "All roads lead to Rome." As pilgrims we are provided something infinitely better: 12 gates that lead to the throne of the King of kings—our equal opportunity Savior.

Asher, Naphtali, and Manasseh

Of the tribe of Asher twelve thousand were sealed;
of the tribe of Naphtali twelve thousand were sealed;
of the tribe of Manasseh twelve thousand were sealed. Rev. 7:6.

God's great mercy, whereby we are granted everlasting life, is emphasized again in the second of the four tribal triads. Asher, like all the other sons of Jacob, was not all bad. He was, because of his pleasant personality, "acceptable to his brethren" (Deut. 33:24, KJV). But the people of Asher were known in other far less complimentary ways as well. One was their reputation for withdrawal in moments of crisis, their unavailability in times of need. So pronounced was their tendency for uninvolvement that they are not listed among the tribes numbered in David's army (1 Chron. 27:16-22).

Naphtali's descendants, on the other hand, exhibited great bravery in battle. Their weakness was lack of gratitude; a trait that earned for them one of Christ's most scathing condemnations (Luke 10:12-15).

Manasseh, a grandson of Jacob, nevertheless provided full tribal status. His inclusion with his brother, Ephraim, both children of Joseph who did not have independent tribal status, was pronounced and significant in Israel's history.

Even though denied the blessings of the firstborn, Manasseh, the older of Joseph's sons, became, as predicted by the dying Jacob, the father of a great nation (Gen. 48:19). The decision of some of his descendants to join with several other tribes in remaining on the eastern side of the Jordan raises serious questions about this tribe's judgment and was the cause of considerable problems for them and their brethren.

The fact that one of the gates bears their name attests to God's powers to deliver from the ranks of "me first" sinners, individuals with a "Jesus only" attitude. This is something wonderful and amazing; something so much better than the greed and selfishness so easily and so pervasively harbored in the human heart.

Simeon, Levi, and Issachar

Of the tribe of Simeon twelve thousand were sealed;
of the tribe of Levi twelve thousand were sealed;
of the tribe of Issachar twelve thousand were sealed. Rev. 7:7.

The first two tribes mentioned in the third triad of the redeemed are Simeon and Levi, both Jacob's sons by Leah. Their description by their dying father Jacob as "instruments of cruelty" (Gen. 49:5) is most starkly seen in their massacre of the Shechemites in retaliation for the rape of their sister Dina (Gen. 34).

Simeon's fierce spirit of reprisal was so pronounced in his descendants that they became legendary as a people of hostility. Their mean-spirited address toward others stunted not only their acceptance with neighboring tribes, but also their individual growth and prosperity as well. In fact, the tribe of Simeon eventually became so small and ineffective that it was absorbed by the other 11.

Levi was also a diminutive tribe. Though awarded the privilege of the priesthood because of their brave stand in the matter of the golden calf (Ex. 32:25. 26), their tendency for revenge contributed mightily to the pronounced hypocrisy of their order and to their being denied territorial inheritance in Canaan.

The people of Issachar, spoken of by Jacob as seeing that "rest was good" (Gen. 49:15) because of their love for ease, eventually became servants for all the other tribes. Their occupation with material matters blunted their spirituality and their patriotism. They were a people known not for "going out" but for dwelling in their tents (Deut. 33:18). Issachar was one of the least influential of all Israel's tribal units.

Simeon, whose cruelty reduced his ranks to extinction, Levi, whose posterity was riddled with hypocrisy and pretense, and Issachar, whose love of ease made this people subservient to their brethren—will all be there.

We will also be there if we repent of our sins and accept the gracious provisions of His love—including the painful trials whereby we are prepared for life eternal.

Zebulun, Joseph, and Benjamin

Of the tribe of Zebulun twelve thousand were sealed;
of the tribe of Joseph twelve thousand were sealed;
of the tribe of Benjamin twelve thousand were sealed. Rev. 7:8.

Zebulun's weakness was one of wanderlust, a reference mentioned by Moses to describe the tribe as "going out" (Deut. 33:18). Their strength was that of valor; they distinguished themselves as warriors. They stood with Barak in his conflict with Sisera; with Gideon versus the Midianites, and with David against Saul. Their history, however, is stained by the debilitating tendency of itinerate wandering.

Joseph is also one of the names written on heaven's gates. Other than what might be seen as his exaggerated sentimentality (notice his repeated weeping: Gen. 42:24; 43:30; 45:2, 14; 46:29; 50:17), Scripture does not record for him any particular weakness. However, inadequacy in child-rearing endeavors is suggested by the fact that his lineage includes few, if any, outstanding descendants.

Benjamin, the youngest of Jacob's sons, fathered a generous and talented people whose primary weaknesses were stubbornness and bad judgment. So doggedly determined and impractical was their fervor that they, on one occasion, went so far as to make war against all of the other 11 tribes—and with predictably dire consequences (Judges 20). The inclusion of their names upon the gates further establishes the unfathomable compassion of our long-suffering God.

Please notice that the names of two of the "encampment tribes" do not appear upon heaven's gates: Dan, whose desire for deception and criticism earned him Jacob's description as a biting serpent (Gen. 49:17), and Ephraim, renowned for idolatry (Hosea 4:17).

The lesson here is also clear: that while God's love is endless, the sins less likely to release the sinner to repentance are faultfinding and false worship. Neither sin is of itself unforgivable, but as history attests, both are peculiarly blinding and binding. With the joyous inclusion of 10 tribes, the saddening loss of two and their substitution by two others, we are wondrously warned of both sin's disastrous results and God's all-conquering grace.

Heaven on Earth

Nevertheless we, according to His promise, look for new heavens and a new earth in which righteousness dwells. 2 Peter 3:13.

Heaven is not only the future home of glory, but it is also, figuratively, the present state of grace. By their relationship with Him, Christ's followers are citizens of a better world; for those who earnestly seek it, heaven is, in a real sense, a present reality.

How is it possible for us, amongst all of life's woes, to experience a foretaste of the future glory? We do so by the happy state of being that is a consequence of an ever-sweetening relationship with Jesus. We can know heaven now in our hearts, in our homes, and in our churches by surrendering completely to His will and continuing in constant devotion to His Word.

This is the essence of the prophets comments: "If the people of God would appreciate His Word, we should have a heaven in the church here below. Christians would be eager, hungry, to search the Word. They would be anxious for time to compare scripture with scripture and meditate upon the Word. They would be more eager for the light of the Word than for the morning paper, magazines, or novels. Their greatest desire would be to eat the flesh and drink the blood of the Son of God. And as a result their lives would be conformed to the principles and promises of the Word. Its instruction would be to them as the leaves of the tree of life. It would be in them a well of water, springing up into everlasting life" (*Testimonies for the Church*, vol. 8, p. 193).

The year now ending did not produce the promised return of Christ and the coming of the glorious kingdom; we hope and pray that the year now beginning will. But this is a matter reckoned in God's time. We have not the power or authority to control the apocalypse; what we do have is the command and, by His grace, the power to drink deeply from the fountain of life, to take up our cross and follow Him, to shun the broad and walk in the narrow way of life, to trust His Word, to lean upon His promises, to love and serve one another, and to live for Him one day at a time—forgiven by His blood and covered by His robe. When we do, heaven begins below.

From Visible Nothing to Invisible Something

We do not look at the things which are seen, but at the things which are not seen. For the things which are seen are temporary, but the things which are not seen are eternal. 2 Cor. 4:18.

All that we see in the world about us is temporary; that is, destined to pass away—to be no more. All that our sensory apparatus allows us to know will someday be nonexistent; the disease of "no more-ness" dooms our world and all its appointments. There was a time in which these tangible objects did not exist, and there is a time ahead in which they will no longer be. They are sure to our senses, but lack "forever-ness." Being transitory and expendable, they are, in the language of eternity, a visible nothing.

But heaven is different! We do not see or know heaven with our sensory apparatus. Heaven is unseen; it is unavailable to our touch and taste, but its appointments, in contrast with those of earth where we do see, are eternal. They are everlasting; untouched by the virus of decay or "no more-ness."

Peter, in describing this reality, states, "Blessed be the God and Father of our Lord Jesus Christ, who according to His abundant mercy has begotten us again to a living hope through the resurrection of Jesus Christ from the dead, to an inheritance incorruptible and undefiled and that does not fade away, reserved in heaven for you" (1 Peter 1:3, 4).

Because the appointments of heaven are eternal, they are indeed a "something." That is, they possess everlastingness. But the problem is that they are an "invisible" something. This means that the process of salvation includes turning from the visible nothingness of this world to the invisible "something-ness" of the world to come; from the tangible but temporary realities of this life to the unseen but eternal rewards of the life to come. And this is the work of faith.

Our generation is not known for its faith. We are trained to believe only the provable—faith in the unseen is not an option for scientism and "hardwired" technology. No wonder Jesus asked, "When the Son of man cometh, shall he find faith on the earth?" (Luke 18:8, KJV). The answer? Yes, He will! How do we know? We know because John saw 144,000 living saints redeemed when Jesus returns (Rev. 14:3, 4). And he described them as those who "keep the commandments of God and the faith of Jesus" (verse 12).

A Matter of Confidence

Therefore do not cast away your confidence,
which has great reward. Heb. 10:35.

William Cummins Davis, prominent American preacher of the early 1800s, was one of many prelates of his day who, having studied the 2300-day prophecy of Daniel 8:14, preached about and fully expected the coming of Jesus and the end of the world sometime in the middle 1840s. Davis' specific calculations were expressed in the following poem:

"In ['47] we may hope
To find the world without a pope;
When 30 more expel the evil,
We'll find the world without a devil;
Add three years more and 42,
We'll find the world without a Jew;
The pope, and devil, known no more;
Until the 1000 years are o'er;
And Jew and Gentile now the same,
Rejoice to wear the Christian name:
The glorious dawn of ['47],
Will introduce new earth and heaven."
—L. E. Froom, *The Prophetic Faith of Our Fathers,* vol. 4, p. 222.

But it did not happen for Davis, and it has not happened for the generations of believers who have since hoped with earnest fervor.

How do we explain this seeming delay? We do so first of all by remembering that God's view of time is not as ours. A thousand years are for Him "but as yesterday," and a "millennium of millenniums" less than the flash of energy that lightens our horizons on a stormy night.

Second, we do so by remembering that since all humans die soon—too soon compared to eternity, and since the first order of business after resurrection will be audience with Christ—it is accurate for all of us to regard His second coming as soon and "very soon."

And third, we do so by remembering that all of God's promises are conditional and that His not having come yet is not a commentary about His faithfulness, but a statement about our need for complete surrender to the "something better" of His matchless love.